THE BIBLICAL REMBRANDT

FOR BETTY

יפה וחכמת־לב

THE BIBLICAL REMBRANDT

HUMAN PAINTER IN A LANDSCAPE OF FAITH

John I Durham

JOHN I DURHAM

MERCER UNIVERSITY PRESS
MACON, GEORGIA

MUP/H658

1400 Coleman Avenue
Macon, Georgia 31207

First Edition.

Book design by Burt & Burt Studio

∞The paper used in this publication meets the minimum requirements of American National Standard for Information Sciences—Permanence of Paper for Printed Library Materials, ANSI Z39.48-1992.

Library of Congress Cataloging-in-Publication Data

Durham, John I, 1933-
The Biblical Rembrandt: human painter in a landscape of faith/
John I Durham.—1st ed.
p. cm.
Includes bibliographical references and index.
ISBN 0-86554-886-2 (hardcover: alk. paper)
1. Rembrandt Harmenszoon van Rijn, 1606-1669—Criticism and interpretation.
2. Rembrandt Harmenszoon van Rijn, 1606-1669—Religion.
3. Bible—Illustrations.
I. Title.
N6953.R4D87 2004
759.9492--dc22
2004020509

Printed in Canada

CONTENTS

μετὰ πάσης εὐχαριστίας

I have a broad inventory of gratitude as I reflect on what follows. Gratitude to Rembrandt, of course, for a gift that can never be measured. Gratitude for the access to Rembrandt's works granted by museums around the world and for the kindness of their keepers and curators. Gratitude to a host of Rembrandt scholars and to the art historians who have presented the larger sweep of drawing and painting and who have shown Rembrandt in his context. Gratitude to those who have stimulated some of what follows by their invitations. Gratitude to the providers of books and tools that have made my labor an easier joy. Gratitude to the libraries that have made available rare and expensive volumes and to the librarians who have searched out and directed me to resources. I list the museums in which I have studied Rembrandt's works at the end of this book. Following each chapter, I provide sources and suggestions for readers who may wish to go a greater distance along the path I have taken in this book.

I am grateful of course to Marc Jolley and Edd Rowell of Mercer University Press. Edd actually asked for this book when it was no more than a rumor, without having seen a single sentence. Marc, along with his gifted production team, has brought these pages and pictures into print with a scrupulous grace and a patient attention to the smallest detail. And I would be remiss if I did not state my thanks to the design team of Jim and Mary-Frances Burt for their creative wedding of text and images.

No reproduction of a work of art, however fine, can be more than a suggestion, and sometimes indeed barely a hint of the work itself. I urge the reader to see the original works at every opportunity, and to that end I include in the text below the location of each painting discussed. The graphic works are far less accessible, though they can be seen in frequent special exhibitions. The collections of Rembrandt's graphic works that I found most helpful were those of the Prentenkabinet of the Rijksmuseum, those of the British Museum, and those of the Ashmolean Museum, Oxford.

I must mention here my particular thanks to Wake Forest University in Winston-Salem, North Carolina, for the invitation, extended by Professors Emmett Willard Hamrick and Carlton T. Mitchell, to give the Albritton Lectures of that university on "The Biblical Rembrandt" in April 1987. The essential material of those lectures, though in much revised form, is present in the pages that follow.

I also name here Wade and Susan Doshier of Dallas, Texas, and Rancho Santa Fe, California whose generosity and kindness across the last twelve years have permitted me both the leisure and the security necessary for the contemplation and the work that gave me this book.

Finally, however, but actually first of all, my fullest gratitude is to my wife Betty. She is both companion and inspiration, with the grace of a lovely flower and the bending strength of a tall tree. She keeps me surrounded with loveliness and reminds me of my vast good fortune. Yet more than any of that, she has both saved my life and given me my life. No man could ask for more, and it is thus to Betty that I dedicate *The Biblical Rembrandt.*

John I Durham
Meadow Creek Mountain
24 December 2001

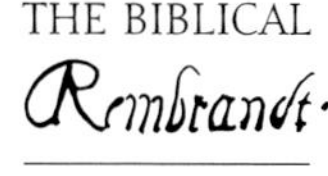

1

TO BEGIN WITH

Yet another book about Rembrandt and his oeuvre? Why? There are so many, and they are so fat, so heavy, and frequently so much alike. And a good number of them have come to us from scholar-historians, trained in looking, and possessing the technology to see beneath Rembrandt's surfaces right into his very pigments and his canvas and board foundations. Sometimes they can even peer behind his finished work and show us how he changed his mind and revised a painting, or even an etching, in the process of its creation.

As for myself, I am neither an art historian nor the son of an art critic, to take a turn of phrase from the prophet Amos, but rather a teacher of *Tanak* and a tender of its Hebrew roots. My career has been a thrilling romp through the Bible, with a primary concentration upon what is called in my Christian tradition the

Old Testament. Such skill as I may claim lies in an attempt to understand the Bible and its history, not in the explanation of art and its history.

Yet some fifty years of experiencing the biblical text have given me the hubris to set forth a summary of some forty years of experiencing Rembrandt. I regard Rembrandt's works on biblical subjects the supreme achievement in the long history of biblical drawing and painting. This is true, I think, because Rembrandt came to the Bible not through the traditions of liturgical art and pious decoration, but as a believer.

Thus do I defend myself against the derisive hoots of the art elite by stating here that I do not intend what follows as "yet another book about Rembrandt." It is far more a tribute, a fan letter, a thank-you note, and an appreciation of an important dimension of Rembrandt's oeuvre that has been often noted and much used in "Rembrandt Bibles" and in the illustration of biblical stories, but written about only sparingly and usually in passing. Indeed, what I have set forth below has been for me a dialogue of student with teacher, a dialogue guided by the Bible I am still studying, and a dialogue in which Rembrandt continues to give me lessons.

The Bible was, for Rembrandt, a sourcebook and a mirror of the human situation, a vision of what might have been, and of what might be, and so at last a sourcebook of faith. Not an orthodox faith, by any measure of orthodoxy—but, then, can real faith, faith at its most personal, ever really be orthodox?

Rembrandt remains in the popular mind very much *the* painter of all time, and his name has been applied to a range of products, from oil pigments (a logical sales pitch) to toothpaste (pray, why?). When Hollywood decides to present a thriller involving the theft of a priceless work of art, the work stolen may well be a Rembrandt, even if it is represented as being in the wrong place, as in the 1999 film *Entrapment.* If the intention is to present the trappings of vast personal wealth, the paintings on the mansion walls may well be led by a Rembrandt, as in the 1996 film *Absolute Power.* Rembrandt himself has been portrayed on the movie screen, most notably perhaps by Charles Laughton in a 1936 film directed by Alexander Korda that is far more Laughton dressed as Rembrandt and storming about with a pouting scowl than any reasonable representation of

Rembrandt. Rembrandt's biographers have had a field day guessing what his life was like and what sort of person he was. And selections of his works continue to appear, sometimes in reproductions so poor that the originals are barely recognizable and sometimes in good likenesses, though never yet with the clarity of detail and richness of color and texture the paintings, in particular, need if a proper impression of Rembrandt's genius is to be received by the non-specialist viewer. Perhaps CD-ROM technology will give us the much-needed gift of accurate reproduction, with a wedding of excellent digital reproductions and specific commentary/annotation. A hint of what is possible may be seen in the publication *Rembrandt the Printmaker*, which presents on CD-ROM all the states of all of Rembrandt's etchings, along with brief annotation.

The bibliography of Rembrandt studies continues to grow, as it has done since Rembrandt's own time. The number of works attributed to him has both expanded and shrunk across the years. At present, we are in a period of revisionism as regards his paintings, in particular, owing in large measure to the important work of the Rembrandt Research Project (RRP), which has to date published its work only on the paintings done from 1625 through 1642, the output of eighteen of Rembrandt's forty-five years of painting (or forty-three if the years from which we can date no paintings, 1649 and 1668, are omitted). A few of the deletions from the Rembrandt canon made in the RRP's *A Corpus of Rembrandt Paintings* have already been strongly contested, and the work of the RRP team will no doubt continue to be assessed and revised, though its contribution to the study of what had become, for an array of reasons, an inflated catalog can hardly be overvalued.

The attempt to be sure about whether a Rembrandt *is* a Rembrandt, a work that can with certainty be declared to have been done by Rembrandt himself, important though it is, has nevertheless spawned more than a little confusion. The popular press, ever eager to pursue and present a shocking story, has perhaps overly enjoyed the removal of celebrated works from their Rembrandtian pedestals. The newspaper accounts of "deattribution" (ugly and awkward word) have nearly always oversimplified a very complicated process of study. Museum curators and trustees have risen to the defense of their Rembrandts, sometimes with understandable irritation. Treasured survey volumes have had to be revised, and some passionate prose has been made to blush. Perhaps the most unfortunate result of the reassignment of a painting, to one of Rembrandt's pupils, or to the still more distant limbo of "Rembrandt's Circle" or "Rembrandt's Studio," has been the impression that such a reassignment somehow lessens the importance of the work in question, as art, or as of value for knowing Rembrandt.

A catalog entry on Rembrandt criticism for a fascinating exhibition titled "Rembrandt: The Master and His Workshop" and held in Berlin, Amsterdam, and London in 1991–1992, noted that despite dramatic advances in the analysis of Rembrandt's oeuvre and an ever more detailed reconstruction of Rembrandt's historical and cultural context, "confusion flourishes as never before." Current scholarly treatises refer to "the visible Rembrandt" and "the invisible Rembrandt," to "the true Rembrandt," to "the nasty Rembrandt," "vindictive" of spirit and "untrustworthy," to Rembrandt the "*pictor economicus*," a self-promoting "entrepreneur," and to "Rembrandt" as a category, viewed as "a cultural text rather than a historical reality." And paintings that have been removed from the Rembrandt canon by the RRP on the basis of elaborate historical and scientific analysis have been retained in the Rembrandt canon by similar arguments and sophisticated scientific tests. The most compelling example of the defense of rejected works to date was a 1995–1996 exhibition in New York titled "Rembrandt/Not Rembrandt in the Metropolitan Museum of Art: Aspects of Connoisseurship."

Each of these studies and essays, and all of them together are of value, from the ones that may strike the admirer of Rembrandt as outlandish and even disrespectful to those that seem more balanced (more in keeping with the "traditional" view, which is once again rapidly evaporating). Given the worth to the human family of Rembrandt's art, any study that prompts a look, even a glance, at even one of his paintings or etchings or drawings is of worth. And the wide range of our ignorance about the historical Rembrandt not only makes his life and character fair game to those of us who care about his work and his life, but also establishes the need for every scrap of information we can gather, even information that turns out to be untenable and therefore false. A large part of knowing, after all, is learning what can be set aside.

While I have learned a great deal that is both valuable and stimulating in my survey across the years of Rembrandt studies both popular and specialist, I have sought in the pages that follow to avoid the attribution debate by dealing for the most part with works that are generally agreed at present to be from Rembrandt's hand. I say "at present" because despite the increasing availability of ever more specialized (and expensive) processes for the identification of the time and context of works of art more than three and a half centuries old, attribution remains a very subjective undertaking. The few works I discuss below that are regarded "at present" as only perhaps from Rembrandt's own hand I note as such.

I find myself wondering with increasing frequency whether we should not begin to think of works as Rembrandt's when they are obviously from Rembrandt's *mind*, whether they were done only in part by his hand or by not even so much as a single brushstroke or etching scratch or line drawn by his own hand. Rembrandt's gift to us is by no means entirely a gift from his hand. We must not forget our debt to his eye, to his mind, to his heart, to his spirit, to his skill, to his example, and to his inspiration as a teacher. Some of his pupils are said to have signed *his* name to *their* paintings so the works would fetch a higher price. In a way, so signing the work of their hands was probably more honest than signing their own names, for what they created, in spite of limitations their teacher did not have, was in essence a creation of Rembrandt. All of us who have been taught are extensions of those who taught us, and every real teacher must be honored by honest (and even dishonest) imitation. Rembrandt was no more an exception to this fact of life than were his pupils, as even a cursory comparison of his early works with those of his teacher Pieter Lastman makes obvious.

Yet there remains a question beyond the attribution of Rembrandt's works, beyond the sources that he used, whether consciously or unconsciously, beyond his technique, beyond the scientific analysis of his materials, beyond the purpose, the commission, the provenance of his works. This question concerns meaning and thus is one that can only be approached subjectively. Nor is it a question merely of what Rembrandt *intended* by a given work, what that work meant to him, as important as that is. A work of art, completed by its creator, has a life of its own. It may come to mean less or even more than the artist who gave it that life would claim for it. It may indeed come to mean something very different from what that artist had in mind, even something that would never, perhaps *could* never, have occurred to that artist.

A fundamental premise of my work, one that I reached only after many years of looking at Rembrandt's works drawn from texts in the Bible, is that Rembrandt's works reflect belief. That Rembrandt was not a devout churchman is one of the certainties of his otherwise uncertain biography. But that he was a devout believer cannot in my judgment be denied—there is simply too much faith in the works themselves. That this faith is not to be perceived without faith, I will not deny; thus my study is necessarily a subjective one, one that involved years of looking, but looking always with faith. In the pages that follow, I have attempted to set down a summary of what I have seen, looking with faith. Am I right about Rembrandt? Finally, only Rembrandt could say. Am I right about what I have seen in his biblical work? Read the texts and look at the works themselves, at the originals whenever possible, and judge for yourself.

At the end of a beautifully presented and lucid commentary on the technical study of Rembrandt's paintings, Ernst van de Wetering, now head of the ongoing RRP, has written a moving essay titled "Perspectives on the Quality of Rembrandt's Art." This essay—coming as it does after ten chapters dealing with such technical matters as Rembrandt's "canvas support," his palette, his brushwork, his "binding medium"—strikes me as having even greater impact than it might otherwise carry. For at the end of some 264 pages dealing with what can be objectively analyzed in the paintings of Rembrandt, van de Wetering suggests that Rembrandt combined an amazing imagination with the lifelong honing of an incredible skill: a skill for transmitting what he imagined onto paper and canvas and panel and copperplate. What Rembrandt drew and etched and painted is what Rembrandt *was*: "Time and again I feel myself drawn into Rembrandt's spaces where figures and objects—but I myself as well—get a specific weight and balance. And in a way that is certainly difficult to prove, this is in part due to my conviction that this space is not 'made' but has 'become'; and that this is so because its maker did not 'make' but 'was.'"

Is it too much to say that knowing Rembrandt's work is, finally, the only way we can really know Rembrandt? I think not, if we keep always in mind that our knowing is always complicated by who *we* are. And this, of course, is one explanation of the wide range of conclusions that continues to be drawn from experiencing Rembrandt. However informed our looking may be, we cannot escape *ourselves* as we look at, and then think about, Rembrandt's gift to us.

Across the years of his career, from 1625 until his death in 1669, Rembrandt painted, etched, and drew more than seventy self-portraits: a greater number by a considerable margin than any other well-known artist either before or since his time. And this total does not include his likenesses of himself in a variety of works on biblical themes (see chap. 2) and at least once in a "history painting." The self-portraits have been variously taken as autobiographical indices to the story of his life, as a means of knowing the "inner" Rembrandt, even as an indication of an almost brutal honesty in self-expression, and as practice pieces early on that in due course became statements of a state of mind. While there may be elements of truth in each of these interpretive approaches, no one of them can be sustained across the span of the self-portraits, not least because they often do not mesh with the events that we know were occurring in Rembrandt's life when he created them. Rembrandt's most ebullient self-portrait, for example, the 1658 depiction of himself as a potentate-grandee (now in the Frick Collection), was painted in what we know to have been one of the most difficult years of his life.

Autobiography, by its very nature, requires arrogance, and no one has as much right to be arrogant as does a genius. Rembrandt, amply supplied with both genius *and* arrogance, may well have thought from time to time about depicting himself as a kind of corrective to portraits done by his pupils and his friends and perhaps even by his detractors. I believe, however, that Rembrandt's self-portraits were far more often an exercise in what Bernard Berenson famously (and infamously) called "seeing and knowing," the "contradiction between looking and knowing," the "compromise...between retinal vision and conceptual looking." In my view, with his self-portrayal Rembrandt was penetratingly involved in the work of the Artist, the One among us who can see what the rest of us cannot see, and so knows what the rest of us, without the Artist's help, cannot know. In the self-portraits,

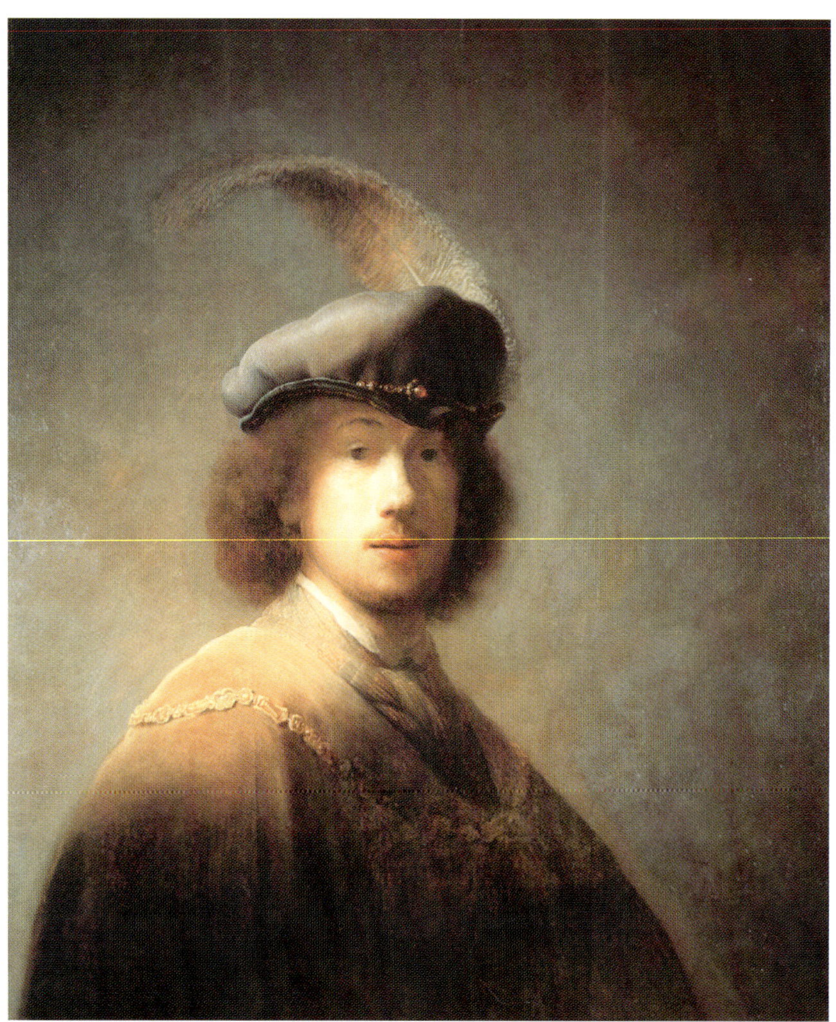

Self-Portrait, 1629, Isabella Stewart Gardner Museum, Boston

Rembrandt was working at seeing and knowing, by attempting to see what he could see whenever he chose, his own visage, and by attempting to know what that seeing had to teach him: not about himself, but about art—painting, etching, and drawing. What we may learn about Rembrandt the person as we study these self-representations is important, but it is limited because we cannot know Rembrandt's mind. What we may learn about art from them is also important, for Rembrandt was, and is, a master teacher. But the most important insight these works offer us, finally, is not about Rembrandt and not about art, but about ourselves—about what we see and refuse to see and about what we will permit ourselves to know.

In the chapters that follow, I comment on some of Rembrandt's self-portraits as they seem to me to have relevance for my reflections on this human artist in the landscape of his faith. But just here, I think of five of them, one from each decade of his evolving career, each in its own way an essay in what I believe to be Rembrandt's seeing and knowing.

In this work on the facing page from 1629, purchased by Bernard Berenson for Isabella Stuart Gardner in 1896, the twenty-three-year-old Rembrandt looks out at us with his mouth just opening as though he is about to speak. His fancy outfit, sometimes interpreted as a statement of ambition, is probably no more than an exercise of his rapidly growing skill as a painter. In 1629, he was still in Leiden, stretching himself along with Jan Lievens and waiting for his first "big" commission. He has looked at himself and seen some of what most of us see at the beginning of our careers, and he has presented himself as most of us have at that stage, as better looking than he was. But what was he about to say? I doubt that his comment would have been about his outfit, or his ambition, or his hope. I wonder instead whether it may not have been a statement about painting, a remark praising the career he had chosen, a confession of excitement about what he had created looking in a mirror, and maybe even a speculation about how he might do it differently the next time.

Self-Portrait, B 21, 1639, Teylers Museum, Haarlem

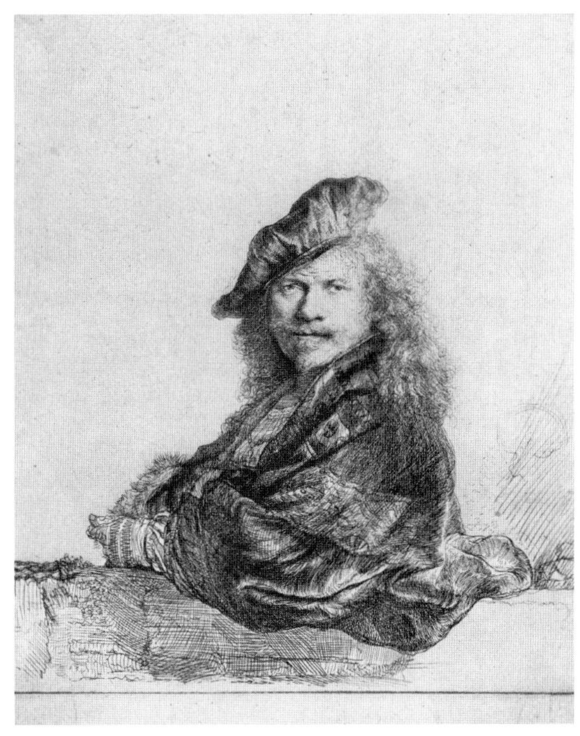

By 1639, Rembrandt, ten years older by the calendar, has become a master artist decades advanced in terms of his skill. He looks out at us with complete assurance, though with serious intensity: his brow is wrinkled, and his lips are closed. He does not appear about to speak; instead, he seems to be deep in thought. His use in this etching of portraits by both Raphael and Titian has often been mentioned, and cited in support of the theory that Rembrandt intended to represent himself as the worthy recipient of the artistic mantle of those two great Renaissance masters.

I wonder, however, whether any such notion was in Rembrandt's mind as he created this etching. He had seen the Raphael work at an auction and made a quick sketch of it *with revisions* (his improvements?!). From it, he took his pose. The Titian work, he had seen in the collection of a Portuguese diplomat and diamond merchant, and from it he took the massive sleeve. But what he has given us is a dramatically different work, one in which he leans out over the wall, locks eyes with us, and pulls us into his world by pulling himself into ours. He had looked at the Raphael and Titian works, both of which are much more self-contained, and then proceeded to create his own work, a quite new and different achievement. His look out at us is totally engaging, impossible to ignore, and I suspect he had no idea of trumping any other artist, from the Renaissance or any other time. As in the 1629 self-portrait done in his hometown of Leiden, this work from the big city of Amsterdam ten years later was a statement of where *he* was at that moment, and what it suggests is that there was more, much more, to come.

Self-Portrait, B 22, 1648, Prentenkabinet, Rijksmuseum, Amsterdam

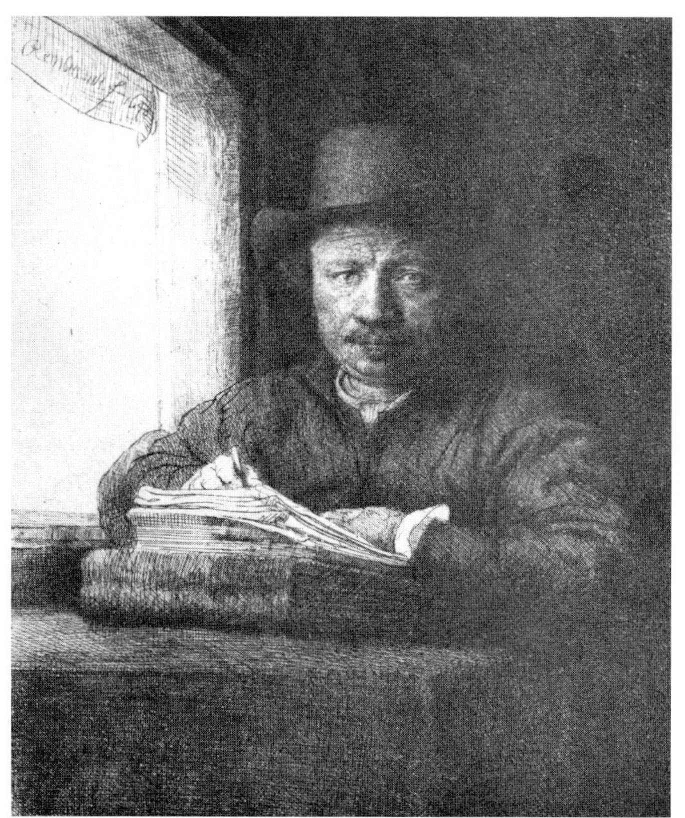

That more is well represented in an etching from 1648. Gone are the fancy clothes, the revision of poses seen and costumes admired—Rembrandt presents himself simply clad and solemnly at work, etching a plate cushioned on a folded cloth resting on two books. His left hand holds the plate steady while he works the plate with the etching tool in his right hand. He has interrupted his work, and looked up. Is he looking at himself, in a mirror as he etches this self-portrait? Of course he must have been at some stage in the creation of this work. But in his concept of this self-portrait is he also looking out at us, as in the self-portraits of 1629 and 1639? In my opinion, this latter option is the case here—he is once again looking

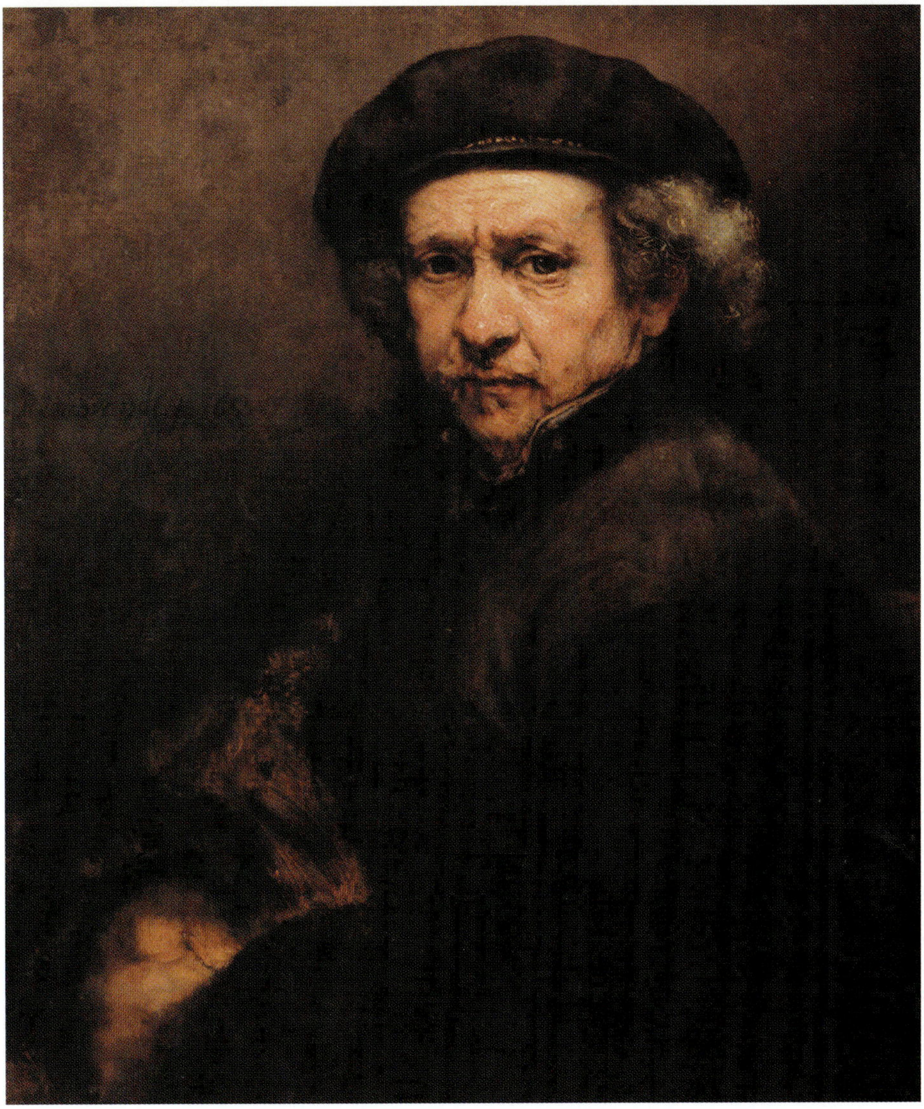

Self-Portrait, 1659, National Gallery of Art, Washington

out at his viewer, this time in a workaday outfit and busy at the work that entranced him most days of his life. His statement seems to me to be, "This is what I do, and this is who I am," and it is not by any means a statement of apology. I do not doubt for a moment that Rembrandt ever thought of doing anything else, and I do not doubt that he considered his work the highest vocation. In this self-portrait from mid-career, he dispenses with every hint of pretence and any hint of display and gives us as honest a picture of himself as he ever created. In a way, almost every subsequent self-depiction is a restatement and an exegesis of this one. And each one of them seems to me to call us to a parallel honesty.

Eleven years later, for example, Rembrandt painted a *Self-Portrait with Beret and Turned-Up Collar*, now in Washington's National

Gallery of Art. The pose is different from most of the self-portraits in that Rembrandt's body is turned toward the left; but the face, the look, the dress are a variation on the etching from 1648. Though his hands, clasped in his lap, are not holding this time the tools of his work, and though he is clearly more than a decade older, with more wrinkles, a puffier face, and more gray hair, he still looks out at us with his "this is me" look, as if to say, "I am Rembrandt, the painter, and my work is what I think about, in one way or another, nearly all the time, right now included."

X-ray photographs of this self-portrait reveal that, to begin with, Rembrandt gave himself a working house cap of the sort he is wearing in such works as his 1660 *Self-Portrait at the Easel* (now in the Louvre), in which he is holding a palette, brushes, and a maulstick. For some reason, however, he replaced the cap here with the dressier black beret with gold beading—not, I believe, because he was attempting to play down his profession. I think it more probable that by 1659, he no longer felt the need of any such allusions to his work unless he was specifically representing himself painting, as in the self-portrait of 1660 and the *Self-Portrait with Two Circles* of 1665–1657, now in London (Kenwood House). In this *Self-Portrait with Beret and Turned-Up Collar*, he *is* painting, he is Rembrandt, and he is still thinking about painting, still working to be yet better, and he looks out at us with the assurance of this reality.

In the year of his death, Rembrandt painted at least two self-portraits. Of the two, the first is probably this *Self-Portrait at the Age of 63*, now in London's National Gallery. Once again, x-ray photography suggests that he may originally have given himself a paintbrush and a house cap such as the one he painted over in the work from 1659. And once again, I suggest, he deleted these specific allusions to his identity as superfluous. He is clearly older, and he appears to be weary, but he still looks out at us with intensity and with the reflective air of someone who is far from finished with learning, with improving, with creating.

As always, it is an arresting face. It gives no hint of impending death, despite its honest representation of sixty-three years of living and labor. It is not a defeated face, not by any measure, despite the loss and the grief and disappointment it has witnessed. I believe it is a face that somehow sums up what draws us so irresistibly to Rembrandt's

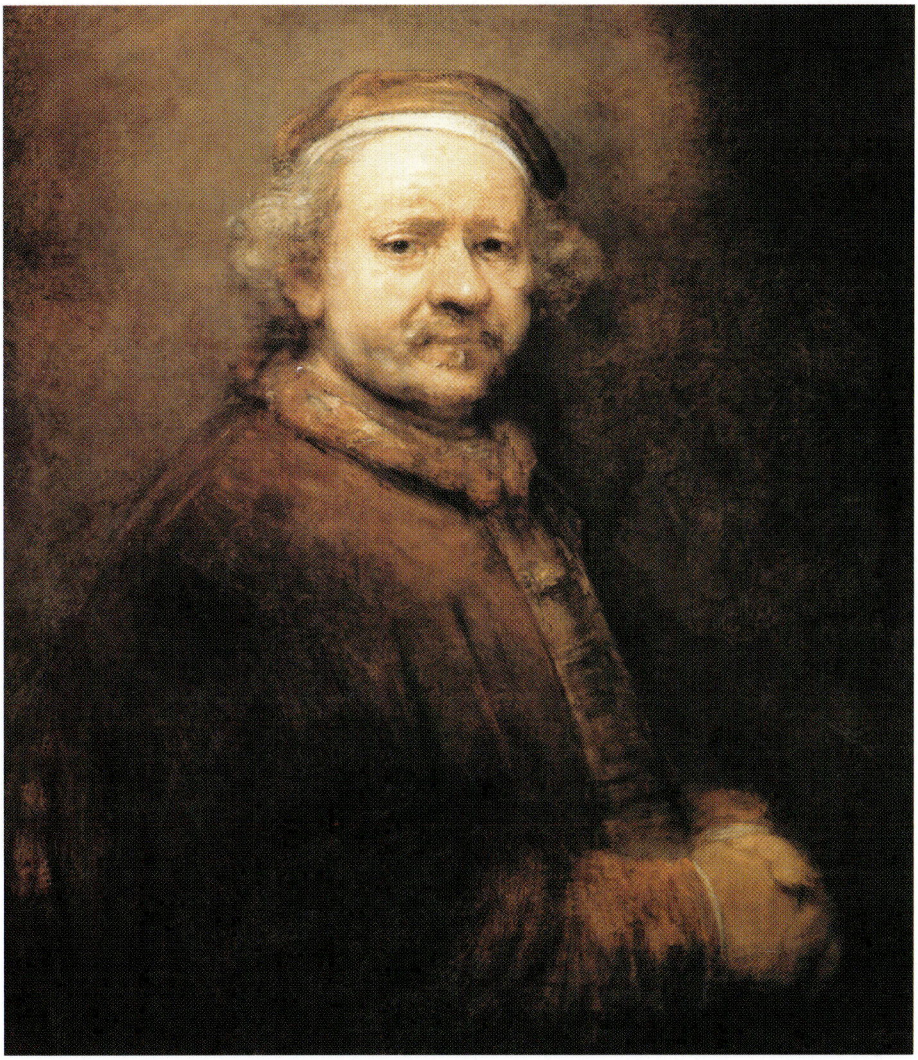

Self-Portrait, 1669, The National Gallery, London

work: it is honest, suggesting spirit, even soul, and it is in some way impossible to define or to describe how and what and even who we are ourselves. Given the sheer number of his self-portraits across the span of his career, not to mention the many ways Rembrandt gave himself to so much of what he painted, etched, and drew, I am bound to wonder whether any artist in history has so seen and known himself as Rembrandt did. Only Van Gogh, who idolized Rembrandt, can be said to have come anywhere near such self-perception.

Those peering, studying, understanding, living eyes draw us into these paintings and help us somehow to define and to know ourselves. They look out at us, and we can feel them seeing us. I find it intriguing that in the majority of his self-portraits, in each of his three media, Rembrandt is looking straight at his viewer. It can be argued, of course, and has been argued, that he was working with a mirror before him as he made the self-portraits and that this makes the look at us inevitable. Such an argument, however, cannot be sustained. For one thing, Rembrandt does not always look at us in his self-portraits. For another, many of his portraits, of men as well as of women, also depict that direct look at the viewer.

The importance of a careful representation of the eyes of a sitter has been a fundamental emphasis in the art of depicting the human face for a very long time, for the very obvious reason that "dead" eyes compromise an otherwise perfect representation of any face. Sometimes an artist shades or in some other way obscures the eyes, thus avoiding this problem. Rembrandt himself did so now and then, for an array of reasons, as Simon Schama's fascinating 1999 book with its *double entendre* title *Rembrandt's Eyes* repeatedly asserts. The eyes can be manipulated in a painting, an etching, a drawing, as an effective means of expression, but they must be presented as alive, as *seeing* eyes, eyes that have intelligence and emotion behind them if the face into which they are set is to be believable.

For Rembrandt, believable eyes, living eyes, seeing eyes, even eyes looking at something we cannot see were not a problem, but an asset. I think it not excessive to call him a virtuoso of vision, both with regard to what he saw and also with regard to the way in which he represented seeing. In the pages that follow, I will celebrate this gift repeatedly, but here I want to note that the five self-portraits I have listed above seem to me to call attention in advance to Rembrandt's astonishing retinal sensitivity and his continual reference to both his seeing and our seeing across the extent of his oeuvre. Is it any wonder that he was entranced by the story of Tobit's blindness and its cure, returning to it again and again in paintings, in etchings, and in drawings? Can we be surprised that he most often represents himself in his self-portraits looking out at us, with a direct and penetrating concentration, almost as if we are ourselves subjects of a work he is about to undertake? I find myself struck, as I look at his work, with the feeling that my own looking is being guided, enhanced, educated, and above all stretched into truth.

In some of his most moving biblical works, as I will note in the chapters that follow, Rembrandt pulls us into his depiction of the moment by presenting eyes that see what we must imagine, eyes that look beyond the picture plane but by no means beyond the range of meaning the narrative suggests. And sometimes he places himself into the biblical moment, looking not at those alongside him but at us, as if to be sure *we* are seeing and to lock our look into the event he has imagined. As in his self-portraits, he looks us into looking at him, so in his re-presentation of the biblical moments that drew him, he pulls us into seeing what he has seen, sometimes by teaching our eyes how to see, but most often by pulling our minds into seeing what his mind has seen.

I wonder whether this gift of Rembrandt to us may be the most valuable of all his many gifts. What we can see with our eyes, the paintings and the etchings and the drawings of his biblical oeuvre that remain to us, wondrous as they are, present to us perhaps an opening, a step into what the Bible is really about, going beyond the text to what gave us the text in the first place. If I am right in this conjecture, Rembrandt may well have been attempting to help us look beyond his biblical pictures—he may even have been inviting us to *complete* those pictures by putting ourselves into them, as he appears to have put himself into the moments he depicted, sometimes literally and always conceptually. Did he always succeed? Of course not. Thus he never stopped working at it, despite all that happened to him, despite all that he brought on himself, despite his incredible success, and despite the rejection he received. At the end, he was still trying to help us look into ourselves by looking into the Bible through his excited grapple with it.

Am I suggesting too much and loading Rembrandt's biblical works with a burden they will not bear? Perhaps. But I wonder whether I may be hinting at another dimension of the Rembrandt effect, that magnetism of his work that still defines art throughout the civilized world by his name. There is an invisible pull in his best work that tugs at us again and again. This attraction is real on an almost universal range—artists, art historians, art "critics," collectors, casual museum-goers, even tourists on "must-see" itineraries planned by someone else find themselves drawn to "the Rembrandts." The images that take root in our very spirits and grow there, defining us somehow, are over and again images Rembrandt has left us. His paintings in particular lay hold on us, and we cannot forget them, in part of course because we do not want to, and in part also because they add to what we are. They are the work of genius, but they tell us about our humanity and remind us at the same time that genius is human too. They complete us by calling on us to complete what they begin, by opening to us a world that we realize, as we reflect on it, is really our own world as well as the world of Rembrandt and Abraham and Jeremiah and Tobit and the shepherds in the stable and a ragged, broken prodigal son weeping into his father's embrace and two astonished men in Emmaus seeing what they had been unable to believe.

Is the greatest part of Rembrandt's legacy to us perhaps what is *not seen* in his pictures? Have I written a book full of biblical pictures to present the belief that Rembrandt's ultimate biblical gift to us is something *beyond* his pictures, something that comes into being only when our response is blended with his paintings and etchings and drawings to create something new and different and yet the same for all of us? Or am I dealing here with that next step that art at its best always sends us to, the amalgam of the artist's work and our own response to that work creating something further?

I have been on a journey with Rembrandt and his Bible. It has been a journey of forty years, and it is not anywhere near an end yet. The chapters that follow are the map of how far along in that journey Rembrandt and I are just now.

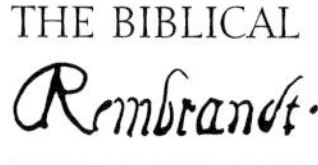

SOME SOURCES AND SUGGESTIONS

The translations of the Hebrew, Greek, and Aramaic texts from the Bible that appear throughout this volume are my own, unless otherwise noted.

The 1999 Jon Amiel film *Entrapment* begins with the theft of Rembrandt's *Bathsheba with King David's Letter*, though the painting is presented as stolen from New York, rather than from the Louvre in Paris where it is located. The 1996 Clint Eastwood film *Absolute Power* begins with the burglary of a mansion filled with paintings, jewels, and cash—the first painting to be seen is Rembrandt's *The Suicide of Lucretia*, which is not in a private collection, but in the Minneapolis Institute of Art. The obvious copies used by the filmmakers are readily recognizable, but by no means exact replicas. The 1936 Alexander Korda/Charles Laughton film is currently once again available. There is a 1942 German film, *Rembrandt*, directed by Hans Steinhoff, and also a 1999 French film by the same title, directed by Charles Matton.

The work of the RRP published to date is available in *A Corpus of Rembrandt Paintings*. Volume 1 (1982) deals with paintings produced in the years 1625–1631; volume 2 (1986), with paintings from the years 1631–1634; and volume 3 (1989), with paintings from the years 1635–1642, ending with *The Militia Company of Captain Frans Banning Cocq*, known in popular parlance as "The Night Watch." Two further volumes were originally promised, to deal with the paintings through the year of Rembrandt's death in 1669. The volumes that have appeared are magnificently presented and include precise descriptions of each work covered, along with elaborate technical data, excellent black-and-white photographs of the paintings, x-ray and infrared photographs, enlarged photographs of details, general commentary, and notes on sources and influences and provenance. These volumes are the work of a panel of Rembrandt specialists, and their work of revision, an attempt to arrive at a more justifiable canon of Rembrandt's paintings, has provoked considerable criticism, not least from museums whose "Rembrandts" have had doubts raised about them or have even been removed entirely from their exalted status and relegated to the "Circle of Rembrandt," or even cast into an outer darkness beyond that circle. No serious study of Rembrandt's paintings can afford to neglect this work. I refer to it in the pages that follow as *Corpus*.

By the time the third volume of the *Corpus* was published, the RRP had lost by death two of its original members, and all save one team member were approaching retirement; early in the final decade of the twentieth century, the approach the original team had followed thus underwent a major shift in procedure. The designation of three categories of attribution (A: "Paintings by Rembrandt," a total of 146 works by the conclusion of volume 3; B: "Paintings Rembrandt's authorship of which cannot be positively either accepted or rejected," a total of 12 works by the conclusion of volume 3; and C: "Paintings Rembrandt's authorship of which cannot be accepted," a total of 122 works by the conclusion of volume 3, of which number the majority did not look much like Rembrandts to begin with) has been abandoned as too rigid, and the team/committee approach has been replaced by a director who with the help of his staff will consult a wider range of specialists. The current head of the project is Ernst van de Wetering, who was appointed to the RRP team in 1970.

A number of "catalog" volumes have appeared, with reproductions of various quality, purporting to present Rembrandt's paintings "complete." The problem, of course, is that the list of Rembrandt's works will not stand still—it swells, is reduced, is revised, and has remained in flux from Rembrandt's own day for a variety of reasons. The volumes of Abraham Bredius (*The Paintings of Rembrandt*, 1935; fourth edition revised by Horst Gerson, 1971), Horst Gerson (*Rembrandt Paintings*, 1968), Bob Haak (*Rembrandt: His Life, His Work, His Time*, 1969), Christian Tümpel (*Rembrandt: All Paintings in Colour*, 1993), and Gary Schwartz (*Rembrandt: His Life, His Paintings*, 1985) are convenient general sources with texts in English translation. In the pages that follow, Rembrandt's paintings are identified by their known or proposed date and by their present location, owing to the complicated and sometimes confusing variance in the different catalog numberings.

Reproductions of the etchings of Rembrandt are variously available. Particularly good are the publications of Karel G. Boon (*Rembrandt: The Complete Etchings*, 1963), Christopher White and Karel G. Boon (*Rembrandt's Etchings: An Illustrated Critical Catalog*, 1969), and Christopher White (*Rembrandt as an Etcher: A Study of the Artist at Work*, 1969 and 1999). Gary Schwartz's *Rembrandt: All the Etchings Reproduced in True Size* (1977) has the advantage of doing just what the title advertises, thus giving a feeling for the wide range of dimension in Rembrandt's etching plates. The Rembrandt House Museum in Amsterdam possesses a magnificent collection of Rembrandt's etchings, now permanently on view, and a catalog published by the museum, *The Rembrandt House Museum: The Prints, Drawings and Paintings*, provides good reproductions of at least one state of the etchings owned by the museum. Better still is *Rembrandt the Printmaker* (2000), a CD-ROM presenting all the etchings of Rembrandt in all their states; it is published by Softmachine BV with the cooperation of the Rembrandt House Museum. In the pages that follow, the etchings are identified by their Bartsch numbers (so B 46, B 74, and so on), with Roman numerals indicating the successive "states" (versions) of etchings that Rembrandt altered in successive printings (so B 78:IV). These numbers, assigned in the catalog of Adam Bartsch published in 1797, remain the most readily recognized of all the various listings designating Rembrandt's etchings.

Rembrandt's drawings are handily available in the six-volume work of Otto and Eva Benesch, *The Drawings of Rembrandt* (1973). The Benesch volumes arrange the drawings chronologically (though the works themselves are usually dated by style and by reference to etchings and paintings with visible—and authentic—dates) and are carefully indexed and cross-referenced. In the pages that follow, the drawings are identified by the catalog numbers assigned to them in the Benesch work (so Benesch 60, Benesch 519, and so on).

The Benesch catalog of Rembrandt's drawings has come under increasing scrutiny in recent years, owing in part to interest in Rembrandt's teaching methods and the resultant work of his pupils. The research of Peter Schatborn on the Rijksmuseum's collection of Rembrandt drawings is particularly interesting (see the catalog of the Rembrandt House Museum exhibit of 1984–1985, *Rembrandt as Teacher*; Schatborn's *Drawings by Rembrandt in the Rijksmuseum*, 1985; and his essay "Aspects of Rembrandt's Draughtmanship" in *Rembrandt: The Master and His Workshop/ Drawings and Etchings*, pp. 10–21). Also fascinating is the work in progress of Werner Sumowski, *Drawings of the Rembrandt School*, ten volumes of which, dealing with fifty of Rembrandt's pupils and associates, are currently available in English (1979–1992). Two further volumes are promised, with critical essays to come in the second of them.

Seymore Slive has published a selection of Rembrandt's drawings in two inexpensive volumes under the title *Drawings of Rembrandt* (1985). This work is based on an edition of the same selection of drawings published in facsimile (1888–1911). A still briefer yet representative selection in a single volume (about 100 drawings) has been published by Bob Haak, *Rembrandt Drawings* (1976).

For an interesting general survey of "connoisseurship" and the process of attribution, see Anthony Bailey's *Responses to Rembrandt* (1994), which deals with the so-called *Polish Rider* in the light of its removal from the canon of Rembrandt's paintings by the RRP. Bailey surveys the history of the RRP, as well as the reception its work has received up to 1994.

The assertion that "confusion flourishes as never before" in Rembrandt criticism is made by Jeroen Boomgaard and Robert W. Scheller in an excellent review essay titled "A Delicate Balance: A brief Survey of Rembrandt Criticism" (pp. 106–24 of *Rembrandt: The Master and His Workshop/Paintings* of the catalog to the 1991–1992 exhibition in Berlin, Amsterdam, and London). They assign the notion of a "visible" and an "invisible" Rembrandt to nineteenth-century criticism, and the "true Rembrandt" is their characterization of Rembrandt criticism in the four decades just past.

The "nasty Rembrandt, vindictive and untrustworthy" represents, though only in part, the view of Gary Schwartz in *Rembrandt: His Life, His Paintings* (1985). Rembrandt is described as "entrepreneur" and "*pictor economicus*" by Svetlana Alpers in *Rembrandt's Enterprise: The Studio and the Market* (1988). And "Rembrandt" as a disembodied category apart from Rembrandt the man and artist is the view of Mieke Bal in *Reading "Rembrandt": Beyond the Word-Image Opposition* (1991).

The catalog to the Metropolitan Museum of Art exhibition titled "Rembrandt/Not Rembrandt," published in 1995, devotes one volume to "Paintings: Problems and Issues" and a second volume to "Paintings, Drawings, and Prints: Art-Historical Perspectives." Though the focus is primarily on works in the Met's collection, the essays and critical entries range more widely and make a substantive contribution to the attribution debate.

A helpful review of the influence of Pieter Lastman on his pupil Rembrandt can be found in the essay by Christian Tümpel titled "Pieter Lastman and Rembrandt" in the catalog for a 1991 exhibition of the Rembrandt House Museum, *Pieter Lastman: The Man Who Taught Rembrandt.*

Ernst van de Wetering's *Rembrandt: The Painter at Work* (2000) has been aptly characterized by Ernst Gombrich as something like a "look over Rembrandt's shoulder while he painted." (His "Epilogue on Quality," from which the quotation on page 8 above is taken, may be found on pp. 273–81.)

Bernard Berenson's essay *Seeing and Knowing* was published in 1953; a subsequent edition published by the New York Graphic Society included illustrations not suggested by Berenson.

The catalog to a 1999–2000 exhibition of London's National Gallery and the Royal Cabinet of Paintings in The Hague, Mauritshuis, *Rembrandt by Himself*, affords the most helpful survey of Rembrandt's self-portraits (and includes, in its commentary on the painted self-portraits from 1642 on, references to an unpublished volume 4 of the *Corpus*). Also valuable is the thesis-derived study of H. Perry Chapman, *Rembrandt's Self-Portraits* (1990). Christopher Wright (*Rembrandt Self-Portraits*, 1982) and Pascal Bonafoux (*Rembrandt: Self-Portrait*, 1985) provide reproductions of most of the self-portraits, arranged more or less chronologically.

2

HUMAN PAINTER OF THE HUMAN CONDITION

Sometime during the year 1625 in a room in a windmill on the Rhine River in the Dutch city of Leiden, a nineteen-year-old man labored to get "just right" his painting of the biblical moment described in Acts 7:58, the stoning of Stephen, the first Christian martyr: "So they thrust him out of the city and stoned him (to death). And the witnesses took off and threw down their coats at the feet of a young man called Saul."

Why the young artist chose such a moment for what is believed to be his very first solo work is a matter of intriguing speculation. We know that his teacher, Pieter Lastman, had painted this scene, but we know also that Rembrandt's work is different in arrangement, in detail, in "feel." That the young Rembrandt should have begun his career with a biblical painting is worth remarking, yet what is of far greater interest is what he did with his text, for his painting remains a clear announcement, even if in somewhat rough form, of what was to come throughout the next forty-four years.

The young Rembrandt knew the work of other artists in Holland and beyond. He had just completed nearly four years of apprentice study with two well-known painters, and he had lived for six exhilarating months in Amsterdam in the Golden Age Simon Schama has so effectively described as an "embarrassment of riches." Rembrandt knew the traditions, the symbols, the clichés, and the poses of both classical art and acceptable ecclesiastical art, and he rejected the lot, for the most part, from the very beginning of his career. Why?

The narrative of Acts 7 is the biblical equivalent of a riot ending in a lynching. It is an account of violent murder at the hands of a mob of religious fanatics, encouraged by an assemblage of insecure religious functionaries, as Acts 6:9–15 makes clear.

Stoning of Stephen, 1625, Musée des Beaux-Arts, Lyon

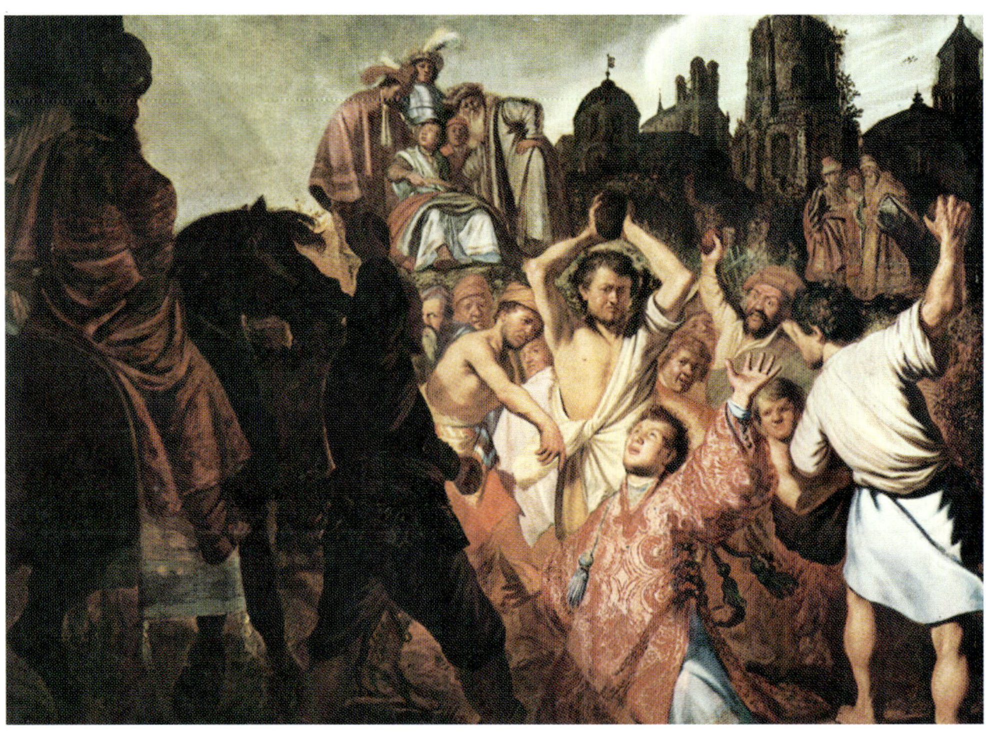

Rembrandt saw no reason to prettify the candid biblical account or to present it as anything more than the shocking reality it is. It was the murder of a man innocent of the wrongdoing of which he was accused. Angels flapping around and offering hands of comfort and laurel wreaths might have made the painting more acceptable to Dutch Catholics, but there were no angels on the scene in the text, so the young painter would not include any. His one concession to the transcendent is based solidly on the verses just preceding the moment of the stoning, Acts 7:55–56:

> Stephen, however, full of the Holy Spirit, his eyes fixed on heaven, saw the glory of God, and Jesus standing at God's right. "Look!" he said, "I see the heavens split open, and the Son of Man standing at God's right!"

Rembrandt gives us a shaft of light slicing diagonally down from above onto a Stephen oblivious to his situation, his arms out as if in preparation for an embrace, looking right into what no one else present even notices.

Kenneth Clark said, "Rembrandt never allowed himself to be deflected from the truth by the beautiful falsehoods of classical imagery." I would add that he also never allowed himself to be blinded to the reality of the Bible as a human book for humans by the need of the church to be comfortable.

Thus Rembrandt had no commissions, great or small, from the Roman Catholic Church, and of course none from his own anti-iconic Dutch Reformed Church.

What Rembrandt gives us in *The Stoning of Stephen*, now in Lyon, is just exactly what he read in his Bible: a public execution by stoning, outside the city gate, on the testimony of more than a single witness, the witnesses throwing the first stones, and the crowd then joining in, as specified in Deuteronomy 17:6–7. He even presents the "young man called Saul" holding the coats of the witnesses (Acts 7:58).

Yet there are also some elaborations on the biblical text by the young Rembrandt himself. They are logical speculations, but nevertheless additions to the brief biblical narrative: an official presence on horseback, looking on, giving the somewhat detached consent of ruling authority. Behind this officer, his standard-bearer also watches. The young Saul points toward the rock-hurling witnesses while turning his head to speak to a man to his right. At a distance, on the right of the painting, three old men are in animated conversation—is one of them Gamaliel? Is he defending the execution?

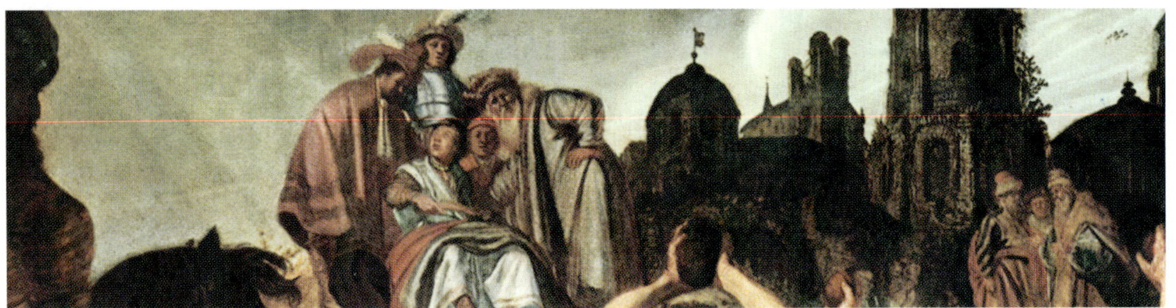

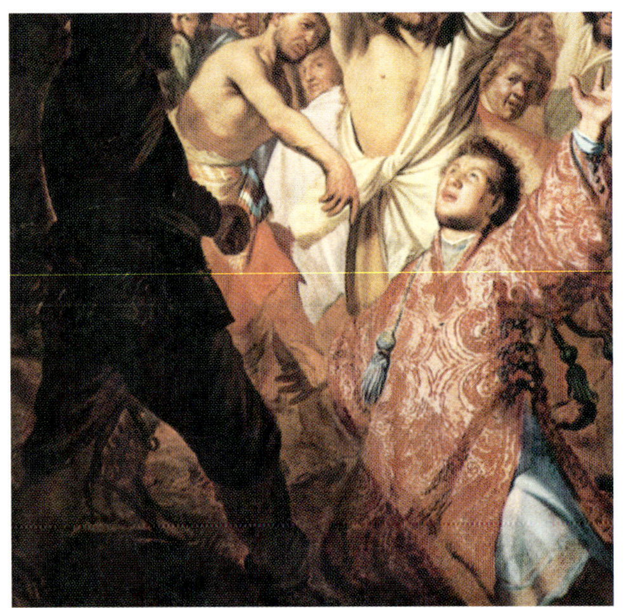

There, in front of the mounted official's horse, only partially visible between the legs of the stone-thrower facing Stephen, is a dog, a repeated presence in some of Rembrandt's depictions of biblical scenes. And peering out at us from a position just above and behind Stephen's head is Rembrandt himself—a bit of confession perhaps, a statement at least, and of a kind Rembrandt made across at least twenty-five years.

Despite all these Rembrandtian touches, this earliest known Rembrandt painting looks so little like what made Rembrandt famous that even the museum that has owned it since 1844, the Musée des Beaux-Arts in Lyon, did not recognize it as a Rembrandt until Horst Gerson declared it to be so in 1962.

Yet looking back at this painting now, through the expanse of Rembrandt's art, we can see the genesis of the conviction that permeates virtually the entire Rembrandt oeuvre, a conviction that is obvious, to one degree or another, in all of his works on biblical themes. For want of some better general term, I call this feature Rembrandt's *humanity*. It is his lifelong attempt to be honest: with his sources, with his viewers, and above all both with and about himself. John Russell calls Rembrandt "someone we can go to in time of trouble" and asks,

> How is it possible that a homely old Dutchman who lived more than 300 years ago should know so much about us? Yet he does. Where the great Italians put forth a daunting ideal of human beauty, and where a great Frenchman like Poussin subordinates our

psychic untidiness to an Olympian sense of order, Rembrandt is right in there with us, putting up with people who are no better looking than we are and taking it for granted that human life is by its very nature disorderly and imperfect.

There are many examples of this humanity in Rembrandt's paintings, etchings, and drawings, whether his subject is classical, historical, contemporary, or biblical. Even his commissioned portraits show it, as for example the painting that is perhaps his most well-known work, *The Militia Company of Captain Frans Banning Cocq* (for many years incorrectly called *The Night Watch*), now in Amsterdam. This work was a revolution in group portrait painting: Rembrandt set aside the customary "class picture" format his patrons may have expected and presented them instead forming up and striding forth to their assigned patrol. His painting is alive with bustle and movement and racket, and his eighteen paying customers are surrounded by a context that presents them *in medias res*, with their powder-boy running, two children watching, a dog barking, and an

The Militia Company of Captain Frans Banning Cocq, 1642, Rijksmuseum, Amsterdam

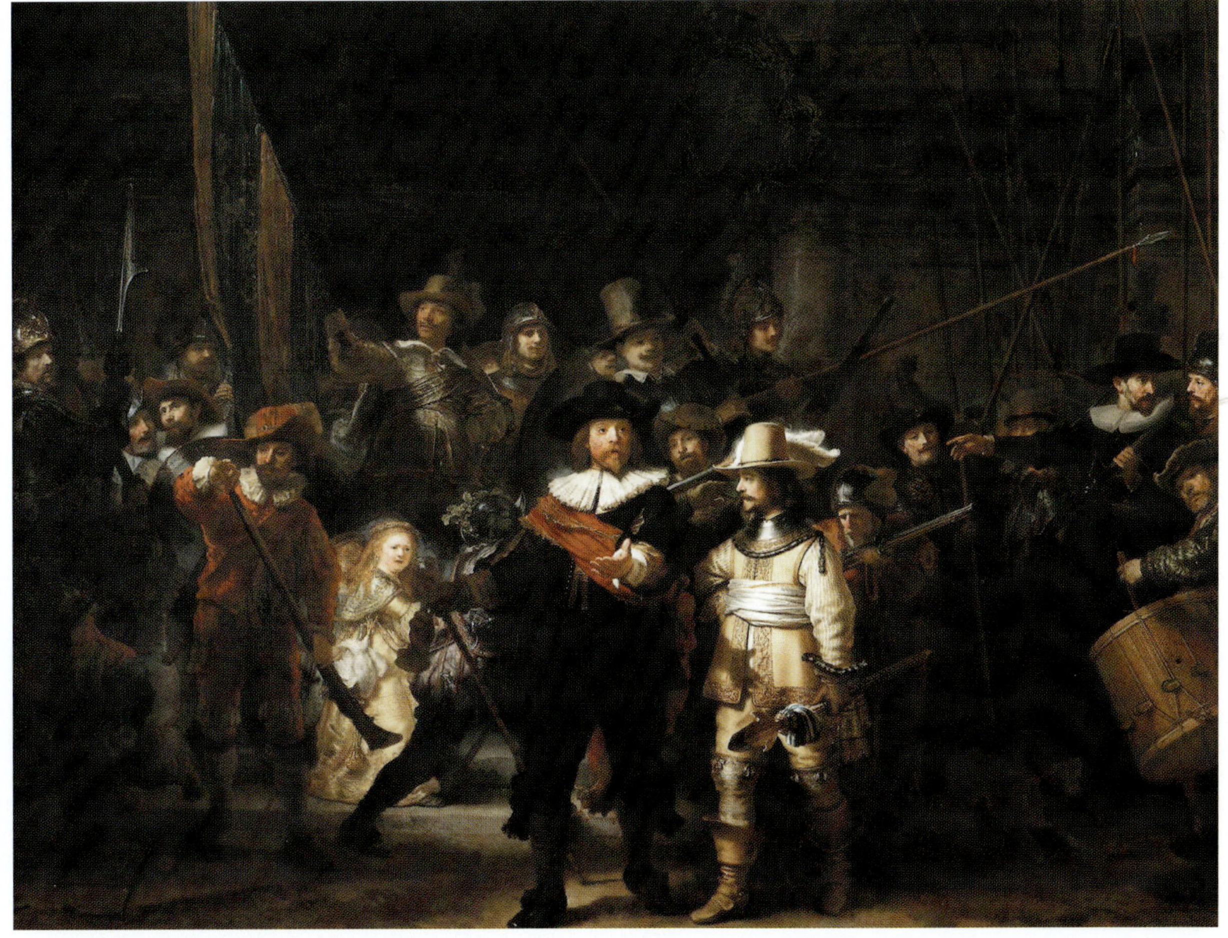

assortment of onlookers, including the artist himself, peeking out at the spectacle from behind, along with an array of symbols and characteristic activities connected with the company, and even the names of the *Kloveniers* themselves, inscribed on a great shield placed on the archway through which the captain's company is moving to do their duty.

There is little wonder that this magnificent (and huge: as Rembrandt painted it in 1642, 158.27 x 200.78 in.) work was received with enthusiasm, both by the company it depicts and also by the public astounded by its dramatic originality. The popular fiction that the painting was refused by its commissioners, ridiculed by the public, and marked the beginning of a career decline for Rembrandt, *à la* Alexander Korda and Charles Laughton, is without even a hint of support. Indeed, Rembrandt received important commissions for group portraits in 1656 and 1662 from Amsterdam dignitaries, some of whom were associates of a few of the "shooters" portrayed in the 1642 painting (see *The Anatomy Lesson of Doctor Joan Deyman* and *The Syndics of the Cloth Merchants' Guild*).

The Frame Maker Herman Doomer, 1640, Metropolitan Museum of Art, New York City (left)

Portrait of Margaretha de Geer, 1661, The National Gallery, London (right)

Rembrandt's portraits of individuals also represent a departure from what may be called static portraiture, the stiff, "posed" look and flattering portraiture, the fawning likeness designed to tickle a patron's ego. Rembrandt again and again seems to capture the soul of his sitters, an essence of what we may imagine them to have been like along with what they really looked like. Unlike the portraits painted by many of his contemporaries, and even by some of his students, Rembrandt's portraits do not appear to flatter—rather, they seem to present the truth of the person depicted, including that part of the truth that a photographic physical likeness does not reveal. Many examples come to mind, but I list here only three, two favorites and a chuckle.

Portrait of Marten Soolmans, 1634, Paris (private collection)

1. *The Frame Maker Herman Doomer*, painted in 1640, now in New York's Metropolitan Museum, presents to us the straightforward countenance of an honest craftsman, confident and unpretentious, a plain man plainly dressed, and caught with just a hint of an amused smile as he is about to speak. His son Lambert became a pupil of Rembrandt, and it is easy to imagine that the father and the artist were friends.

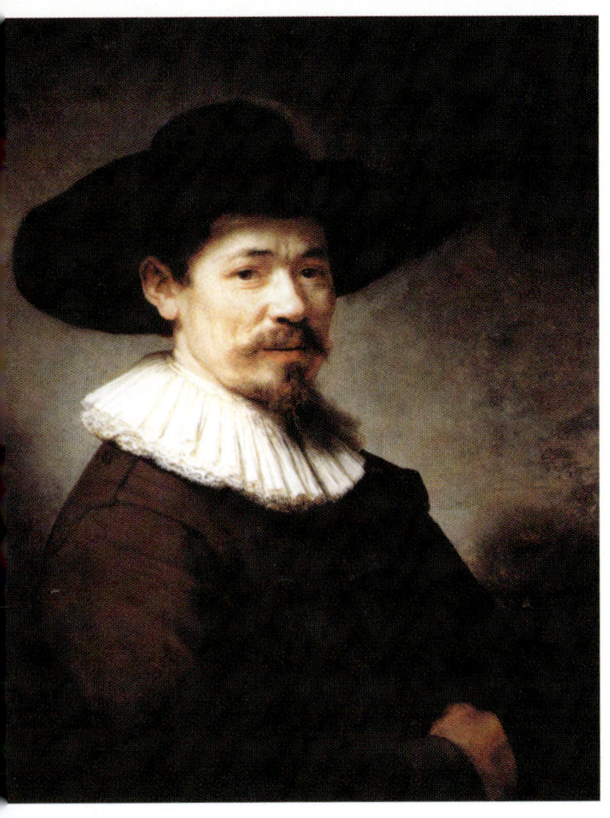

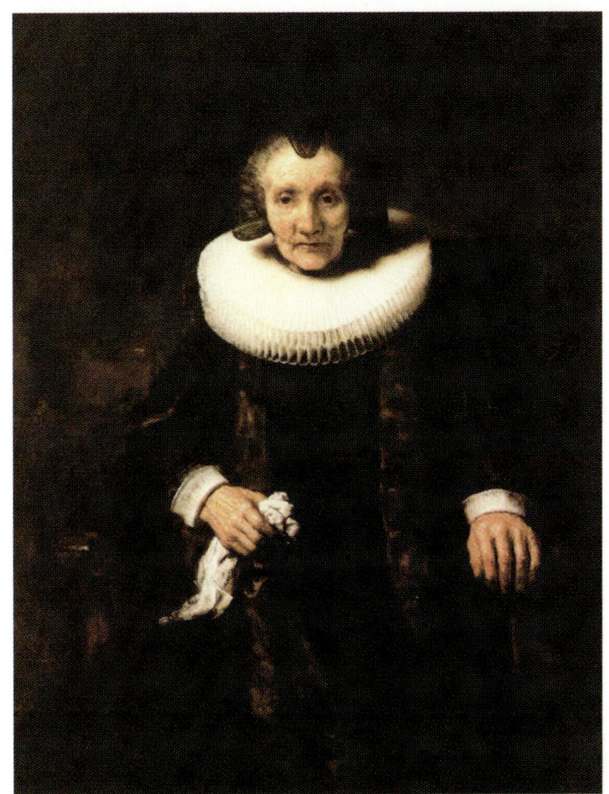

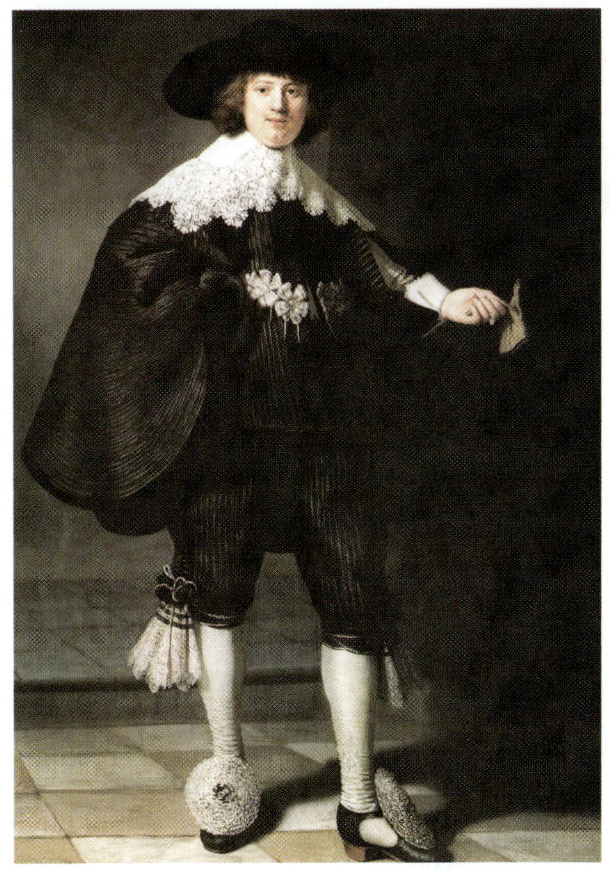

2. *Portrait of Margaretha de Geer*, painted in 1661, now in London's National Gallery, presents to us a no-nonsense lady in old-fashioned dress, not entirely happy with the fatigue and cramped joints of posing, a woman of much wisdom who is by no means reluctant to share it, as she appears in the process of doing. It is easy to imagine that Rembrandt found her delightful and painted her with affection. Indeed, he painted her portrait twice in 1661, the second time a half-length with a hint of a smile.

3. The chuckle I include is the *Portrait of Marten Soolmans*. Painted in 1634 and now in private ownership, it presents to us a pompous, over-decorated dandy who might be said to be "over the top" feet first. In 1634, Rembrandt needed work, and the

money it produced, and he would hardly have offended a paying patron. So once again he has been honest and presented Marten (and in a separate portrait, his wife) just as they presented themselves. If there is little animation in Marten's face, it is no doubt because there was little there, and if his portrait seems lacking the presence of Herman Doomer and Margaretha de Geer, well.... I find myself imagining Rembrandt painting Marten Soolmans' incredible shoes with more interest than he could find in Marten's face, and no doubt with an inner smile outwardly stifled.

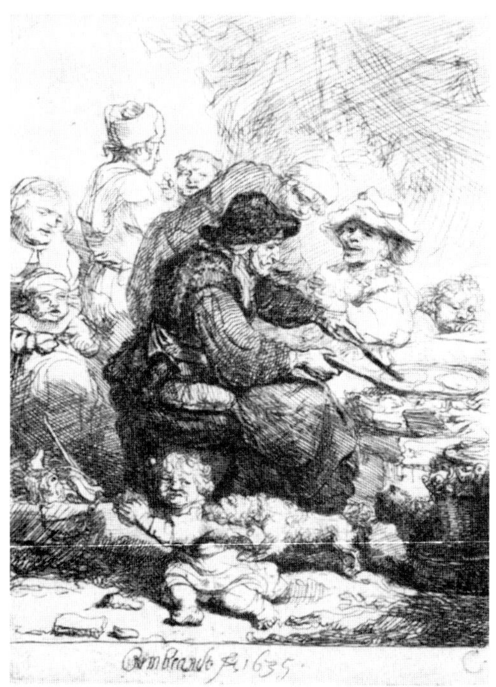

Pancake Woman, B 124, 1635, Prentenkabinet, Rijksmuseum, Amsterdam

There are etchings and drawings also that attest to what I am calling Rembrandt's humanity, his attraction to the real, his sensitivity to the truth of the human comedy. I think, for example, of the charming *Pancake Woman* of 1635, with its dog attempting the theft of the little lad's pancake while the vendor, oblivious to his distress, keeps making *panenkoeken*.

The Naughty Boy, Benesch 401, around 1635, Kupferstichkabinett, Staatliche Museen, Berlin

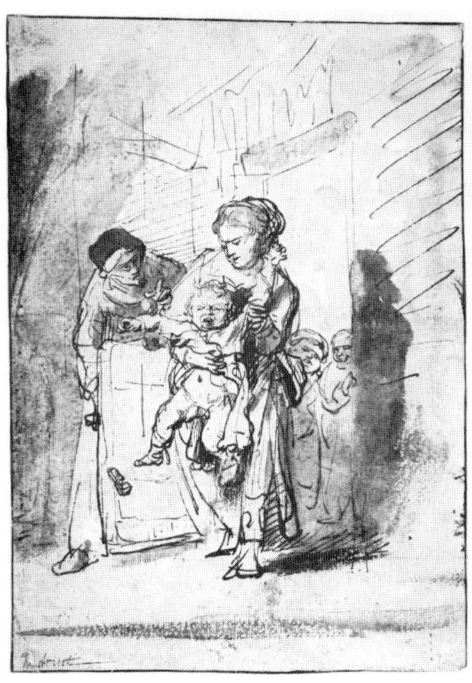

And then there is the drawing of *The Naughty Boy*, from about the same period, recording a scene from life that is unfailingly amusing to those save the ones who are its stars: the frustrated mother attempting unsuccessfully to restrain her limber, slippery, squirming child; the flailing, kicking, angry child, yelling a protest and throwing its toy; the grandmother (or even worse, the mother-in-law) giving unwanted advice with a wagging finger; and the two siblings, one laughing, one worried, just in the door behind.

A great many such examples might be presented to demonstrate Rembrandt's sensitivity to the human in any of his works portraying persons. It is a characteristic even more dramatically obvious in his works on biblical themes, my primary interest here. Indeed, we may well find this feature more obvious still in Rembrandt's biblical works because we bring baggage to the Bible that Rembrandt did not carry.

Two years after he painted *The Stoning of Stephen*, the young artist turned his hand to *St. Paul in Prison*, a painting now in Stuttgart that may present the most human St. Paul in art. There is no specific text for this work, just the various accounts of Paul's multiple imprisonments (Acts 16:23–24; 24:22–23, 27; 26:30-32) and testimony from Paul's own hand, as in Phil. 1:12–14. My guess is that Rembrandt had in mind the less restricting Roman imprisonment described in Acts 28:16, given his obvious inclusion of an unused shackle, various creature comforts, and the biblical testimony that Paul wrote letters during his two years of arrest in Rome.

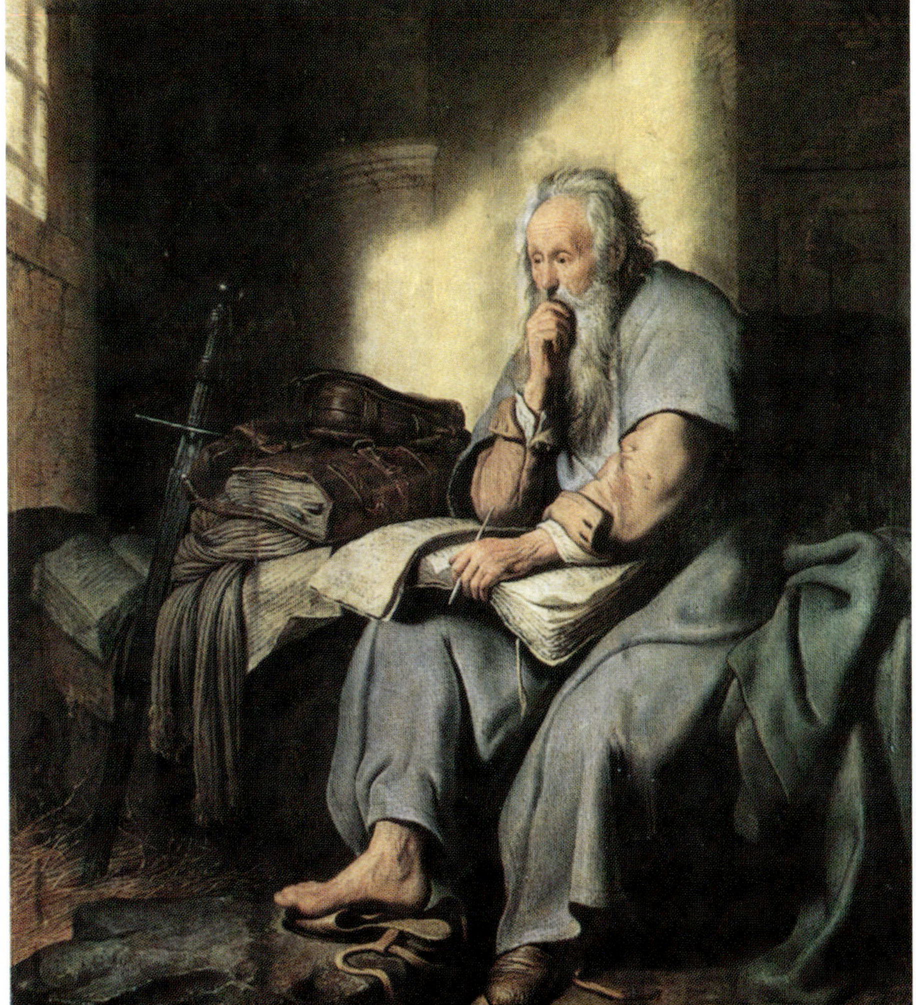

St. Paul in Prison, 1627, Staatsgalerie, Stuttgart

Here, then, is an old Paul: no halos, no angels, no piercing holy genius glare, just an old man surrounded by his books, one shoe kicked off to relieve what looks like a bunioned foot and toes with corns, paper at the ready, pen in hand, and that thinking look beyond where he is into the nearness of how to write down what he feels. It is not the look of writer's block, but the struggle to express a reality too large for mere words. Rembrandt was no writer—the 674-page collection of documents relating to his family, his life, and his work includes just seven letters, each of them having to do with his work. No great adjustment is required, however, to see in St. Paul's struggle for expression in words Rembrandt's struggle for expression in painting and etching and drawing.

Rembrandt does make one concession to traditional Christian symbolism in this painting: the sword leaning against the bed or bench upon which the old apostle is sitting with his book and paper, an attribute of the saints who were martyred or known as militant evangelists. Both militancy and martyrdom could of course be claimed for Paul.

There is also the curious feature of the large stone on which Paul rests his bare foot. This stone may be an allusion to the second part of Paul's life: his foot unshod because it is on holy ground (Exod. 3:5) and set on the rock of faith in God (Ps. 18:1–3 or 40:1–3 or 144:1–2). I think this unlikely, however; the rock may be no more than a memory of an engraving by Willem Swannenburgh of Leiden.

Christ in the Storm on the Sea of Galilee, 1633, Isabella Stewart Gardner Museum, Boston, stolen on March 18, 1990, and still missing

In 1633, Rembrandt painted what, surprisingly, given Holland's dominance of the sea in the seventeenth century, is his sole seascape. It is *Christ in the Storm on the Sea of Galilee*, alas now lost to us following the infamous raid on Boston's Isabella Stewart Gardner Museum in 1990.

Once again, Rembrandt gives us reality: a real storm on a real sea, with real peril, real fear, and one really seasick disciple. There is here not one false or melodramatic pose: the disciples who are not frozen with fear or praying or beseeching Christ are fighting the ship's rigging, sails, and tiller for their lives.

The helmsman is making a mighty effort to keep the vessel off the huge rock to the left, Patrick O'Brian's dread "lee shore." Another disciple is attempting to reach the gaff hook, jutting out forward, to fend the craft off from the certain destruction of the rocky shore, but

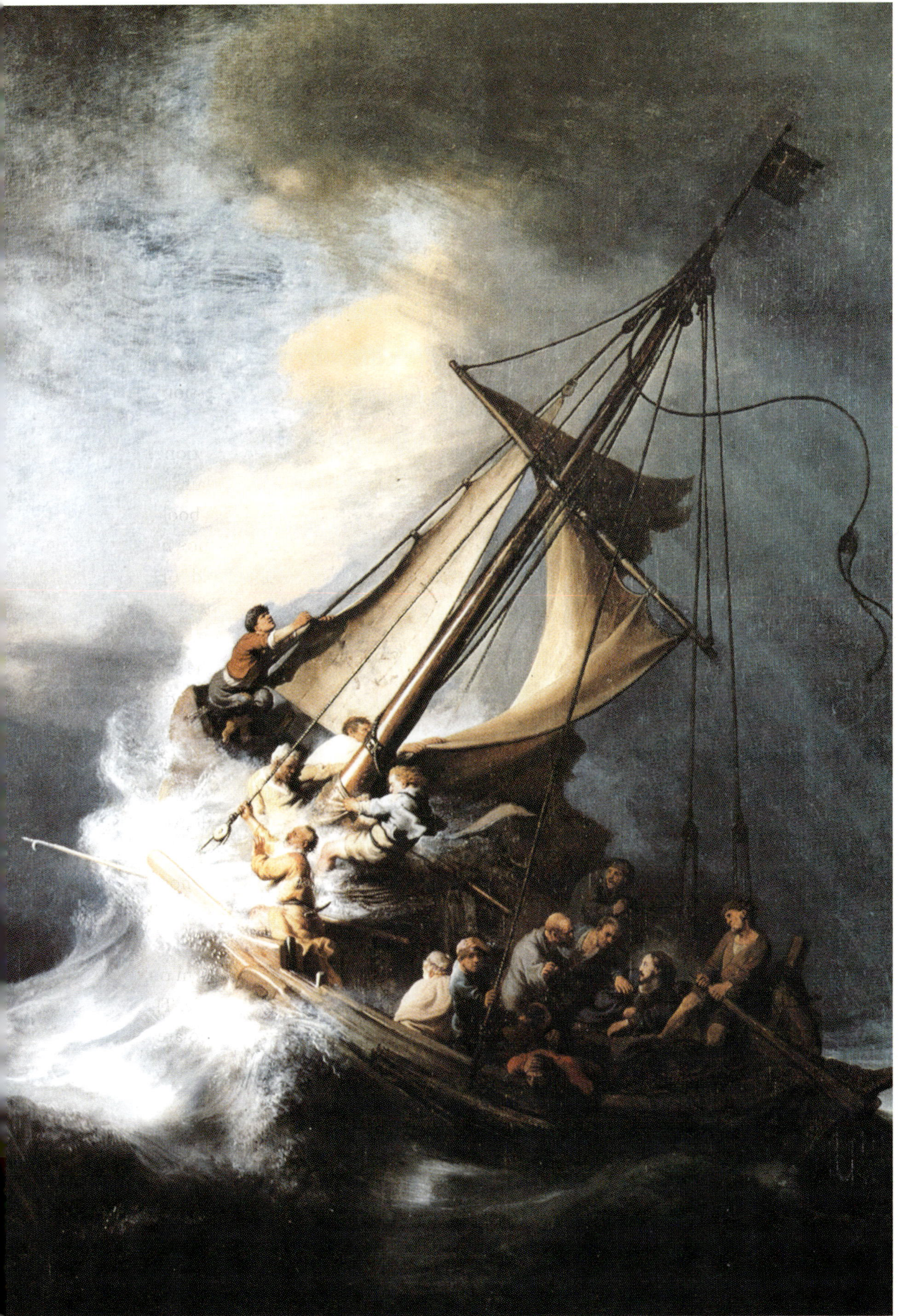

it is all he can do to pull himself into position by the stay he grasps with his right hand. A second stay has broken loose and swings wildly and dangerously with its lower block still attached. Three disciples are struggling with the mainsail, two of them pulling it about the base of the mainmast, a third tugging at the part of it still drawing. A fourth disciple attempts to lower the foresail, which seems to be skewing the boat stern-on toward the fearful rock.

Two disciples are pleading with Christ to "do something," and one on each side aft seems to be in a paralysis of fear. Of the remaining figures, one is apparently bent in prayer; two face each other just within and just outside the boat's small cabin, perhaps frozen in terror. The remaining disciple is ill. It is interesting that Rembrandt has given us fourteen disciples.

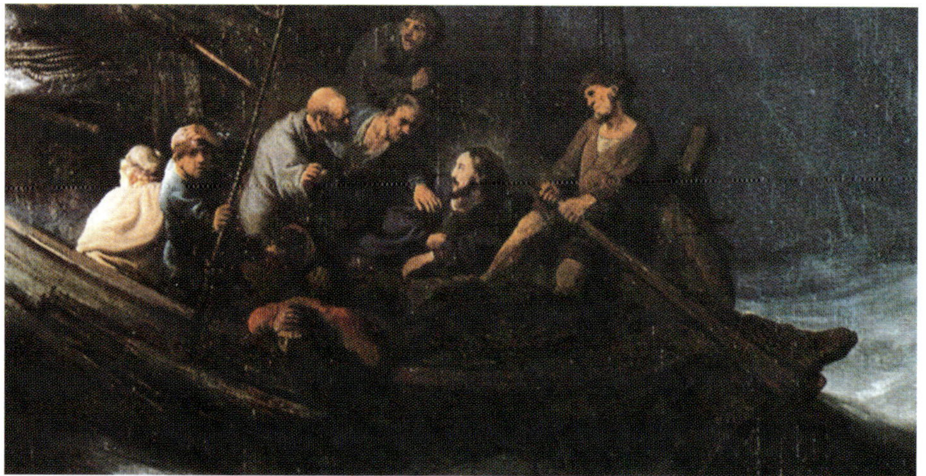

Only Christ remains calm. So Matthew 8:23–25:

> Then he went aboard the boat, his disciples following. A sudden violent storm blew down upon the lake, the waves all but swamping the boat. But he was sleeping! So they drew near and woke him, shouting, "Lord, rescue! We are going down!"

Rembrandt has captured to perfection the moment with this wild and dangerous, wet and pitching storm. I have been in such a storm on the Sea of Galilee in 1992. It came without warning, with a blue sky and the sun shining, and it threw waves over the top deck of a double-decked tourist boat. The Israeli dailies published pictures of the event, with reports of the damage it caused. Rembrandt did not know

Galilee, of course. But he was a Dutchman, and he knew about storms at sea. He also knew the end of this powerful story, and at the top of his painting, left, the sun is already breaking through.

In 1628 or 1629, Rembrandt began a series of paintings based on the story of Samson; altogether, he would do at least five such paintings, the last of them in 1641, and across the years from around 1632 or 1633 to about 1656, he did about a dozen drawings of moments from Samson's history. In the first of the paintings, he undertook to illustrate the moment in the story just before Delilah cuts the Danite's hair, long because of his Nazirite vow (Judg. 16:1–19): *Samson Betrayed by Delilah.*

This work, now in Berlin, presents a somewhat coarse-looking Delilah lifting a lock of the long curls of a sleeping, helpless Samson as two understandably scared Philistine soldiers sneak into the room, one with the shears that are to break the big man's Nazirite vow and so sap his incredible strength. The complete vulnerability of the Danite hero, Delilah's willing treachery, and the creeping fear of the

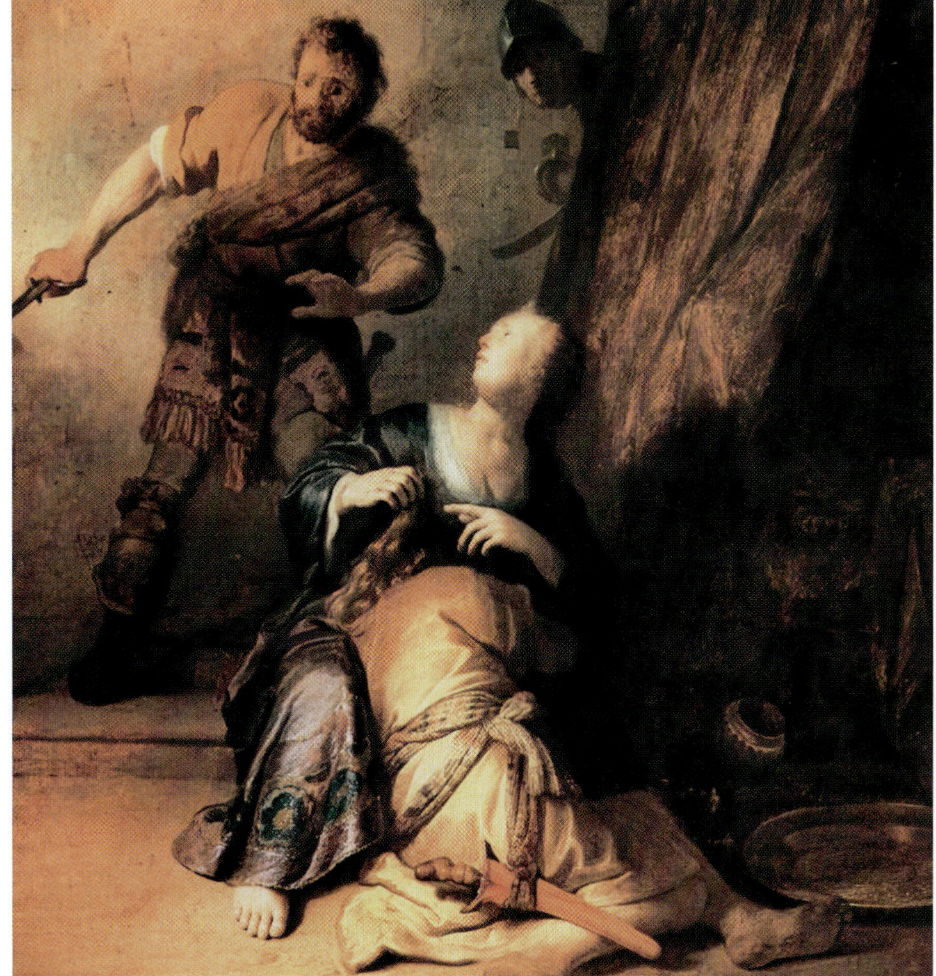

Samson Betrayed by Delilah, 1629-1630, Gemäldegalerie, Staatliche Museen, Berlin

tiptoeing Philistines are presented with great drama and tension, and Rembrandt, as usual, follows his text quite literally: "And so she lulled him to sleep on her lap, and then she summoned a man; next, she sheared off the seven locks of his head, thus managing to bring him low. Thus his power left him." (Judg. 16:19)

Seven or eight years later, Rembrandt painted a huge work (some 10 x 8 ft.), depicting the next moment in the narrative, when Samson, deprived of his mighty strength, is wakened, seized, and blinded by the Philistines. It is *The Blinding of Samson*, now in Frankfurt. And once again, Rembrandt is faithful to his chosen text:

> And then she [Delilah of the Wadi Sorek] warned, "Philistines are on top of you, Samson!" He was immediately awake, and he said, "I'll just go out and get rid of them as I usually do." He was unaware that Yahweh had turned away from him. Thus the Philistines held him down, and gouged out his eyes. (Judg. 16:20–21a)

The Blinding of Samson is easily the most violent work Rembrandt ever created. To some of Rembrandt's contemporaries, steeped as they

The Blinding of Samson, 1636, Städelsches Kunstinstitut, Frankfurt

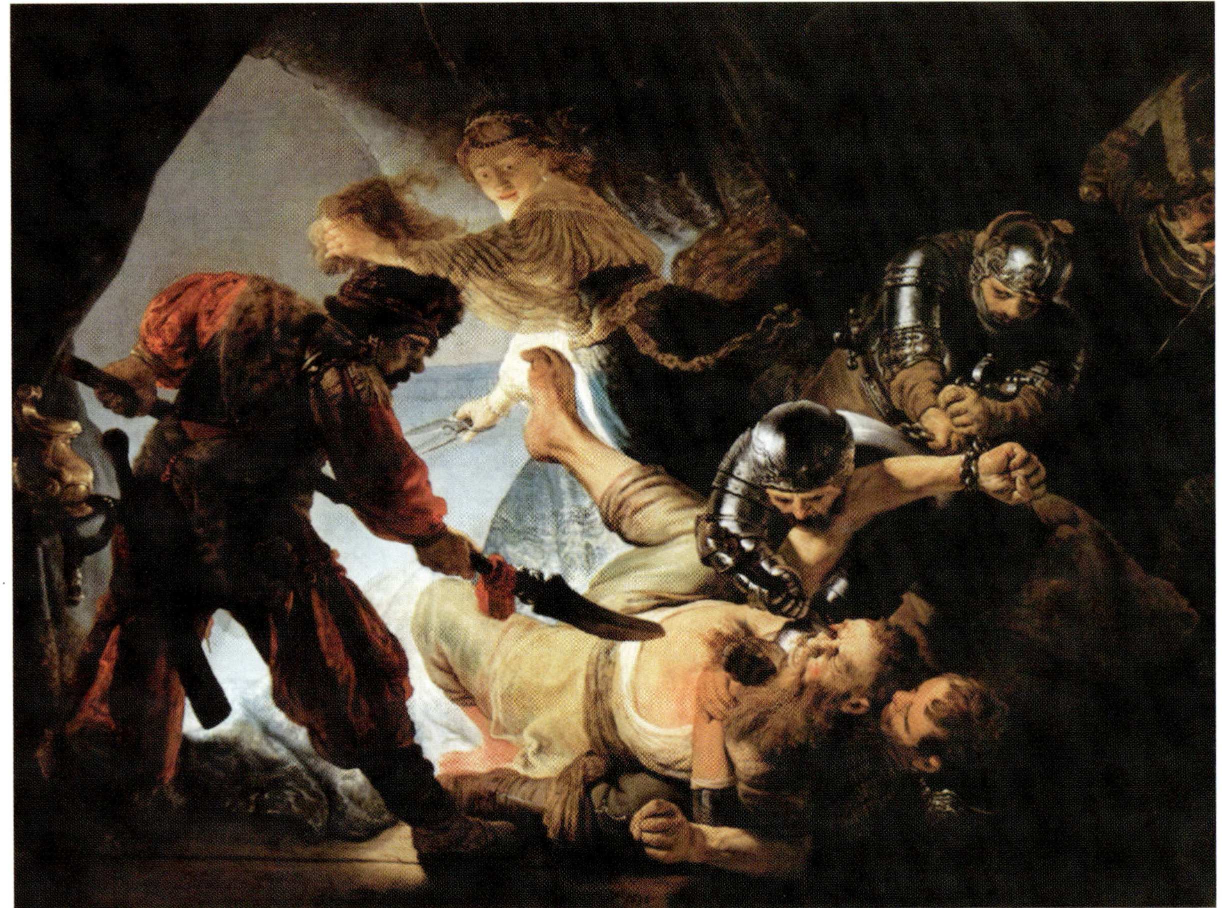

were in the curlicue pleasantness of Baroque painting, it must have been both hideous and ugly. It still has the power to shock, even in this age jaded with violent images from movies, not to mention television newscasts.

As a testimony to Rembrandt's human view of Holy Scripture, this painting is unequalled. It rewards long looking and concentrated study. I stood before it in 1984 for such a long time that the Städelsches Kunstinstitut guards began to watch me in nervous shifts. In composition, as in detail, it is a riveting portrayal of a moment of violent agony.

Rembrandt presents the tense fright of the Philistine soldiers by their actions, their posture, their faces. They *know* this Israelite's terrible reputation, and they are not all that sure that a haircut is going to save them from being smashed. Samson's Nazirite vow (Judg. 13:4–5 and Num. 6) of course had no significance for them.

The soldier on the left holds his partizan at the ready, much as a battering ram might be grasped: his stance, in silhouette, suggests power, but his face is wide-eyed and open-mouthed terror. So also is the face of the man with raised sword (*and* protecting shield)—his fear is equally obvious, and he is as ready to run as he is to slash.

The *three* soldiers in heavy armor are in a frantic struggle to subdue and control the writhing Danite champion. One, failing an attempt to lock a manacle around Samson's flailing right arm, has quickly wrapped the manacle's chain around his right wrist, twisting it so tightly that the wrist is bleeding. Another has fallen under the struggling body of Samson and has a lock hold around Samson's neck and under his left arm; this soldier is holding on for dear life, and Samson's bucking head has jarred his helmet off. The third Philistine soldier is trying to aid this wrestling one, seizing Samson's heavy beard with a gloved left fist and pressing down on Samson's neck while with his right hand he is jabbing a *kris* into Samson's right eye.

This *kris*, an ornate dagger with a wavy blade (used by Rembrandt more than once), is an Indonesian weapon. Rembrandt's fascination with exotic garments and unusual weapons is well known, as is the longstanding Indonesian presence in Amsterdam, where to this day a big night out is a *rijsttafel*, a dinner in an Indonesian restaurant. The soldier holds the *kris* not by its handle, but by the middle of its

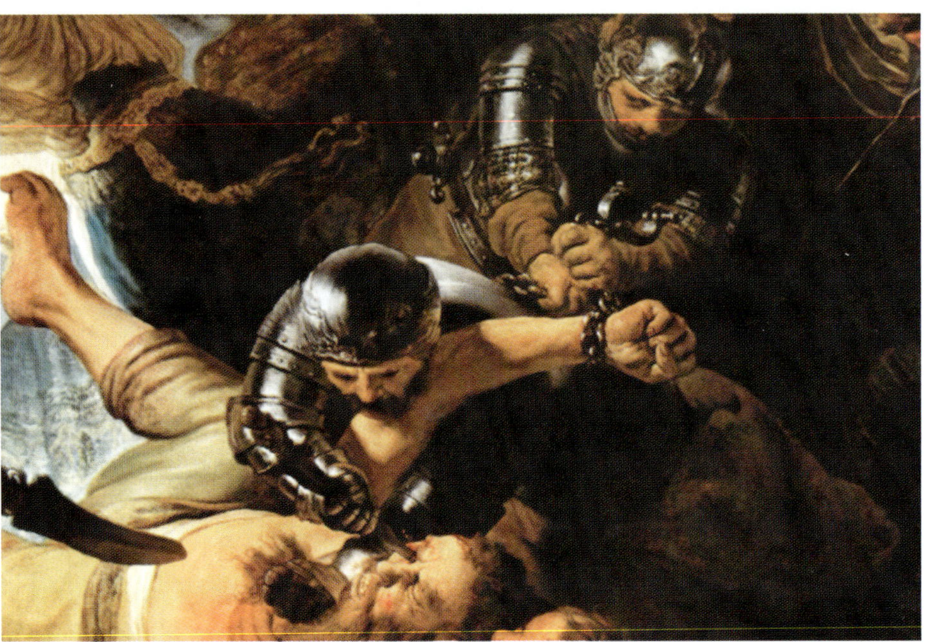

curving blade, for accuracy of aim amidst the furious struggle, and blood is spurting from Samson's eye socket.

Samson himself, though much weakened by the departure of the blessing presence of Yahweh (Judg. 16:20d) is still powerful, and he kicks with his right knee, pushes with his left foot and leg, butts backward with his head, and tries in vain to bring his clenched fists into action. His muscles strain. His teeth are gritted. The toes of his right foot are curled with the tension of his pain and struggle. His scalp is lacerated and bleeding from Delilah's hasty, anxious, ragged haircut.

Delilah rushes out of harm's way, overturning in her haste what appears to be a chair upholstered with heavy brass nails, but she looks back in fascinated fear. Her right hand still holds the scissors she has just used, her left hand the mass of Samson's lifetime of hair. She is beautifully dressed and bejeweled, her delicate bracelet and teardrop earring a testimony of Rembrandt's lifelong penchant for pearls. The expression on her face speaks fear, astonishment, a mixture of victory and regret, and the surprise (and hope) that this haircut, after three failed attempts to weaken this huge man (Judg. 16:4–16), may actually do the job. This Delilah is more elegant, by far, and much less common in appearance than the Delilah of *Samson Betrayed by Delilah.*

There are yet many details in this huge painting of the twenty-year-old Rembrandt, details of what can only be called "prettiness," despite the violent, even gory, moment being depicted: the beauty of

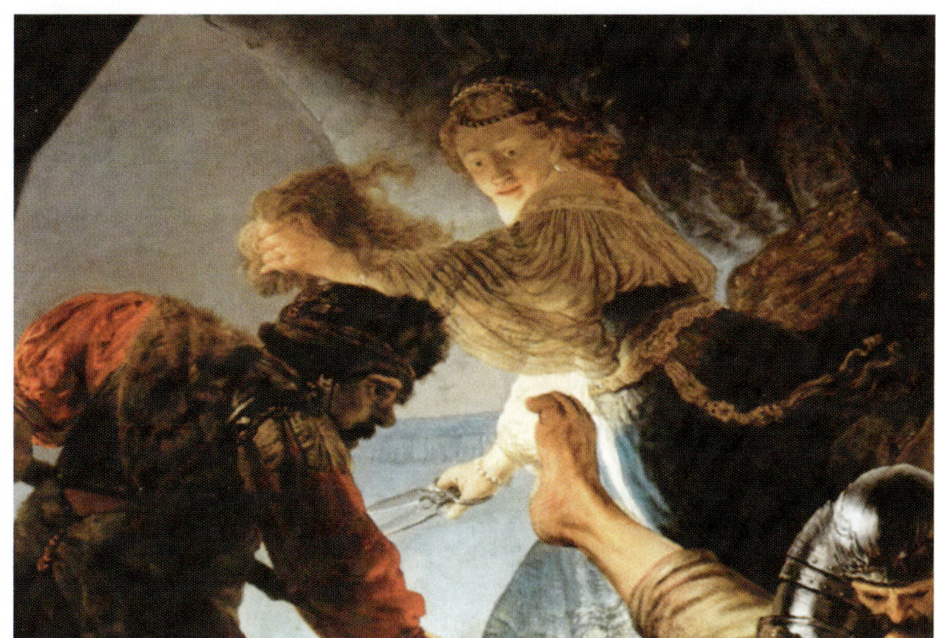

the drapery in this bedchamber of Delilah, the tumbled bedclothes on the floor, the gilded pitcher and basin on the stand with the heavy, gold-trimmed cloth and the gold-tipped belt at the left, the parted curtain through which Delilah lunges, the fringed blue hanging in the next room, and of course the gorgeous and delicately painted costume of Delilah herself.

No detail is more telling or more moving, however, than the play of light dazzling its way across the skirt and the face of Delilah and the writhing body of the prone Samson into the black darkness at the right of the painting. Rembrandt has given us the drawing curtain of Samson's blindness, closing from right to left. Delilah, his temptress, rushes into the light Samson will never see again. And knowing the story of Judges 16, as Rembrandt undoubtedly did, we are given the feeling that the pain and first darkness of this horrific moment are nothing compared to what Samson is to know in the days to come, to his people Israel a failure, grinding grain in a Philistine prison.

A great many more examples of what I am calling Rembrandt's humanity in his works on biblical texts and themes might easily be given. It is a characteristic that I will mention repeatedly in chapters to come. *The Blinding of Samson* is in many ways, however, the ultimate expression of what remained throughout Rembrandt's life a consistent feature of much of his art, indeed a feature of nearly all of it. He did not again present so violent a human struggle in a single work, and as he grew older his human touches grew far more subtle, and more moving as well.

Just four years after he had painted *The Blinding of Samson*, Rembrandt painted *The Visitation*, now in Detroit, a gentle and moving depiction of familial and feminine connection in its portrayal of the moment of Mary's meeting with her kinswoman Elizabeth. Elizabeth and her husband Zechariah had been given in their old age, as had been Abraham and Sarah, the gift of a child (Luke 1:5–25). When the angel Gabriel came to Mary in Nazareth to announce her impending pregnancy by the Holy Spirit, he told Mary, "Your kinswoman Elizabeth is pregnant with a son in her old age: this woman who was called barren is in her sixth month" (Luke 1:36). Immediately following this event, Mary quickly journeyed to the hill town near Jerusalem where Zechariah and Elizabeth lived, identified only by tradition as Ein Kerem. As she arrived and greeted Elizabeth, Elizabeth felt the child in her womb move, and she was aware of the presence of the Holy Spirit (Luke 1:39–45). Rembrandt chose this moment, this greeting, and this response, this special communication between two miraculously blessed women, as the moment for a painting suffused with a palpable sense of family affection and spiritual expectation.

Zechariah is present, following his wife onto the front steps of their rather grand house, helped along by the steadying shoulder of a young boy. Joseph is there, leading by the house to shelter and provender the animal Mary has ridden on their long journey. A servant-girl, standing on tiptoe, helps Mary with her heavy cloak; a little dog watches Joseph and the donkey; a peacock and his family stir out to see what's up; a large city in the background, identified as Jerusalem by the presence of the temple, has an array of people moving about.

But all this is secondary to the center of the painting, where Elizabeth, cane in hand, embraces Mary, speaking and looking heavenward as she does. Mary looks respectfully into the old woman's face and reaches around her shoulder with her right arm, as a cloud hovers above them both, seeming to embrace just the two of them. Elizabeth's words, as reported by Luke (1:42b–44), are:

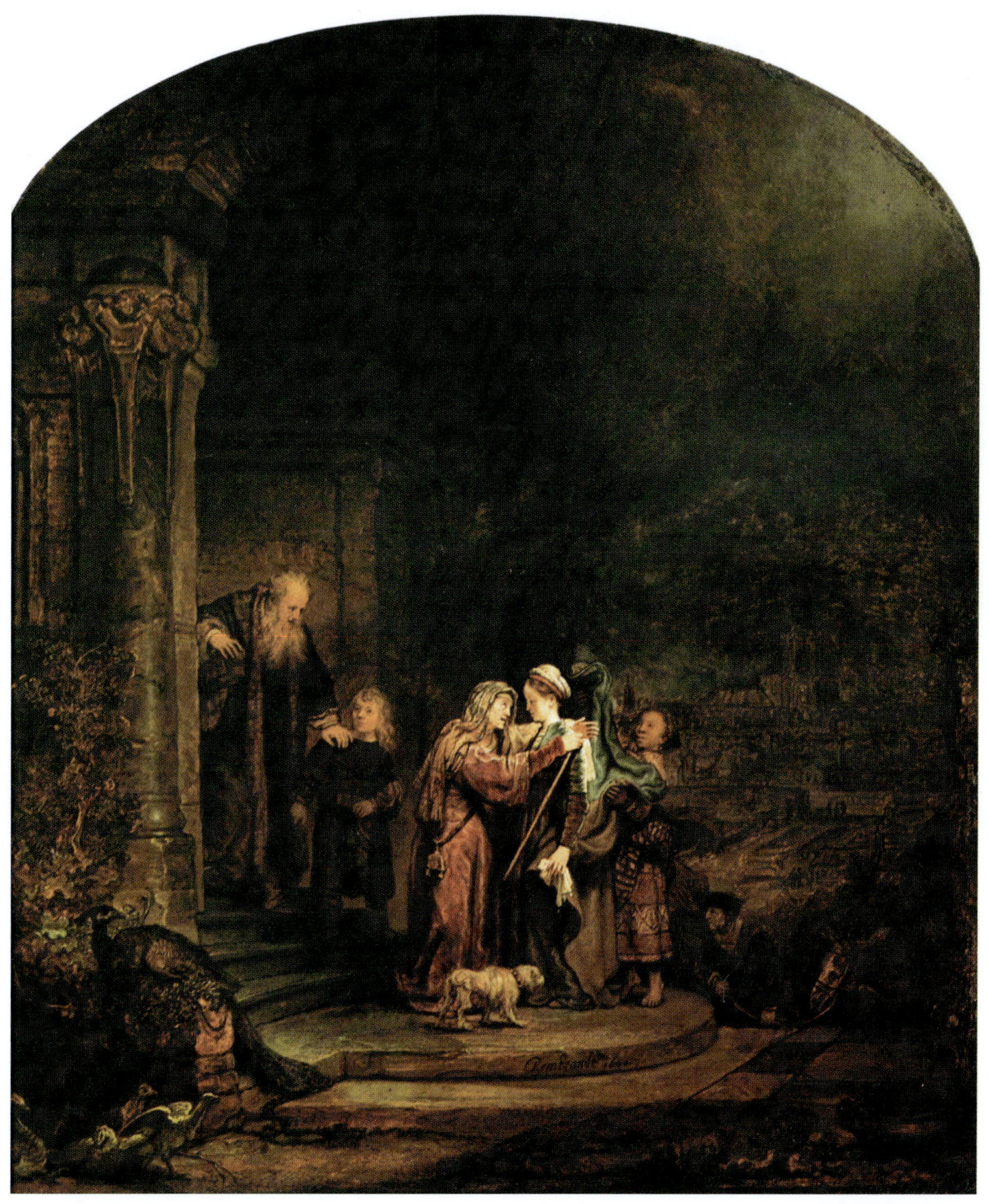

The Visitation, 1640, Detroit Institute of Arts, Detroit

You are blessed above women, and the child in your womb is blessed! And how is it that *I* am visited by the mother of my Lord? Indeed, the minute I heard the sound of your greeting, the child I am carrying moved with delight in my womb!

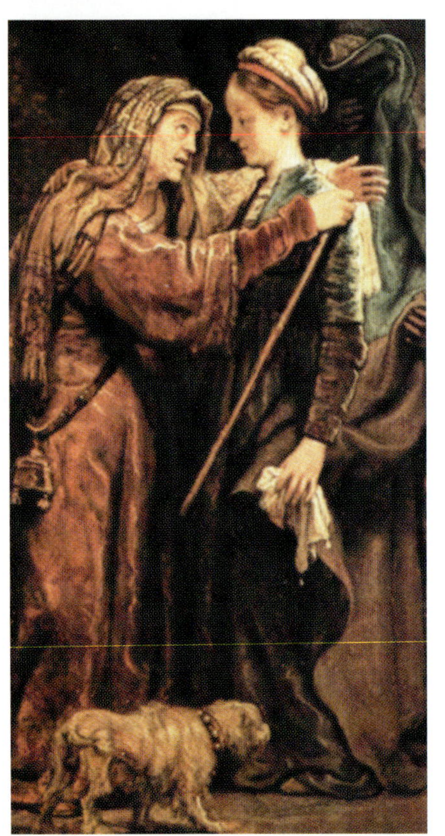

This moment of Elizabeth's speaking is the moment Rembrandt sought to depict, and he did so by placing the two women in a sort of spotlight that falls from a luminous cloud at the top right of the painting. Elizabeth appears to be looking up toward this cloud as she speaks to Mary, and the light illumines Mary's back and Elizabeth's embracing left hand, lifted as if to pat Mary affectionately. The dark cloud over the heads of the two women is Rembrandt's suggestion of the presence of the Holy Spirit felt by Elizabeth, and of course in this same chapter of Luke's Gospel, felt by Mary as well.

Yet it is not this cloud nor the heavenly light that gives this painting its sense of intimacy—that is provided by the humanity of this domestic setting, a happy arrival that calls up trips home, visits to grandmother's, with everyone excited, even animals noticing the departure from the usual, and each member of the household in an unaccustomed place, doing the right but different thing. And in the middle of all this movement, the two women: one old, one young, both pregnant by an act of God, and a connection between them that is beyond anything either of them is saying, miraculous in its ordinariness and somehow here an enhancement as well as a reflection of the divine blessing upon them in this unique moment.

Across the entire range of Rembrandt's biblical works, this humanity is an obvious feature, and in works such as *The Blinding of Samson*, a feature that has been the occasion of much discussion, not all of it is complimentary to him. Some have considered it crude, even coarse. Others have thought it a young man's protest, never fully outgrown by Rembrandt, against the establishment, the shared language of the artists' guild of Rembrandt's time. Still others have held him to be too much influenced by the "dirty feet, ragged clothes, and rotten fruit" of the great rascal of Italian art, Caravaggio. Kenneth Clark gave a fascinating television lecture on the subject, titled "The Rebel." And a number of art historians have thought Rembrandt out of step with tradition, with society, with his time, with his patrons, with his customers, certainly with organized religion, and even with art itself.

All of this can be both supported and disproved, and variously has been. I suggest, however, that there is a middle ground between adoration and deconstruction, and though I attempt here to demonstrate that middle ground by reference to Rembrandt's works on biblical themes, I believe it can be supported throughout his oeuvre.

A German contemporary of Rembrandt, Joachim von Sandrart, in a work published in 1675, wrote, "He did not at all manage to consider his own station, but always associated only with lowly people who also hindered him in his work." The range of Rembrandt's art suggests, rather, that he was interested in the people who impressed him as *real*, whatever their station in life. If this did not go down well with those who considered themselves of higher station, Rembrandt simply did not care. I doubt that he ever even thought about it. His seven letters to his early patron Constantin Huygens reveal in their deference an anxiety about money he badly needed, not any awe of a courtier highly placed.

At the beginning of this chapter, I called attention to the dog in *The Stoning of Stephen* as a repeated presence in Rembrandt's works on biblical texts. In the Apocryphal story of Tobit and his son Tobias, a dog is mentioned twice (Tob. 6:2 and 11:4) and is thus an obvious feature of works based on the narrative of Tobit, particularly for so careful a reader of the biblical text as Rembrandt. Yet there is no dog in the account of Stephen's martyrdom, nor is any dog present in more than thirty different biblical stories from Genesis to Acts into which Rembrandt places one. A variety of animals turns up in Rembrandt's drawings, etchings, and paintings as logically present in works both secular and religious in theme—pastoral scenes include sheep and cows, for example, and martial scenes include war horses. There are ducks and swans in streams and canals and peacocks in settings suggesting wealth. But dogs, when Hagar and Ishmael are turned out by Abraham, when Joseph is telling his dreams to his family, when Gabriel makes his astounding announcement to Mary, when the infant Jesus is presented to Simeon and Anna in the temple in Jerusalem, when Jesus is preaching and healing the sick, when the resurrected Jesus is dining with the two disciples from Emmaus, and even added (!) to a copy sketch of da Vinci's *Last Supper* that Rembrandt made from an engraving he had seen in 1635?

There is no apparent reason to think of Rembrandt as particularly fond of dogs. Only twice did he prepare a work depicting a dog alone: the small *Sleeping Puppy* of 1640, B 158, and *A Sleeping Dog,* Benesch 455, that reappears in a grisaille painting of 1633, *Joseph Telling His Dreams* (now in Amsterdam). He showed much greater interest, to judge by the number of works depicting them, in lions and elephants. A self-portrait of 1631, *The Artist in an Oriental Costume, with a Poodle at His Feet* now in Paris (Musée du Petit Palais), includes a dog with the hair shorn from its hindquarters and looking a bit embarrassed. The attribution of this work to Rembrandt has been questioned, but it is accepted as correct by the RRP. The poodle with its rump shaved may have been included as a sort of status symbol, a hunter as an accessory to the "oriental," that is, Middle Eastern, costume Rembrandt has given himself. I see no reason to assume that this uncomfortable-looking dog should be regarded as a favorite pet—indeed, it was added to the painting later to replace what Rembrandt may have considered a problem with the bottom of the work, as x-ray photography and a copy of the painting *sans* dog show.

So why so many dogs in so many biblical works, particularly in works drawn from narratives in which no dog is present? A dog in the drawing of Esau selling his birthright to Jacob (Benesch 607) seems a reasonable presence, of course, as Esau had just come in from a hunt; so also a dog in a painting with the shepherds squeezing into the stable to see the child the heavenly host had told them about or in a painting of the crowd arriving to gawk at the lad David presenting the severed head of the Philistine giant Goliath to King Saul (see chap. 3), to cite three examples.

But what about a dog in a drawing of Gabriel's annunciation to Mary (Benesch 994) or in a painting, an etching (B 37), *and* a drawing (Benesch 527) of Joseph relating his dreams to his family, or in an etching of the presentation of the infant Jesus to Simeon and Anna in the temple (B 49), or in a drawing of the moment of Pilate's surrender of Jesus to the political pressure of religious authority (Benesch 927)?

I believe all these dogs in biblical works are yet another example of Rembrandt's humanity. They have no iconographic significance, and they are certainly no part of any received artistic tradition. No major artist before Rembrandt put dogs into the Bible on such a scale. Rembrandt's dogs are one more way of presenting the Bible as a human document, albeit a document about divine reality. Rembrandt was ever anxious to make clear, in every way he could think up, that the people of the Bible were real people living in a real world, surrounded by the creatures, the vegetation, the things that made his own landscape so continuously entertaining. His saints have no halos, and they are not shocked by the sight of dogs doing what dogs will do, simply because of what they are. Some of Rembrandt's dogs proved so embarrassing to some viewers that they cited them as evidence of his eccentricity, his crudeness; other viewers doubted that so great and spiritual an artist as Rembrandt could have put dogs into such "holy" scenes and suggested that the offending animals had been added by other hands or that the works in which they appear are really not works by Rembrandt. The problem of such critics, however, was not really Rembrandt, but themselves. Rembrandt put the dogs in because he was a human painter painting human scenes, even about divine moments, for human eyes. I call attention to these dogs of Rembrandt in the works I include in the chapters that follow, as I did above discussing *The Stoning of Stephen.* I cannot resist including a few of them here that make no appearance in later chapters because they seem to me so specific an example of Rembrandt's entry into the biblical world that intrigued him as a valid world because it was, for him, a real world.

There is a moving etching of 1637 depicting the moment when Abraham, nagged by a jealous Sarah, turns Hagar and her son by Abraham out into the wilderness. Rembrandt was obviously working from the second version of the expulsion, Genesis 21:8–14, in which Abraham himself sends Hagar and Ishmael away (in the earlier narrative, in Gen. 16:3–6, it is Sarai, before her name change (Gen. 17:15) who made Hagar "miserable," so that she ran away). Thus does Rembrandt give us a weeping Hagar, setting off with her little son Ishmael, compelled by an Abraham distressed by this "thing very wrong" (Gen. 21:11): his trouble shows on his face, and by the ambivalence of his hands and feet, which are literally divided between the two worlds his two sons will now face. Sarah peers from a window with the unabashed glee of having had her way, and little Isaac, standing by his mother's skirts, peeps from the doorway. Then there is Rembrandt's addition to the narrative—the little dog, running down the steps to follow his young master who is setting off toward

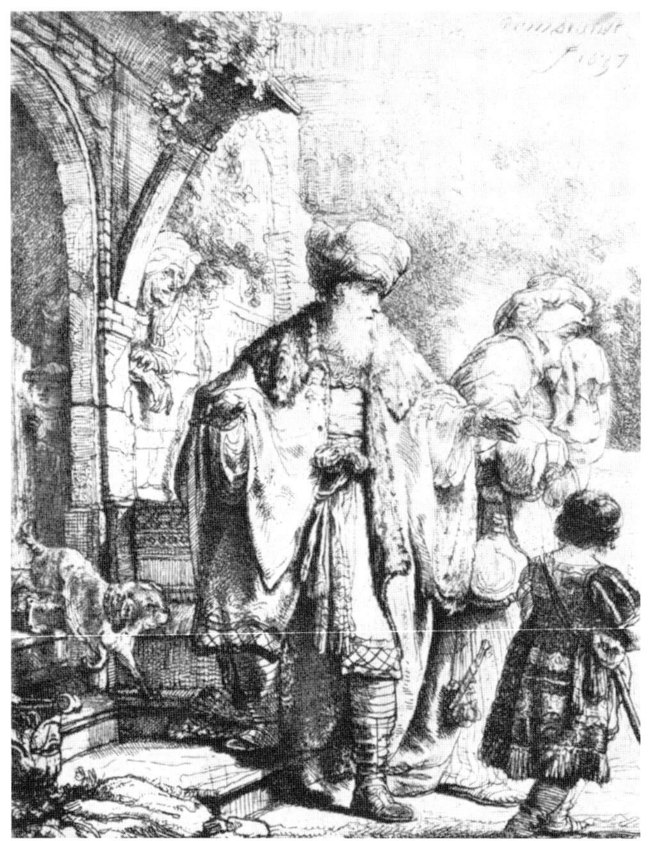

Abraham Casting Out Hagar, B 30, 1637, Albertina, Vienna

the wilderness with a determined step, his back turned toward Abraham and the only home he has ever known. This dog is a charming touch: the one creature in the scene whose loyalty appears undivided, moving without any division of spirit to go with the outcast son.

In two drawings done later, one in the early forties and one in the early fifties (Benesch 916), the dog is still present and still following the two outcasts; in this earlier of these two works, it comes down the steps and *around* both Hagar and Abraham to follow Ishmael, heading out this time with his bow and quiver (Gen. 21:20). Abraham seems to bless this son, even as he comforts the weeping Hagar, while Sarah peeps around the door slightly opened in the background.

The biblical narrative to which Rembrandt gave more dogs than any other is the story of Tobit and his son Tobias. Rembrandt created at least a dozen works on moments from the Book of Tobit in which he included the dog, mentioned twice in the text simply as "the dog" (ὁ κύων). The most touching of these works is surely the etching of

The Dismissal of Hagar, Benesch 524, early 1640s, British Museum, London

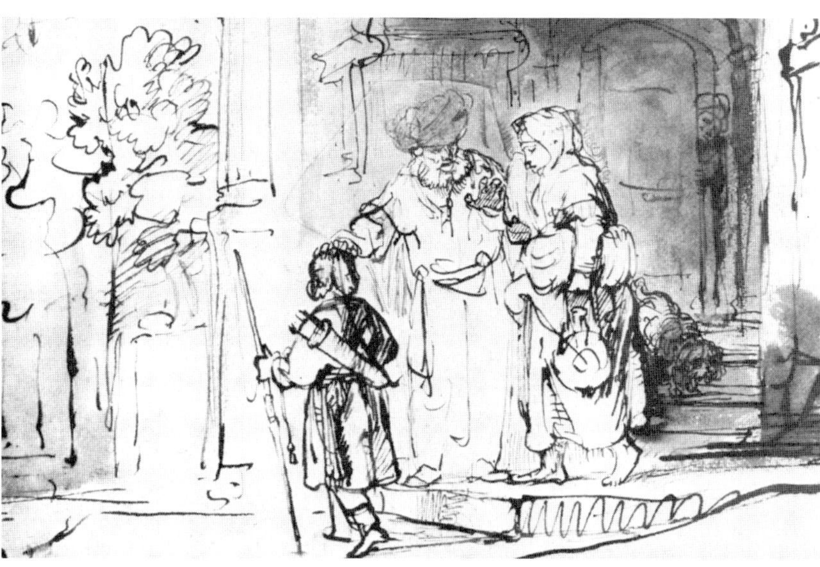

1651, in which the dog appears to be attempting to keep the blind old Tobit from colliding with the wall in his attempt to find the door, a work I discuss below (B 42—see chap. 7). There are two drawings, however, one from the late forties and one from the early fifties, that seem to me to attest to Rembrandt's use of a dog to add a human touch to the story of Tobit. In the first of them, the little dog is leaping up onto Tobias as though begging to go along on the impending journey, while the angel Raphael, with wings only *we* can see (Tob. 5:4–17), speaks with Tobit and Anna in the guise of Azariah, a relative. In the second of them, which appears to be from Rembrandt's hand only in part, the little dog is leaping up onto Tobit in happy greeting, as Anna embraces her returning son and Raphael/Azariah looks considerately at the ground. The antics of the dog in either drawing are entirely familiar to anyone who has ever been befriended by a dog.

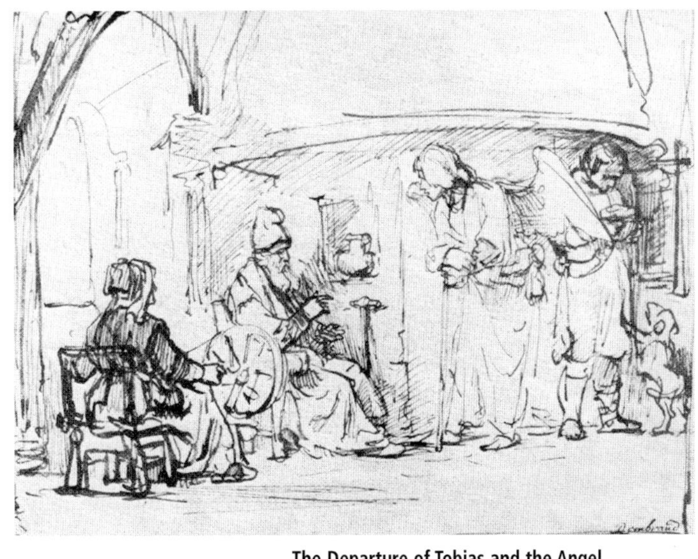

The Departure of Tobias and the Angel, Benesch 597, late 1640s, Albertina, Vienna

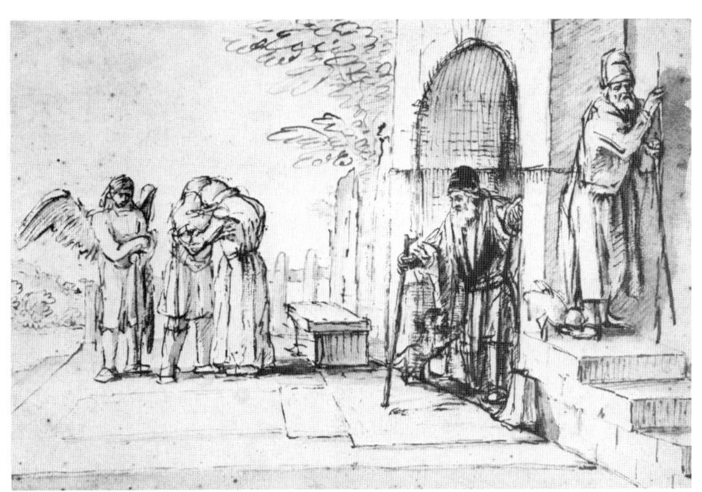

The Return of Tobias, Benesch 881, early 1650s, Kupferstichkabinett, Staatliche Museen, Berlin

The single work into which Rembrandt put more dogs than any other is his grisaille of 1634–1635, now in Berlin, *John the Baptist Preaching* (see next page). There are dogs fighting, dogs coupling, and one dog that appears to be voiding its bowels, and their presence in a painting depicting the preaching of John the forerunner (Matt. 3:1–12; Mark 1:1–8; Luke 3:1–9; and John 1:19–28) has provoked a wide range of tut-tutting and theologizing interpretation for at least three and a quarter centuries, some of it from surprising sources. In my view, we need look no further to understand these dogs than the biblical statement that people were crowding out from "Jerusalem and

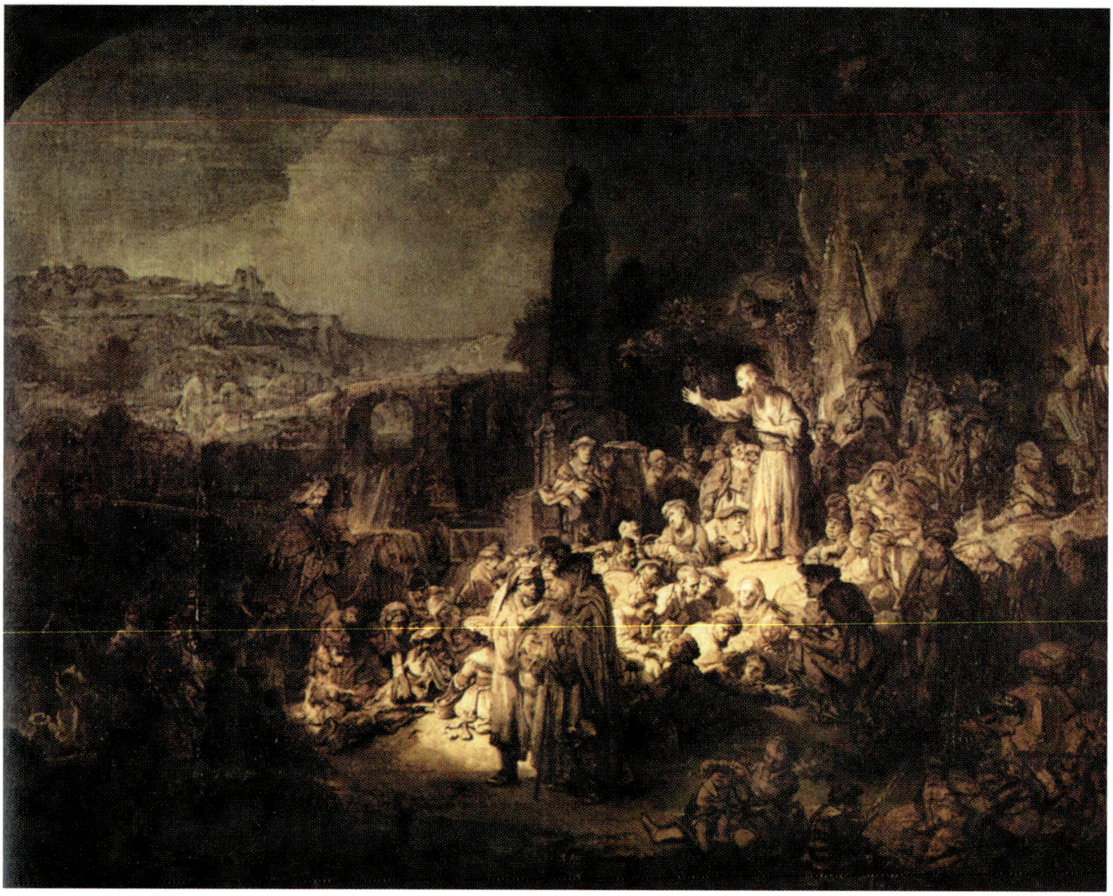

John the Baptist Preaching, 1634-1635,
Gemäldegalerie, Staatliche Museen, Berlin

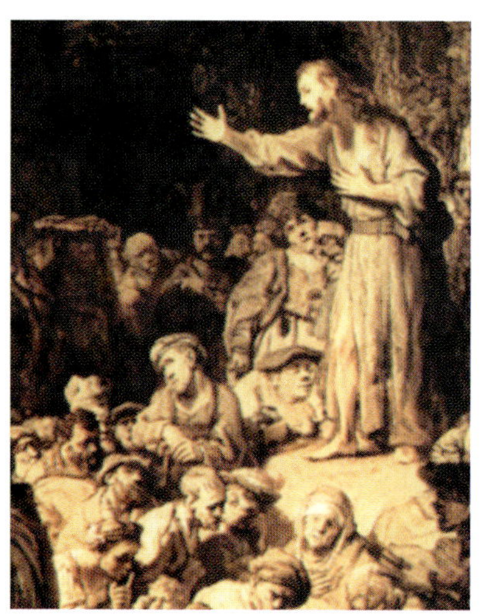

the whole of Judea, and the whole of the region along the Jordan" (Matt. 3:5) to hear John. Their activities are not unusual and are by no means out of place or inappropriate in a gathering outdoors along a riverbank.

Rembrandt has gone to considerable trouble in this work to depict the wide variety of people the text suggested to him, some of them exotic and some of them entirely at home in such a setting. Many of them, indeed, are paying no more attention to John's sermon than the dogs or, for that matter, the horse, the camel, or the monkey Rembrandt also included. Once again, Rembrandt has attempted to present the scene as he thought it must have been to those who were there—a crowd that came out to hear an eccentric holy man who was causing a stir. He considered it more like the local fair than some holy occasion, and the dogs are but one of the array of touches he included to insist that the event was real. Rembrandt was not given to

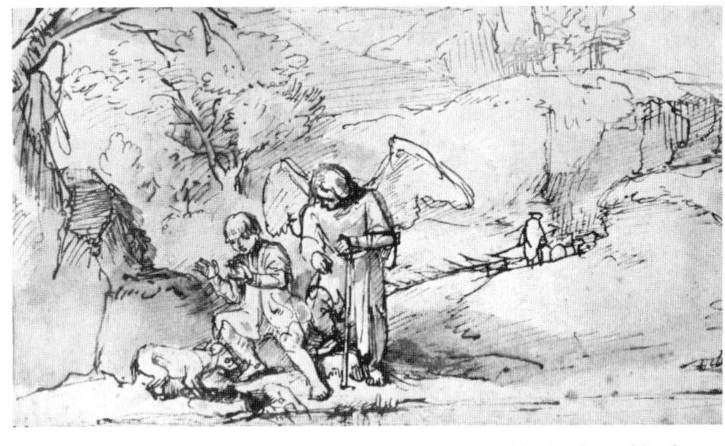

Tobias Frightened by the Fish, Benesch 638, around 1650, Kobberstiksamling, Statens Museum for Kunst, Copenhagen

elaborate symbolism, even when it was a part of the legacy of art he knew, nor did he fill his biblical works with hidden meanings. The events of the biblical story were, for him, *real* events, so real that he frequently imagined himself a part of them; in this painting, indeed, he appears to have included a self-portrait, placing himself in front and to the left side of John, wearing a plumed hat, his hand on his chin, and looking somewhat lazily away from the preaching John and out toward us.

Rembrandt's dogs display a variety of reaction in the scenes in which they are placed, thus adding to the impact of each given work. So the dog accompanying Tobias on his journey to Ecbatana in Media is terrified, just as his master is, at the attack of the fearsome fish by the River Tigris (Tob. 6:1b–4) in two drawings, one from the mid-forties (Benesch 559), in which the dog cowers behind Tobias, who is jerking back from the fish, and in the one above from five or six years later, in which the dog draws back in fright.

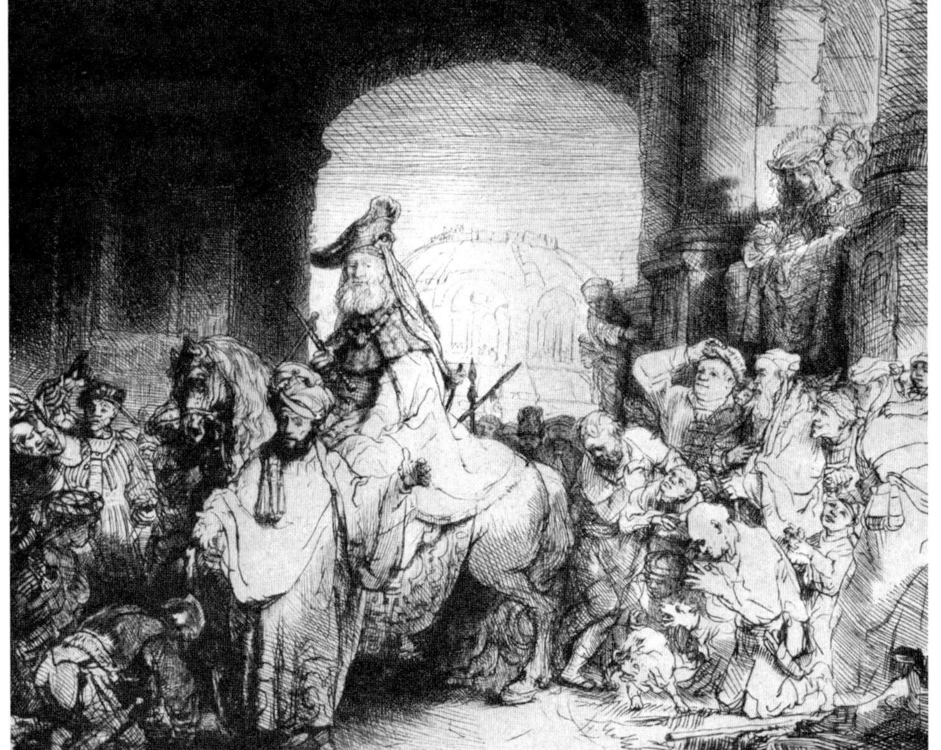

The Triumph of Mordecai, B 40, 1641, British Museum, London

As Mordecai rides in regal splendor through the crowded streets of Susa (see previous page), preceded by a humiliated Haman and watched from a balcony by King Ahasureus and Queen Esther (Esther 6:1–11), two dogs, frightened by the spectacle, growl and bark in anger in an etching from 1641.

And in an etching from 1634 of the Supper at Emmaus when the risen Christ is known "in the breaking of the bread" (Luke 24:35), a somewhat emaciated-looking dog stands in readiness for another morsel, looking up from the bone he has gnawed clean.

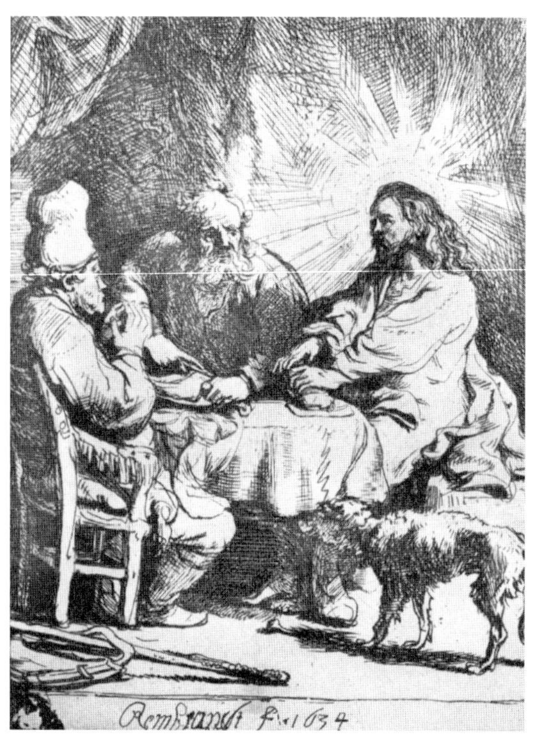

The Supper at Emmaus, B 88, 1634, British Museum, London

In an etching of the same moment from 1654 (B 87, see chap. 6), the dog is following a servant away from the table, yet turning to look back, no doubt wondering whether the sudden motion behind him may mean the drop of something edible.

Rembrandt also put dogs into some of his non-biblical works, as in *The Pancake Woman* mentioned earlier in this chapter. But the appearance of dogs in Rembrandt's non-biblical oeuvre is far more limited—only about half as many dogs turn up in these works, though they make up nearly two-thirds of his total output. For the most part these works are what may be called genre scenes: landscapes, hunting scenes, a variety of persons accompanied by pets or even working dogs, four mythological scenes, and even the famous commissioned group portrait incorrectly called *The Night Watch*, in which a dog barks with excitement and fear at the racket made by the drummer beating the assembly for the guard.

In the biblical works, however, excepting only those based on the Book of Tobit, the dogs are not mentioned in the texts Rembrandt was following and must therefore be reckoned a deliberate insertion. Whenever Rembrandt made any variance from what is stated in the biblical text, he did so, in my opinion, to create a feel of reality in the action, the moment, the event he was depicting. These "biblical" dogs of Rembrandt are thus an obvious and continuing example, in some fifty-five separate works, of his attempt at verisimilitude, his "humanizing" of narratives that too much religious art, in his view, had presented as otherworldly and "sacred." It was an attempt that came to be emulated by Rembrandt's pupils: they included dogs in biblical scenes based on their teacher's work, as well as in scenes that Rembrandt drew without a dog and in scenes based on biblical texts that he did not choose to depict.

Thus is Rembrandt's biblical art suffused with humanity because Rembrandt knew his own humanness and was quite unable to view the people of the Bible, or the people of history and mythology, or his own contemporaries, or for that matter even God, except in human terms. Here was a man who in his passion to draw sometimes used whatever was at hand, an envelope whose shape he used to advantage sketching a church steeple (Benesch 1311 recto and verso), even a proof page of a theological treatise for a study of a female nude (Benesch 1114a). In an etching he made in 1641, *Three Oriental Figures*, he was apparently so engrossed in his work that he forgot, when he signed and dated the second state, to inscribe his signature and the date in reverse on the plate—thus they are backwards in the initial impressions. As he matured, he appears to have made fewer and fewer concessions to the tastes of his sitters or his patrons, and his works on biblical themes present a Bible he *experienced*, a Bible that was real to him because he read it as a book about himself. I suspect it was of no matter to him whether his Stephen or his Paul or his Samson appeared as anyone save he himself thought they should—not because he was arrogant or a rebel or unsophisticated, countrified, but because that is how they were to him. They were human beings, after all, just as he was. And without their humanity, and enrobed in some saintly holiness, they had no meaning for him.

As for God, Rembrandt was to struggle for an understanding of how God is both to be known *and* represented for the whole of his life.

SOME SOURCES AND SUGGESTIONS

Simon Schama has written an entertaining and delightful "Interpretation of Dutch Culture in the Golden Age," appropriately called *The Embarrassment of Riches* (1987). It is a readable scholarly book (a rarity indeed) and one that gives us Rembrandt's context almost with its sounds and smells. Also of interest, though far less fun, is John J. Murray's *Amsterdam in the Age of Rembrandt* (1967). For an entertaining tour that sets one foot in Rembrandt's Amsterdam and one in late twentieth-century Amsterdam, see Anthony Bailey's *Rembrandt's House* (1978).

The superb (and superbly produced) survey of Bob Haak, *The Golden Age: Dutch Painters of the Seventeenth Century* (1984), ranges across the artistic Elysian fields of Rembrandt's period and provides a fascinating comparative review of Dutch art in Rembrandt's century. Also rewarding: the catalog to the 1981 exhibition of the National Gallery of Art in Washington, the Detroit Institute of Arts, and the Rijksmuseum, *Gods, Saints & Heroes: Dutch Painting in the Age of Rembrandt* (1980). More briefly still, but helpful as a quick survey, is Christopher White's *The Dutch Painters: 100 Seventeenth Century Masters* (1978).

Biographies of Rembrandt are numerous, though limited by the scarcity of information about his life. I suggest Christopher White, *Rembrandt* (1984), and Mariët Westermann, *Rembrandt* (2000), for brief surveys. For surveys in much fuller detail, I recommend Bob Haak, *Rembrandt: His Life, His Work, His Time* (1968), and Christian Tümpel, *Rembrandt* (1993). Kenneth Clark, who seems never to have written an inelegant line, left us two helpful summary works: a brief account, *An Introduction to Rembrandt* (1978; the sentence quoted on p. 23 above comes from p. 57), and the more specialized but very informative *Rembrandt and the Italian Renaissance* (1966). In this latter work, on p. 30, Clark notes, "Of course, anything that Rembrandt does is crammed with humanity." Two brief but packed articles by S. A. C. Dudok van Heel provide excellent surveys of recent research: "Rembrandt van Rijn (1606–1669): a changing portrait of the artist" in *Rembrandt: The Master and His Workshop: Paintings* (1991) and "Rembrandt: his life, his wife, the nursemaid and the servant" in *Rembrandt's Women* (2001). A fascinating and most helpful survey of early (though scarcely trustworthy) biographical information about Rembrandt has been put together by Seymore Slive: *Rembrandt and His Critics 1630–1730* (1953). And the lengthy entry by Ben Broos on Rembrandt ("I. Life and Work") in *The Grove Dictionary of Art* is a model of clarity, now available in a separate format in *From Rembrandt to Vermeer: 17th-century Dutch Artists.*

For Gerson's account of his identification of *The Stoning of Stephen* as Rembrandt's, see *Apollo* 77 (1963, p. 371 ff.).

John Russell's winsome appreciation of Rembrandt in a *New York Times* review of a Pierpont Morgan exhibition, "Rembrandt Etchings: Landscapes and Portraits" (11 September 1977, 33[D]), is the source of the quote on pp. 24-25 above. He titled his piece "Why We Can't Find Fault with Rembrandt," and as usual for Russell he has given us *multum in parvo.*

The Rembrandt Documents (1979) is an indispensable assemblage of every known document having to do with Rembrandt's life, arranged chronologically. Like a look, albeit a bureaucratic one, right into the painter's existence, it is both fascinating and frustrating, but invaluable. Its frequent inclusion of facsimile printings of documents often gives the feel of their time. I cite it hereafter as RD.

The Artist in an Oriental Costume, with a Poodle at His Feet, 1631, Musée du Petit Palais, Paris

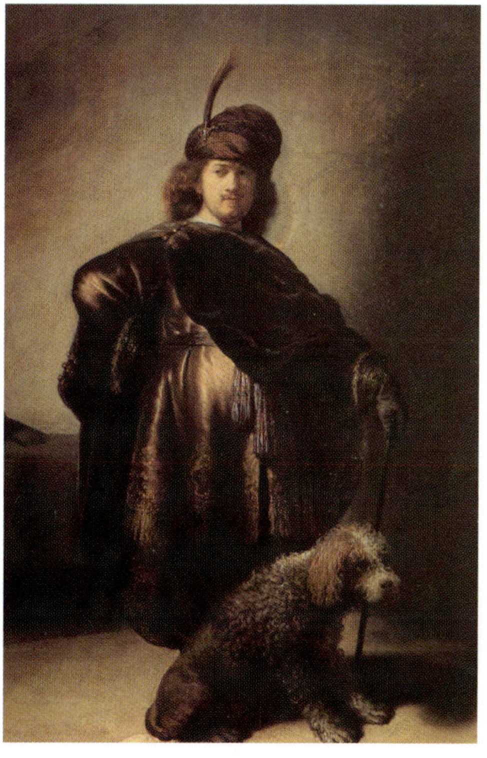

Rembrandt's love of exotic weapons, luxurious fabrics, small animal specimens, and curiosities of all sorts is delightfully described in the catalog to an exhibition of the Rembrandt House Museum held in 1999–2000 under the title *Rembrandt's Treasures.* Particularly fascinating is the essay by Roelof van Gelder and Jaap van der Ween, "A collector's cabinet in the Breestraat: Rembrandt as a lover of art and curiosities," and the essay by Ben Broos, "Rembrandt and his picturesque universe: The artist's collection as a source of inspiration."

Seymore Slive's *Rembrandt and His Critics* includes a summary (and the full German text, Appendix D, pp. 208–209) of Joachim von Sandrart's brief "biography" of Rembrandt in his work with a *fourteen-line* title, briefly known as *Teusche Academie der Edelen Bau-, Bild- und Mahlerey-Künste.* Sandrart's comment that Rembrandt was hindered by the low company he kept ("und sich jederzeit nur zu niedrigen Leuten gesellet, dannenhero er auch in seiner Arbiet verhindert gewesen") has often been quoted, but given the list of Rembrandt's known patrons is best taken with a cellar full of salt.

At right is Rembrandt's self-portrait of 1631, with the poodle, added at a later time. This painting, Rembrandt's only full-length self-portrait, is known in its original, non-poodle form, in a copy by one of his pupils (for a color reproduction, see *Rembrandt by Himself*, cat. no. 29b).

Rembrandt's drawing of an engraving of Leonardo da Vinci's *Last Supper* in the refectory of Santa Maria delle Grazie, Milan, with the dog added in the right corner.

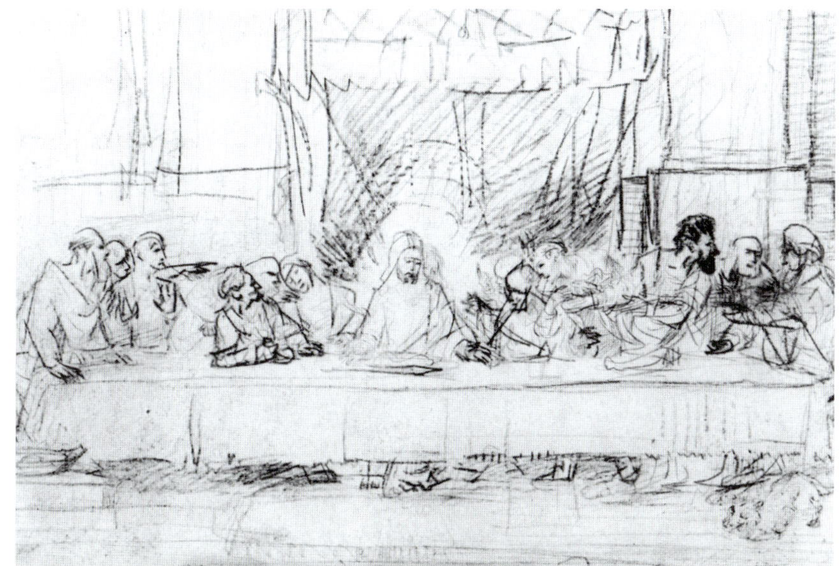

Drawing of **DaVinci's Last Supper**, Benesch 443, 1635, Metropolitan Museum of Art, New York

The impact of Rembrandt's dogs on his pupils can be seen in the extensive survey of Werner Sumowski, *Drawings of the Rembrandt School*, which runs at present to ten volumes. Such pupils as Ferdinand Bol, Lambert Doomer, and Gerbrand van den Eeckhout included dogs in drawings based on works by Rembrandt and also in works of their own on texts on which we have no known Rembrandt drawings. See, for example, Sumowski 130x, 253x, 445x, 460x, 637, 644, 700x (x following a number indicates drawings Sumowski considers "drawings of unquestionable authenticity based on stylistic criteria," instead of "authentic drawings," those including a signature, or those linked to etchings and paintings of the artist under consideration).

Rembrandt's drawing on the flap of an envelope, from around 1652/53.

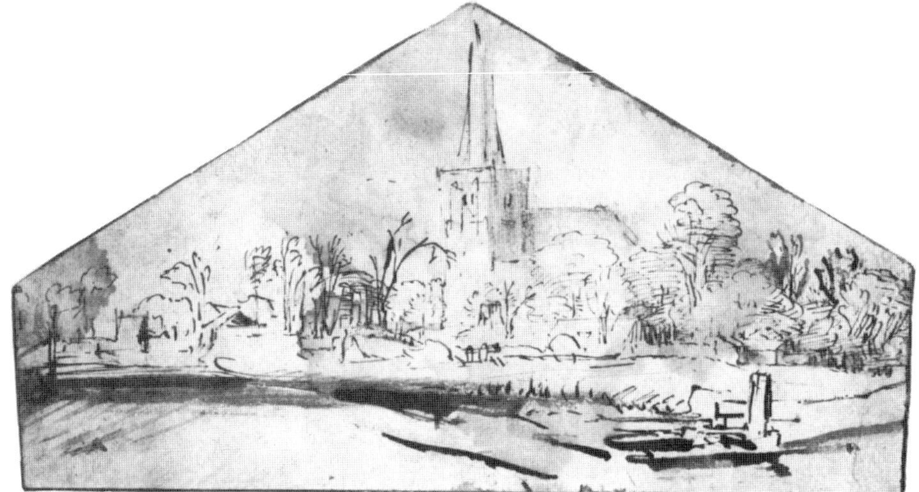

The Church of Diemen, Benesch 1311 recto, 1652-1653 (private collection)

3

REMBRANDT'S BIBLE

In the Rijksmuseum in Amsterdam, there is a likeness of an old woman reading a heavy book. It was painted by Rembrandt in 1631, his twenty-fifth year. From the eighteenth century at least, this work and an array of similar ones have been thought to be likenesses of Neeltje (or Cornelia), Willemsdochter van Suyttbroeck, Rembrandt's mother. She would have been sixty-two in 1631, and the similarity of the face of the woman in this painting with that in a number of other paintings, etchings, and drawings, all of them from roughly the same period and all of them also linked in popular tradition with Rembrandt's mother, gives plausibility to such an identification.

This is true whether Rembrandt actually intended a portrait of his mother or was using her likeness to represent the prophetess Anna. My interest is in the fact that the elderly lady is reading from a large book, her worn and wrinkled (and beautifully painted) hand moving across the lines of text as she does.

Whether the unreadable lines on the pages open to her are Rembrandt's attempt to suggest Hebrew seems to me unlikely, not least in view of the apparent direction in which her hand is moving. Such a suggestion would aid the identification of the woman as the prophetess Anna, but what is more certain is that Rembrandt has given us an old woman reading what has every appearance of a Bible.

A painting from about three years later by seventeen-year-old Gerrit Dou, one of Rembrandt's earliest pupils, presents a very similar

An Old Woman Reading, 1631, Rijksmuseum, Amsterdam

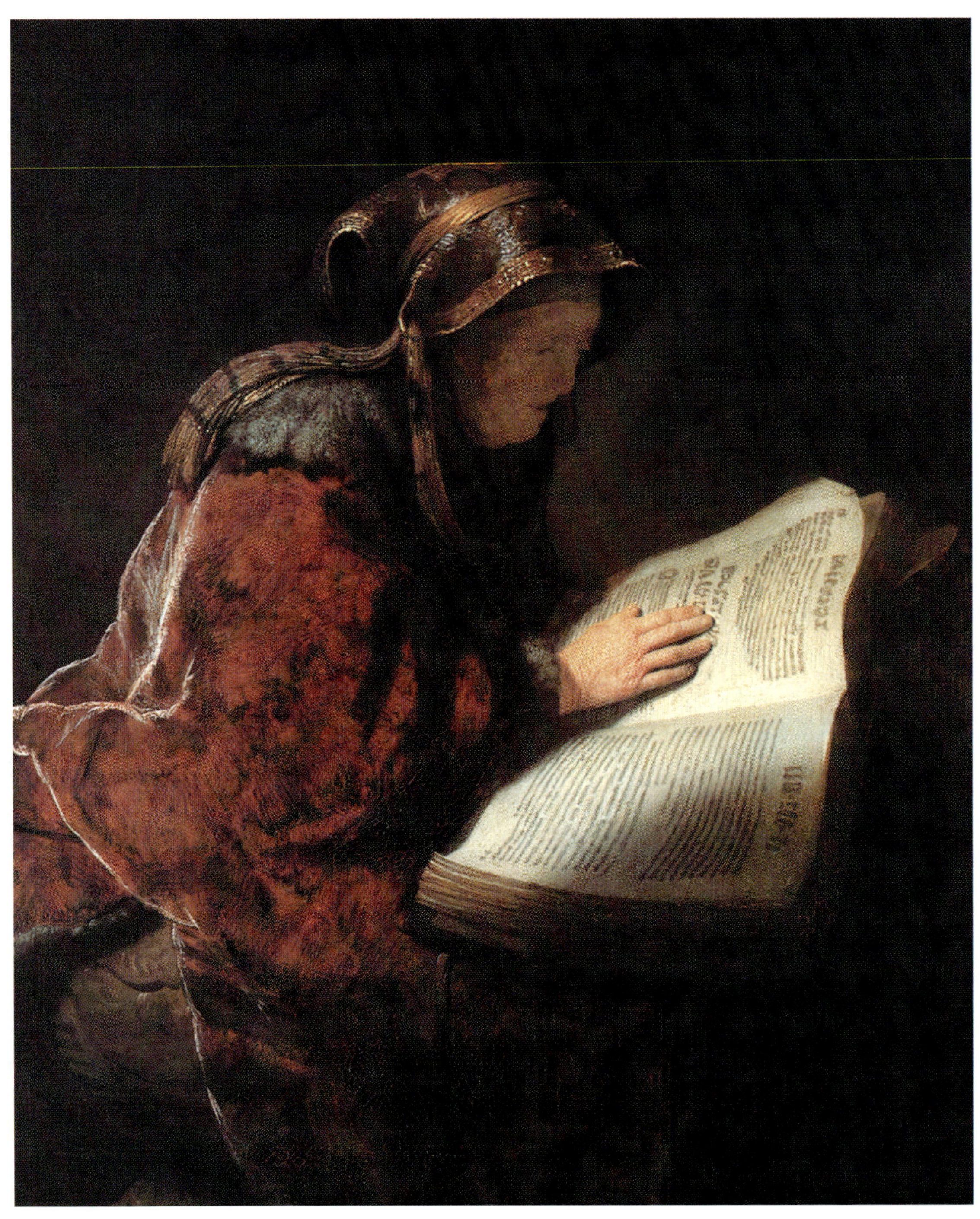

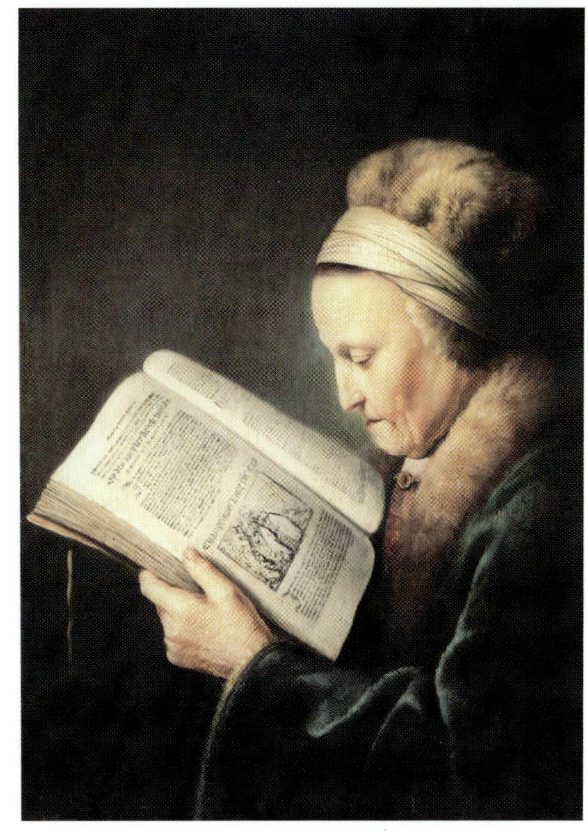

Gerrit Dou, **Old Woman Reading**, 1634, Rijksmuseum, Amsterdam

old woman in a very similar (though reversed) pose, clearly reading from the Gospel of Luke. It too has long been reckoned a likeness of Rembrandt's mother, and Dou painted it around the time Rembrandt was leaving Leiden for greater things in Amsterdam.

My attention is attracted by the image of the elderly woman reading the Bible, an image that must have been recorded in Rembrandt's mind at an early age. Rembrandt's portraits of the woman thought to be his mother are done with obvious affection, and his inclusion of a Bible on her lap in this work may well be a special memory.

The family of Rembrandt's mother was staunchly Roman Catholic. His father's family was Roman Catholic as well, but Harmen, Rembrandt's father, had left the Catholic Church for the Protestant Dutch Reformed Church at some point in his life prior to his marriage. Rembrandt's parents were married on 8 October 1589 in the Dutch Reformed Pieterskerk in Leiden. Harmen's earliest will, recorded on 1 March 1600, leaves the whole of his property to Neeltje, but specifies that she should bring up their children "in the fear of God throughout their minority." Thus, by family history as by his childhood context, the Bible must have had a significant presence in Rembrandt's early life.

That the Bible was important to Rembrandt throughout his life is not to be doubted, nor is his upbringing in the faith of Dutch Reformed Protestantism. His education in the "Latin School" of Leiden from the age of seven until he was fourteen would have added to Rembrandt's Protestant patina. The motto over the door of the Latin School to this day reads "*Pietate, Linguis et Artib.liberalis* (Piety—Languages—Liberal Arts)," and the school in Rembrandt's day emphasized Latin as a living language, along with the strict religious teaching of John Calvin. Students were expected to attend *two* Sunday services, and on Monday they were given a test on the sermons of the day before.

Whatever his childhood enthusiasms, Rembrandt did not cling for long to the "true religion" of John Calvin—in fact, I am inclined to doubt that he ever found it very attractive. By early adulthood, he showed impatience with religious orthodoxy and pious stuffiness, an impatience that is quite evident in his work.

Though Rembrandt's first three children, none of whom survived infancy, were baptized in Amsterdam's Oude Kerk (as also was his illegitimate daughter with Hendrickje Stoeffels, Cornelia), and his fourth child, Titus, was baptized in Amsterdam's Zuider Kerk, Rembrandt clearly moved farther and farther away from any regular connection with the Dutch Reformed Church, for a number of reasons.

The only contemporary testimony concerning Rembrandt's religious interests comes to us from the *Cominciamento* of Abbot Filippo Baldinucci, who drew much of his information from a Danish student who studied with Rembrandt from 1642 until 1644, Bernhardt Keil. Baldinucci reported that Rembrandt had become a Mennonite. That Rembrandt associated with members of the Mennonite community is amply demonstrable, but that he became a Mennonite is highly unlikely. He certainly associated with a variety of other religious and freethinking groups in Amsterdam, and with the Jewish community there as well. Despite much attention to the subject of Rembrandt's religious affiliations, however, nothing can be established with certainty because hard evidence is scarce.

What cannot be gainsaid is Rembrandt's early and lasting affection for and fascination with the Bible. This is clear even from the number of his drawings, etchings, and paintings of which the Bible is the source: in rough estimate, about one-third of Rembrandt's prodigious output. The 1656 inventory of Rembrandt's possessions required by his application for *cessio bonorum* includes, among its 363 items, item 285, "an old Bible." The inventory of Rembrandt's estate made on 5 October 1669, the day after he died, includes among the items "in the inner chamber," only one book, "a Bible." And the presence of a large number of works on biblical subjects in the output of even the earliest years of Rembrandt's career (almost fifty from the Leiden years, 1625–1631) and right through his life to his death raises two important questions: (1) What was the Bible to Rembrandt, and (2) how did Rembrandt use the Bible in his art?

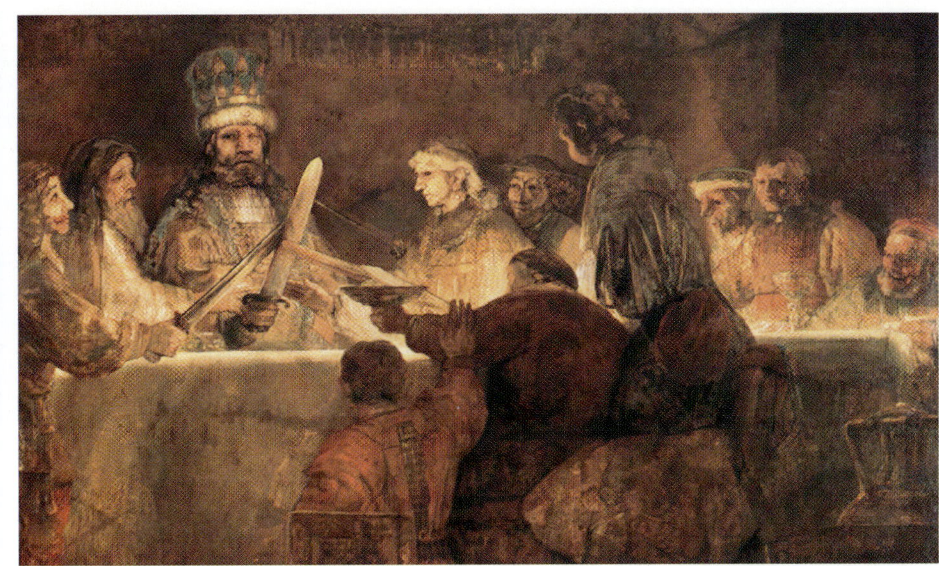

Conspiracy of the Batavians, 1661-1662, Nationalmuseum, Stockholm

Rembrandt scholars have written much about Rembrandt's turning to the Bible as a source for history painting, a genre popular in his time. They often pair the biblical stories with those from Greek and Roman mythology and history, also a source for history painting. While this point is well taken, it is hardly sufficient to explain Rembrandt's approach to the Bible. For one thing, Rembrandt's depiction of mythological and historical scenes is a fractional part of his oeuvre in comparison to his works depicting biblical scenes. For another, not one of the mythological/historical works belongs to what may be called Rembrandt's best, apart from what is left of the *Conspiracy of the Batavians* (reduced in size from 236 x 236 in. to 77 x 121) from 1661 or 1662, now in Stockholm.

In the battered face of the one-eyed old warrior Claudius Civilis, there is testimony of Rembrandt's humanity. And in this fragment of the work that must have been, there is an echo of the astonished eagerness of the disciples in a much earlier work, the 1629 *Supper at Emmaus* (now in the Musée Jacquemart-André, Paris), in the placement of the source of light, in the warriors kneeling in profile, and in the chair overturned by sudden movement (see next page).

So what *was* the Bible to Rembrandt? For one thing, the Bible that so intrigued Rembrandt was, as Kenneth Clark has said, picking up a witticism from G. K. Chesterton, *his* Bible. Rembrandt simply would not allow his access to Scripture to be limited by any set of restrictions, whether imposed by the history of art or by the dogmas of the theologians and the notions of preachers. Clark's summary statement is trenchant:

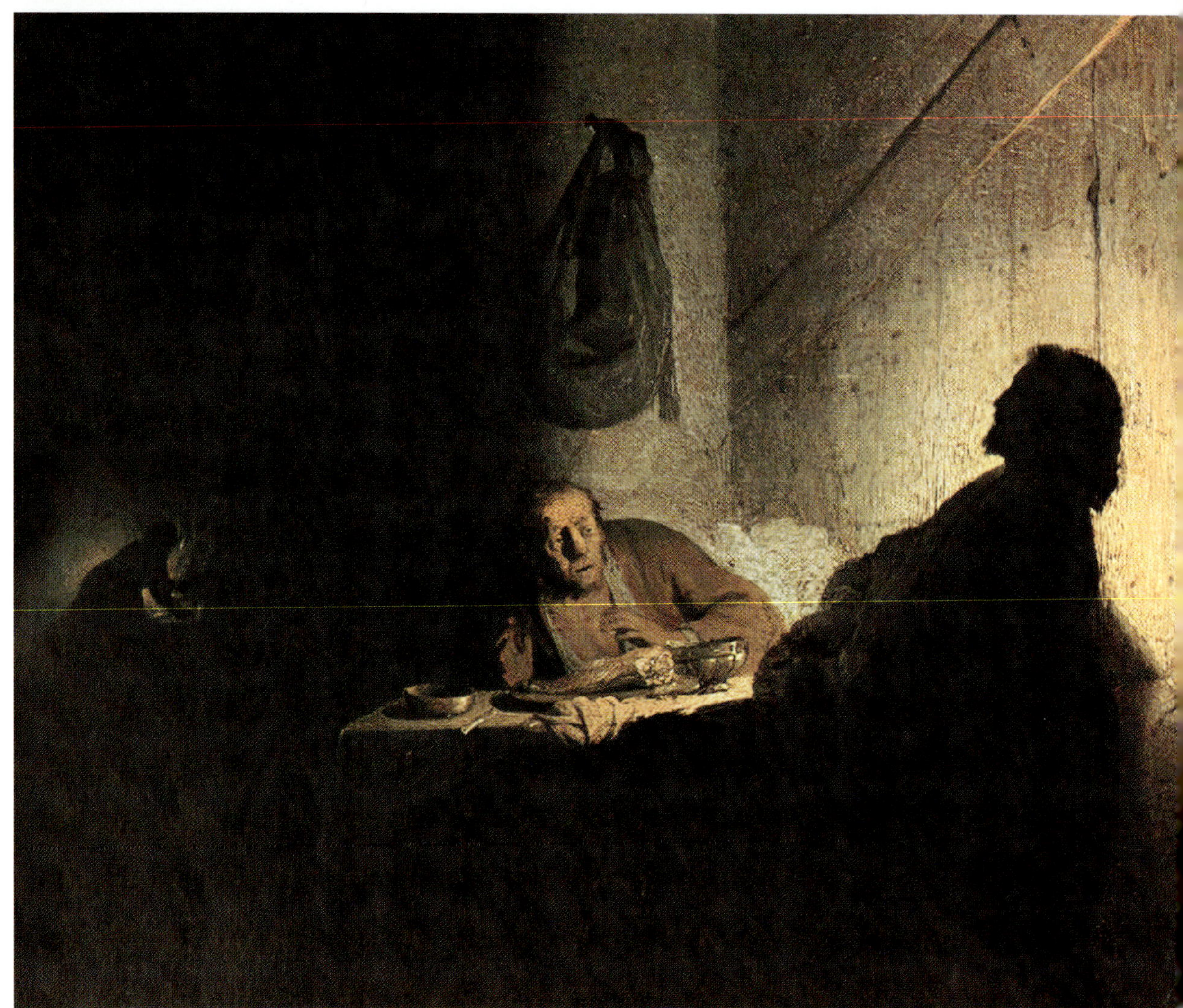

Supper at Emmaus, 1629,
Musée Jacquemart-André, Paris

> In the end the Bible he illustrated was *his* Bible, that part of Holy Writ which supported his own convictions, those episodes that illustrated his own feelings about human life and…the Divine intervention on which it depended.

Willem Visser 'T Hooft's comment is similar:

> We cannot construct any "system" from Rembrandt's choice of subjects or his handling of them. Nor could this be expected. He was a painter and not a theologian. He went his own way, which does not mean that he ruled out any stimulus he might receive from his acquaintance with members of the Reformed, the Remonstrant, the Mennonite, the Catholic, the Jewish, or the humanist community. One thing only is certain: he lived with his Bible. He was in truth "*homo unius libri*."

These comments, and others similar to them, are on target, but they do not go far enough. In my view, Rembrandt, as he matured, did more, sometimes far more, than illustrate the biblical moments that gripped him. And the undoubted fact that he came to the Bible with fresh eyes does not tell us why he came so frequently to the Bible in the first place.

For an answer to the question of what the Bible *was* to Rembrandt, we have to go beyond the view that the Bible was a handy source for the history painter, not least because no other artist in seventeenth-century Holland or anywhere else, Rembrandt's own pupils included, turned to the Bible with anything approaching Rembrandt's frequency. We also have to go beyond the assertion that Rembrandt approached the Bible as a human book about human people, a statement embarrassing because it is necessary.

Without faith, Rembrandt's biblical works can be approached solely as works of art—in an astonishing number of cases as great works of art. That approach is both entirely justified and vastly rewarding, as the massive bibliography of Rembrandt criticism over more than three centuries attests. I propose, however, an approach that adds another dimension to the understanding of these works. It is an approach that both learns from and builds upon the work of art history and criticism, but goes beyond what is comfortable to those who give us that work. It is in its nature an approach that can have no proof, as faith—just because it *is* faith—can never have any proof.

Yet this approach has added to my experience of Rembrandt a dimension I have found nowhere else. It has enabled me to converse with him in many hours of holding in my hand his drawings, and etchings he made and printed and touched up himself, and of standing with a kind of happy knowing before his paintings in their diaspora around the world.

Whatever images Rembrandt had filed away in his visual memory—and they were many, and he appears to have drawn on them almost subconsciously—he appears always to have begun his biblical works with the biblical text. His biblical oeuvre suggests that he lived with the texts he chose, internalizing them, seeing places and people he knew in them, and reading them through those people and those places, and above all, through his own life in its day-to-day pleasure and pain.

I think Rembrandt allowed the biblical text to speak to him before he ever began, with his gift, to attempt speaking of the biblical text. This is never an easy discipline to achieve, for none more difficult than for the Bible scholar, and close to impossible for the preacher. Yet Rembrandt mastered this discipline, I believe, to such an extent that it came to inform much of his work, even all of his best work, whatever its theme. Thus, when he came to the representation of a given biblical moment, that moment was real to Rembrandt because he had experienced it—he had become a part of the moment, and the moment had thus become a part of him.

In a way, the Bible became for Rembrandt a kind of diary, an account of moments in his own life. How else are we to explain his frequent insertion of his own face, his own person, into such a large number of his biblical works? He is undoubtedly looking out at us, as I have noted already (chap. 2), in *The Stoning of Stephen*, and in *David with the Head of Goliath before Saul* (now in Basel), both from the early years in Leiden. He makes an appearance in *The Raising of the Cross* and *The Descent from the Cross* (both now in Munich). He is the central presence in *The Prodigal Son in the Tavern* (now in Dresden), from the early years in Amsterdam. It is Rembrandt who is one of Jacob's sons in an etching of 1638, *Joseph Telling His Dreams*, and he is even peeping out behind Peter's bald head in the large *Christ Preaching* (the so-called "Hundred Guilder Print") of the late 1640s.

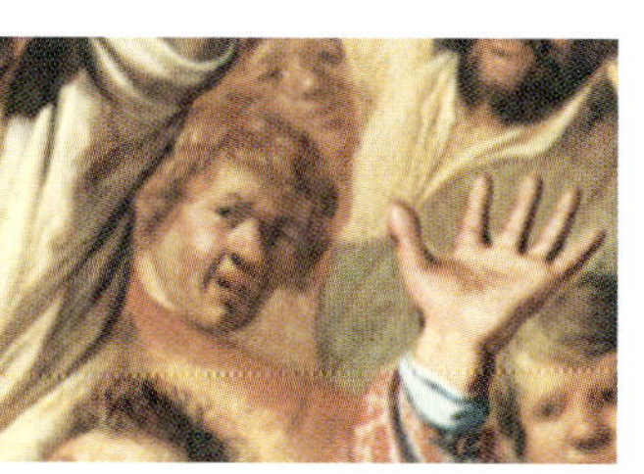

Detail, **The Stoning of Stephen,** Lyon

Rembrandt presents himself here as a somewhat alarmed presence, a participant who may be having second thoughts about what is taking place. I wonder whether he was asking himself the question that often rises as we read such accounts: What would I have done had I been there? Ten years after he painted this work, he was still thinking about Stephen's death, and he etched this moment of violent martyrdom just a bit farther along in its process: Stephen has already cried out, "Lord, don't hold them responsible for this sin" (Acts 7:60). His body is limp, his head is lolling back, his mouth is gaping open, his eyes appear to be rolling upward—he is near death, and the two men with stones raised, one of them a giant with a huge block, are about to finish this murder. The "glory of God" still shines down from heaven, this time from the right and onto the almost unconscious

Stephen's back and head. Rembrandt has compressed his depiction of the death of Stephen, focusing this time almost wholly on the brutality of the event. There is no Saul/Paul now, no Gamaliel, no authorizing official presence on horseback, no excited barking dog, and no Rembrandt. Or is there? Has Rembrandt put himself in by just an eye and a nose, as he was to do in *The Militia Company of Captain Frans Banning Cocq* (see chap. 2) and in the etching *Christ Preaching*?

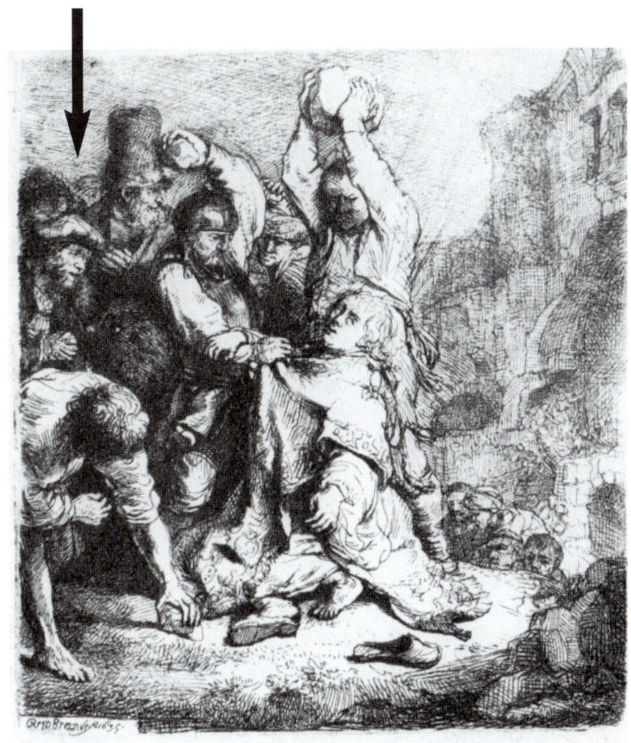

The Stoning of St. Stephen, B 97, 1635, Prentenkabinet, Rijksmuseum, Amsterdam

David with the Head of Goliath before Saul (see next page), painted in 1627 and now in Basel, presents the moment mentioned in 1 Samuel 17:54, 57: "Then David picked up the head of the Philistine, and so brought it to Jerusalem.... And when David returned from defeating the Philistine, Abner took him in hand and brought him into Saul's presence, holding the Philistine's head."

Rembrandt gives us David on his knees, with the huge head of Goliath, open-mouthed and with a cowlick, cradled in his arms. Just behind David stands Abner, holding the Philistine giant's considerable sword, a detail Rembrandt picked up from 1 Samuel 17:51. The old man bending to look at David's grisly souvenir probably represents the old prophet Samuel, who had previously anointed David to be king of Israel in place of Saul, whom Yahweh has rejected (1 Sam. 16:1–13), though Samuel is not mentioned in 1 Samuel 17. Saul himself is the rotund figure in the gorgeous outfit who reaches out to restrain Samuel, either from blocking his view or from appearing to bow toward David.

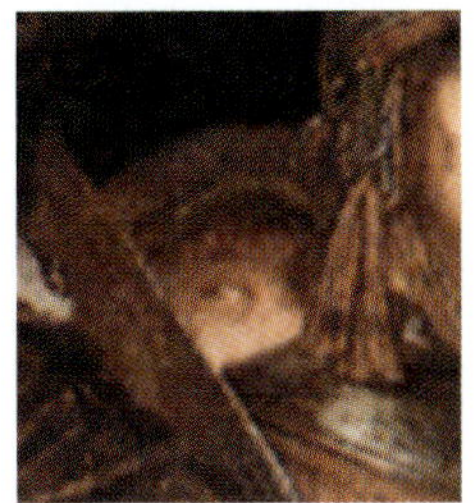

Detail, **The Militia Company**

Though Rembrandt has somewhat obviously based his composition on a history painting of his teacher Lastman (*Coriolanus and the Roman Women*, now in Dublin), the event he presents is totally different, and he includes the kind of details that make even his early works both interesting and entertaining: a dog barks, understandably,

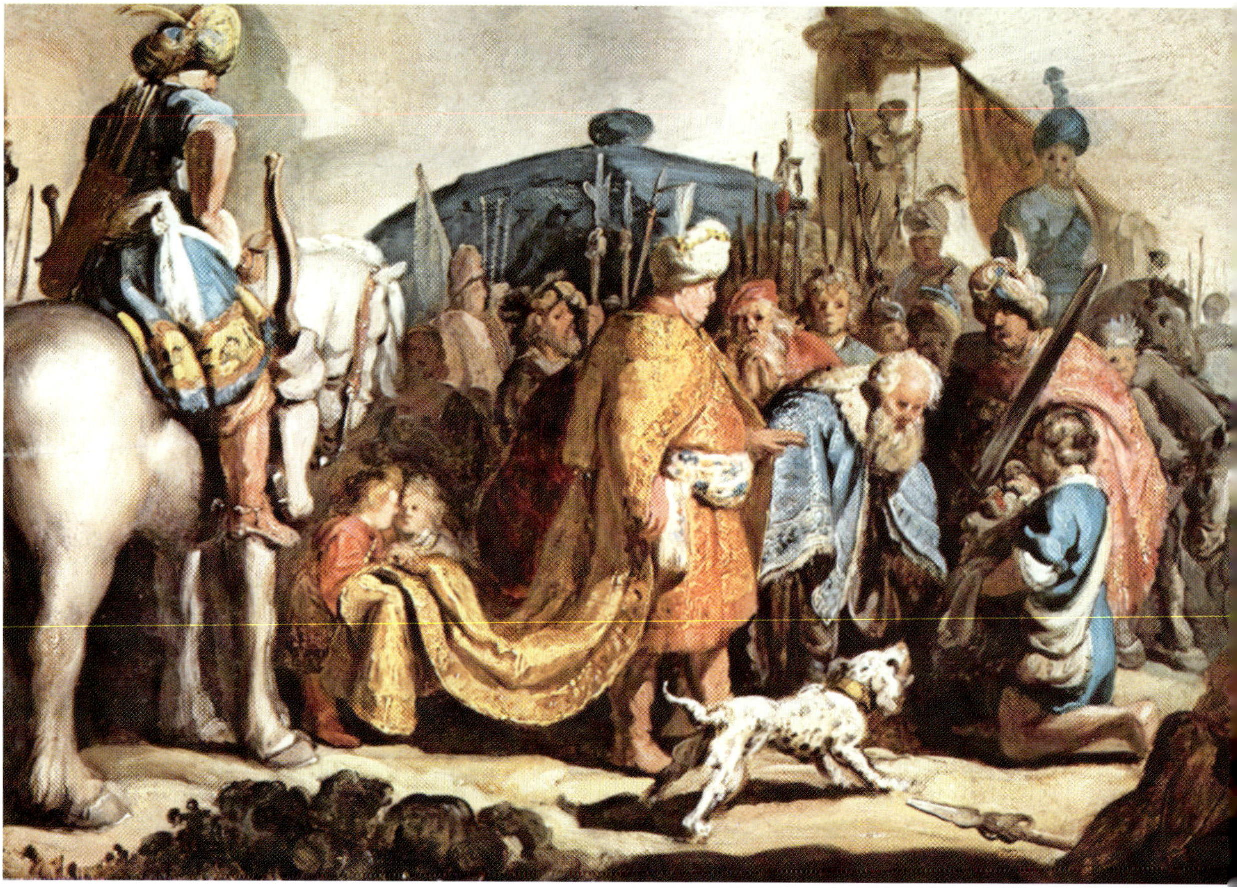

David with the Head of Goliath before Saul, 1627, Öffentliche Kunstsammlung, Basel

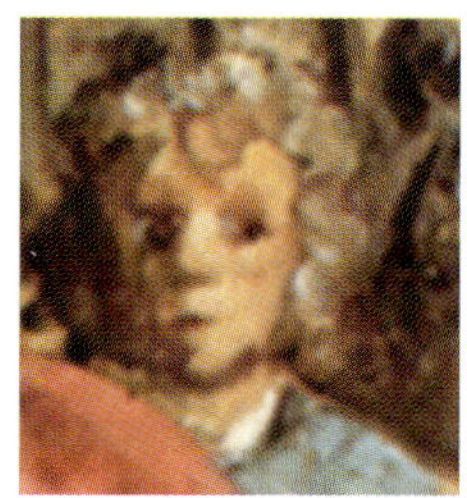

at David's horrific burden; the two little lads who bear Saul's impressive royal train are having a completely non-deferential chat; the young Rembrandt himself squeezes in with the crowd to see the spectacle; and at the extreme left, there is a mounted figure generally held to represent Saul's son Jonathan, who, in addition to his bow and his quiver of arrows, has the same right arm akimbo position that Rembrandt was to give to the so-called *Polish Rider* some thirty years later. I believe, indeed, that both these mounted archers with arm akimbo may well represent Jonathan (see pp. 107-108).

Rembrandt has filled his space in the picture's background with onlookers, a natural assumption for so stupendous and remarkable a victory. Even at this early stage of his career, he was *thinking* about the events he depicted and representing them in accord with his own experience and emotions.

In 1633, Rembrandt painted *The Raising of the Cross* and *The Descent from the Cross*, two pictures of an eventual series of seven that constituted his first big commission. Five of the seven works dealt with the crucifixion, burial, resurrection, and ascension of Christ; the

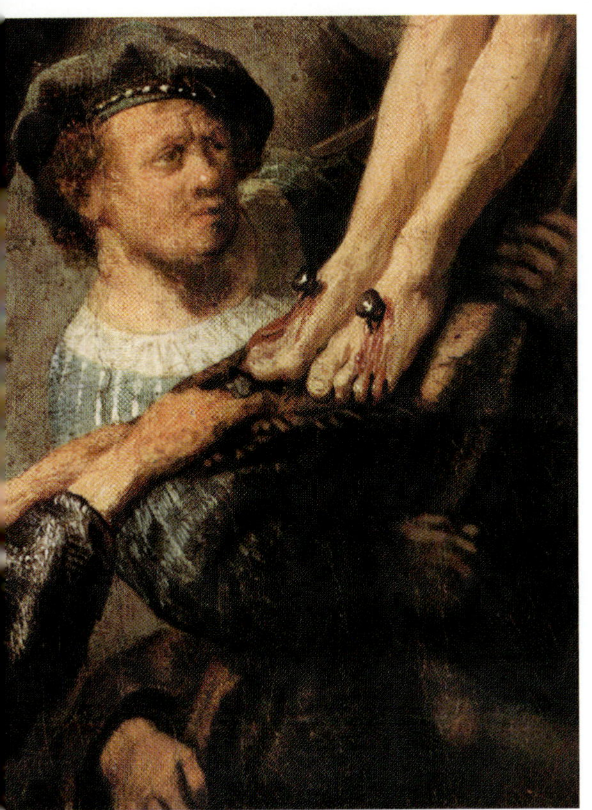

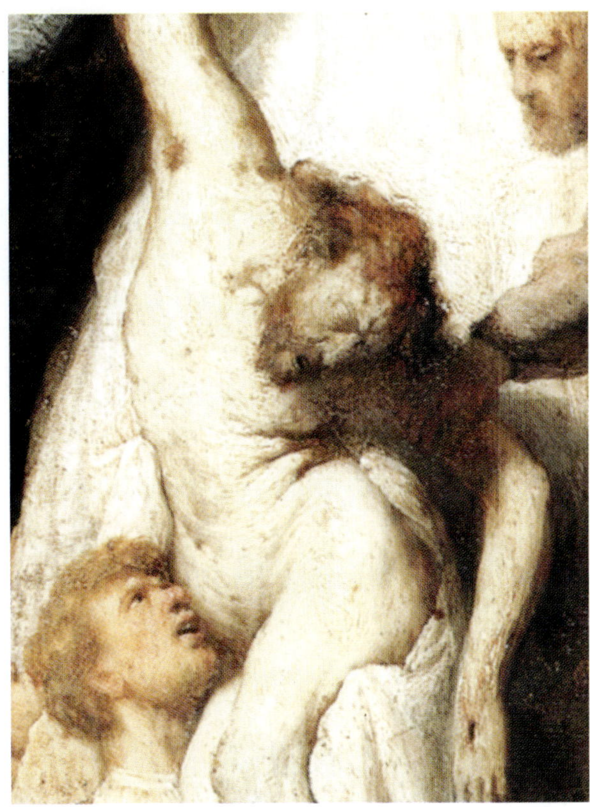

The Raising of the Cross, 1633, Alte Pinakothek, Munich, detail (left)

The Descent from the Cross, 1633, Alte Pinakothek, Munich, detail (right)

other two appear to have dealt with the adoration of the shepherds and the circumcision of the infant Jesus (this last work was lost by early in the eighteenth century). I find it intriguing that Rembrandt included his own likeness only in the paintings that deal with the crucifixion, a fact on which I comment more fully below (chap. 5); I include here the self-portraits in those two works.

In each of these two paintings, both now in Munich, Rembrandt presents a realistic scene, one that appears to have been deeply felt. In *The Raising of the Cross*, Christ is clearly suffering, and in *The Descent from the Cross*, Christ is clearly dead. Both pictures are devoid of the classical beauty intended to provoke reverential awe—instead, they present the ugliness of unjust suffering and death. I believe it not too much to suggest that Rembrandt intended to provoke grief and the shame of guilt and that he included himself in the grip of both.

In 1635, perhaps a bit more than three years after his move to Amsterdam, Rembrandt painted *The Prodigal Son in the Tavern*, now in Dresden. He is the prodigal son, raising his glass to us as he laughs, with his wife Saskia sitting on his knee, her back to us, but turning to look at us as well. It is a work that has stimulated considerable discussion, ranging from whether Rembrandt intended for himself and

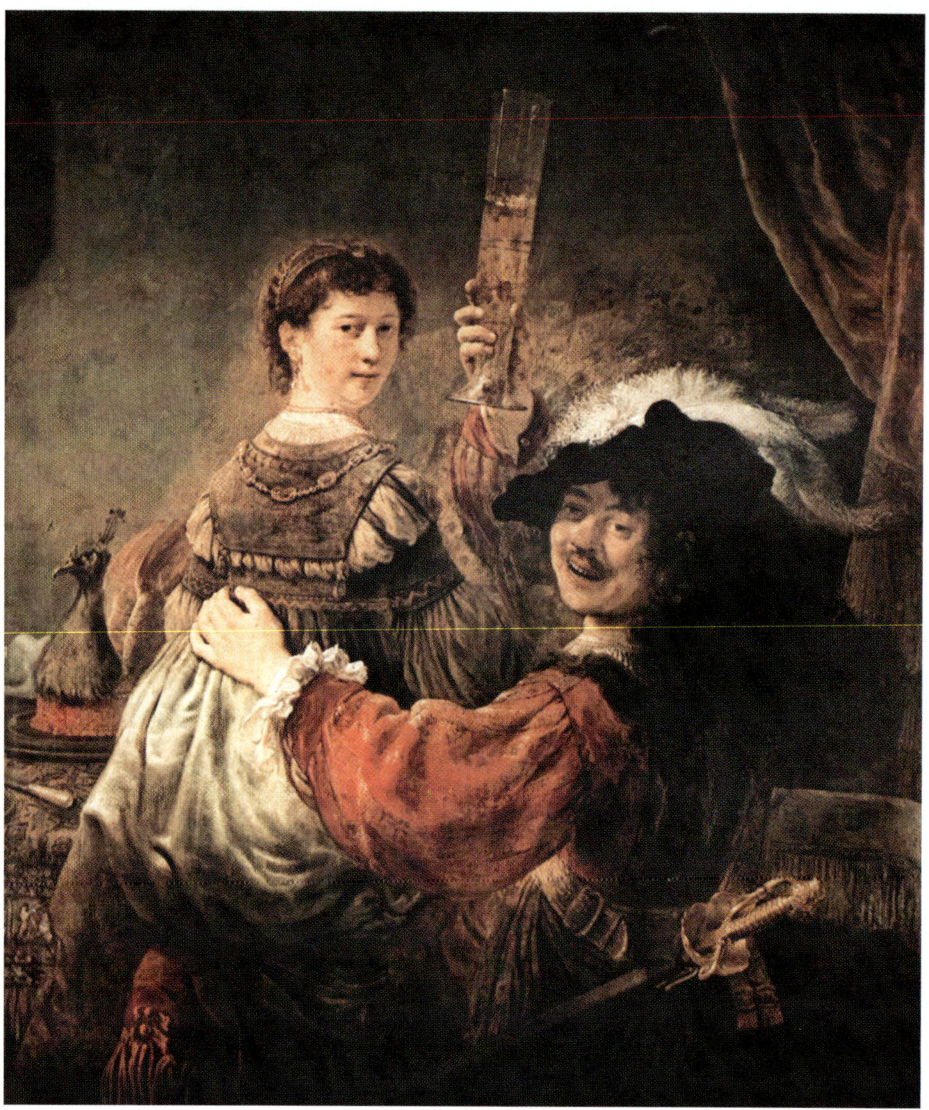

The Prodigal Son in the Tavern, 1635, Gemäldegalerie Alter Meister, Dresden

Saskia really to be recognized, to the notion that he was giving the raspberry to his in-laws, who were critical of his lifestyle, to the view that the work is not connected to the biblical parable of the prodigal son at all.

I think this work is certainly a product of Rembrandt's fascination with the story of the prodigal son, his father, and even his mother and his older brother—he drew, etched, and painted a series of at least fifteen works on the story from around 1632–1633 to the time of his death thirty-six years later (see chap. 6). Nor is his likeness here, and Saskia's, to be considered incidental, just faces handy as models for the painting. Here again, Rembrandt has read the Bible as a book about himself. He saw himself in its stories, and he saw those stories as real, the narrative accounts of real persons whose experiences were not that different from his own, and whose difficulties and mistakes and triumphs and celebrations had value for his own life. If he could think of himself as a participant in the martyrdom of Stephen, as a spectator at the lad David's triumphant return to Jerusalem, as one of those who crucified Jesus, and as a follower who received the dead body of Christ when it was lowered from the cross, why should we be troubled at his presentation of himself as the partying prodigal son, and of Saskia as one of the prodigal's female companions in the high living of the far country? I doubt that Rembrandt was attempting to tell his in-laws anything or that he was sounding a general warning about high living. He was yet again expressing his lifelong confession of the value of the Bible and its relevance, not as some sacred list of do's and don'ts, not as a holy compendium of stuff about saints, but as a gift that serves as a kind of mirror to us. "Look in the pages of the Bible," he might have said, "and see yourself." I believe, indeed, that he did say that, in the way he could speak so eloquently, in such works as this one.

Three years after he had painted himself as the prodigal son, Rembrandt depicted himself as one of Jacob's twelve sons in an etching based on the narrative of Genesis 37:9–11, the second account of Joseph reporting a dream (in the first such account, in Gen. 37:5–8, there is no mention of the presence of Jacob):

> Then he dreamed yet a second dream, and he bragged it out to his father [added by LXX] and his brothers. This is what he told: "Pay attention: I have dreamed still another dream—and look here, the sun and the moon and eleven stars were bowing down low to me."
>
> But when he bragged this out to his father and to his brothers, his father scolded him, saying to him, "What is this dream that you have dreamed? Are we really to come, I and your mother and your brothers to bow down low to the ground to you?"
>
> And consequently, his brothers were jealous of him, though his father mused over the incident.

Rembrandt gives us an earnest Joseph, leaning forward toward his father, his hands extended in demonstration of the "bowing down low" (the best part of the dream, from his point of view) and more than a hint of a smile of pride on his face. Jacob looks straight into the

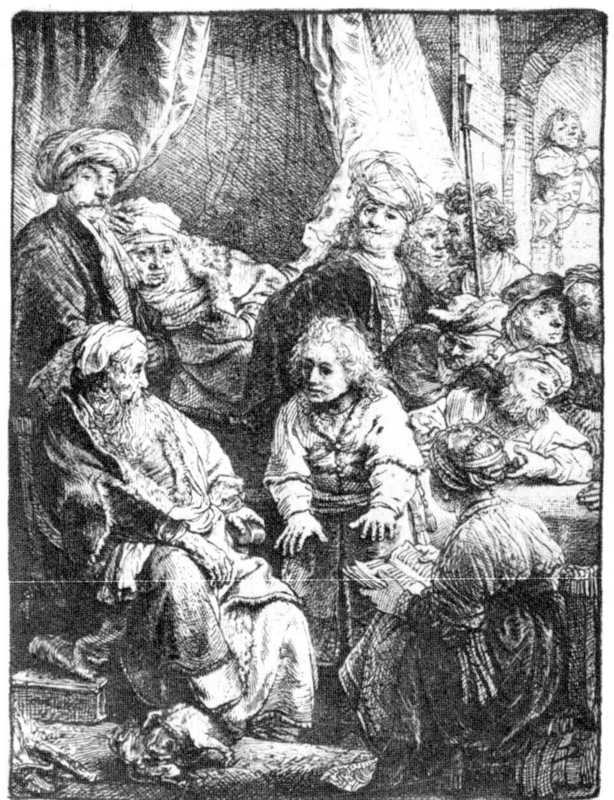

Joseph Telling His Dreams, B 37, 1638, Prentenkabinet, Rijksmuseum, Amsterdam

face of this cheeky love-son, his lips parted in the beginning of his rebuke. Rachel ("your mother") looks on from her bed with a weary and somewhat frightened expression. And the twelve sons are all there, though one of them is out of the picture to the right, just the fingers of his left hand visible, and the brother to Joseph's immediate left looking toward him with some affection. I suggest that the face we do not see may be intended as the face of Benjamin, the youngest of them all, and Rachel's second love-son. Rembrandt stands just behind Joseph, his arms akimbo, with something like a smirk on his face. I wonder whether he has represented himself as Reuben, the brother who was later to offer his two sons as surety to Jacob for the safe return from Egypt of Benjamin (Gen. 43:1–10). The brother immediately behind Jacob and to Rachel's right with the pop-eyed expression must surely be Judah, Jacob's firstborn, to whom Joseph's dream of ascendancy would have been the greatest affront.

In the midst of this jam-packed family scene, a composition no doubt designed to suggest the intimacy of this most important of Old Testament families, a sister looks up from a book she has been reading to her father, and in the left foreground another of Rembrandt's dogs is busily licking himself. This is, after all, a real family get-together, with everyone gathered and gathering (a late arrival hurries toward the doorway at the right top of the scene) around, and only the family pet is unconcerned by Joseph's outlandish *hubris.*

Rembrandt's appearance in his composite and compressed depiction of the whole of chapter 19 of Matthew's Gospel, *Christ Preaching* (see chap. 6), is just a head from the mouth up, no doubt representing one of the disciples or followers of Jesus given his position just behind

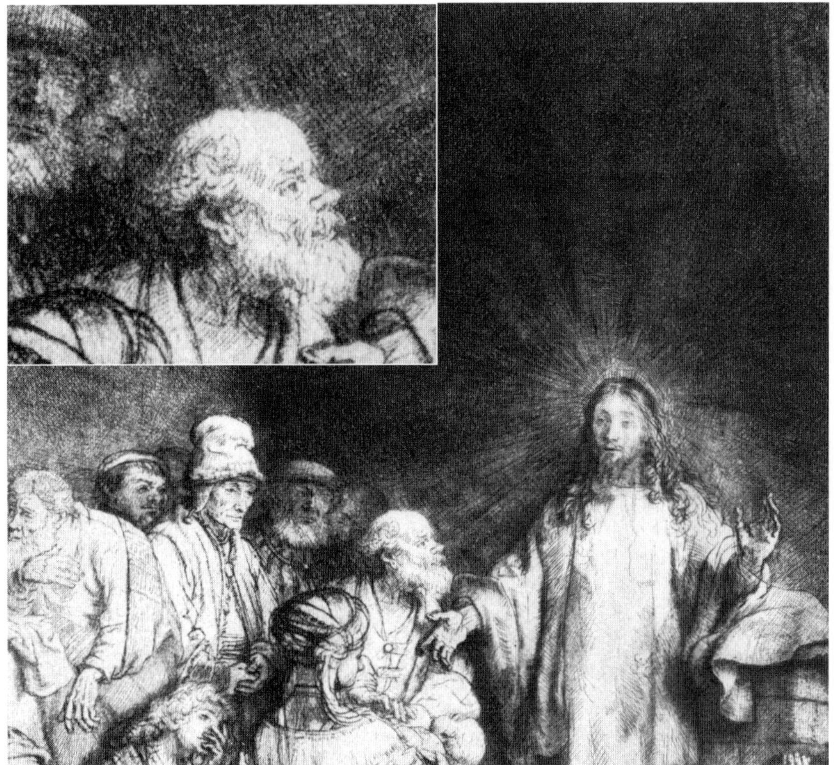

Christ Preaching,
B 74, 1640-1650,
Prentenkabinet,
Rijksmuseum, Amsterdam,
detail

and between Peter and the bearded man with the striped robe. Even so, it is more than we have in the etching of *The Stoning of Stephen* of 1635 (see page 61).

This is to list but a few of the biblical paintings and etchings into which Rembrandt placed his own face, a face so familiar to us from his amazing autobiography in self-portraiture. Some of these Rembrandt sightings are almost certainly imaginary. But more of them are not, and whatever else may be said about them—that they are self-puffing, or rebellion, or confession, or the simple need for another face—they are clear evidence of how seriously Rembrandt took the Bible.

I believe the Bible was for Rembrandt what his mother's devotion to it declared it to be—*the* book above every other book. His affection for painting books and manuscript folios is obvious from the number of times he did so—they appear in more than forty works. Of this number, at least half appear to represent the biblical text, in part or as a whole. And such representations of books and manuscripts they are! They are depictions to warm the heart of any book collector/addict, with palpable pages and the patina of much loving use. In a painting of 1628, now in Melbourne's National Gallery of Victoria, *Two Old*

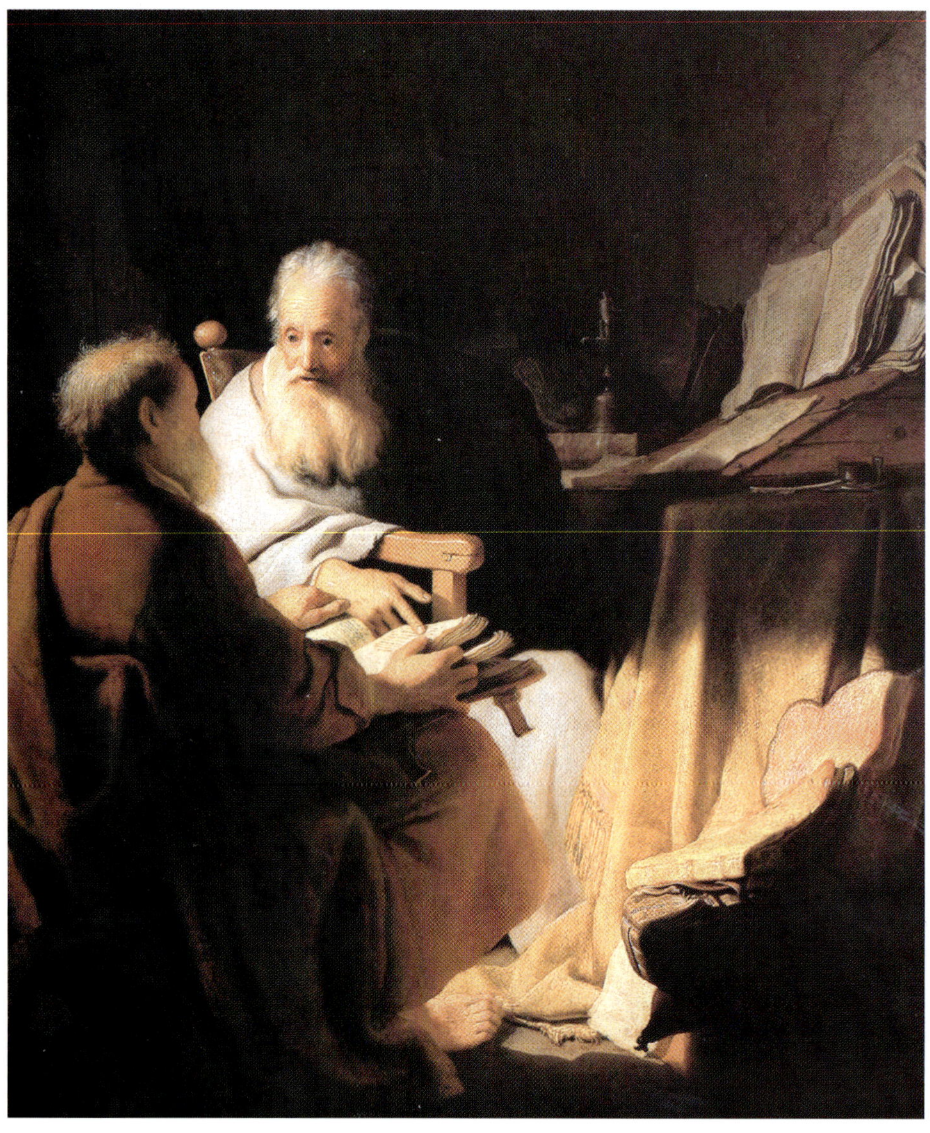

Two Old Men Disputing, Probably Saint Peter and Saint Paul, 1628, National Gallery of Victoria, Melbourne

Men Disputing, Probably Saint Peter and Saint Paul, the text Paul is exegeting to Peter fairly glows in the light that falls also onto the stack of books at the bottom right.

In *Judas, Repentant, Returning the Pieces of Silver* of the following year, the holy text the seated priest is reading, with its visible Hebrew letters, seems suffused with a brightness that falls onto the fateful silver pieces scattered across the floor (see chap. 4). In the series of depictions of the Apostle Paul, books and manuscripts are prominent, not least in Rembrandt's own *Self-Portrait as the Apostle Paul* from 1661, now in Amsterdam. Here, too, the text Rembrandt/Paul is

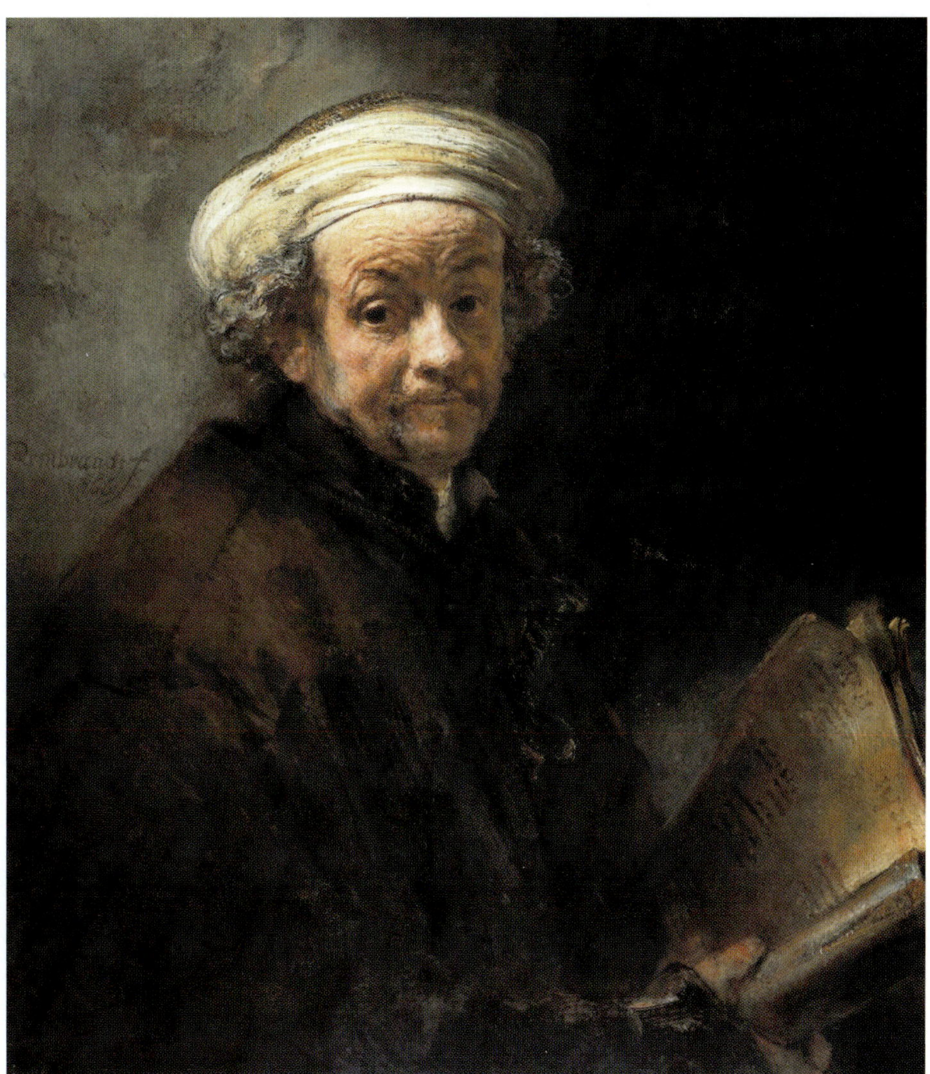

Self-Portrait as the Apostle Paul, 1661, Rijksmuseum, Amsterdam

holding is illumined, its curling pages tempting one to turn them. (See also the pile of books in *St. Paul in Prison*, chap. 2.)

In some ways, Rembrandt's most astounding representation of books and manuscript leaves is to be found in an early painting done in Leiden in 1627, and now in Berlin. It is titled *The Rich Man from the Parable* by the RRP and has been held to represent the wealthy landowner who amassed treasure for himself but had no regard for the richness of relationship with God (Luke 12:16–21).

Rembrandt gives us a man expensively clad who is scrutinizing a coin he holds in his right hand, close to a candle he is lifting with his left hand. Additional coins are scattered on the table in front of the man, and a fat moneybag sits at his left elbow on a stack of books. He is surrounded, all but closeted, by an array of books and manuscript sheets: on his worktable, hanging from a shelf above him, and draped over what appear to be pegs in the wall. A manuscript sheet across from him and a fat book protruding from behind it have what appears to be an imitation of Hebrew characters, but they seem to be intended as no more than a suggestion—the letters spell nothing and appear to be upside down. Perhaps Rembrandt intended to suggest biblical texts the rich farmer is ignoring, transfixed as he is on his money.

Is this painting, with its avalanche of pages, leaves, sheets, bindings, and books thick and thin, nothing more than a young painter's rollicking display of incredible skill, a twenty-one-year-old going over the top in the exhilaration of his astounding gift? Or is it an artist-bibliophile's tribute to his passion for the written and printed word? I think neither—Rembrandt does not seem to have surrounded himself with a great many books unrelated to his print and drawing collections. His interests appear to have been far more visual than literary. And his frequent depiction of books and folio volumes, apart from those representing the interests and professions of persons whose portraits he etched and painted, are predominantly connected in one way or another with the Bible. I suggest, therefore, that in his painting of pages, his mind was never far from the pages of the Bible, even when the pages he presented, as in *The Rich Man from the Parable*, did

The Rich Man from the Parable, 1627, Gemäldegalerie, Staatliche Museen, Berlin

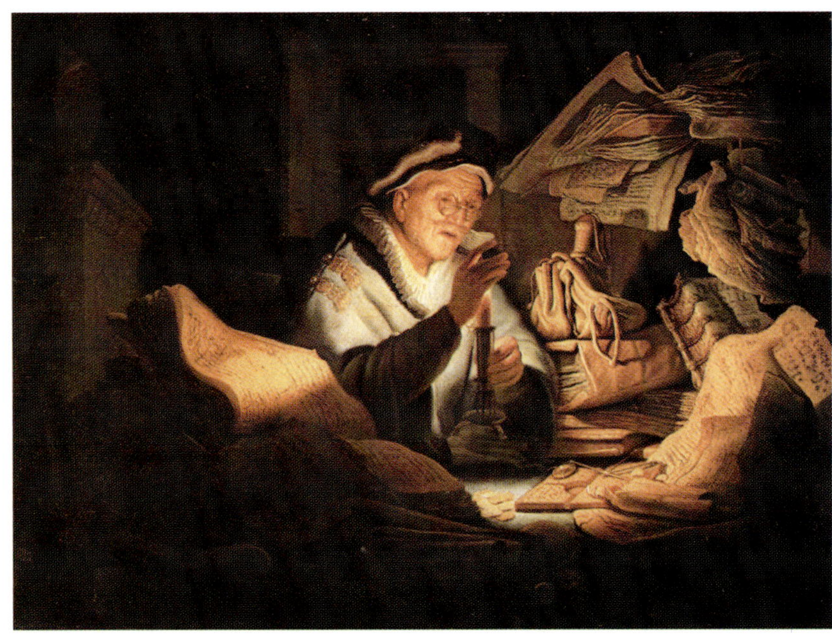

not depict biblical pages. The Bible for Rembrandt was simply *the* book, the book that he obviously read often and read thoughtfully, *the* book that was more than book and more than information. It was probably the first book he ever saw, and he may well have seen it in his mother's lap. It may have been the last book he ever saw, in 1669. One can hardly doubt that he saw it frequently throughout the years of his life.

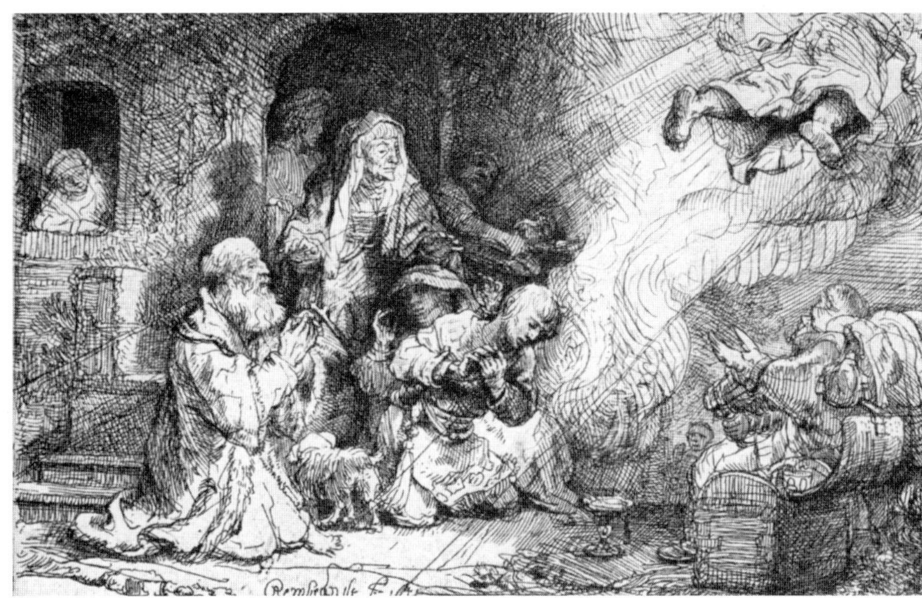

The Angel Departing from the Family of Tobias, B 43, 1641, Fitzwilliam Museum, Cambridge

Rembrandt also saw his Bible thoroughly, reading it with a mind unprejudiced by the theological patina of too much preaching, reading it with an eye for its lively and honest inclusion of detail, and reading it as a real report rather than as some ossified chant. His works based on the biblical text contain an amazing amount of biblical detail, detail that attests a careful and open-minded reading of the Bible. I have noted already his repeated inclusion in works dealing with the story of Tobit of the dog that accompanied Tobias on his trip to Media, a dog that is mentioned but two times in the fourteen chapters of the Book of Tobit (see chap. 2). In his 1641 etching of the moment when the angel Raphael ascends to heaven following the healing of Tobit and the celebration of the marriage of Tobias and Sarah (Tob. 12), Rembrandt also includes a chest and a donkey-load of the treasure given to the couple by the bride's father Raguel, a gift mentioned once, in Tobit 10:10. This part of Raguel's gift becomes a component of the scene of departure because of the decision of Tobias and Tobit to give Raphael, whom they know to this point only as Azariah, "half of all that he brought back" (Tob., 12:4), a payment far beyond the drachma per day expense money plus "something more" promised him (Tob. 5:15-16).

In an etching of 1645 depicting the moment when Isaac, going up Mount Moriah with Abraham, asks the heart-wrenching question, "Look here—the fire and the wood, but where is the lamb for the burnt-offering?" (Gen. 22:7), Rembrandt depicts Abraham explaining to his son that "God will see to the lamb himself, my son" (Gen. 22:8). The two have paused in their journey up the mountain. Isaac holds the load of wood against himself as he listens to his father. Abraham

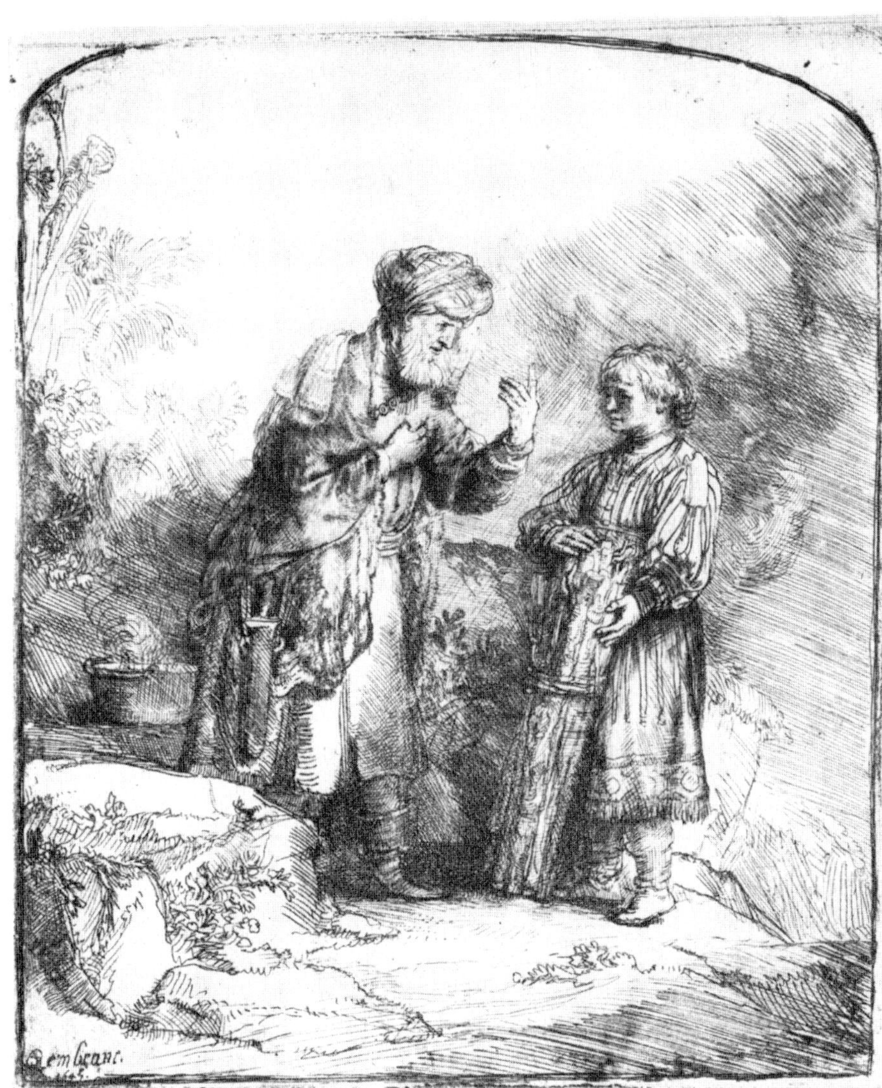

Abraham and Isaac, B 34, 1645, Prentenkabinet, Rijksmuseum, Amsterdam

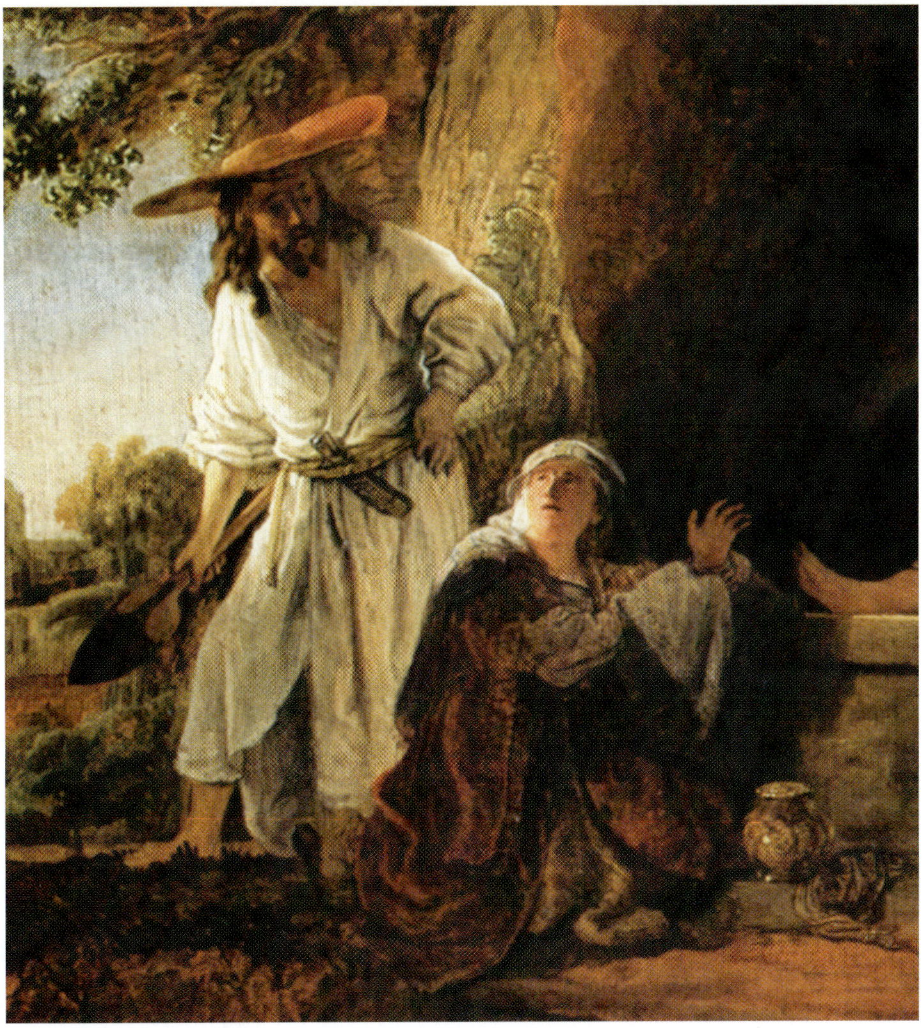

The Risen Christ Appearing to Mary Magdalene, 1638, The Queen's Gallery, Buckingham Palace, London, detail

appears to clutch his heart as he speaks, and the knife for the sacrifice, the knife that falls in mid-air from Abraham's startled hand in the painting of the moment of the sacrifice done ten years earlier (see chap. 4), is safely in its sheath by Abraham's side. The fire to which Isaac alludes is *behind* Abraham, well away from even an accidental touch by the boy. Rembrandt has caught and represented perfectly the poignant precautions taken by the old father: "So Abraham took the wood for the burnt-offering and placed it on Isaac his son, while he took in his own hand the fire and the knife" (Gen. 22:6).

A painting of 1638, now in the Queen's Collection, Buckingham Palace, *The Risen Christ Appearing to Mary Magdalene*, shows Rembrandt's practice of reading *all* the texts connecting with a moment he was depicting. The narrative on which the painting is based, John 20:14–17, makes no mention of the aromatic oil or spices (ἀρώματα) Mary and the other women brought to the tomb to anoint Jesus' hastily buried body—only Mark (16:1) and Luke (24:1) record this detail. It is, however, a detail Rembrandt caught, and at Mary's feet, as she sits on the steps leading to the tomb, is an ointment jar and a cloth for the anointing the women had come to perform.

In 1645, Rembrandt painted *The Holy Family with Angels*, now in St. Petersburg. This work is not typical of his biblical works in that there is no text depicting any such domestic moment in the life of Joseph and Mary and the infant Jesus. Rembrandt gives us what amounts to a genre painting of what, but for the tumble of protecting cherubs, could be an intimate domestic scene in the home of a Dutch craftsman. Mary and the book she is holding, a book that appears to be a Bible, are in a brightness that seems to fall from the spill of little angels. The cradle of the sleeping baby Jesus is lit by this same light, but only the child's hand is illumined—no halo of light surrounds his head. A fire burns on the brick hearth, and Joseph labors by an unseen source of light beyond the chimney hood, with his very modern-looking brace and bit hanging at the ready on the wall. Rembrandt's biblical detail in this work, indeed the only feature of the painting that links it to the Bible at all, lies in the object of Joseph's work: he is fashioning a yoke. Rembrandt has read Matthew 11:28–30, which reports Jesus the teacher inviting those who are listening to him to "take my yoke [ζυγόν] upon you, and learn from me by experience.... Indeed my yoke fits well and my load is easy to carry" (vv. 29a–30). The inclusion of this yoke is yet another indication of Rembrandt's familiarity with his Bible.

I have cited here none of Rembrandt's many biblical drawings, mainly because they are so largely works of the moment, works on the way to much greater detail, works that are often his shorthand, his planning of things to come. But no etching or painting on a biblical text is devoid of Rembrandt's close attention to his Bible—they are works of imagination, certainly, but an imagination disciplined and informed by a diligent study of the Bible itself. There is ample evidence that Rembrandt also studied the classical texts that were the basis of his works on mythological and historical themes. One of his late masterpieces, *The Conspiracy of the Batavians*, which survives now in Stockholm only in fragmentary form (see page 57), provides in itself dramatic support for his care in gathering information about a moment in secular history. But when he turned to the biblical text in

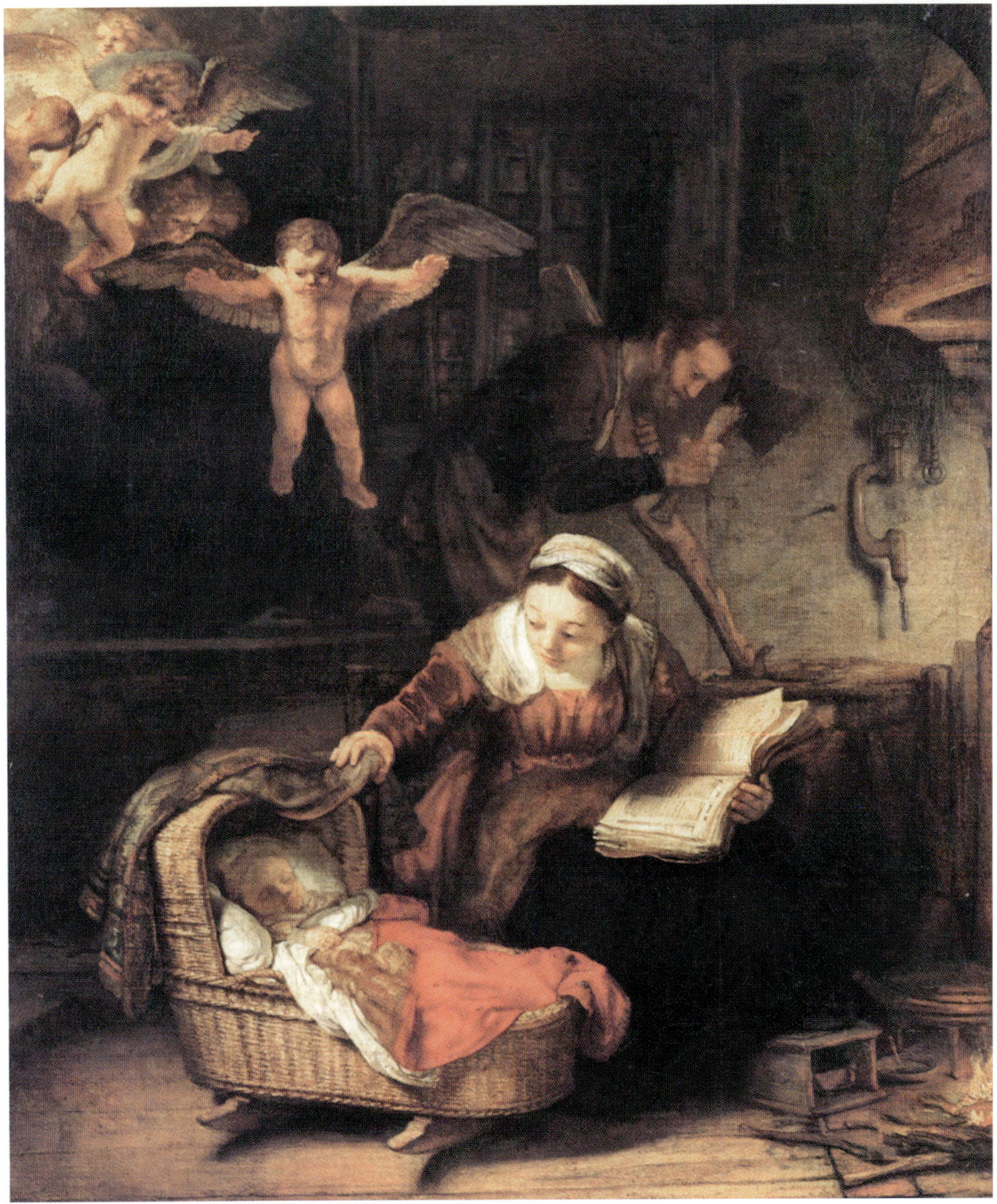

The Holy Family with Angels, 1645, State Hermitage, Winter Palace, St. Petersburg

his preparation for a painting or an etching, Rembrandt seems, on the basis of the resultant works, to have been even more absorbed in the pertinent texts than at any other time. Why?

In that the Bible was of God, it was for Rembrandt *The Holy Bible.* The Bible appears to have been the first book of his life—not only as the first book he experienced, but also as the book of first importance to him. But in that it was *of* the human family and *for* the human family, the Bible was for Rembrandt a book about the people he saw and knew and loved, and the people he painted and taught and sometimes disagreed with and sometimes disliked. The Bible, for Rembrandt, was ultimately about *him.* In its stories, he recognized himself. What more reasonable, then, than that he should be drawn into its stories, that he should pore over its pages, and that he should literally put himself right into some of the biblical moments he depicted?

Right through his life, Rembrandt kept and put to work this fascination with his Bible. As his very first known work, *The Stoning of Stephen,* was drawn from the pages of the Bible, so also was his final work, the work still on his easel at the time of his death, *Simeon with the Christ Child in the Temple,* now in Stockholm (see chap. 7), a work taken from the Bible. Into that very first work, Rembrandt placed himself, peering out at us from the vicious mob that is smashing Stephen's life away. In time, however, Rembrandt came to put himself into some of the biblical moments he depicted without using any likeness of his face at all—his final *Simeon in the Temple* is one such work, I believe. And it is these works, more than all the rest, the works in which he is present not by self-portrait but by what must be called faith, that make clear to us what the Bible was for him.

It was indeed *his* Bible that Rembrandt presented in his biblical works, as Kenneth Clark said. But Rembrandt, human and honest old Rembrandt, gave us an art that makes the Bible we read, all of it, more fully *our* Bible as well.

SOME SOURCES AND SUGGESTIONS

Information about Rembrandt's parental background can be found in RD, under the heading "Antecedents: 1484–1605" (the summary of the text of Harmen's earliest will is on pp. 37–38), and of course in the beginning chapters of the standard works on Rembrandt's life and art (as, for example, the volumes of Bob Haak, Christian Tümpel, Horst Gerson, and Gary Schwartz, who presents (pp. 18-20) a helpful Rembrandt family tree prepared by P. J. M. de Baar of the Leiden archival office). The entries on catalog numbers 1–5 in *Rembrandt's Women* provide an interesting survey of ten portraits by Rembrandt of his mother, from 1628 to 1631.

The catalog to an exhibition held in 2000–2001 in Washington's National Gallery of Art, London's Dulwich Picture Gallery, and Mauritshuis in The Hague of works by Gerrit Dou provides a comprehensive summary of the life and work of an artist who became Rembrandt's student, perhaps even his very first pupil, at thirteen: *Gerrit Dou, 1613–1675: Master Painter in the Age of Rembrandt* (2000). Dou's painting of the *Old Woman Reading* is now in the Rijksmuseum.

This photograph of the motto above the door of the Latin School in Leiden was made on 24 April 2001.

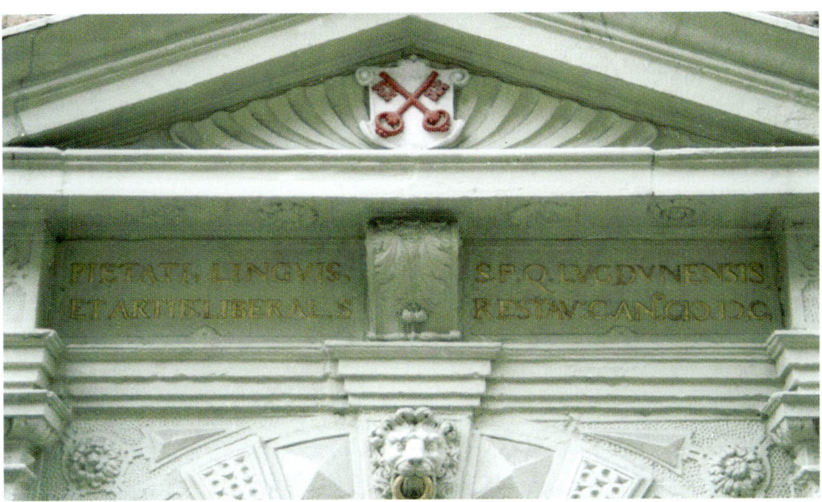

Seymore Slive (*Rembrandt and His Critics*, pp. 104–15) devotes a chapter to Baldinucci's discussion of Rembrandt and his art, including his speculation about Rembrandt's supposed Mennonite connections. Jacob Rosenberg (*Rembrandt: Life and Work*, pp. 180–84) provides a helpful summary on the Mennonite question.

See RD (pp. 344–45, 347) for Rembrandt's application for *cessio bonorum* and for a copy of the inventory (pp. 348–88), which was made on 25–26 July 1656. The only books listed in the inventory not specifically connected with art are, apart from his "old Bible," "15 books of various sizes," item 281—as these unnamed volumes were found in the "art chamber," however, it is reasonable to suppose that they too were related to Rembrandt's work. One longs to know, all the same, what the fifteen titles were. The addition of a new wing adjoining the Rembrandt House Museum in Amsterdam has made possible the utilization of much more of the space in the house in which Rembrandt lived and worked for almost twenty years to represent the residence as it was in Rembrandt's time. Using the 1656 inventory as a guide, the museum has attempted to furnish the "art chamber" with an array of objects and curiosities similar to those listed in the inventory taken on 25–26 July 1656. *Rembrandt's Treasures* provides a fascinating and elegant look at Rembrandt as an avid collector of art and objects useful to him as artist and teacher.

Discussions of Rembrandt's interest in and use of the Bible can be found in a number of works. Many of them are largely books of reproductions with the pertinent biblical texts included, sometimes with narrative summaries. Of these, by far the most elaborate is the six-volume work edited by Hidde Hoekstra and published by Hanssler-Verlag from 1980–1984 under the title *Die Rembrandt-Bibel.* An English translation of this work appeared in a single oversize volume in 1990 under the title *Rembrandt and the Bible.* Neither edition, curiously, includes the works based on texts in the Book of Acts.

A. Hyatt Major contributed a helpful summary essay, "Rembrandt and the Bible," to the winter 1978/79 issue of *The Metropolitan Museum of Art Bulletin*, and Kenneth Clark's "Rembrandt and the Bible" (chap. 5 of *An Introduction to Rembrandt*, 1978), leaves one, as Clark almost always does, hungry for more (the quotation on p. 58 above comes from p. 117). Also helpful is a lengthy essay by Hans-Martin Rotermund, *Rembrandts Handzeichnungen und Radierungen zur Bibel* (1963), available in an English translation under the title *Rembrandt's Drawings and Etchings for the Bible* (1969). Following a brief introduction, Rotermund comments, with considerable summary of the biblical text, on the drawings and etchings in the sequence of the Old and New Testaments: "The First Age and the Patriarchs," "The Life of Moses and the Period of the Judges," "The Lives of Samuel, Saul, and David," "Scenes from the Time of the Kings; the Book of Esther; the Prophets," "Jesus' Birth and Childhood," "Christ as Preacher and Healer," "Scenes from the Gospel According to John," "Jesus' Suffering and Death," "Encounters with the Resurrected Christ," and "The Acts of the Apostles."

More valuable still is W. A. Visser 'T Hooft's *Rembrandt and the Gospel* (1960), a gentle essay from a Christian perspective (the quotation on p. 58 above comes from pp. 29–30 of this work). It was Visser 'T Hooft's chapter on the so-called "Hundred Guilder Print" that stimulated me to begin a study of the details of Rembrandt's works on biblical themes as narrative commentary on the texts they interpreted.

Christian Tümpel's three chapters on what he calls "the Biblical Histories" in his *Rembrandt: All Paintings in Colour* are interesting summaries: "The Biblical Histories of the First Amsterdam Period," "The Biblical Histories of the 1640s: The Hidden Symbolism of New Testament Depictions," and "The Biblical History of the 1650s." His "An Uncommon Subject," on Hagar's expulsion by Abraham, his "The Hundred Guilder Print: and the Suggestion of How the Story Hangs Together," and his "The Language of Pictures: Elimination" are also instructive.

Of special interest is the work of Franz Landsberger, *Rembrandt, the Jews and the Bible* (1972). His references to Rembrandt's use of Hebrew and his fourth chapter, "Rembrandt and the Bible," deal primarily with works on Old Testament texts. Also worth a look for an understanding of Rembrandt's immersion in the biblical texts he found appealing is Julius Held's article "Rembrandt and the Book of Tobit" in his *Rembrandt Studies* (1991).

By far the most extensive resource for the study of the themes pursued by Rembrandt's pupils is the multi-volume work of Werner Sumowski, *Gemälde der Rembrandt-Schüler*, available now in English translation as *Drawings of the Rembrandt School*, ten volumes of which (out of the proposed twelve) have appeared thus far. Sumowski arranges the drawings of Rembrandt's known pupils in three categories: "authentic drawings," those signed or otherwise certainly identified as autograph works; "substantiated drawings," those he believes are "of unquestionable authenticity based on stylistic criteria"; and "attributed drawings," those he suggests only *may* belong to a given artist's oeuvre. A survey of the more than 2,453 drawings thus far collected and published in volumes 1–10 of *Drawings of the Rembrandt School* reveals a number of drawings by some of Rembrandt's pupils that are based on Rembrandt's biblical works and other drawings on biblical themes on which there are no known works by Rembrandt. Five of the fifty artists listed in Sumowski's ten volumes show the greatest interest in biblical subjects: of 220 drawings assigned to Gerbrand van den Eeckhout, who studied with Rembrandt between 1635 and 1640, some 40 are biblical; of 179 drawings assigned to Samuel van Hoogstraten, who studied with Rembrandt between 1640 and 1648, more than 120 are biblical; of 220 drawings assigned to Philips Koninck, who studied with Rembrandt in 1641 and the years immediately following, some 73 are biblical; of 258 drawings assigned to Nicolaes Maes, who studied with Rembrandt around 1648 and following, some 94 are biblical; and of 65 drawings assigned to Constantijn Daniel van Renesse, who studied with Rembrandt from late in the 1640s until the mid-1650s, 41 are biblical. Far the majority of the drawings of Rembrandt's students listed and reproduced by Sumowski are without any reference at all to the Bible—more than 76 percent of them, in fact.

Christian Tümpel deals with the influence upon Rembrandt of Lastman's *Coriolanus and the Roman Women*, *The Stoning of Stephen*, and *The Baptism of the Eunuch* in his essay "Pieter Lastman and Rembrandt" in *Pieter Lastman: The Man Who Taught Rembrandt.*

Rembrandt's self-portraits have been discussed in fascinating detail by H. Perry Chapman in *Rembrandt's Self-Portraits: A Study in Seventeenth-Century Identity* (1990; see particularly his chapter "Rembrandt's Biblical Roles"). The catalog to the exhibition in London's National Gallery and Mauritshuis in 2000–2001, *Rembrandt by Himself* (1999), is exemplary in both text and illustrations; Ernst van de Wetering's essay in this volume, "The Multiple Functions of Rembrandt's Self-Portraits," notes (pp. 21-22) that Rembrandt "knew that his face would be recognized in the history pieces in which he appeared as a 'bit player.'... [Such] was undoubtedly the case with *The Raising of the Cross*...." Also worth a look, mainly for their assemblage of "straight," that is, non-narrative Rembrandt self-portraits, are the works of Pascal Bonafoux (*Rembrandt: Self-Portrait*, 1985) and Christopher Wright (*Rembrandt Self-Portraits*, 1982).

I have no doubt that Rembrandt was aware of Genesis 35:16-20, which notes that Rachel died giving birth to Joseph's younger brother Benjamin, the last of Jacob's "twelve" sons. A depiction of the narrative of Joseph telling his dreams to the family thus should not include both Rachel looking on from her bed and Benjamin as a boy, barely in the etching plate, literally by four fingers, as I have suggested. Rembrandt may have forgotten this biblical sequence, or he may have disregarded it deliberately for dramatic reasons. And of course my guess-identification of the fingers may be wide of the mark. Five years before he made this plate, Rembrandt did a grisaille sketch of *Joseph Telling His Dreams* that gives every appearance of preparation for a painting, but may have resulted instead in this more detailed plate.

An alternate suggestion regarding the yoke Joseph is preparing in *The Holy Family with Angels* is given by Christian Tümpel (*Rembrandt: All Paintings in Colour*, p. 245), who suggests that Rembrandt may have had in mind Isaiah 9:4 (9:3 in Hebrew), which describes God's shattering of the yoke that weighed Israel down as a prophecy of Christ, who would bring deliverance again. I think this interpretation requires a far greater leap than the connection with Matthew 11:28–30, not least because the Matthew text is more directly related to Jesus as the incarnation the angels would bless.

A publication of the Nationalmuseum in Stockholm, *The Batavians' Oath of Allegiance: Rembrandt's Only Monumental Painting* by Carl Nordenfalk, provides a detailed account of *The Conspiracy of the Batavians* and its fate, along with a trenchant discussion of Rembrandt's departure from heroic tradition and his attention to historical sources in his depiction of Claudius Civilis.

4

REMBRANDT'S PICTURES

What Bible was it that Rembrandt saw on his mother's lap? And what Bible was it that he lived with, the Bible listed among his possessions in the inventory of 1656, the Bible that was the sole book found among his things when he died in 1669? We know very little more than that he had a Bible; thus, regarding these questions, no more than speculation is possible.

An Old Testament in Dutch, lacking only the Book of Psalms, was printed in 1477, and it was followed by a variety of vernacular versions of parts of the Bible, and in due course by an array of complete Bibles. The Bible known and used by Rembrandt's parents in their Roman Catholic upbringing was probably an edition based on an authorized translation of Jerome's Vulgate, perhaps the Christopher Plantin edition of 1566 as revised by Plantin's son-in-law Jan Moerentorf in 1599.

The Bible Rembrandt would have seen on his mother's lap was more likely one of the Dutch versions of Luther's German translation, which began appearing in the first third of the sixteenth century. The "old Bible" of the 1656 inventory may well have been this very Bible, as Neeltje died in 1640, and which of her children would have claimed her Bible with greater affection than Rembrandt?

In 1619, the Dutch Reformed Church authorized its own translation of the Bible, the *Statenvertaling*. This version was published in 1637 at the expense of the Dutch government, "the States-General." It became the standard Dutch Reform Bible and was accorded in Dutch religion the place occupied later by the King James Version in American Protestantism. That Rembrandt would have known this Bible, which appeared in his twenty-first year, is virtually certain. He may also have known the earlier *Deus-aes* Bible of 1561–1562, used by Calvinists before 1637, and even the Biestkens Bible favored by the Mennonites for the century and a half following 1560.

Given what we know of Rembrandt's education at the Latin School in Leiden, we can assume that he could have read the text of the Vulgate with little or no difficulty. He may even have been able to make his way through the Koiné Greek of the New Testament, as classical Greek was also a part of the Latin School curriculum, though apparently as an elective study. That he was fascinated with the Hebrew of the Old Testament and studied at least its characters is clear from such works as the early *Judas, Repentant, Returning the Pieces of Silver* of 1629, now in England, and the *Belshazzar's Feast* of 1635, now in London's National Gallery.

This speculation about the Bible Rembrandt may have owned and used, interesting though it may be, is largely irrelevant to a consideration of Rembrandt's biblical works, as no one of these works appears to depend upon any given version of the Bible. A more important point is the inclusion of the Apocryphal books in at least some version of the Bible Rembrandt may have used, given his attraction to the Book of Tobit and his interest in the story of Susanna.

The Apocrypha was, in Rembrandt's day as it remains still, a part of the Roman Catholic canon. While Luther included it in his translation, Calvin and his followers opposed its inclusion fiercely. Rembrandt appears to have accepted the Apocryphal books as Scripture, whatever he may have been taught in the Latin School and whatever version of the Bible was standard in his Dutch Reform tradition. The "old Bible" he perhaps inherited from his mother would have been based on Luther's translation and would have included at least some of the Apocryphal books. And may we not think of the boy Rembrandt hearing the story of Tobit from his mother, who herself had kept it as a part of her Roman Catholic childhood?

Given this importance of the Bible in Rembrandt's life at home in the mill on "De Rijn" and his education in Leiden's Latin School, what could be more natural than his use of the Bible as a sourcebook for his art? To this may be added the fact that his most important teacher, Pieter Lastman of Amsterdam, was much given to painting biblical scenes and had himself studied in Italy from 1603 to 1605 the work of a German painter there, Adam Elsheimer. Elsheimer, like Peter Paul Rubens, had spent time with Caravaggio, that one-man revolution in the painting of scenes from the Bible, in the home of Caravaggio's patron, Cardinal Francesco Maria Del Monte.

Turning to the Bible as a source for his work was for Rembrandt both entirely logical and entirely natural. Some of his early works on biblical moments, as for example *Balaam and the Ass* of 1626, now in the Musée Cognacq-Jay in Paris, and *David with the Head of Goliath before Saul* of 1627, now in Basel, are very nearly copies of paintings by Lastman, despite some irrepressibly Rembrandtian touches.

Rembrandt's depiction of Balaam and the she-ass in a dialogue both furious and affronted, for example, perfectly captures the humor of Numbers 22:27: "So when the she-ass saw Yahweh's messenger, she lay down under Balaam—then Balaam was livid with anger, and he hit the she-ass with his stick." (See next page.)

As the narrative continues, Balaam had so "lost it" to his temper that he answered the she-ass's complaint without noticing anything exceptional, and the conversation goes along at length, the "stubborn" animal with beseeching eye reasoning with the "rational" human seer with gritted teeth (Num. 22:28–30). Rembrandt's version of the moment, though derivative of Lastman's in both theme and composition, captures the biblical text with far greater feeling.

Despite such special touches, however, what Rembrandt did with "*his* Bible" at the beginning of his career may most accurately be called illustration. We have no works of Rembrandt from his six-month period of study with Lastman in Amsterdam. The works that

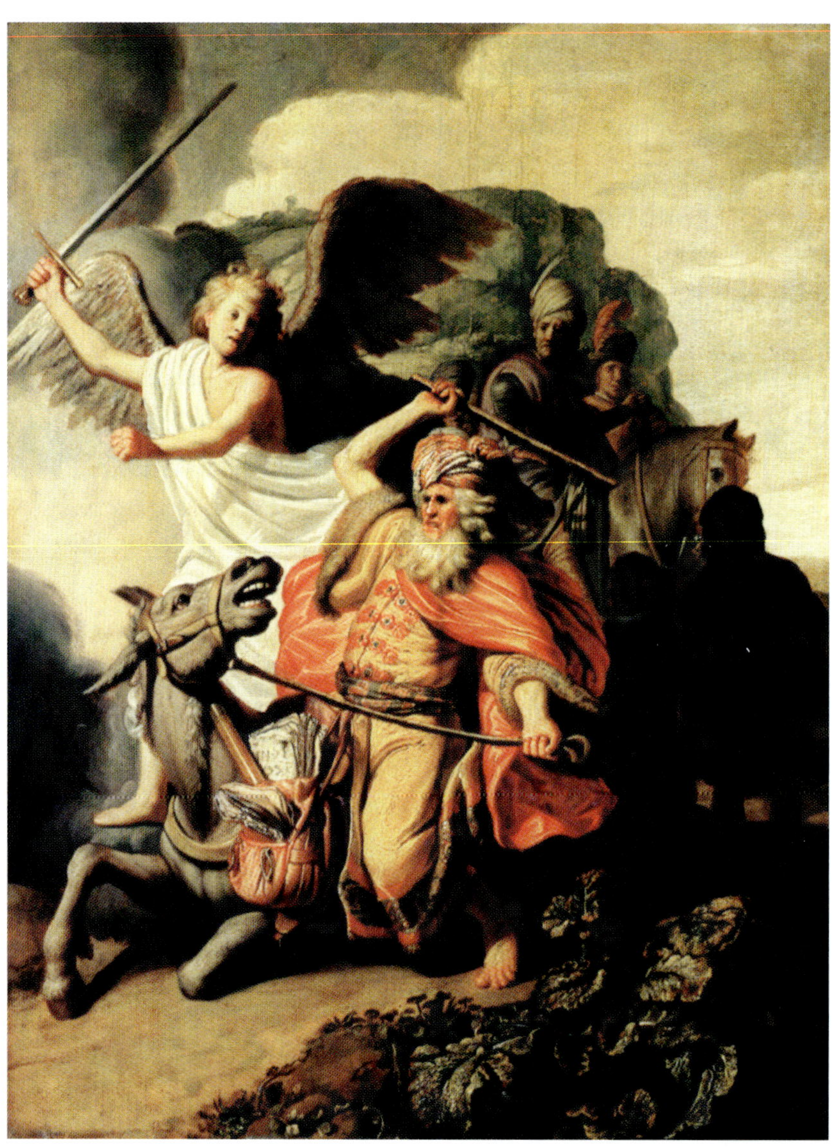

Balaam and the Ass, 1626,
Musée Cognaq-Jay, Paris

can be placed in his Leiden period, 1625–1631/32, and the works from his early years in Amsterdam are what I call "Rembrandt's pictures." Whatever the medium he employed in these works, Rembrandt appears to have intended to picture the biblical moments that attracted him.

I suggest that Rembrandt, to illustrate these moments, began always with the biblical text, whatever previous works or remembered images may have come to his mind. And as he did so, he began entering the biblical world in ways that made that world a part of his experience. I believe it not too much to say that his own world, as he worked, became entwined with the biblical world to such an extent that the gulf between the two often became blurred. His biblical drawings from the Leiden years all appear to be notes to himself, and studies that suggest such a blurring—so, for example, *Judas Repentant*, an obvious study for the painting of 1629 (see page 92).

Judas Repentant, Benesch 8, around 1629 (private collection)

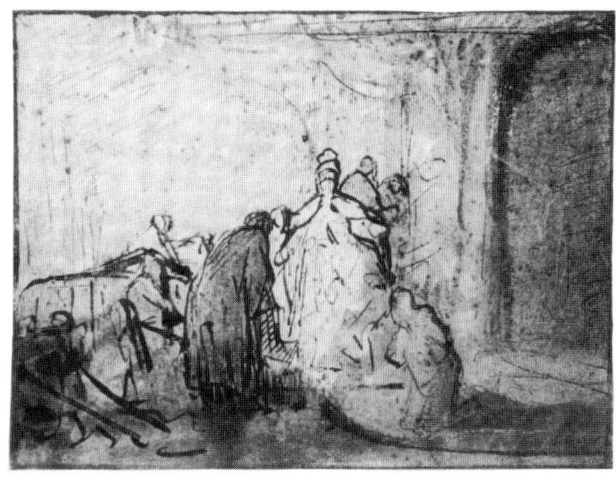

The biblical etchings of this period are tentative explorations of a medium Rembrandt would all but invent. They give us a *Flight into Egypt*, two versions of a *Night Rest* on that flight, a *Presentation in the Temple* (a later version of the painting of 1627/28) and two representations of the *Circumcision*, one of them also a very early plate. The "Night Rest" pieces, of which the one shown here is probably Rembrandt's earliest etching, are samples of what may be called "imagined" biblical moments, in that they are without any specific biblical text. Rembrandt may have been drawn to such a moment by a lovely little painting of Adam Elsheimer, now in Munich's Alte Pinakothek, which he perhaps knew from his teacher Pieter Lastman.

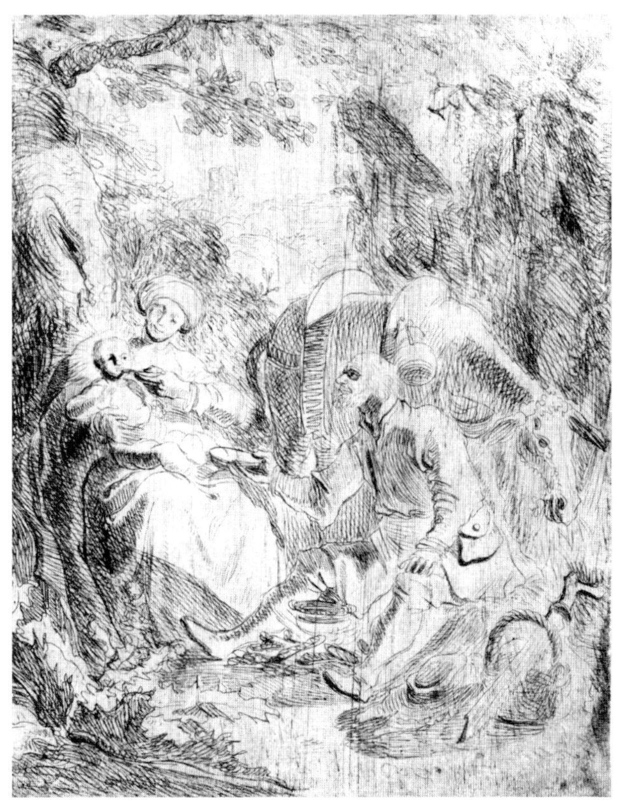

The Rest on the Flight to Egypt, B 59, around 1626, Prentenkabinet, Rijksmuseum, Amsterdam

From the first years in Amsterdam, there is a flood of works depicting biblical moments, all of them illustrative, but more and more revealing Rembrandt's entry, often a very human entry, into the biblical world. The grief of Jacob hearing the deceptive news of the death of Joseph is depicted in an etching of 1633 and in a drawing of 1635. The two years have made a dramatic difference: Jacob's

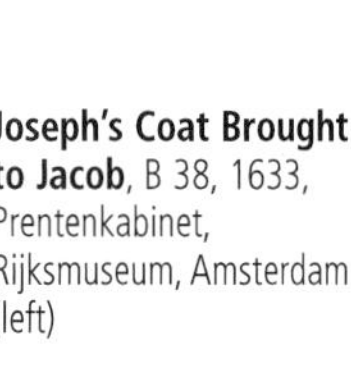

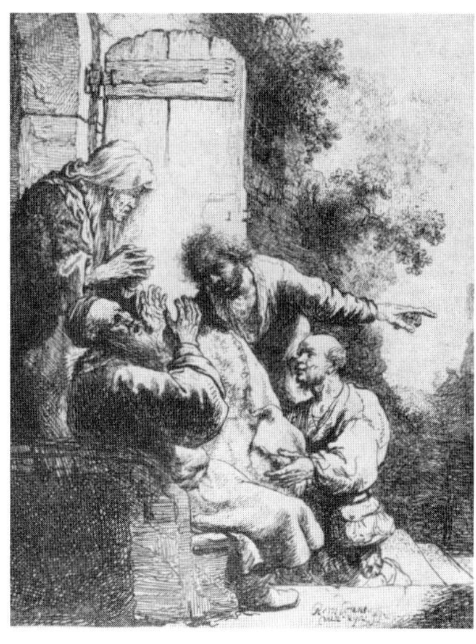

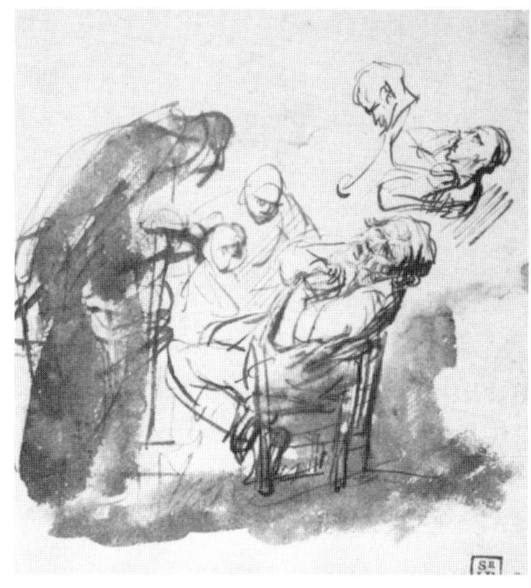

Joseph's Coat Brought to Jacob, B 38, 1633, Prentenkabinet, Rijksmuseum, Amsterdam (left)

Study for Jacob Lamenting, Benesch 95, 1635, Kupferstichkabinett, Staatliche Museen, Berlin (right)

devastation is palpable, more vivid by far in the drawing than in the etching. The old deceiver, who had deceived his father, his brother, and his father-in-law, is now himself so cruelly deceived that he reels back under the news as under the impact of a physical blow.

So Genesis 37:34c–35c: "Then Jacob ["Deceiver"]…grieved for his son for days on end. And all of his sons and all of his daughters tried their best to comfort him, but he was unwilling to be consoled, and he said, 'I will go down to join my son in the grave, still grieving.' "

Touches of Rembrandt's humanity abound in these works of illustration, and they appear to have flown from his mind and his hand during his early years in Amsterdam. There is the solemn paralysis and the tender gentleness of a drawing from 1632 or 1633 of Christ being borne to the tomb.

There is the wagging finger of the scolding, nagging Martha opposite the entranced attention of her sister Mary in the presence of Christ (Luke 10:38–42) in a drawing also from 1632–1633.

Group for an Entombment of Christ, Benesch 60, 1632 or 1633, Kupferstichkabinett, Staatliche Museen, Berlin (left)

Christ Conversing with Mary and Martha, Benesch 79, 1632 or 1633, Teylers Museum, Haarlem (right)

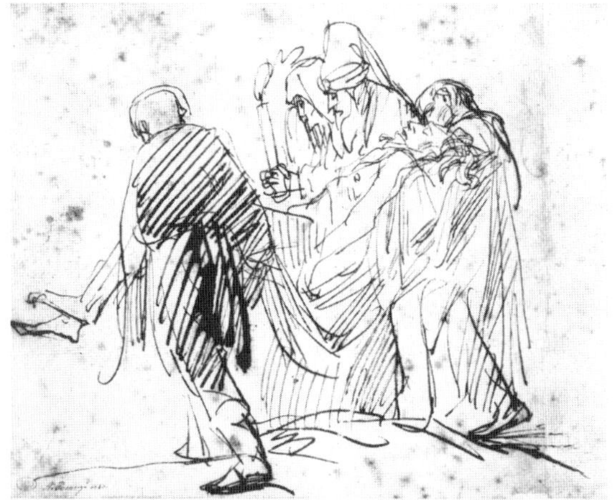

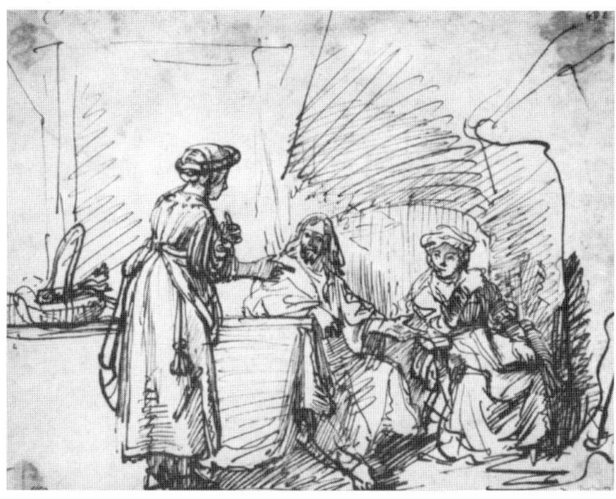

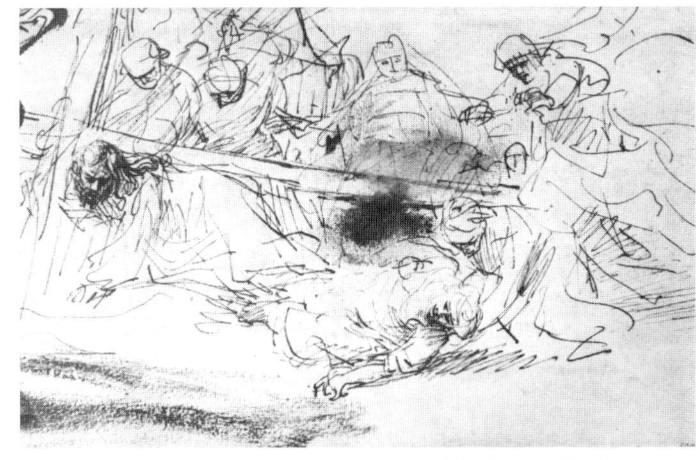

Christ Carrying the Cross, Benesch 97, 1635, detail, Kupferstichkabinett, Staatliche Museen, Berlin

There is the pathos of the drawing of 1635 of Christ falling under the weight of his cross, some of his followers lunging to help him, others reaching to help his mother, who has fainted.

There is the action-packed movement of the turbulent 1635 etching of *Christ Driving the Moneychangers from the Temple*, with the merchant retreating with his basket of chickens, the greedy moneychanger grasping his fat purse, the coins and purse of his leaning companion falling, and the wall-eyed cow, the barking dog, and the general melee of the flight from an angry Christ in the cavernous space of the temple.

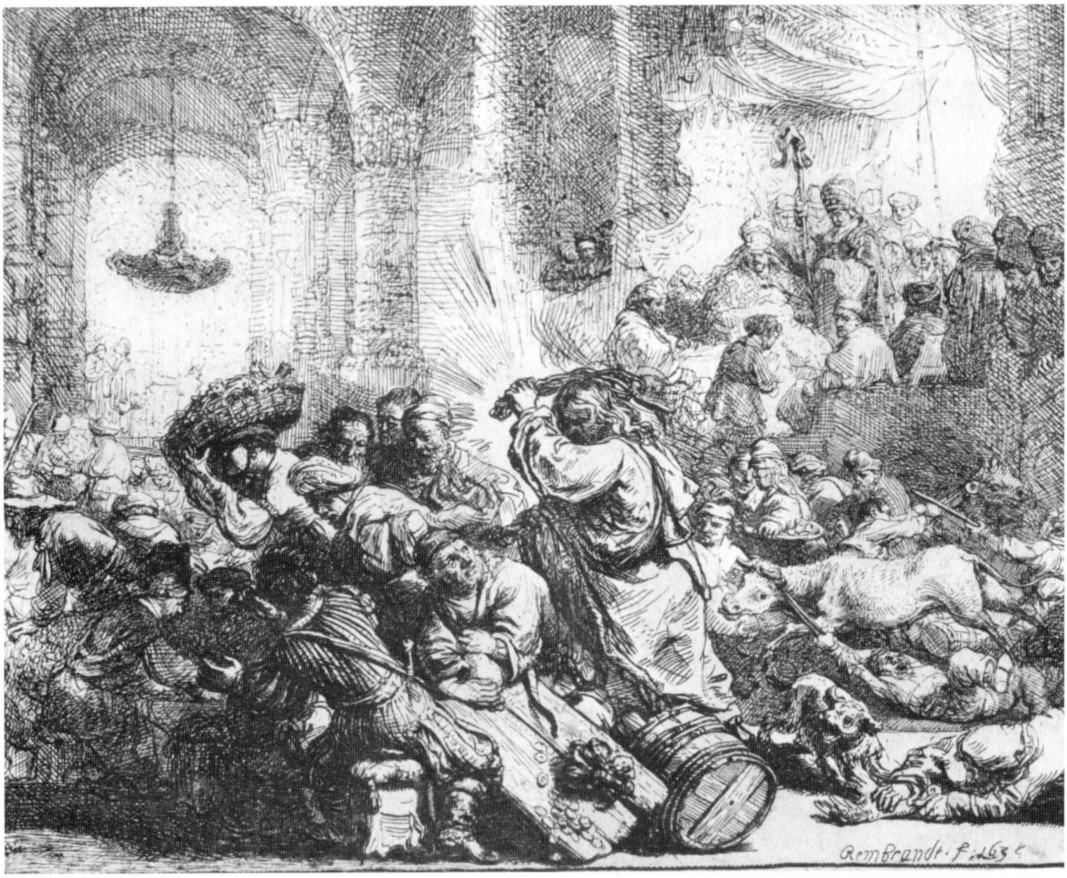

Christ Driving the Moneychangers from the Temple, B 69, 1635, Prentenkabinet, Rijksmuseum, Amsterdam

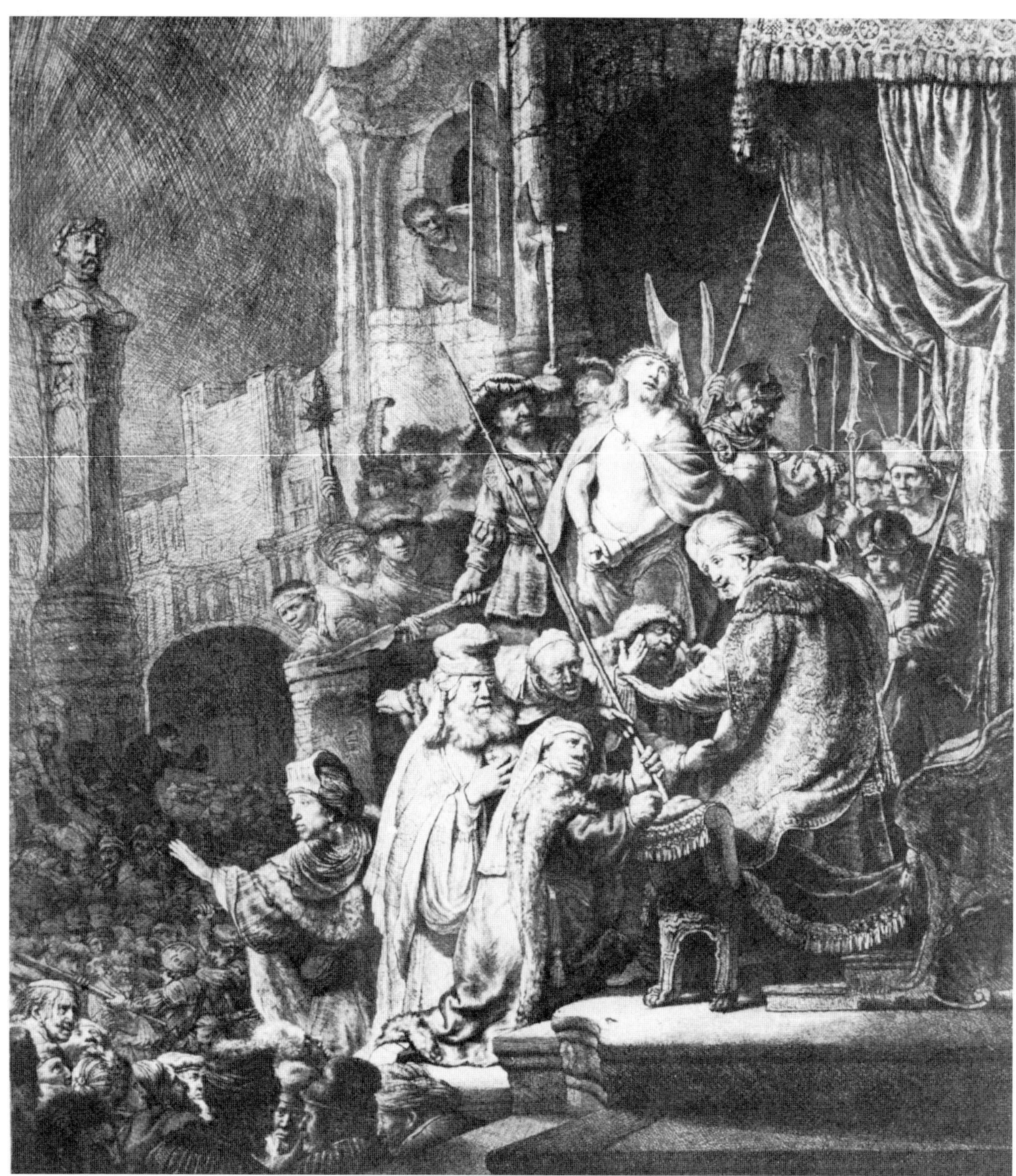

Christ Before Pilate, B 77, 1635-1636, Prentenkabinet, Rijksmuseum, Amsterdam

There is the 1635–1636 etching of *Christ before Pilate*, with its repulsive crawl of temple officials squirming obsequiously toward Pilate in their quest for Jesus' life as the teeming mob below is restrained.

There is the bestial face of the ragged, wasted younger son in the 1636 *Return of the Prodigal Son*, with its bending father, its curious maid, and its rush of servants.

There is the middle-aged pair with sagging bodies in their final moment of innocent nakedness in the garden of Eden in the 1638 *Adam and Eve*, with its chubby elephant in the forest background and the tempting serpent drawn with a reptilian tail, a canine haunch, an avian spur and foot and claw, a bat wing, a wolfish face, and a boar's snout and tusk, holding out yet another piece of forbidden fruit, just to make sure of their fall.

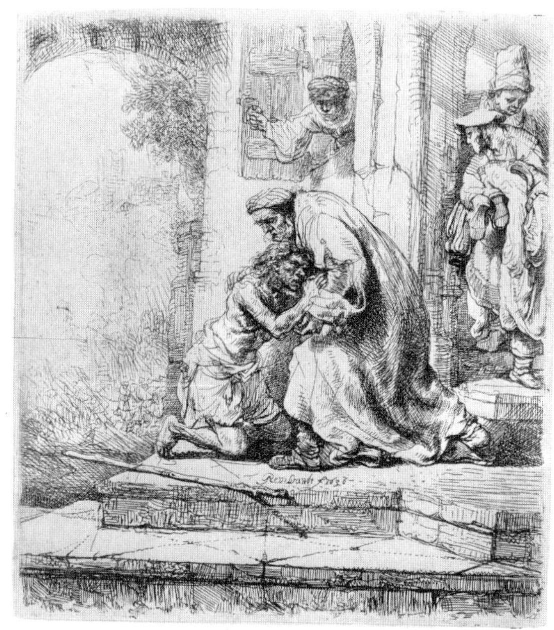

Return of the Prodigal Son, B 91, 1636, Prentenkabinet, Rijksmuseum, Amsterdam

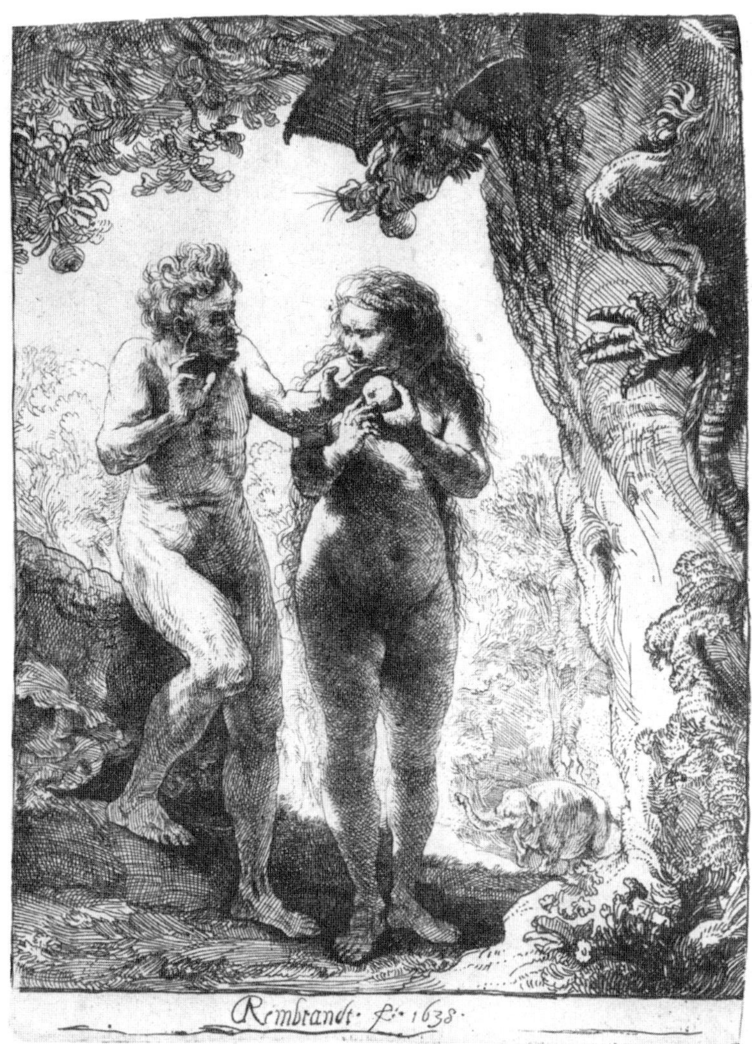

Adam and Eve, B 28, 1638, Prentenkabinet, Rijksmuseum, Amsterdam

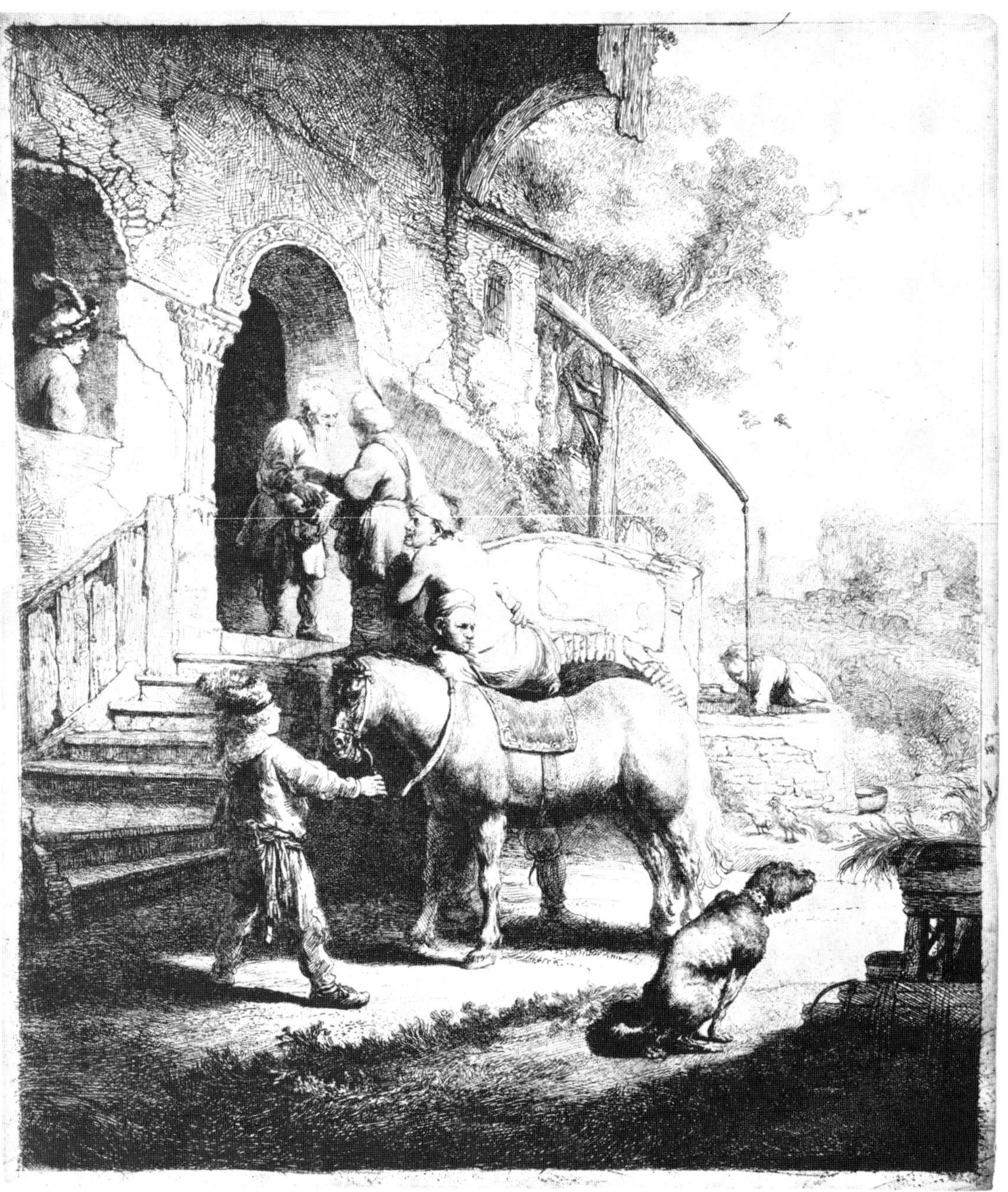

The Good Samaritan,
B 90, 1633, Prentenkabinet,
Rijksmuseum, Amsterdam

And there is the 1633 *Good Samaritan*, with its curious onlooker, its maid drawing water, and that notorious dog defecating in the foreground at just the moment when the Samaritan is negotiating the care of the wounded traveler, who is being lifted, wincing, from the Samaritan's horse.

Rembrandt's pictures, however, are far more than an assembly, even a gifted one, of details that suggest how real the biblical stories were to him. He was attempting to illustrate the texts he chose, but what he achieved in that effort amounts to more than pictorial summary. Beginning with the biblical texts themselves, Rembrandt first experienced the moments he was drawn to, then re-presented them, as though from his own life. In a sense, they *were* moments from his own life, with no particular reference to the past or the future, in art or in history or in society or beyond them. What made those moments true for Rembrandt was their very timelessness. They could, they must, be real for him because of their truth, the truth that would not be limited by any tradition or any system or any laws that human beings might impose on them. Rembrandt's biblical persons are unaware that they are going to be in the Bible, an important point all too often ignored in biblical works of art.

This same view of integrity and of truth is present also in Rembrandt's non-biblical art, from his self-portraits to his doodlings, from works he created for his own amusement to those he did on commission. Along with his incredible gift for mismanaging his finances, it was a view that caused his contemporaries to make his life very difficult at times.

Four paintings from the first decade of Rembrandt's career, two from his time in Leiden and two from his first years in Amsterdam, seem to me to sum up his attempt to re-present biblical moments in the language of his own perception of their truth. They are *Judas, Repentant, Returning the Pieces of Silver* of 1629, now in England, the work that bowled over his early patron Constantin Huygens; *Jeremiah Lamenting the Destruction of Jerusalem* of 1630, now in Amsterdam; *Abraham's Sacrifice* of 1635, now in St. Petersburg; and *Belshazzar's Feast,* also from 1635, now in London's National Gallery.

The narrative of the moment Rembrandt has portrayed in *Judas, Repentant, Returning the Pieces of Silver,* is recorded in the New Testament only in the Gospel of Matthew, at 27:3–5a:

> Then, realizing that he [Jesus] had been sentenced to death, Judas, who had handed him over, changed his mind and gave back the thirty silver pieces to the high priests and the elders, saying, "I have done wrong in handing over innocent blood!" "So what?" they said, "How does that concern us? That's your problem." And throwing down the silver pieces in the temple....

Rembrandt has compressed this narrative into a single moment, the moment just after Judas has thrown down the blood money, a moment when the priests and elders have just made their curt reply. He has suggested the vast and imposing space of a great religious edifice with massive supporting walls and pillars and a vaulted ceiling, his standard architecture for the interior of the temple of Jesus' day. The same interior, suggested in *Simeon in the Temple* of 1631 (see chap. 7), now in Mauritshuis, recurs in *Christ and the Woman Taken in Adultery* of 1644 (see chap. 7), now in London's National Gallery, and in *The Tribute Money* of about 1631, a work now in Ottawa that the RRP has reassigned, I think correctly, to Rembrandt's "immediate circle."

This solid interior is reinforced by, and reinforces, the thick and solid bodies of the high priests and the elders. Their richly colored and sumptuous clothing is echoed by the hanging of drapery and bronze on the pillar behind the seated "chief priest" nearest to Judas.

Judas Repentant, Returning the Pieces of Silver, 1629, England (private collection)

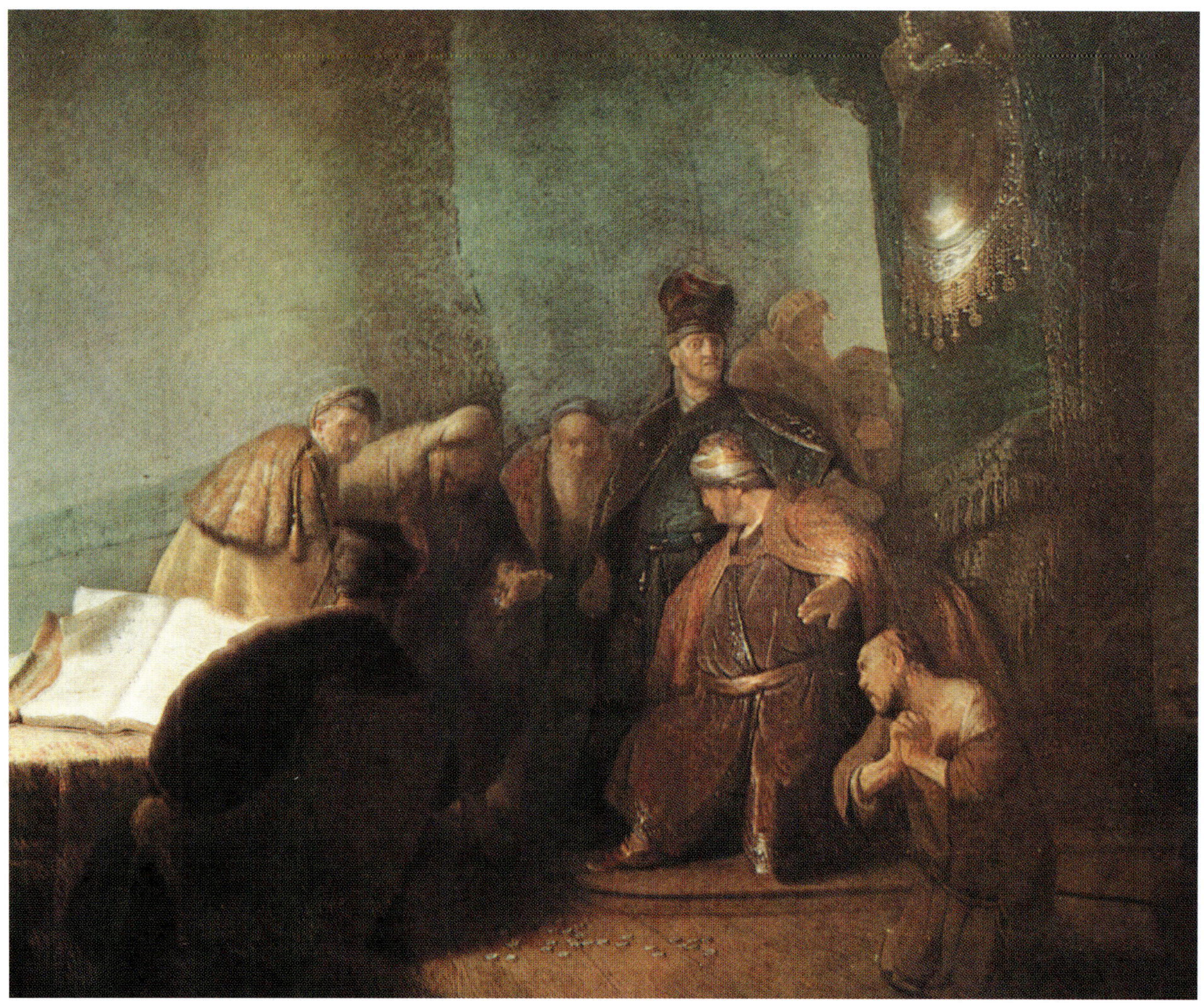

Judas, by contrast, is clad plainly in a brown robe that appears to be slipping from his shoulder, revealing his undergarment. Rembrandt has given us a Judas shut off from human sympathy or help, the Judas who will later hang himself. His visible eye is nearly closed, yet dropping tears; his lips are parted, and the side of his head is bloody from a scalp torn as he has pulled out his hair; his hands are clasped so tightly into one another that they too are bleeding.

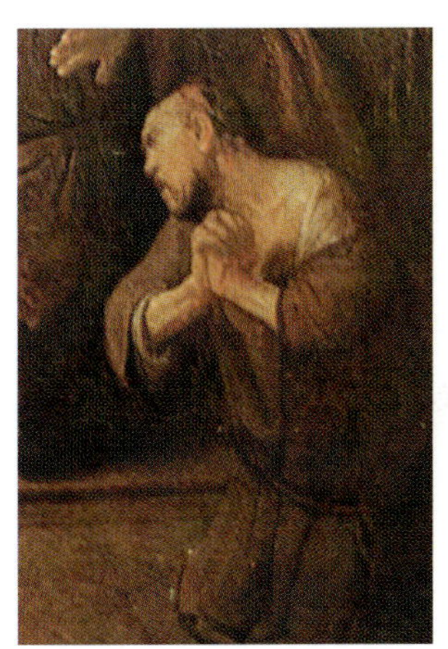

As often in his Leiden years, Rembrandt presents much of the moment in faces. The despairing agony of Judas's face is met by irritation, rejection, indifference, indignation, and in the two faces turned away from him, by greed. Two heads cannot resist turning to see where the coins have landed. These coins, and there are indeed thirty of them, lead the eye from Judas into the gathering of heavy figures of authority to whom he has attempted to return them. And two of these officials, one of whom is looking away from Judas at the coins, have lifted each a hand, palm out, as if to reinforce what they have said and to shove Judas away. Those two hands are like the harsh noise of a door slammed shut.

On the table at the left of the painting a sacred book lies open, its left page pulled up at the top corner as if the reader with his back to us has been interrupted in his reading by the clatter of the silver pieces. Rembrandt has given us some Hebrew letters at the top of this

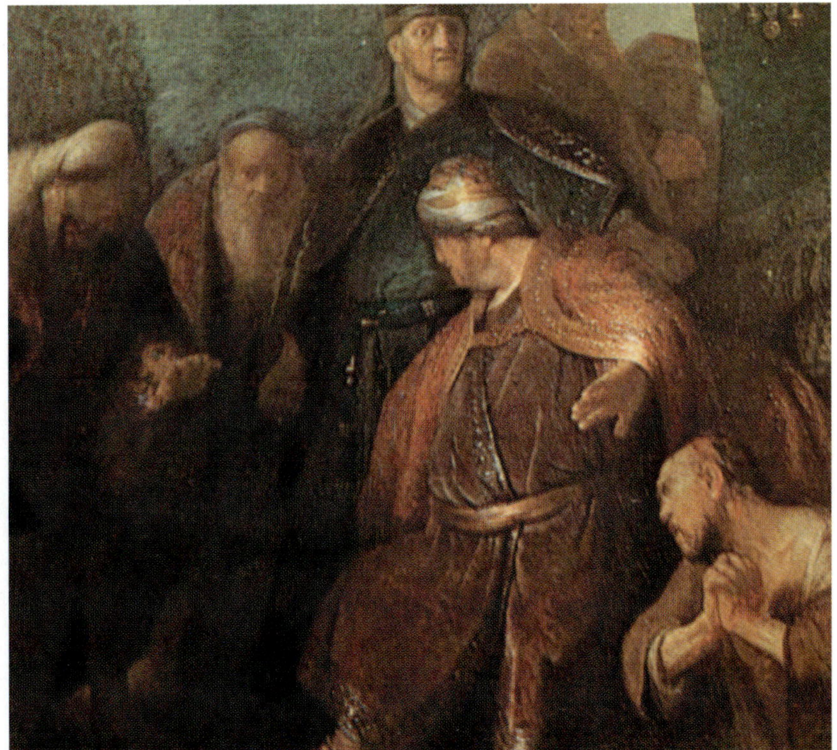

page, as well as at the top of the facing page. These letters can be read only partially, and Rembrandt may have intended only to suggest words.

Two words may be proposed from the letters on the left-hand page; the fourth letter of the first of the words is unclear, as is the third letter of the second of them. I suggest reading these words without adding any letters, giving two possibilities:

לְדֵעָה עוּרֵךְ "to know your blindness"
or
לְדַעַת עֲוֹתֵךְ "to know your mistake (ruin)"

The letters at the top of the right-hand page appear to suggest the special Hebrew name of God, the Tetragrammaton, יְהוָה. If such is the case, Rembrandt was attempting to give the book the most sacred appearance possible.

There are also Hebrew letters embroidered in gold on the left shoulder of the most imposing of the standing figures; they appear, again, to give us two choices:

כֹּהֵן ל "priest for (to)"
or
תּוֹרָה ל "Law (*Torah*) for (to)"

The inclusion of these Hebrew words—along with the thirty coins, the imposing officials, the suggestion of massive architecture, and the dull, patched garment of Judas—was an attempt by Rembrandt to make his moment authentic. I doubt that he studied any Hebrew during his brief time at the University of Leiden, as has been suggested. I think it far more likely that he got his Hebrew from acquaintances in Amsterdam, probably a few letters at a time.

Jeremiah Lamenting the Destruction of Jerusalem, 1630, Rijksmuseum, Amsterdam

All of these features attest Rembrandt's involvement with the tragic moment of Judas' attempt to undo his betrayal of Christ. So also do three drawings that appear to be studies for this painting and the complex evolution of the painting revealed by x-ray photographs.

Yet what is most arresting about this early painting, as Constantin Huygens observed within a year of its creation, is the powerful emotion it projects. Rembrandt has illustrated what *he* would have felt in such a moment, in such a place, in such an awful situation. He

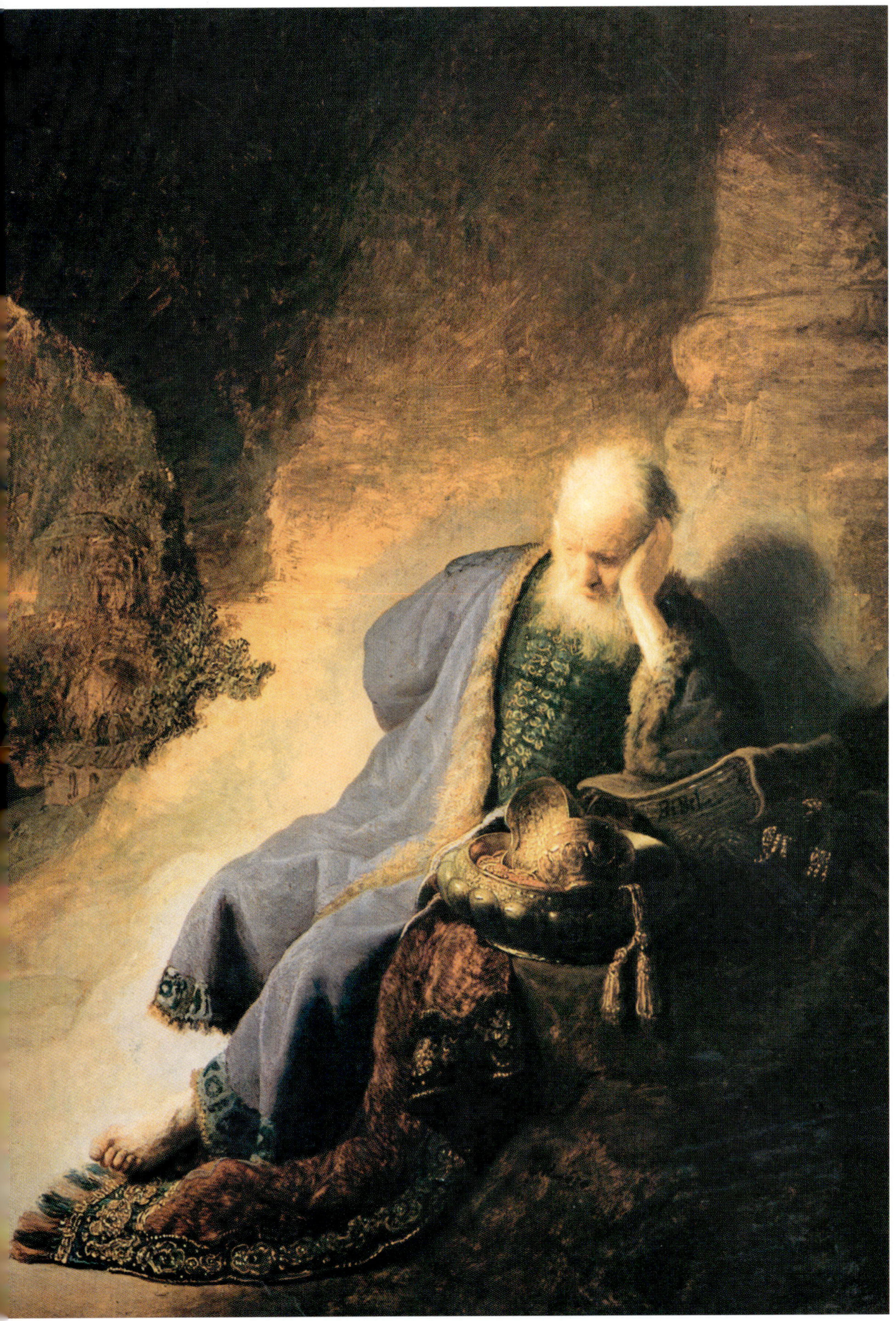

has entered the temple with Judas, and what he has given us is what he *did* feel in that entry.

The very next year Rembrandt painted what may be called his biblical masterpiece from the Leiden years, *Jeremiah Lamenting the Destruction of Jerusalem* (see previous page), now in Amsterdam. It presents a scene both wider and more focused than the *Judas*, yet with an intensity of emotion that is several notches higher because it is presented so much more subtly. Rembrandt had no single text for the moment he re-presents in this work. The painting gives us what may be called a conjecture based upon a synthesis of separate but related texts: 2 Kings 25, 2 Chronicles 36:11–21, Jeremiah 21:1–10, Psalm 74, and Psalm 79, all of which present accounts that describe the history of the Babylonian siege and destruction of Jerusalem in 587–586 B.C.

I consider it unlikely that Rembrandt would have reviewed all of these texts, particularly the texts of the two psalms. He may well have had the passages from 2 Kings and 2 Chronicles in mind, though I think it likely that the immediate catalyst for this painting is 2 Maccabees 2:4–5:

> Included also in this writing was the instruction that the prophet, alerted by God, commanded that the Tabernacle and Ark be sent after him—then he went away onto the mountain that Moses had ascended to see God's Promised Land. When Jeremiah arrived there, he found a hollowed-out place, and he put there the Tabernacle, and the Ark, and the Altar of Incense; then he blocked up the entrance.

If Rembrandt had in mind "Mount Nebo…the top of Pisgah, which is opposite Jericho" (Deut. 34:1) as the location of Jeremiah's lamentation, he would have had to do some squeezing of geography to get the burning Jerusalem, some twenty-six miles away, into the scene to Jeremiah's right. Rembrandt could have had however no more than a vague notion of Middle Eastern geography, just as he could have had no accurate notion of the architecture or the furniture or the dress of biblical times. He considered that which was distant in time and place exotic, and so fascinating, and he simply used his imagination.

Rembrandt has placed Jeremiah on a promontory at a distance from Jerusalem in flames, apparently at the mouth of the sort of cave chamber suggested in 2 Maccabees 2:5, a further hint of which can be seen in the massive pillar behind the prophet's back. To the right of Jeremiah, Jerusalem is burning, and the roaring flames leap up into a sky darkened by thick, roiling smoke.

An array of details suggests the Babylonian siege of the city: at the far left, a soldier climbing a scaling ladder set against a city wall (a detail very difficult to see in a reproduction); a group of soldiers with spears passing under an archway to the right and beneath this figure; a robed person leaving the city by this same approach, headed toward a set of wide steps, hands lifted in despair to cover his or her face.

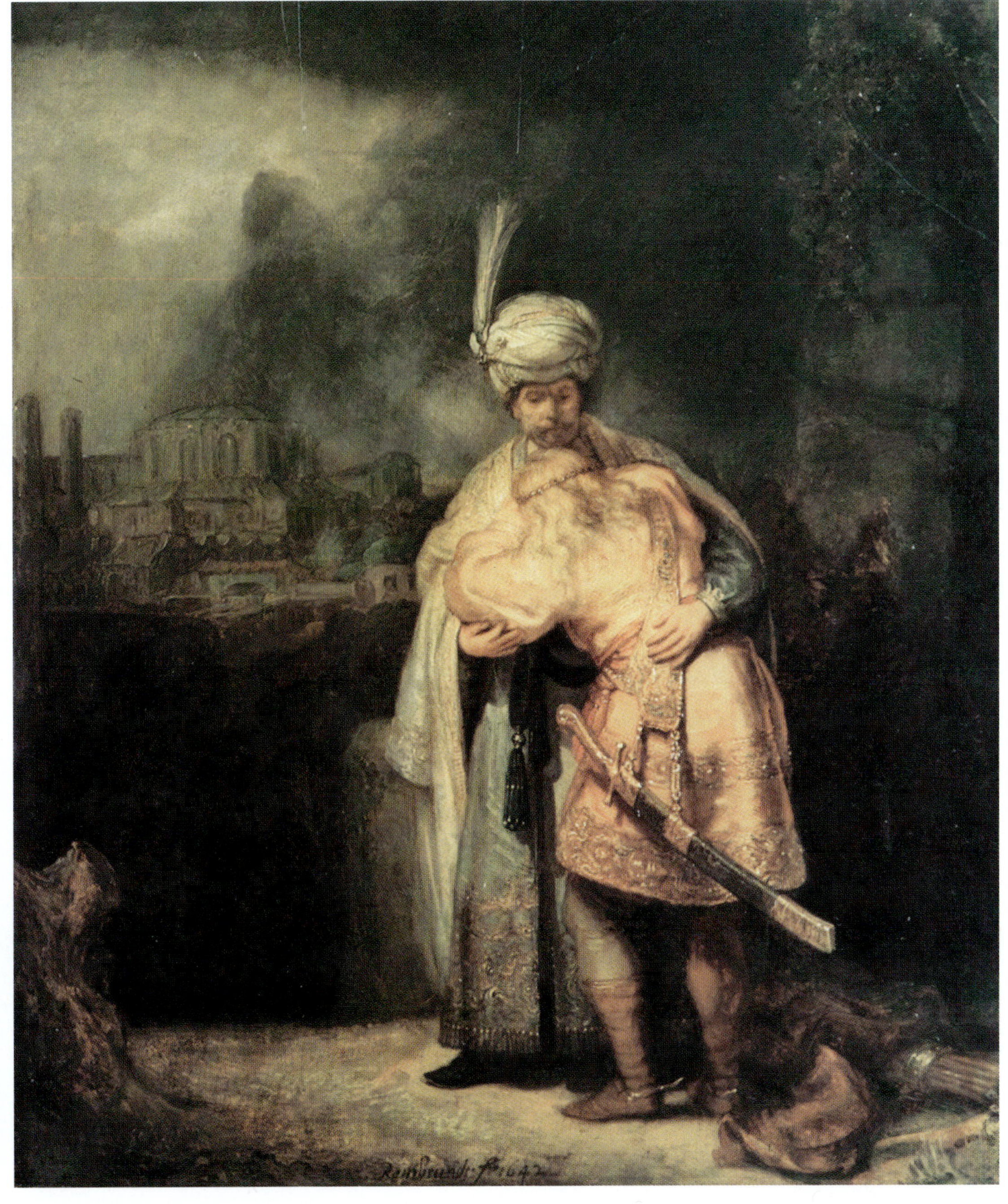

David's Farewell to Jonathan, 1642, State Hermitage, The Winter Palace, St. Petersburg

Peter and John Healing the Cripple at the Gate of the Temple, B 94, 1659, Prentenkabinett, Rijksmuseum, Amsterdam

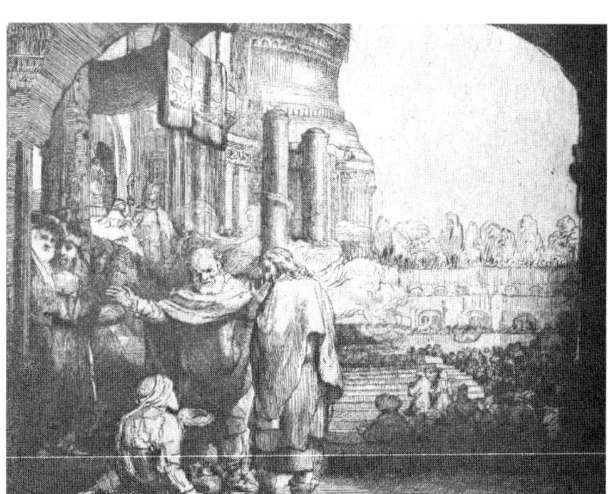

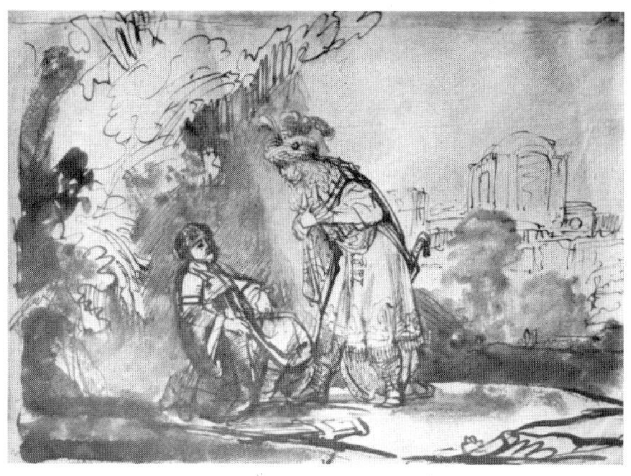

David Takes Leave of Jonathan, Benesch 74a, 1632-1633, The Barber Institute of Fine Arts, University of Birmingham, Birmingham (England)

At the center of the city is a large round-domed building with two tall freestanding columns in front of it, one of them broken. It is Rembrandt's depiction of the temple in Jerusalem, which recurs in a number of his Jerusalem exteriors, most notably a painting of 1642 now in St. Petersburg, probably best titled *David's Farewell to Jonathan* (see previous page). There, too, is the round-domed building, with the two freestanding pillars much more sharply shown.

These pillars are an important clue to the identification of this building as the temple, as they represent the pillars called Jachin and Boaz, the symbols of God's guiding presence in the wilderness, described in detail in 1 Kings 7:15–22. (The RRP, somewhat alone, gives this painting to a pupil of Rembrandt, Ferdinand Bol. This reattribution, which I am inclined to doubt, does not affect my suggestion above, as the domed temple with its free-standing pillars remains a concept original to Rembrandt.) The pillars and the round-domed building are present also in an etching of 1659, *Peter and John Healing the Cripple at the Gate of the Temple.*

This structure appears as well in a number of drawings, as for example in: a David's farewell to Jonathan from 1632–1633 (This drawing is considered by Sumowski the work of Ferdinand Bol, on "stylistic" grounds; I favor the Benesch opinion), a coronation of Solomon from 1637, a triumphant procession of Mordecai from 1640–1641, a Pilate washing his hands from 1653–1654, and a Jesus finding the sleeping apostles in the garden of Gethsemane from 1654.

Of course the anachronism involved in putting the temple built by Solomon into a scene with David presented no problem to Rembrandt, any more than did his use of a single form for the different temple of the time of Jesus and the apostles. He had no way of knowing what either temple looked like nor that the two temple

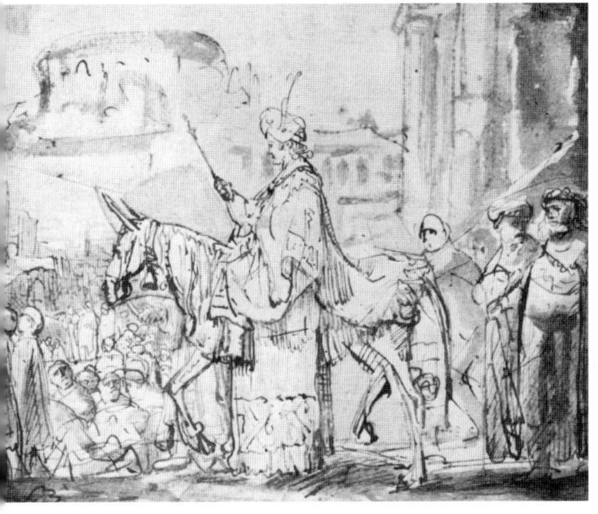

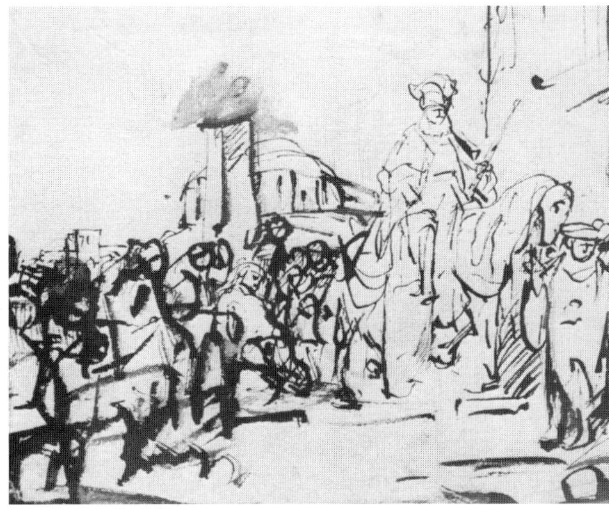

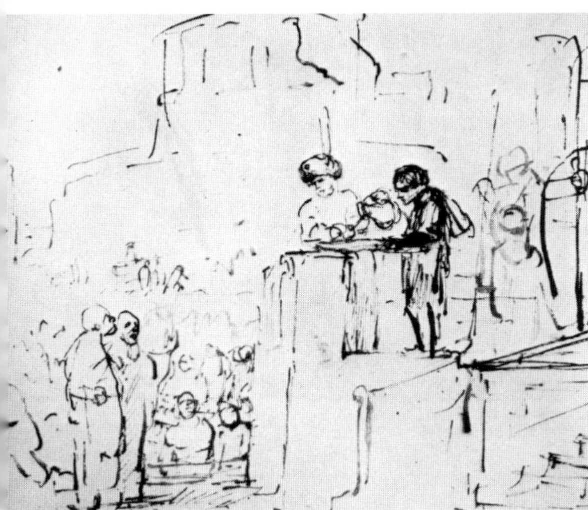

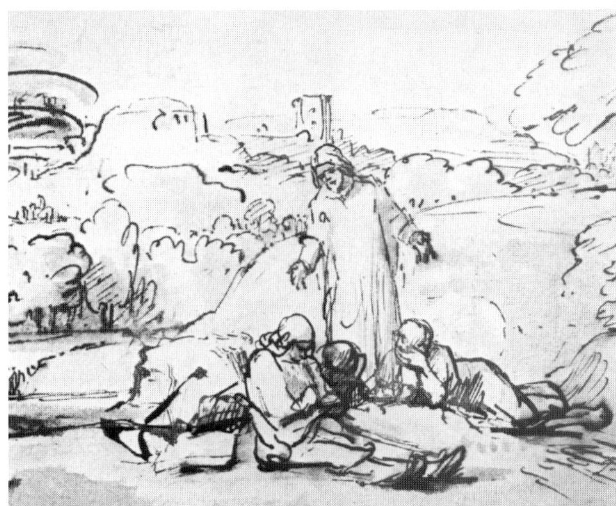

structures were so completely different. He attempted simply to make his temples fit the biblical text.

These various details, of course, were merely Rembrandt's setting for his lamenting Jeremiah, just as are the items Jeremiah has snatched up in rescue from the wanton destruction of the Babylonian soldiers: a gorgeous priestly robe, several vessels of gold, a *Torah* covering, and a great volume of the *Torah* itself, on which Jeremiah, significantly, is leaning, and on which someone afraid we might miss the point has written *BiBeL*, probably after Rembrandt's time. Behind this volume, a jug stands.

At the center of all this, Rembrandt has set the old prophet himself and has given him a posture and a face that show how fully he felt Jeremiah's grief. This prophet had often predicted the destruction of Jerusalem, so often, indeed, that the conquering Babylonians are

Young Solomon Proclaimed King, Riding on the Mule, Benesch 146, 1637, Musée du Louvre, Paris, detail (above left)

The Triumph of Mordecai, Benesch 487, 1640-1641, Ossolineum, Wroclaw (formerly Breslau), Poland, detail (above right)

Pilate Washing His Hands, Benesch 937, 1653-1654, Fogg Museum of Art, Cambridge, detail (below left)

Christ Finding the Apostles Asleep, Benesch 941, 1654, Sterling and Francine Clark Art Institute, Williamstown, Massachusetts, detail (below right)

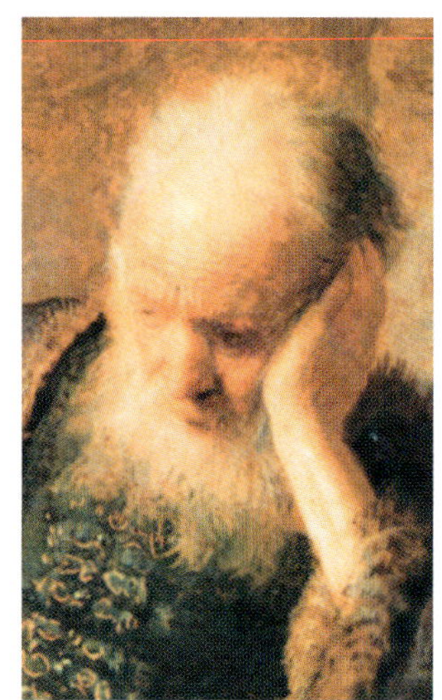

reported to have treated him with special kindness (Jer. 39 and 40, though the text as we have it is somewhat confused). Over and over he had upbraided the people of Jerusalem, high and low, and pled with them to repent. They rejected his words and his person. The king outlawed him, burned his writings, locked him up, and would have welcomed his death with joy. No one believed him, not even anyone in his own family. Yet now, at long last, Jeremiah has been proven right, vindicated, affirmed by event.

Rembrandt's Jeremiah, however, is not celebrating, just as the biblical Jeremiah did not. Rembrandt gives us a Jeremiah whose body is stooped, as under a load too heavy to be borne. His head, bent down, is tilted against a supporting left palm. His mouth is open in the speechless horror of deep grief. He can bear no longer to look upon the death of the city he has so loved and tried for so long to save, so his eyes are turned toward the ground. Even so, they do not see anything, for they are the staring dry eyes that are beyond tears, the eyes of a man whose grief is beyond relief.

This Jeremiah has no satisfaction in the fulfillment of the prophetic word delivered through him. His heart is broken. And Rembrandt's point is unmistakable: here in vivid image is the loneliness of the prophetic word, the difficulty of the prophet's call, and at once the source and strength of the prophet when everything else is gone. For Rembrandt's Jeremiah, nearly struck down by the fulfillment of the word he has proclaimed, leans for support on what finally can be trusted to be true, the word of God. It does not matter that Jeremiah had no *Bibel* such as Rembrandt must have had in mind with his great heavy book. The prophet *did have* the word of God, and this painting suggests that Rembrandt knew he did, by instinct as by his own experience.

Abraham's Sacrifice, 1635, State Hermitage, The Winter Palace, St. Petersburg

About four years after his move to Amsterdam Rembrandt gave us, in 1635, yet another biblical moment in an old man's emotion-filled face, in a painting based on Genesis 22:10–12, *Abraham's Sacrifice*, now in St. Petersburg. The narrative from which these verses are taken is one of the more powerful stories in the first book of the Bible, which is filled with powerful stories. The story is known as the *Akedah*, the "binding of Isaac," or as the "Testing of Abraham," and it has fired the imagination of secular writers as well as biblical commentators across many centuries.

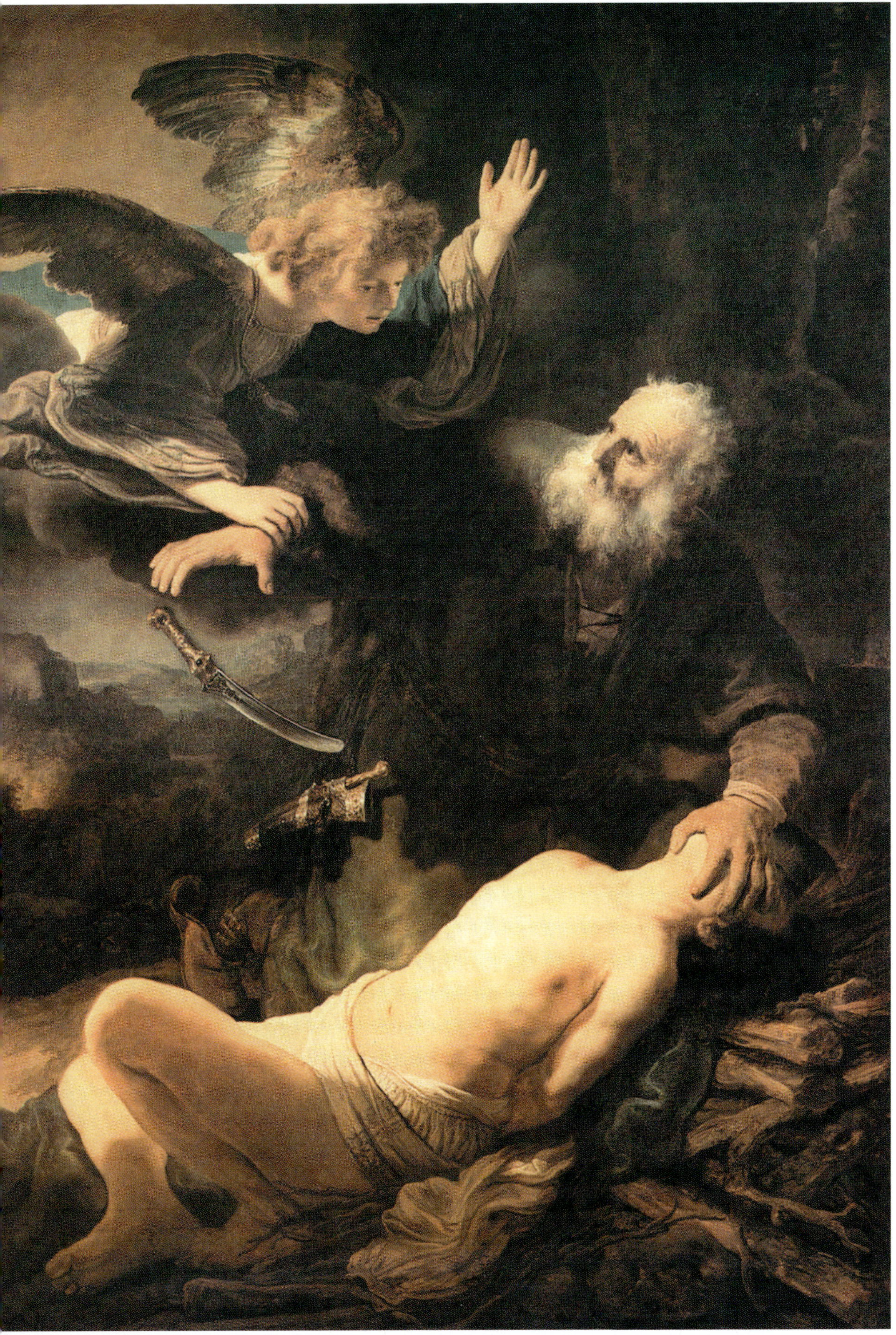

The moment Rembrandt has depicted is the culmination of the story of Abraham's willingness to obey God's command, whatever the cost. It is a story that may be said to begin in Genesis 12, where Abraham is commanded to take leave of his family, his home, his inheritance, and his past. After many adventures and testings, Abraham comes at last to his ultimate test, in the command of God that even begins with the same words as does the command in Genesis 12:1. In that earlier command, God ordered Abraham to cut himself off from his past; in this command, where Isaac is to die by his father's own hand, the old man is to cut himself off from his future as well.

After a heart-stopping narrative of command and travel and poignant conversation and heavy silence between the old father and his adored son, the awful preparations are made, and when barely a heartbeat remains before the knife is to cut short the life of the boy, the divine reprieve comes:

> Then Abraham put out his hand and took up the knife to end the life of his son. But a messenger from Yahweh called out to him from the heavens, saying, "Abraham! Abraham!" And he answered, "Here I am!" So the messenger said, "Don't put out your hand against the lad, and don't do anything at all to him, for now I know for a fact that you have reverence for God: you have not refused me your son, your one and only son." Genesis 22:10-12

That Rembrandt has felt the awful anxiety of this moment is made clear by Abraham's wrinkled face, tears streaming down his cheeks. Rembrandt's involvement in this tense biblical moment is made even plainer by touches that elaborate the stark simplicity of the biblical text: Abraham's left hand covering his son's face as he pushes back the head to cut Isaac's throat; the anxious angel (the traditional translation of מַלְאָךְ "sent one, messenger") not only speaking, but seizing Abraham's right wrist to stop the fatal sweep of the knife in case the old man is slow to hear or to respond; and the knife itself, in mid-air, released in the fright of this startling grip.

The details of the text are also all here. The scene takes place on a mountain; the wood of verses 3 and 7 and 9 is here, carefully placed under the prone body of Isaac. The fire of verse 7 glows in a pot to the right of Abraham's left elbow. The boy's hands appear to be tied behind his back, the "binding" of verse 9.

The impact of the painting comes from Rembrandt's own response to such a terrible/joyous moment. We feel Abraham's agony, his resolve to obey, and his disbelieving relief because Rembrandt has felt them. The powerful Genesis text has touched his humanity. He has put himself on Mount Moriah. And anyone really seeing this painting in the Hermitage has been right there with him.

Another version of this painting, now in Munich, has frequently been assigned to Rembrandt. In composition it is very similar, apart from a relocation of the heavenly messenger, though there are some differences of detail: the ram caught by its horns in a thicket of verse 13 is present, but the fire pot of verse 6 is missing. There is an unusual (and wholly uncharacteristic) inscription on the painting that reads "Rembrandt. Altered. And over painted." The work is perhaps best regarded as a copy of Rembrandt's painting with changes done by one of his pupils.

Also in 1635, Rembrandt turned to Daniel 5:5–6 to paint *Belshazzar's Feast*, now in London's National Gallery, a picture of the moment in the banquet at which the Babylonian king and his guests, drinking wine from the gold and silver vessels taken from the temple in Jerusalem, see the terrible handwriting on the wall:

> At that very moment, the fingers of a person appeared, writing, opposite the lamp stand, on the plaster surface of the wall of the royal palace! And the king saw the back of the hand doing the writing!
>
> At that instant, the king's face changed, and his thoughts turned to terror, his legs began to give way under him, and his knees knocked one against the other.

Rembrandt has re-presented this biblical moment with an array of human touches. The king's nearby companions react with understandable fright: the woman at the right is spilling the wine from a golden temple vessel onto her left sleeve as she lurches back from the writing hand; the woman to the king's right, her mouth open, her eyes bulging as she stares at the hand, has clasped her own hands as if to pray; the old man to her right also looks, dumbfounded; the woman

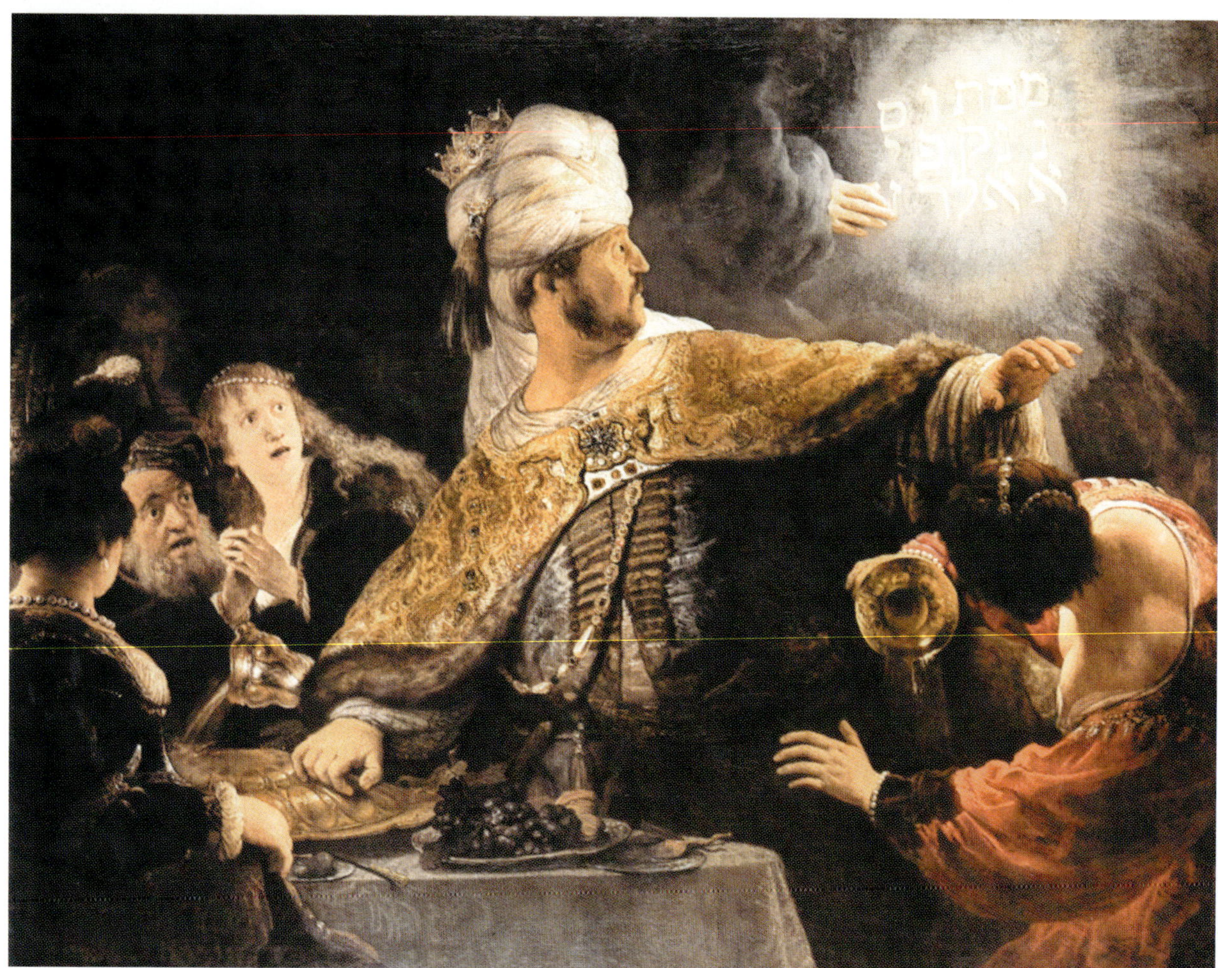

Belshazzar's Feast, 1635, The National Gallery, London

just across from the king has been distracted by the golden wine goblet the king has just knocked over, and turning to see that, she misses the spectacle of the writing.

Belshazzar himself has risen from the table in alarm but leans away from the writing hand and is already attempting to steady himself with his right arm and grabbing fingers. His left arm and hand are rising as if in self-protection, as he turns his head to see the dreadful sight on the palace wall.

The luxurious excess of the clothing of the king and his four near companions (Dan. 5:1 puts the guest list of the men alone at a thousand) is Rembrandt's idea of the exotic Babylonian court. The most striking of Rembrandt's touches in this painting is the hand and its writing on the wall. Rembrandt has given us a very human-looking hand, yet one reaching from what has the appearance of a sleeve of gray cloud. The first and second fingers of the hand are just completing the writing of the last of the letters on the wall.

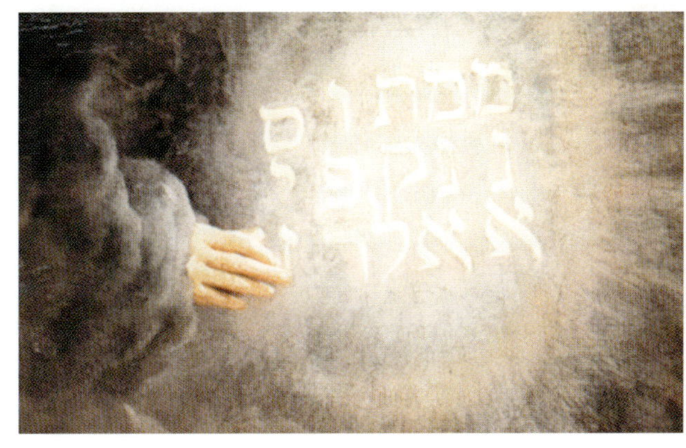

Rembrandt has arranged the letters of the message vertically so that they read as no Aramaic sentence would, from top to bottom, though with the words in their proper sequence, from right to left. The opinion generally held about this writing is that the letters were arranged vertically to render them more mysterious—they make no sense read in the normal order from right to left. Rembrandt may have learned this arrangement from Rabbi Manasseh ben Israel, probably a friend, whose portrait he etched in 1636, and who is known to have published the letters thus in a book in 1639.

What is most interesting about the writing, however, and endearingly human, is the formation of the final letter, the one the hand is inscribing. That letter should be the letter (נ) in its final, elongated form, ן. Rembrandt has the hand forming the letter (ז). That he knew better is clear from the correct form of the top of the letter נ in its two occurrences in the first two words of the writing, yet Rembrandt has this hand (the "back of the hand" of God!—v. 24) writing the wrong letter, certainly in error. The mistake is one of the most common slips of nearly every beginning Hebrew student, for whom the top of the printed letters נ and ז at first, and with limited experience, look alike.

Rembrandt was involved in his picture of Belshazzar's fright. He was struck by the drama of the text, and he was stretching his illustrative skills as well as his technique in painting at this early date—in 1635, he was but 29. That he made a mistake with a language he did not know is not off-putting. If anything, his slip makes him somehow more accessible to us, pulling us further into his experience of the Bible.

Many more such examples of what I have called Rembrandt's pictures, his illustrations, or better, his re-presentations of the biblical moments that drew him into the Bible might easily be listed. A great many years of studying such examples has been a discipline for my eyes, and a delight as well. I have found myself, with Rembrandt's help, seeing more of texts that I had thought I knew well.

As Rembrandt matured, however, in skill as in perception, he moved beyond these pictures into which his imagination and hissense

sense of what is true took him. The more he saw, the more he felt, and that seeing and feeling brought him knowing. This knowing came to sustain him in difficult times, and it gave him a sense of truth that threw him increasingly out of step with many of his contemporaries. Whether he regretted this, we have no way of knowing. What is certain, as his pictures show, is that Rembrandt came to know himself to be a *human* artist.

Yet what truth shone from that humanity onto the humanity of the Bible, opening the Bible's pages with a candor that cuts through centuries of "acceptable" and "spiritual" biblical art and giving real people a sense of biblical reality. The Bible became so real to Rembrandt that he found himself knowing that he might have lived its drama, might have been one of its people. And that knowing, joined to his humanity, reached out toward and into meaning, a meaning that drew Rembrandt beyond his pictures toward the representation of meaning that makes his best work so irresistible to us, and so indispensable as well.

SOME SOURCES AND SUGGESTIONS

A brief summary of the history of the Dutch versions of the Bible (by S. van der Woude) may be found in *The Cambridge History of the Bible*, Volume III (1963), pp. 122-125. Simon Schama has a characteristically entertaining and informative discussion of the view of "Scripture" in the Dutch culture of Rembrandt's day in *The Embarrassment of Riches* (pp. 93-125).

Franz Landsberger (in *Rembrandt, the Jews and the Bible)* suggests that Rembrandt "began" his study of the Hebrew language during his period of matriculation at the University of Leiden – I think this unlikely, not least because Rembrandt spent so short a time in University study (if indeed he spent *any* time there). Landsberger's discussion of the Jewish community in Amsterdam and Rembrandt's involvement with that community is nonetheless helpful: see especially "Rembrandt and the Jews Come to Amsterdam" and his various references to Rembrandt's "meticulous care" with Hebrew words in his paintings.

Julius Held discusses Rembrandt's fascination with the Book of Tobit in an essay from 1964, conveniently reprinted in his *Rembrandt Studies* (revised and expanded, 1991), pp. 118-143. Simon Schama even discusses the Book of Tobit as "Rembrandt's favorite, or at least most compulsively revisited book" (*Rembrandt's Eyes*, p. 238).

On Caravaggio's Biblical paintings, two recent books are particularly interesting: Helen Langdon's *Caravaggio: a Life* (1998; see especially "Conversion and Martyrdom: the Jubilee of 1600" and "The Shock of Humility: the Imitation of Christ") and Catherine Pugilisi's *Caravaggio* (1998; see especially "Most Famous Painter").

Pieter Lastman's influence on Rembrandt's *Balaam and the Ass* and *David with the Head of Goliath before Saul* is helpfully described by Christian Tümpel in *Pieter Lastman: the Man who Taught Rembrandt* under the headings "Rembrandt's study of Lastman in the early Leiden Works" and "Rarely depicted themes". Also well worth a look is the catalog to a exhibition in 2000-2001 of the Isabella Stewart Gardner Museum, *Rembrandt Creates Rembrandt: Art and Ambition in Leiden, 1629-1630.*

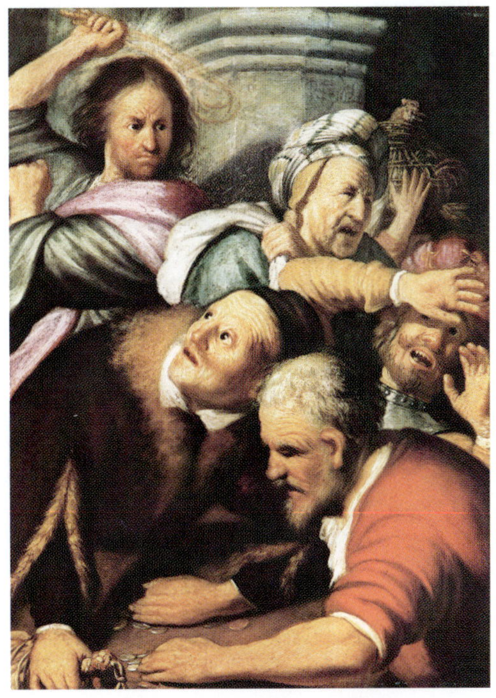

Christ Driving the Moneychangers from the Temple, 1626, Pushkin Fine Art Museum, Moscow

In 1626, almost ten years before he did the etching of *Christ Driving the Moneychangers from the Temple,* Rembrandt painted what can be termed "a close-up" of the same moment, a work now in the Pushkin Museum in Moscow. The coins, the money-changers, the rooster in the basket lifted high and a flailing, angry Christ are presented in a work more crammed than anything Rembrandt ever created.

The discussion of *Judas, Repentant, Returning the Pieces of Silver* in *Corpus*, Volume 1 (A 15), includes two excellent photographs of the Hebrew Rembrandt inscribed, on the pages of the open book on the table and on the left shoulder of one of the standing figures. Also included is a detailed treatment of the x-ray studies of this painting, and reproductions of the three drawings of Rembrandt that are relevant. See also the catalogue to the 1988-1989 exhibition at London's National Gallery, "Art in the Making: Rembrandt," pp. 36-41, for these drawings and an x-ray "mosaic."

An enlarged black and white photograph of the left side of *Jeremiah Lamenting the Destruction of Jerusalem* in *Corpus*, Volume 1 (A 28), shows the soldier climbing the scaling ladder, the group of soldiers with spears and other details of Rembrandt's representation of the Babylonian siege of Jerusalem more clearly than the usual color reproductions. This photograph also reveals more clearly the large round-domed building that I believe to be Rembrandt's representation of the Temple of Solomon.

As regards this building, which turns up repeatedly in Rembrandt's representations of the city of Jerusalem, I wonder whether it might also be a clue to the identification of another painting, tentatively removed from the Rembrandt canon by RRP to the sound of furious debate, the work now in the Frick Collection called *The Polish Rider.* Without meaning to put the cat in with the pigeons, I yet believe it well worth considering whether the building behind and above the man on horseback is yet another depiction of Rembrandt's Temple of Solomon: the round dome is there, and even the freestanding pillars, Jachin and Boaz. If this suggestion is correct, the man on horseback might well be Saul's son Jonathan (the anachronism was no bother to Rembrandt, as I have noted already), on his way out to the secret rendezvous with David – the pre-arranged signal that the coast was clear was to be three arrows shot

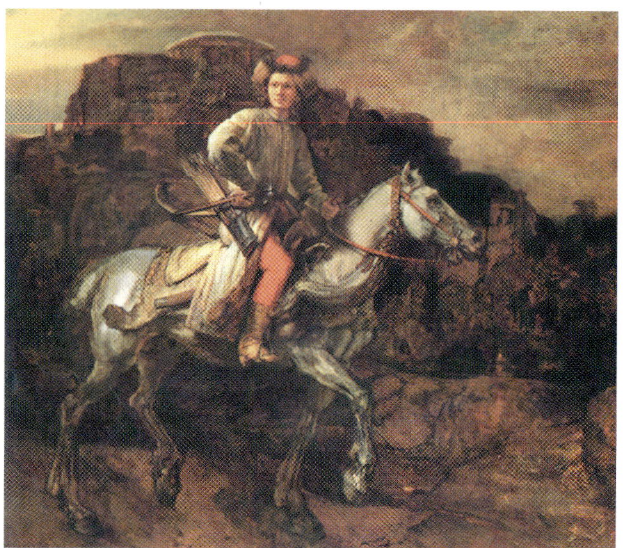

The Polish Rider, 1655, The Frick Collection, New York

as though at a target (1 Samuel 20). See the "Jonathan" in *David with the Head of Goliath*, chapter 3, p. 62. The "Polish" costume of the horseman with the bow and the quiver would be, on such an interpretation, just another example of Rembrandt's love of the exotic.

Extensive discussions of the controversy this work has provoked are aptly summarized by Julius Held in an essay first published in 1944, "The 'Polish' Rider" (in *Rembrandt Studies*, pp. 59-98), and more recently by Anthony Bailey in *Responses to Rembrandt* (1994), the subtitle of which is "Who Painted *The Polish Rider*? A Controversy Considered".

The Munich version of *Abraham's Sacrifice* has the ram caught by its horns, Genesis 22:13, but is without the pot of fire.

Following years of debate about the attribution of this work, and its assignment to several of Rembrandt's pupils, with various touches by the master himself, this version is now generally held to be the work of a member of Rembrandt's circle, with no convincing designation of just who painted what. It amounts to a copy with revisions.

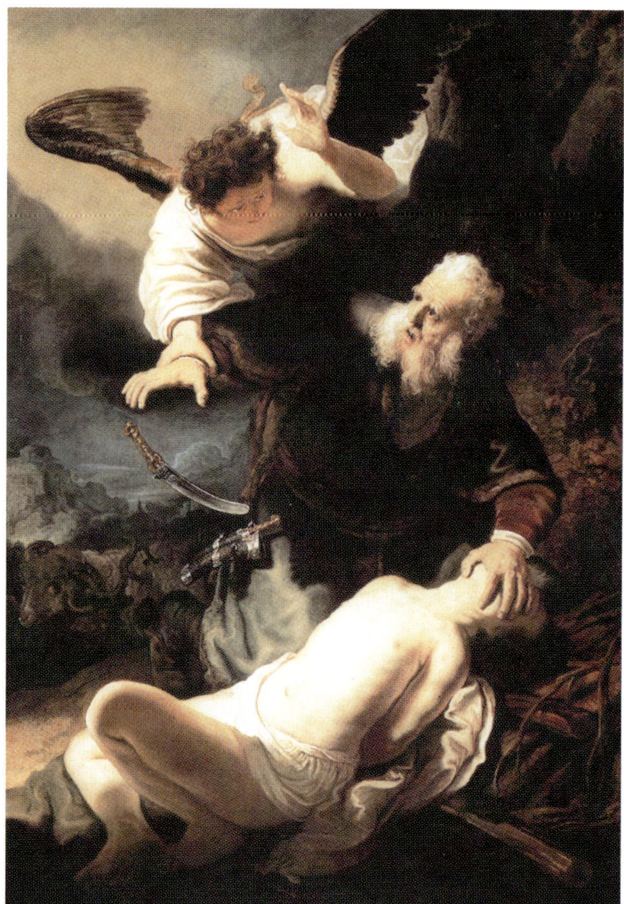

Copy of Abraham's Sacrifice (Rembrandt's circle, 1636), Alte Pinakothek, Munich

Rabbi Samuel Manasseh ben Israel was a neighbor of Rembrandt, who in the mid-1650s asked Rembrandt to prepare four illustrations for his book on "the Glorious Stone," a sort of Messianic speculation drawn from the dream of King Nebuchadnezzar described in Daniel 2:31-45. Rembrandt appears to have had a tough time with the etchings, working and reworking parts of them, and in the end, they were apparently replaced after only a few printings by the work of a Jewish artist, Salom Italia (RD, 325). The Rabbi's book (*De termino vitae*) presenting the arrangement of the handwriting on the wall employed by Rembrandt in *Belshazzar's Feast* was published in Amsterdam in 1639; he set the letters apart from one another by a series of lines—and his final ן is quite correctly drawn. One wonders whether Rembrandt discussed with Manasseh ben Israel the problem of painting the divine message to Belshazzar in 1635, and whether the Rabbi some four years later used the arrangement he had suggested to Rembrandt in his work on the Messianic hope.

5

REMBRANDT'S MEANING

Rembrandt's earliest known works are depictions of biblical events. His first five paintings, in the chronological listing of the RRP, present scenes from Acts 7:58 (*The Stoning of St. Stephen,* 1625), Numbers 22:22–33 (*Balaam and the Ass,* 1626), Tobit 2:11–14 (*Tobit and Anna,* 1626), Matthew 21:12–13/Mark 11:15–17/Luke 19:45–46 (*Christ Driving the Moneychangers from the Temple,* 1626), and Acts 8:38 (*The Baptism of the Eunuch,* 1626), in that order. His earliest etchings include *The Rest on the Flight into Egypt* (Matt. 2:14), and *The Circumcision* (Luke 2:21–38), both from 1626, and among the early drawings there is a Mordecai's triumph (Esther 6:11), based on a 1617 painting of Pieter Lastman, a raising of the cross (Mark 15:24/Luke 23:33/John 19:18), a repentant Judas (Matt. 27:3–5a), and an Emmaus supper (Luke 24:30–31), each an apparent study for a painting.

This list can easily be expanded, but need not be to assert that Rembrandt was interested in presenting scenes and events from the Bible. This interest did not wane at any point in his career, and the unfinished painting on his easel at his death was a biblical work, *Simeon with the Christ Child in the Temple* (Luke 2:25–35), now in Stockholm (see chap. 7).

At the start of his career, as I suggested in the previous chapter, Rembrandt appears to have been attempting to picture the biblical moments that interested him, in part because he was attracted to the stories themselves for a combination of reasons. My question is, what was he attempting to present? Starting out, surely he was attempting an illustration of a moment in a given narrative that caught his interest—a picture, as I put it earlier. Yet even a picture, a re-presentation, involves interpretation.

A narrative on a printed page inevitably presents to a reader's mind a scene, a picture of a description. This is so whatever the skill with which the narrative is set down and however detailed or incomplete that narrative may be. The scene the narrative stimulates, further, is an amalgam, a combination of the narrator's effort and the reader's imagination. As the narrator has experienced and then written his own account of the event or place he recalls, so also the reader of the narrative imagines that event or place in his own way, drawing on his own experience. When the reader then re-presents the narrative, the result is a fourth version of the reality that began the process. The event experienced is reported, the report is read (or heard), and the report is then interpreted and re-presented.

If the narrative being handled is a biblical narrative, an additional level is added to this amalgam, an aura of tradition, an undercurrent of belief. This level is present both in the creation of the narrative and also in its transmission and translation, and then in any interpretation of the narrative, in whatever medium.

Whether the narrative is detailed or not, these levels of interpretation are still present. Even the most expansive narrative requires the reader's imagination, and the narrative that omits much detail, as is often and deliberately the case with biblical narrative, requires even more of the reader's involvement in a re-creation of the original scene.

Authenticity, the accurate representation of historically correct detail, adds yet another dimension to any narrative, but authenticity in his history painting was of little interest to Rembrandt. In part, of course, he had no access to the necessary information. And as his biblical oeuvre shows, he had a much larger objective in mind.

While his earliest works may be called illustrations, and are often derivative illustrations based on works he had seen, Rembrandt soon began to move beyond pictorial re-presentation by including also what at the least may be called some notion of meaning. While any picture is necessarily an interpretation, what I am suggesting is that early on Rembrandt began sometimes to move beyond illustration in his pictures, especially in his most deeply felt pictures, to what I am calling his meaning, the step beyond re-presentation to understanding, an understanding derived more from his own experience than from the narrative with which he began.

Many of Rembrandt's drawings, for example, are like snapshots of scenes and persons and moments he had experienced or imagined (or suggested to his students). They form a kind of shorthand notation, a memory file for future use. They are often primarily pictorial, but even in these notes to himself, Rembrandt sometimes moved beyond illustration to interpretation, the suggestion of meaning. One of the several drawings he made of the miracle of the raising of the daughter of Jairus, for example, presents an interesting counterpoint between human grief at loss and the joy of divine restoration that goes well beyond the biblical narrative in any of its three Gospel versions. According to Mark 5:40, Jesus entered the room where the girl was, accompanied by her parents and his "followers." Luke 8:51 names these "followers" as Peter, John, and James. Matthew 9:25 implies that only Jesus entered the room where Jairus's daughter lay. Mark 5:42 and Luke 8:42 refer to this daughter as a child of twelve; Matthew 9:24–25 speaks only of a "girl" (κοράσιον).

Rembrandt, however, has given us an adult woman, not a child, in a drawing from 1632 or 1633, as also in one additional drawing from the same period, one from 1656, and one from early in the final decade of his life. He has also included a varied number of figures from drawing to drawing: six apart from Jairus's daughter in the work following, four (plus one at the door) in the other drawing from 1632–1633, and seven in each of the two additional drawings. Given his usual strict attention to the biblical text, this is unusual, despite the relative freedom with which he made his drawings, which were largely for his own and his pupils' use only.

My suggestion is that the version of the miracle of Jesus' raising Jairus's daughter here is an example of Rembrandt's meaning, as distinct from his illustration. Jesus is drawn approaching the prone form of the woman who gives every appearance of death: hands open, head to one side, mouth gaping, eyes closed. He has paused to comfort the weeping mother, who wipes tears from her face. Another woman, intended perhaps as a sister, grieves at the foot of the bed. Behind Jesus, a man with hands clasped and head bowed appears resigned to the inevitability of death. Is he a brother or one of Jesus' "followers" wondering if they have not arrived too late to be of help? Another man bends over the head of the dead woman in a moving gesture of the finality of the loss death is. Otto Benesch suggested that this is a physician, who "bends over the head of the dead girl to catch a last flicker of life." As no physician is mentioned anywhere in the three New Testament accounts of this event, however, I think this an unlikely proposal. Rembrandt more probably has given us in this figure the grieving Jairus, who had come to fetch Jesus in the first place. One additional person appears behind the grieving mother, a young man with a cowlick. He looks on with open-mouthed wonder.

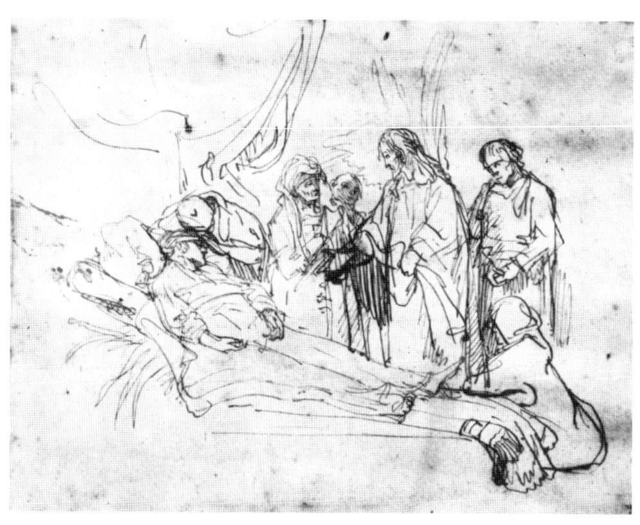

The Raising of the Daughter of Jairus, Benesch 61, 1632 or 1633, Berlin (private collection)

Rembrandt has begun with the narrative of the Gospels, then gone well beyond it to present what I am calling his meaning. He gives us in the figure of Jairus's daughter stark death; in the figure of the father, the desolation of loss; in the figure of the mother, the flowing tears of grief; in the figure of the boy, awe in the nearness of death; in the figure of the man behind Jesus, resignation to the reality of death; and in the figure of the woman kneeling at the foot of the bed, the disorientation death brings.

And then there is the figure of Jesus, drawn taller than anyone else in the scene, radiant with confidence and comfort (and the hint not of a halo but of a brightness around the head and the shoulders—Rembrandt's recurring version of the feeling presented by Bach's warmth of strings around the voice of Jesus in the *St. Matthew Passion*). Jesus reaches with his right hand to touch the crying mother, looking toward her and perhaps speaking to her, even as with his left hand he grasps his robe to keep it from impeding his movement toward the lifeless body he is about to bring to life again. In this figure of Christ, Rembrandt presents the cancellation of the range of grief spread everywhere else in the drawing.

His meaning is unmistakable, and it is precisely true to the point of the story the Gospels present. This story is not about death and defeat; we are given instead a moment of life and victory. That Rembrandt felt this deeply is clear from the lengths to which he went to make the counterpoint unavoidable.

When Rembrandt turned mind, eye, and hand to the same biblical moment more than once, and over a period of time, as he did to story of Jairus's daughter, he was often doing work preliminary to a painting or even an etching. As no such more finished work on this narrative is extant, we are left to assume that this was a project he never got around to, one of many from which he was deflected, both by biblical moments even more meaningful to him and by the pressures of life.

A more extended example of what I am calling Rembrandt's meaning, indeed what might almost be called an obsessive example, may be seen in his career-long preoccupation with the Passion of Christ. And no moment in that final week in the narrative of the Gospels appears to have moved him more than the crucifixion itself. Of the events mentioned in the four Gospels, from the betrayal of Judas to the entombment, there are some 89 drawings, 34 states of 12 etchings, and 9 paintings. Of this total of 132 different re-presentations of 109 scenes, no less than 21 (30 if each separate etching state is counted) deal with the crucifixion itself. And these works range in time from 1631, when Rembrandt was 25, to around 1658, when he was 52.

Near the beginning of this ongoing sequence of works on the crucifixion are two works in the series of Passion paintings done for Prince Frederick Hendrick of the House of Orange soon after Rembrandt's move to Amsterdam: *The Raising of the Cross* and *The*

Descent from the Cross from 1633, both now in Munich's Alte Pinakotek. (Rembrandt's work on the entire series is fascinatingly documented in his correspondence with Constantin Huygens, the prince's secretary.)

Each of these two paintings is an example of what I have called "Rembrandt's pictures," but with an important feature that makes them examples also of what I am here calling "Rembrandt's meaning"—in each, as I have noted (chap. 3), there is an unmistakable self-portrait.

In *The Raising of the Cross*, Rembrandt presents himself in a rich blue-green beret and tunic, both arms around the upright of the cross, both hands grasping the rough wood, and leaning with the strain of helping three other men, one pulling and guiding, two pushing, to heave the cross into the hole dug for it. The shovel with which this digging has been done stands stuck into the soil in the right foreground (and reappears, notably, in Picasso's *Crucifixion* of February 1930). Rembrandt's brow is wrinkled, his lips pursed, and his eyes still have a distant look of concern, despite some loss of detail owing to what the *Corpus* calls "poor preservation." The expression has an appearance of regret and discomfort. He is looking beyond the bleeding feet of Christ just below his chin, looking beyond the scene and the moment of which he has made himself a part (see the detail from this painting, chap. 3).

Every kind of suggestion can of course be made about Rembrandt's self-portraits, as Rembrandt himself left us no key to their interpretation. The suggestions range from theological imposition to downright eisegesis, and from a notion of self-advertisement to a sort of psychological self-examination, all the way to the theory that Rembrandt simply needed a *tronie*, a head to fill the blank space in a painting. The possibilities were informatively (and beautifully) reviewed in a 1999 exhibition of London's National Gallery and the Mauritshuis Museum called "Rembrandt by Himself."

My own view is that Rembrandt always intended something with his obvious self-portraits, as opposed to his more incidental and partial self-portraits. And what he intended with this likeness of himself in *The Raising of the Cross* is what moves this painting from the illustration of a biblical moment to a statement about the meaning of that biblical moment. I think Rembrandt is making a

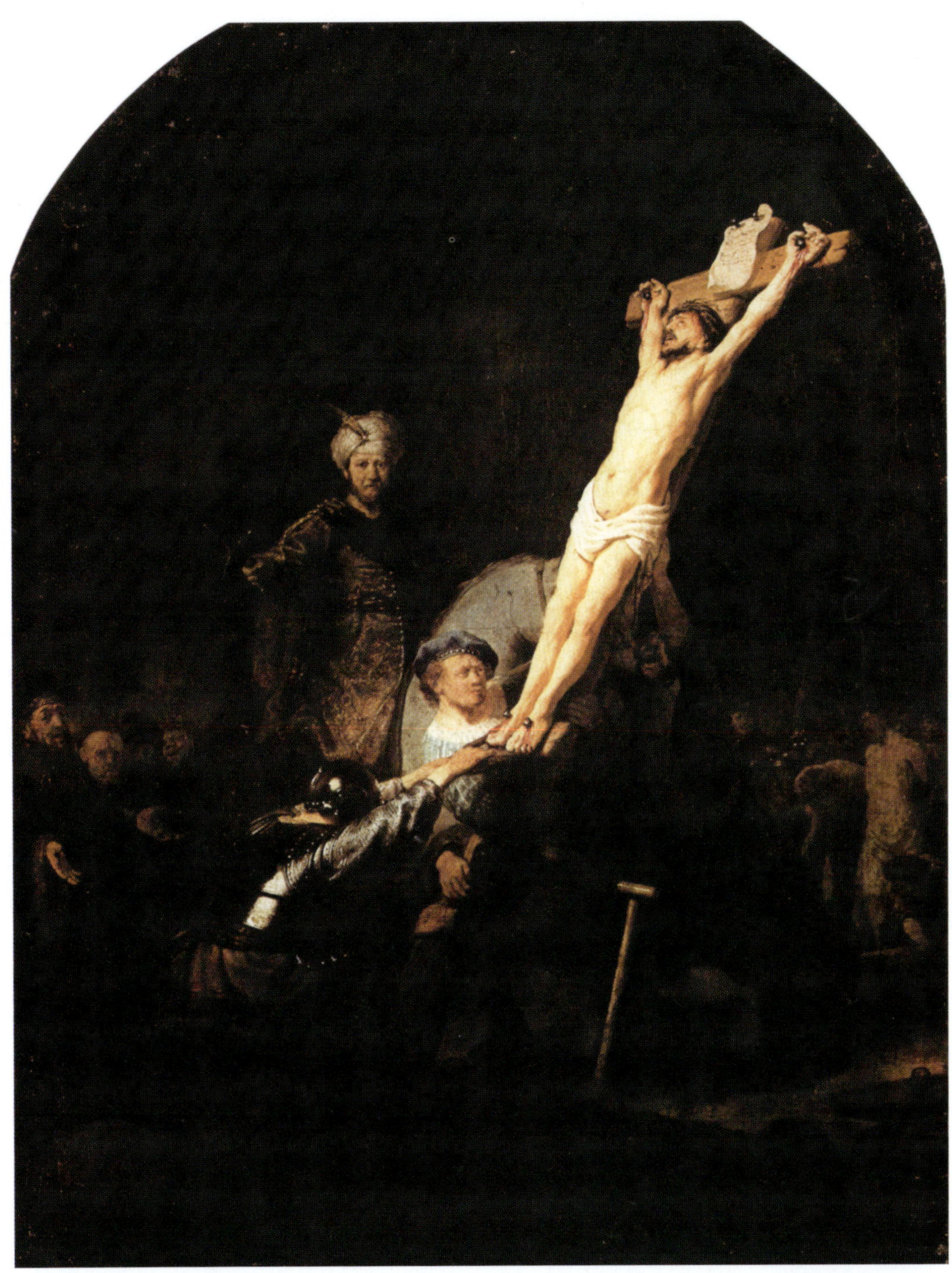

The Raising of the Cross, 1633, Alte Pinakothek, Munich

personal statement. His self-portrait in this work is not a statement of the universal responsibility of humankind for the crucifixion, as has sometimes been argued, but a statement of his own involvement in an event that he contemplated throughout his life. He was there. He did not want to be there, and he was wrong to be there, but he *was* there,

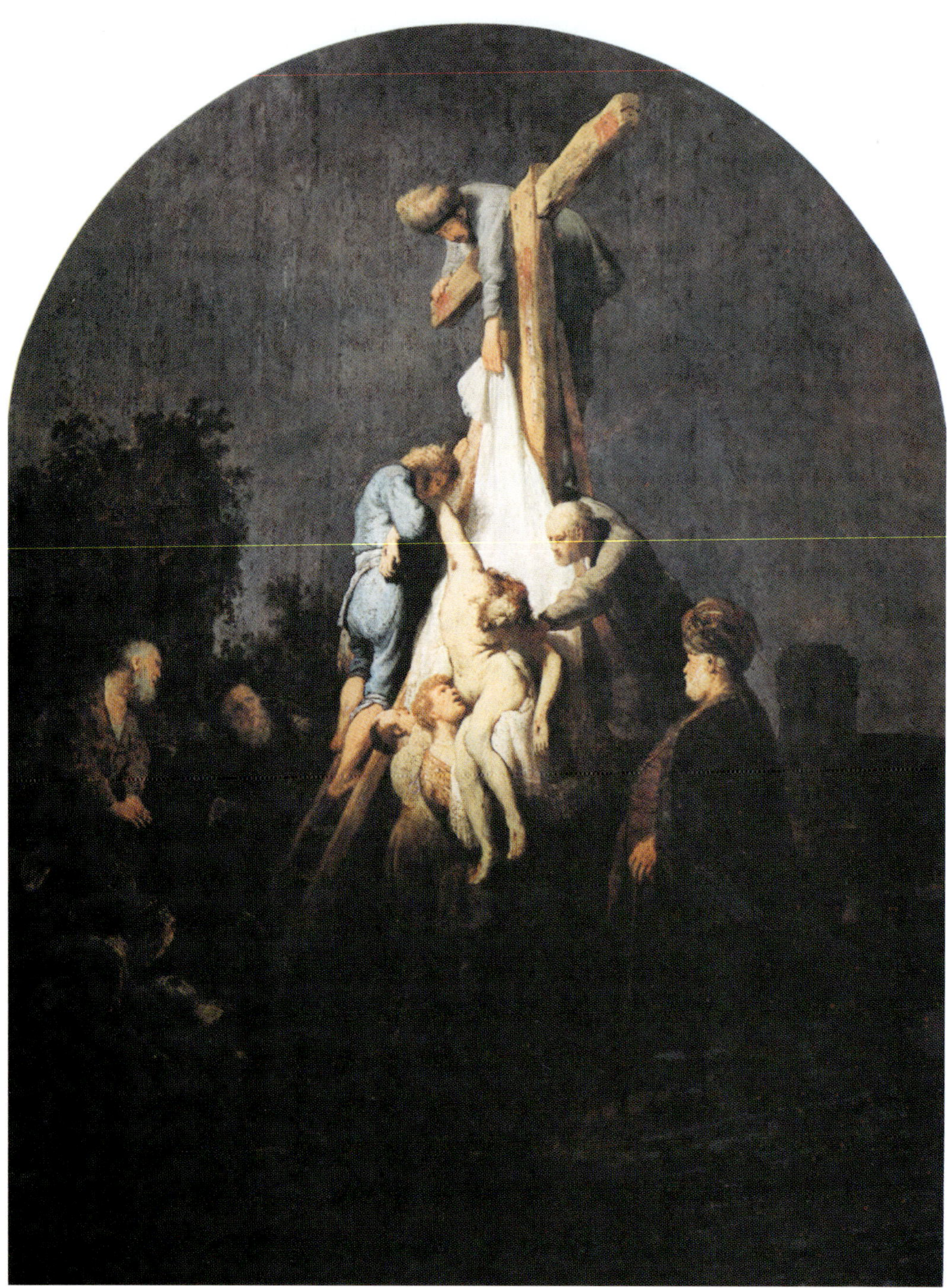

The Descent from the Cross, 1633, Alte Pinakothek, Munich

and sorry about being there. I suggest that he has painted himself in a moment of regret and the resolve to do better.

In *The Descent from the Cross*, probably painted in the same year, Rembrandt presents himself as a richly clad young man who is helping to receive in the cradle of his arms the limp body of Christ being taken down from the cross. Some have seen the man on the ladder holding Christ's right arm as a self-portrait. I think it unlikely that Rembrandt would portray himself twice in a single painting, unless the man on the ladder is to be considered a mere *tronie*. The young man receiving the body being let down is an obvious and intentional self-portrait, as a comparison with the 1628 self-portrait in the Rijksmuseum, the 1629 self-portraits in Munich (see below, p. 138) and in the Hague, and several etchings and drawings from this period suggests.

Rembrandt here gives himself a younger face (see the detail from the painting, chap. 3) than in *The Raising of the Cross*. He looks up at the dead body of Christ, the left side of his face against Christ's lower abdomen, with undisguised awe and adoration. I am tempted to wonder whether this may not be the earlier of the two paintings and the more traditional of the two in meaning. Here, Rembrandt seems to be declaring his belief in and his love for Christ. In *The Raising of the Cross*, he gives himself an older appearance, and a wiser one as well, as he considers the implications this moment has for his own life.

Against the reasonable objection that I am suggesting more meaning than Rembrandt intended, I call attention to the following works that may support my view of what the crucifixion meant to Rembrandt. There is an etching from 1633 that revisits *The Descent from the Cross* (and may be from Rembrandt's hand only in part) in which the man on the ladder holding the limp left forearm of the dead Christ is probably a self-portrait—compare the two etchings reproduced here with the face of the figure grasping Christ's left arm.

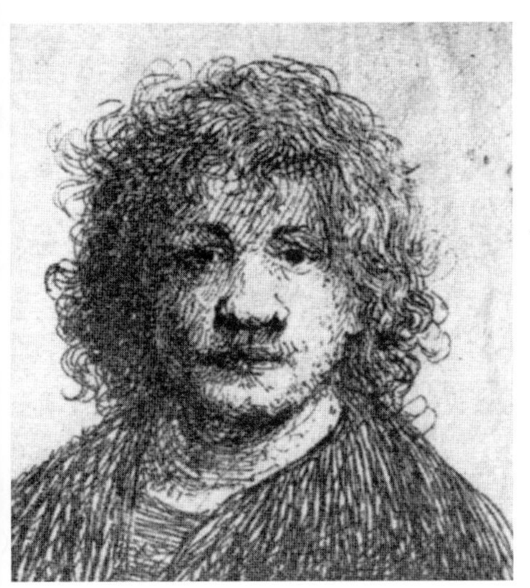

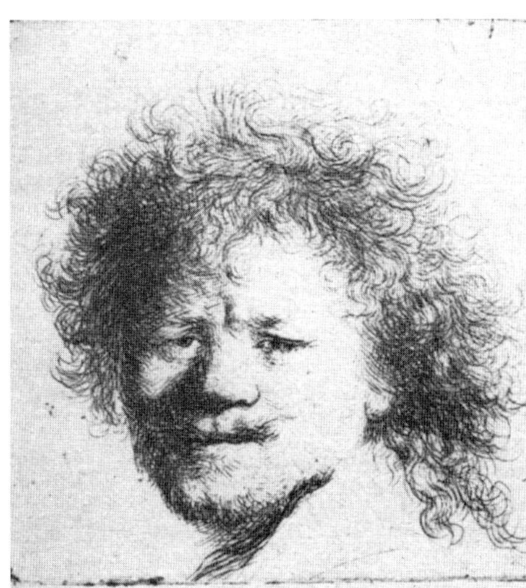

Self-Portrait, B 4, 1628, Prentenkabinet, Rijksmuseum, Amsterdam (left)

Self-Portrait, B 8, 1631, Prentenkabinet, Rijksmuseum, Amsterdam (right)

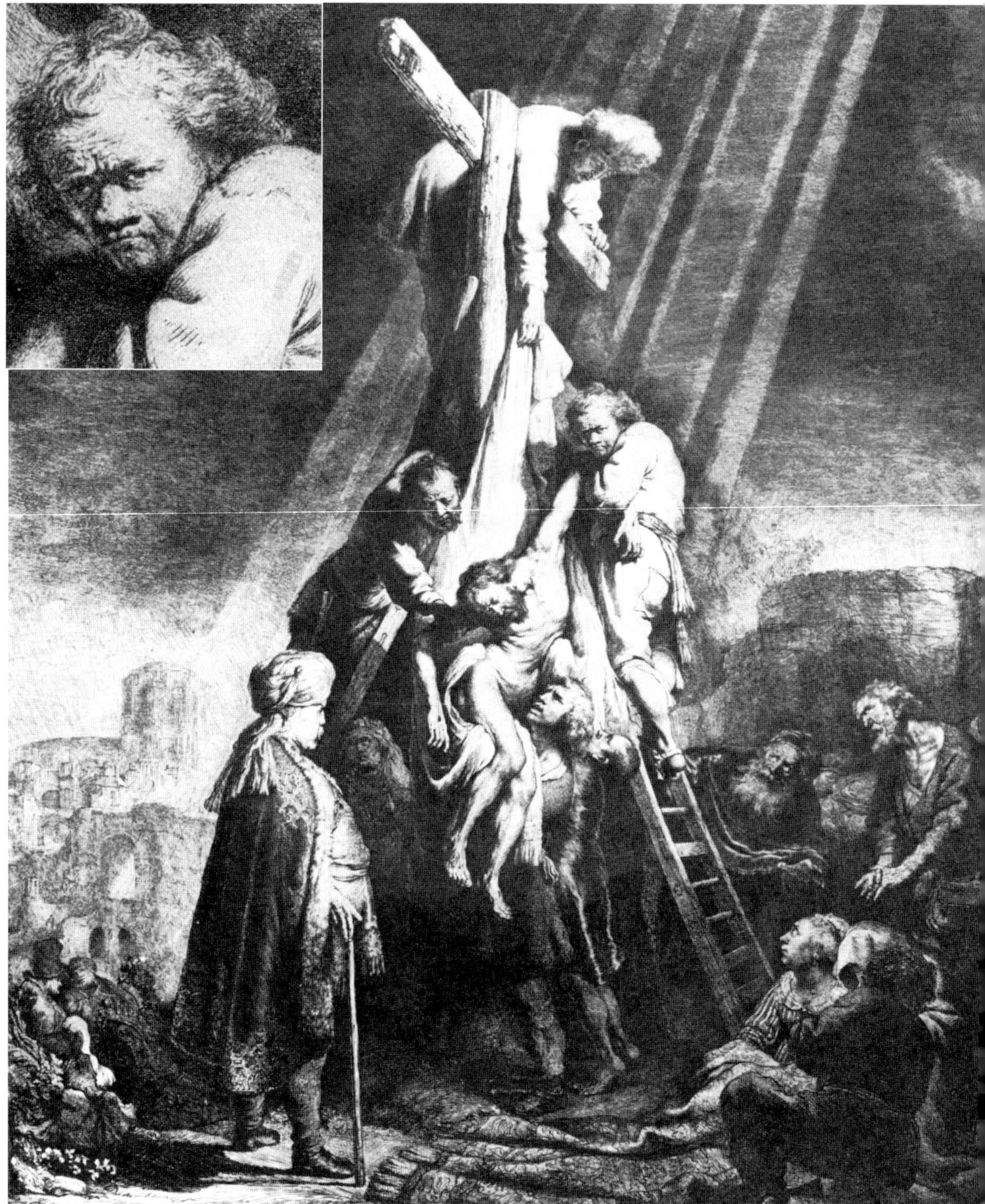

The Descent from the Cross, B 81, 1633, Prentenkabinet, Rijksmuseum, Amsterdam

The expression Rembrandt gives himself here is one of pain, regret, and distraction from the work at hand, despite a precarious position on the rungs of a ladder. I suspect he may intend to suggest a mixture of guilt, outrage, and fear of what may come next. The reach of the old man to the right of the ladder who holds a garment to cover the naked body of the dead Jesus is moving in its pathos, as are the wringing hands of the follower at the right and the woman and the man waiting to receive the body on what has the appearance of an expensive carpet. Has this rug been provided by Joseph of Arimathea, who stands, cane in hand, looking solemnly at the procedure? The shaft of light falling down from heaven onto the cross and the four men lowering the limp and grotesquely stretched body of Jesus anticipate an etching of 1654, *The Descent from the Cross by Torchlight.*

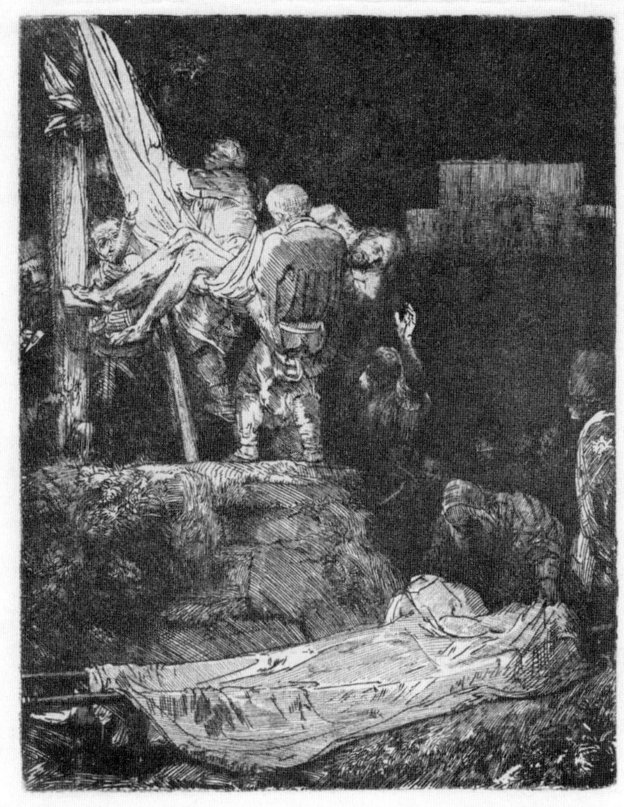

The Descent from the Cross by Torchlight, B 83, 1654, Prentenkabinet, Rijksmuseum, Amsterdam

Here, the light comes not from heaven but from a torch held by the man at the base of the cross. It shines onto the knees and legs of the dead Christ and washes across his face and onto a hand reaching up to receive and help to lower the body onto the makeshift stretcher being spread in readiness below.

Two years earlier, Rembrandt had done an etching of *The Adoration of the Shepherds* in which he used the same contrast of darkness and brightness to present Christ as the Light of the World,

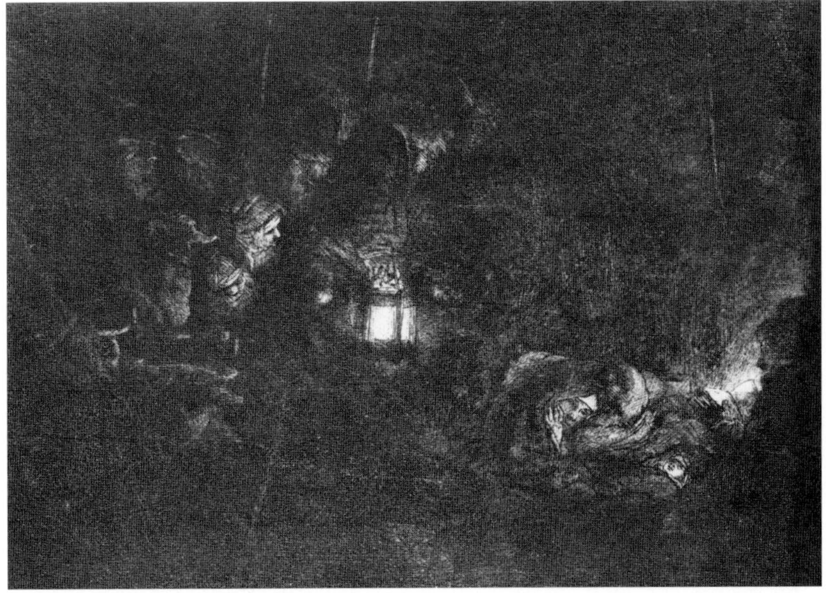

The Adoration of the Shepherds (a Night Piece), B 46, 1652, Prentenkabinet, Rijksmuseum, Amsterdam

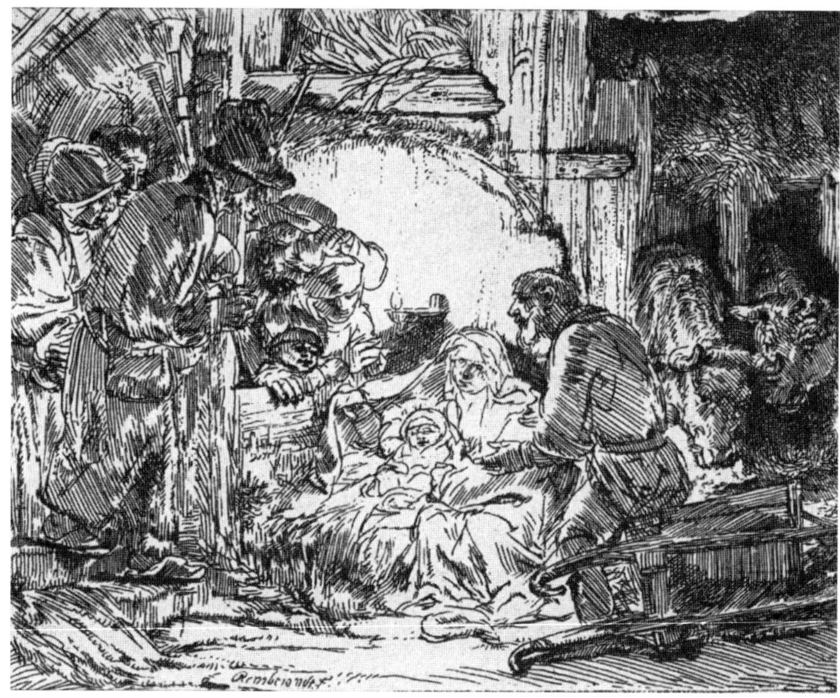

The Adoration of the Shepherds with the Lamp, B 45, 1654, Prentenkabinet, Rijksmuseum, Amsterdam

1. **The Adoration of the Shepherds**, 1646, Alte Pinakothek, Munich

2. **The Adoration of the Shepherds**, 1646, The National Gallery, London

3. **The Three Crosses**, B 78:I, 1653, Prentenkabinet, Rijksmuseum, Amsterdam

lumen de lumine. So also *The Adoration of the Shepherds with the Lamp* from 1654.

There are two paintings of *The Adoration of the Shepherds* from 1646, one of them now in London, the other now in Munich, in which the infant Jesus is bathed in light from an unseen source. Indeed, these paintings nearly give the impression that the Christ child *is* the source of the brightness at the center of these works.

While Christ as a source of light is certainly not Rembrandt's invention, his repeated use of chiaroscuro in connection with the nativity and the crucifixion is exceptional, and may be taken as yet another evidence of the meaning these events had for him.

The most compelling example of Rembrandt's meaning in his representation of the Passion is a drypoint work of 1653, *The Three Crosses*, which seems to have started out as a composite of the Gospel narratives of the crucifixion, with a focus on the moment described in Mark 15:39, so: "When the centurion standing just across from him saw that he died thus, he said, 'For a fact this man was a Son of God!'"

Rembrandt took this work through four states in which he made changes, and the prints that remain of each state reveal a dramatic experimentation with the inking of his plate to augment his meaning. The original work presents a scene full of activity and one including all the persons mentioned in the Gospels as present at the crucifixion as well as some not mentioned in the New Testament at all.

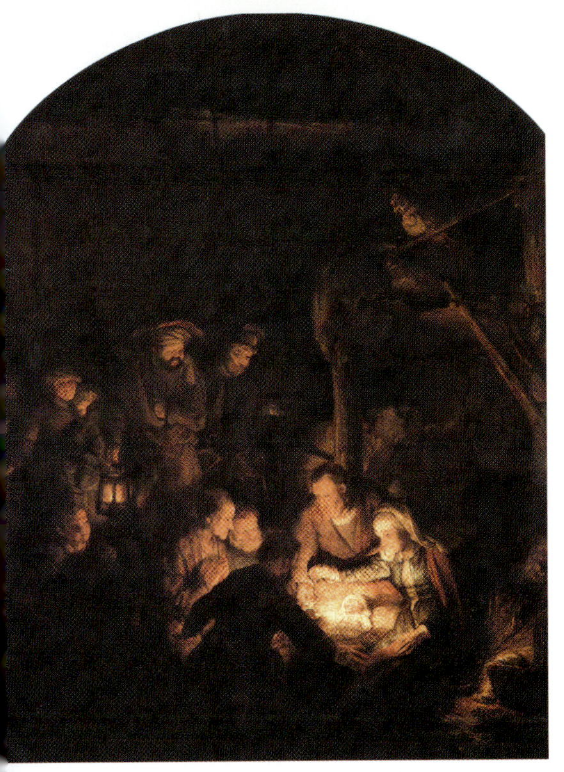

1.

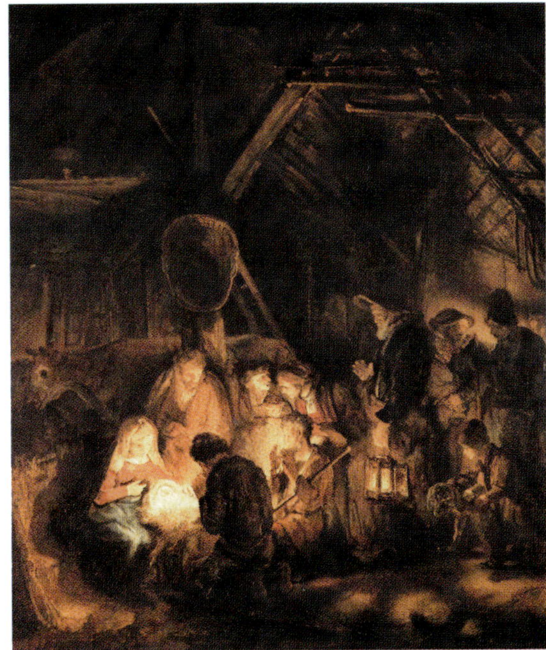

2.

3.

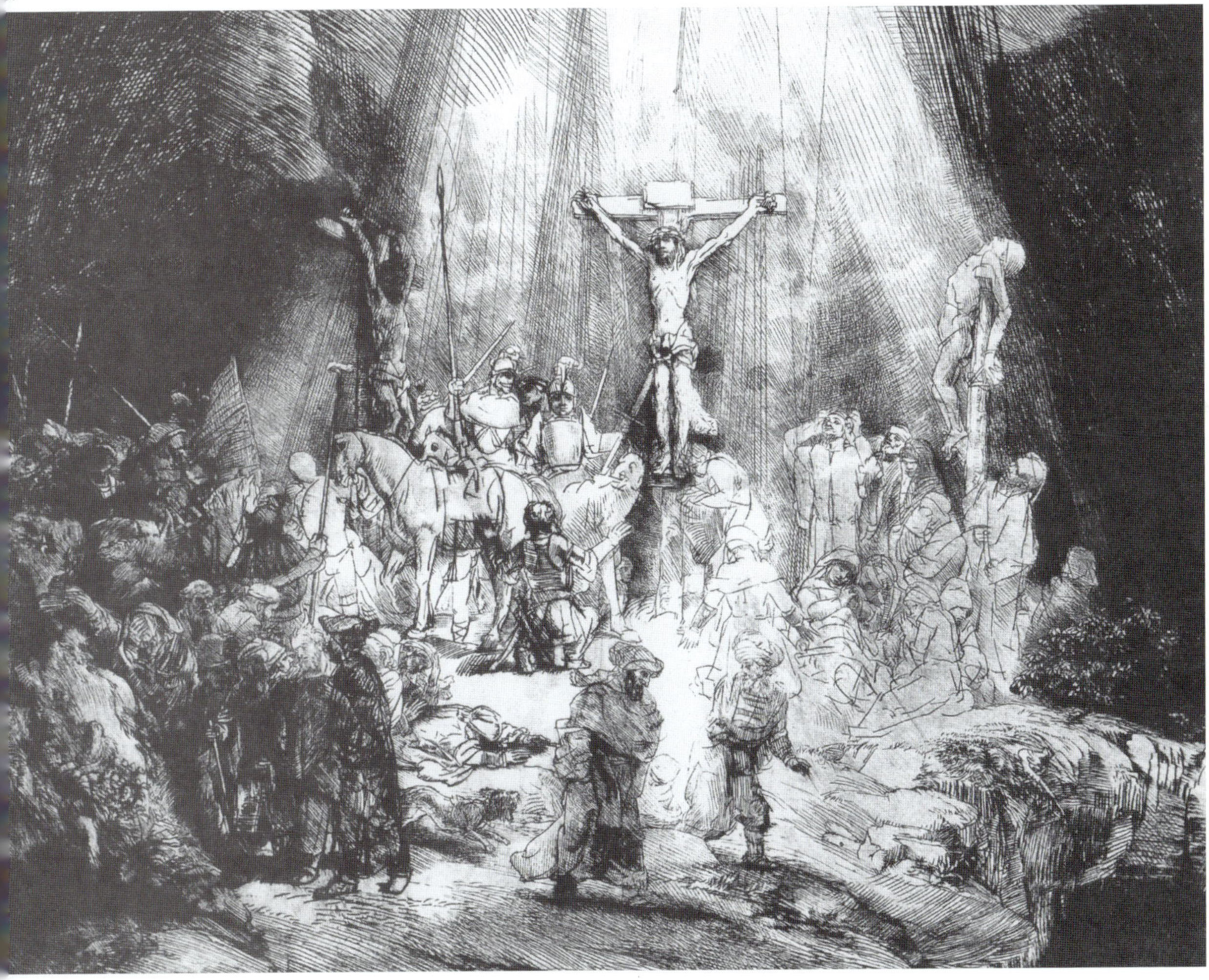

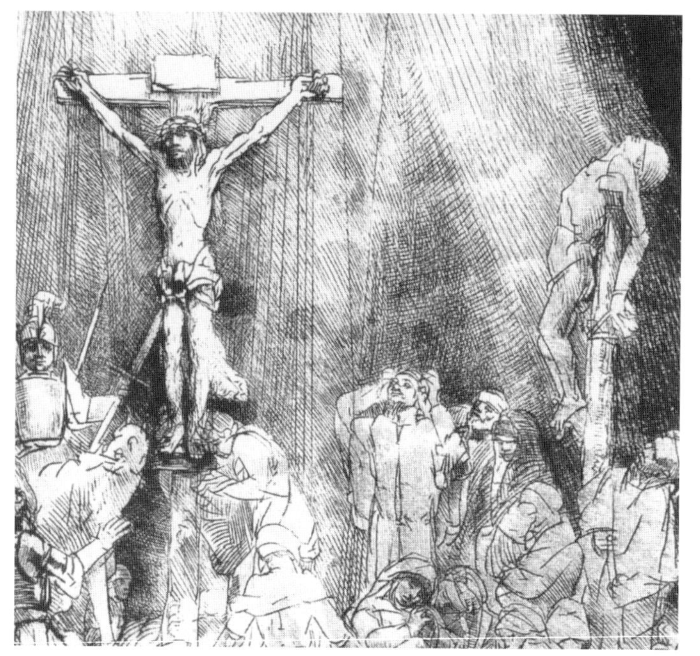

B 78:I

The two thieves crucified to the left and the right of Christ are there, facing him. At the right of Christ's cross, his grieving followers are gathered, his mother sunk to the ground with her back to Christ, Mary Magdalene bending at Christ's feet but turning to look at his mother, John with his hands raised to the side of his head, and others standing, sitting, kneeling, distraught.

In the left foreground, there is a compact group of mourners and sightseers. A bearded man is being helped away—he has usually been identified as Simon of Cyrene, who was forced to help Christ carry his cross (Mark 15:21). One man has turned away from the scene with his hand over his eyes; another has fallen prostrate to the ground; others look down or away, their faces vacant, their expressions numb. One man still holds the pole with the sponge soaked in wine offered to Jesus a moment before (Mark 15:36). In the center foreground, two well-dressed men hurry away, one of Rembrandt's dogs running and barking after them. Are they representative of the "passersby" (Mark 15:29) who abused him as they walked along? I consider this far likelier than the proposal that they are Nicodemus and Joseph of Arimathea, who would hardly be hurrying away from this event.

B 78:I

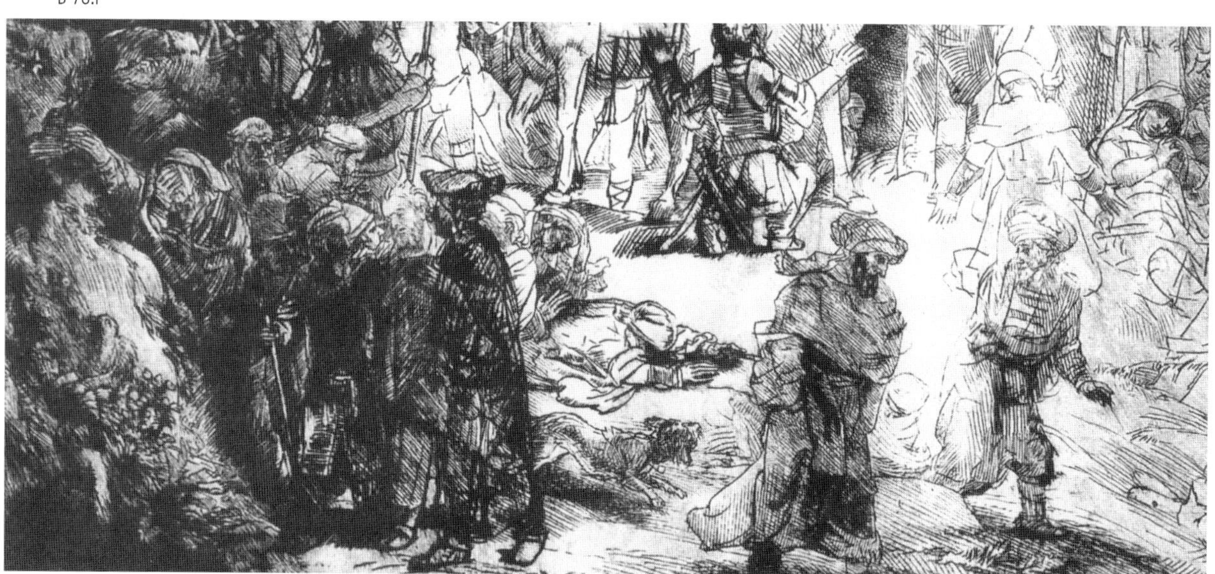

At the center of the work is Christ, bathed even in the most heavily inked impressions in layers of light shining down from above. His mouth is open in death; his body is rigid in the strain of his nailed hands and feet. And beneath the cross at the left of Christ, the centurion kneels, his hands thrown up in awe as he looks up at Christ. His company of mounted soldiers appears not to know where to look; one of them turns to whisper to his companion. Only the faceless groom holding his officer's horse seems to have turned his glance toward the kneeling man.

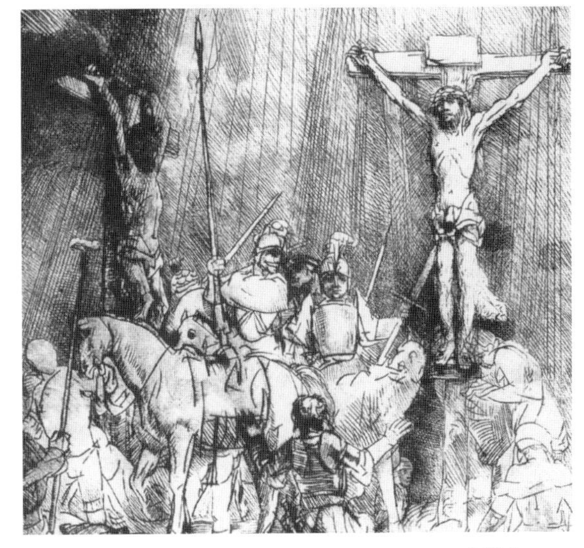

B 78:1

Rembrandt's meaning is clear—in every way that has occurred to him, he has attempted to re-present the biblical moment of the death of Christ as a devastating tragedy for those who believed, but more, as a dazzling burst of light to the unlikeliest one to come to belief, the centurion in charge of the detail assigned to execute this trouble-maker from Nazareth. I think it not too much to suggest that

The Three Crosses, B 78:III, 1653, Prentenkabinet, Rijksmuseum, Amsterdam

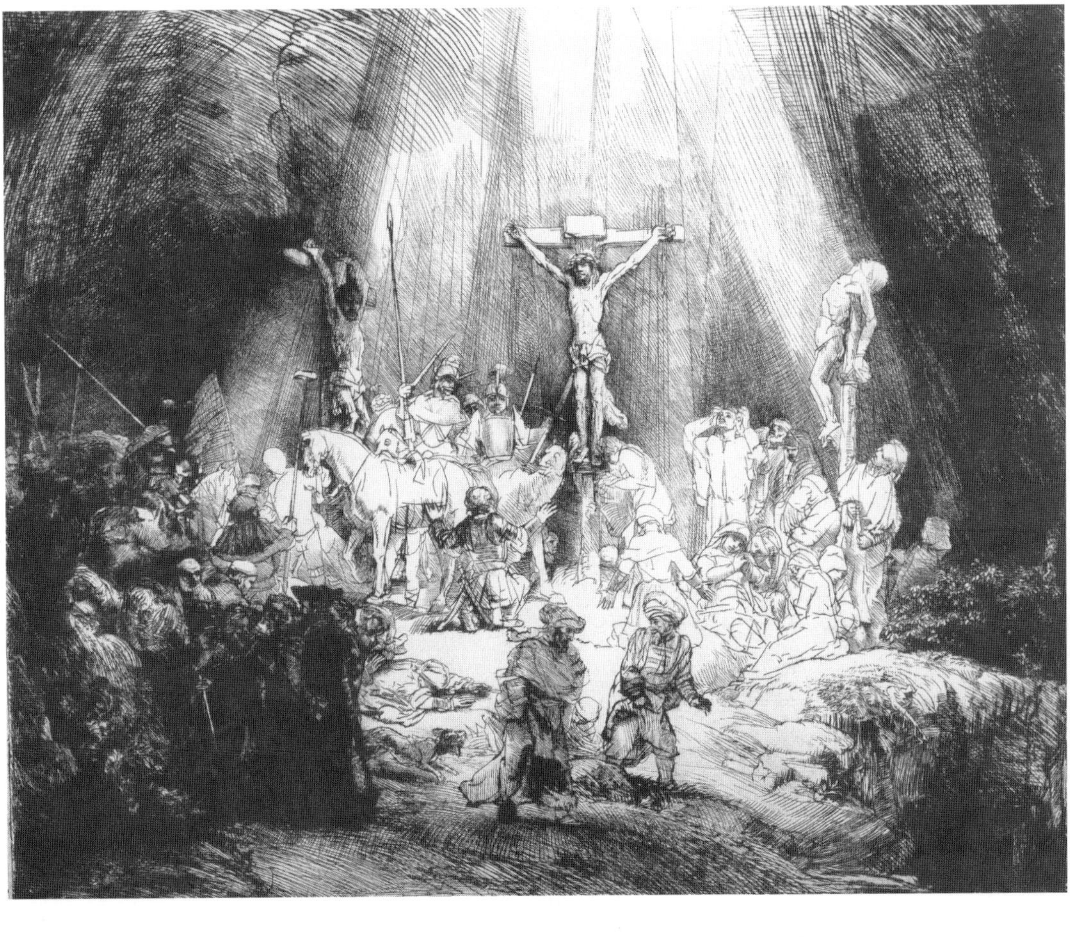

Rembrandt thought of himself in terms of this centurion and that he hints as much not by the device of a self-portrait, but by his choice of the narrative that presents the outsider coming to hope and even joy amidst the despair and grief of the insiders. By 1652, Rembrandt was very much an outsider, as far as the Dutch Reformed Church was concerned. And in any case, he has caught and multiplied the very point by contrast that the three Synoptic Gospels make.

The drypoint technique Rembrandt employed for *The Three Crosses* was far closer to drawing than the technique of etching with an acid bath and yielded a freer, more spontaneous result. As the drypoint stylus leaves a line far less deep than a line cut through a wax ground by acid, however, the drypoint plate is erased by wear much more rapidly. Thus, Rembrandt was forced as much by necessity as by his second thoughts to create the second and third states of this work. He made but a single change in the second state, but in the third state

The Three Crosses, B 78:IV, 1653, Prentenkabinet, Rijksmuseum, Amsterdam

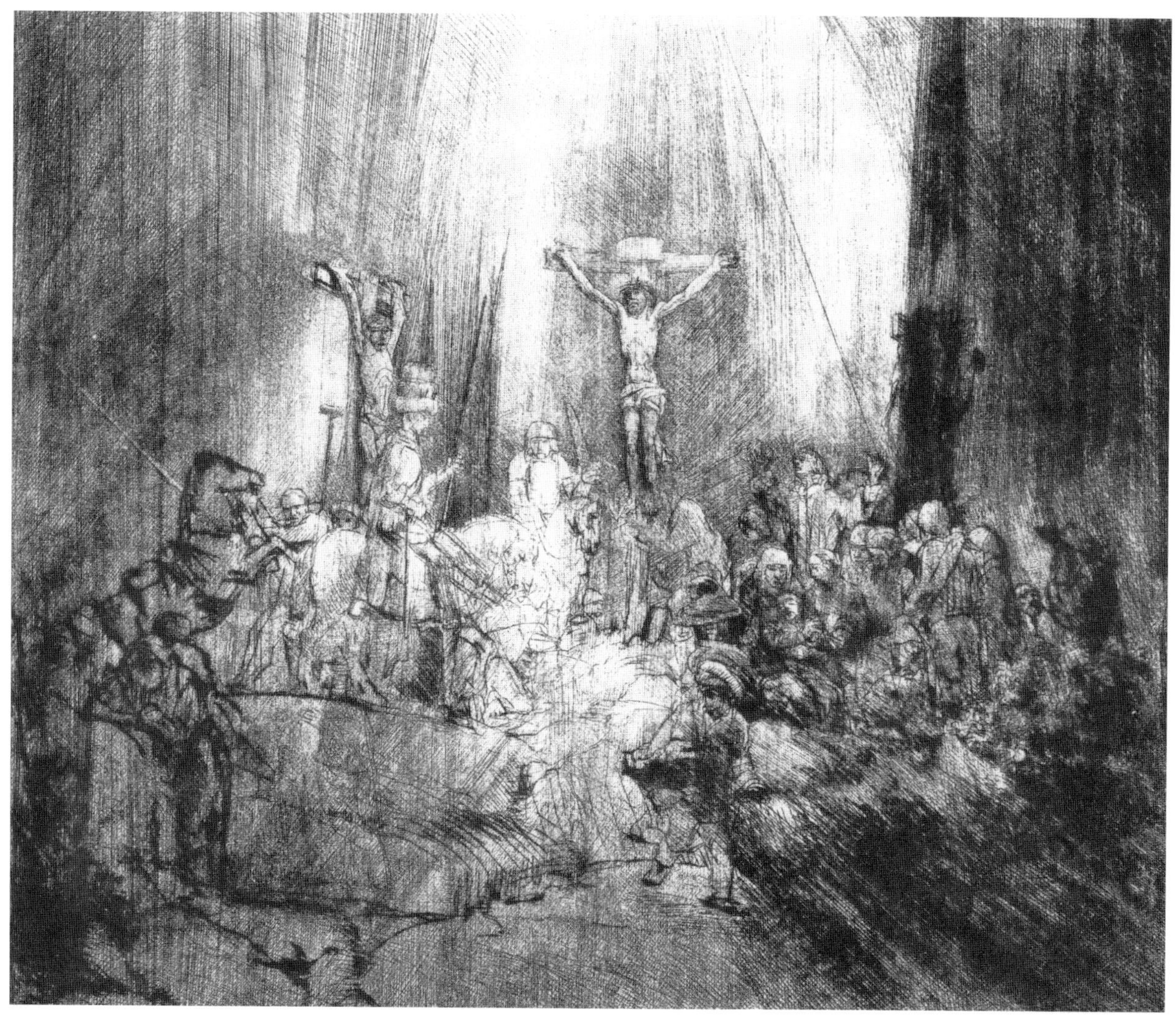

he greatly reduced the appearance of activity at the left and center foreground, bringing into still sharper focus the bright center with its shower of light upon the scene of the crucifixion. To this third state, (see p. 123) Rembrandt added his signature and the date 1653, suggesting that he had finished the work.

As this third version of the plate wore down, however, Rembrandt found himself unable to leave *The Three Crosses.* Out of necessity, certainly, but also no doubt by intention, he created what amounts to a new work, one that presents in a still more dramatic way what I am calling Rembrandt's meaning. By heavy burnishing, Rembrandt virtually erased the group of figures in the left foreground, removed one of the two departing figures and the dog from the center foreground, and redrew the grieving group of Jesus' followers to the right of the cross, increasing their number by half. Mary the mother now faints away, with closed eyes and open mouth; John now reaches out his arms as if to embrace the dead Christ on the cross; there are alterations to the face and figure of Jesus; the figure of the kneeling centurion has been made far less prominent; the mounted detachment to the left of the cross and behind the centurion has been reduced to one menacing soldier, in heavy armor and with drawn sword; and to the left of the centurion, two new figures have been introduced: a groom struggling to control a rearing horse, and a man on horseback with a lance at the ready in his left hand, wearing the same curious tall hat that is to turn up in a work of 1661, *The Conspiracy of the Batavians* (see chap. 3), now in Stockholm. It is worth wondering whether Rembrandt intended here the approach of

B 78:IV

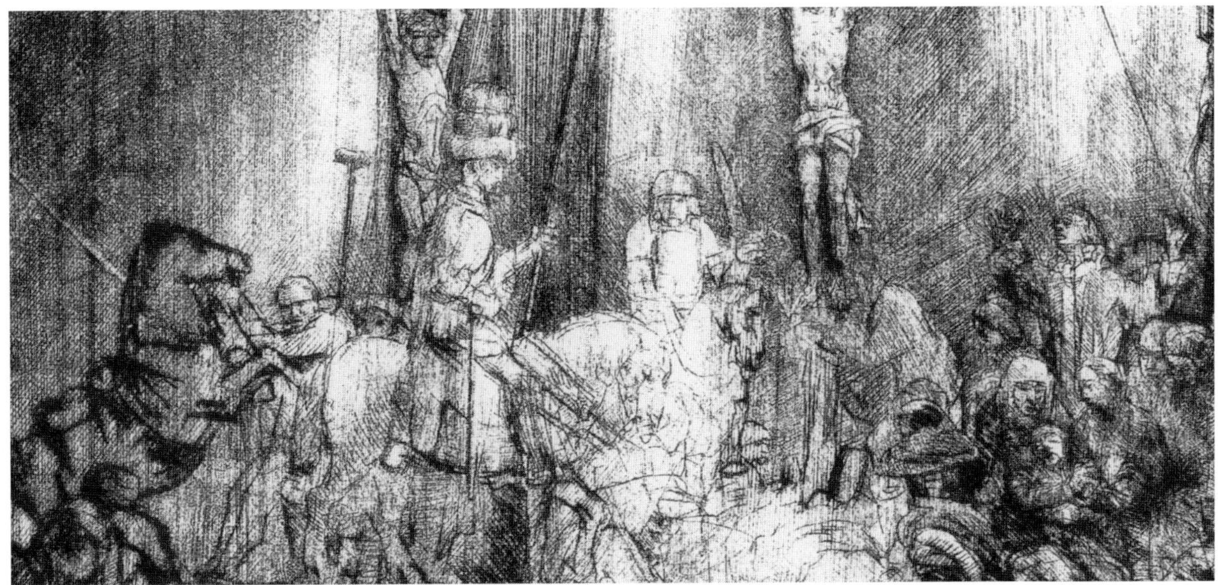

the soldier whom only the Gospel of John mentions (19:34) as piercing the side of the dead Christ with a spear.

The use by Rembrandt in this completely altered version of *The Three Crosses* of images from Italian art has been often noted. Kenneth Clark proposed in his Wrightsman Lectures that this usage "argues a deep understanding of the mechanism of the unconscious."

Yet far more telling still is Rembrandt's statement in this work of the meaning the crucifixion had for him. In this fourth state of *The Three Crosses*, Rembrandt created his ultimate contemplation of a biblical event that he thought about through most of his career. A fifth state exists, but it reveals no changes by Rembrandt's hand.

For all the grief and emotion and movement and expression and contrasting response he so powerfully re-presented in the first three versions of *The Three Crosses*, Rembrandt came finally to the view that what mattered most is what had happened on the cross itself. In even the darkest, most heavily inked impressions of the plate, copies that are very nearly studies in gray and black, the light cascading down upon Christ from above is unmistakable. Not only is the darkness that fell over the whole earth at the sixth hour (Mark 15:33) virtually palpable in this fourth state, but it now represents the appearance of the parted veil of the temple, disclosing the holiest place of God's presence, the holiest sight human vision could experience: "The sun failed; the veil of the Temple was torn down the middle" (Luke 23:45).

Only Luke reports this rending, another hint that Rembrandt must have read all the Gospel accounts of the crucifixion as he worked on this plate. What he has given us in *The Three Crosses*, in each state, is a rending apart of all the distractions that obscure for us what the crucifixion is really about, whether those distractions are personal or doctrinal or professional in nature. This meaning is given its fullest expression in the much different final version of the plate, where every distraction is shoved aside and where even the new figures of the soldier with the raised sword and the soldier with the tall hat and the lance seem suspended in their movement by the holiness of the moment.

The final versions of *The Three Crosses* are thus a distillation, a re-presentation of the very essence of God's death on behalf of the human family, the human family taken one at a time. There can be little doubt that Rembrandt had here moved beyond depiction to a

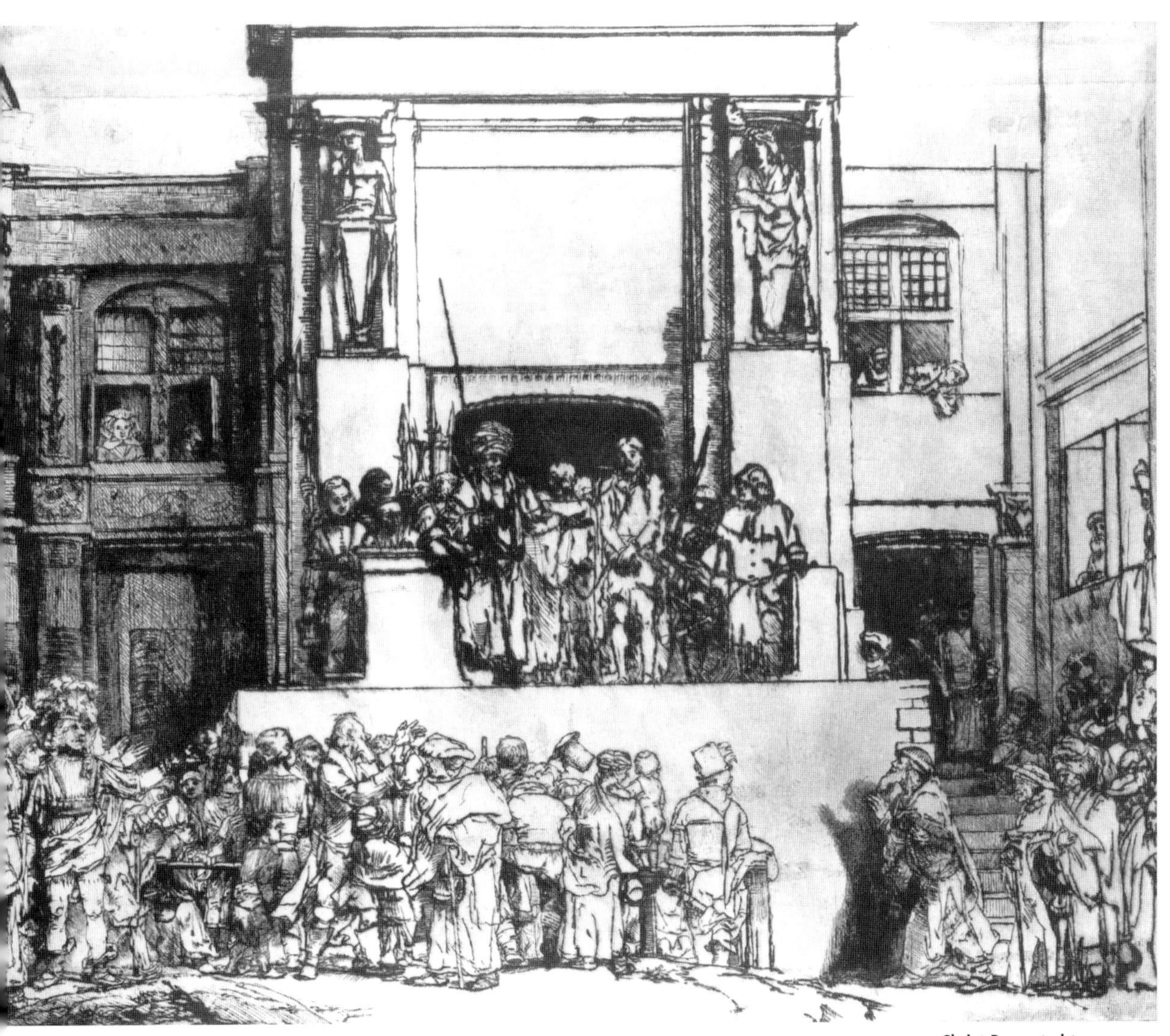

Christ Presented to the People, B 76:I, 1655, British Museum, London

statement of significance, and any real statement of significance must always be personal.

Additional examples of what I am calling Rembrandt's meaning in his re-presentation of biblical moments come to mind. From his Passion works alone, there are the eight states of *Christ Presented to the People* from 1655, a dramatic leap forward from the etching of 1636 (B 77; see chap. 4), where the officials of the temple who want Jesus removed from their list of problems swarm toward Pilate, one of them even tugging at the governor's clothes. In the first five states of this *Christ Presented to the People*, Rembrandt drew a crush of accusers and spectators crowding in from the left and the right beneath a platform on which an abused and sad Christ stands bound alongside Pontius Pilate and an array of guards and officials.

In the left foreground, there are priests and beggars, guards and old men, women and children, one old woman with a cane turning her back on the group above, and even a man doffing his hat. Just above this mob, to the left, a woman with an elaborate headdress peers from a window onto the scene below, and to her left, through a second window, a soldier can be seen moving away from her. Rembrandt apparently had in mind the detail in the narrative reported in Matthew 27:19: "But even as he [Pilate] was in place for judgment, his wife sent along to him this message: 'Do nothing to that innocent man; I have had an awful dream about him this very day.'"

From two matching windows on the right, two women gawk at the proceedings, one of them hanging precariously out to see around the column atop the platform. In the right foreground, additional accusers and onlookers surge in, and one old man with a long beard raises a hand and looks up toward Christ, his shadow falling across the base of the platform as he moves forward.

The group surrounding Jesus and Pilate on the raised platform includes an array of armed guards; a young man in the left corner with a jug and a basin, a reference to another detail of the story included only by Matthew, at 27:24c ("he took water, and washed his hands"); beside this young man an official who has the appearance of a scribe or record-keeper; and between Pilate and Jesus a scowling man with thinning hair. This latter figure is usually taken for Barabbas, an identification I am inclined to doubt—the man does not appear to be bound, as such a criminal would be. Indeed, he may even be holding a rope attached to Jesus' wrists, and he has what looks like some sort of purse at his belt. Perhaps Rembrandt had in mind an official who has conducted Jesus to this place of judgment.

Rembrandt did this work in drypoint, as he had *The Three Crosses* of two years before, and thus it too wore down far more quickly than a more deeply inscribed acid-etched plate would. He made changes and adjustments through five states, including a reduction of the height of the plate by 2.5 cm, but the alterations affect the appearance of the plate, for the most part, only in its details.

With the sixth, seventh, and eighth states, however, Rembrandt arrived at an altogether new work, a work in which the distraction of the crowd has been reduced to a minimum. I wonder whether he began this dramatic revision out of the necessity forced upon him by

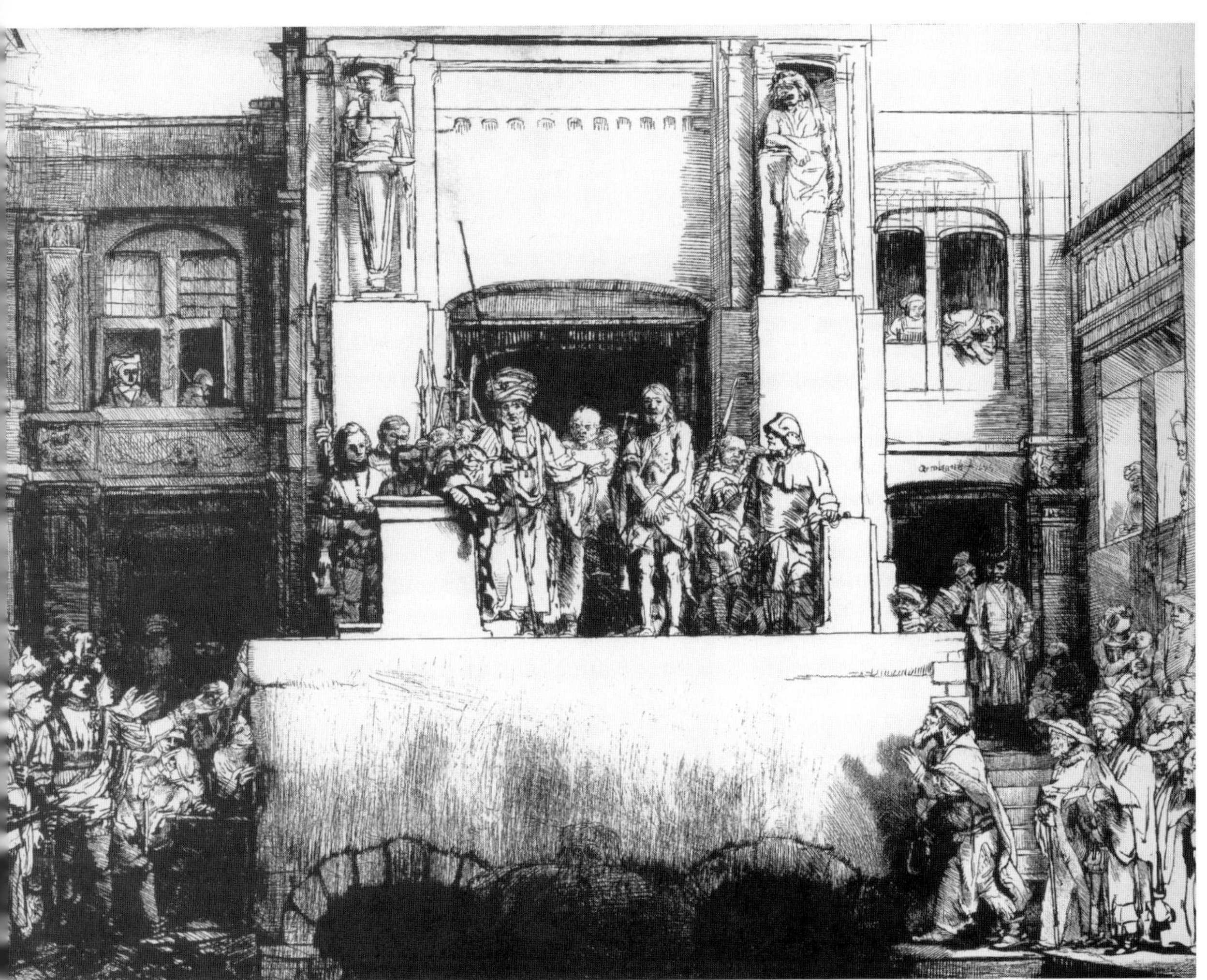

Christ Presented to the People, B 76:VIII, 1655, Prentenkabinet, Rijksmuseum, Amsterdam

the wear of the plate, or if he found himself unable to finish the work until he achieved the same concentrated focus that he managed in *The Three Crosses*. As in *The Three Crosses*, he came finally to present Christ as the absolute center of the work. The pushing, ogling, shouting crowd is gone; the officials remain and, interestingly, the women and children to the left and the right of the platform. No one has been removed from the platform, but Christ has been moved forward, made to appear more alone than ever and intensely sad in condemnation.

It is an astonishing distillation, and one that leaves little doubt about the meaning this moment had for Rembrandt. As so often in his depictions of the events of Jesus' Passion, he gives the impression of having been there. Only in the seventh state did he put his signature onto the plate, over the entry way to the right of the platform.

Many more than these few examples of what I am calling Rembrandt's meaning come to mind. There is, for example, a wonderful nativity sequence, consisting of eight etchings across the years from 1634 to 1654, ten paintings across the years from 1628 to 1669, and twelve drawings across the years from 1635 to 1655, and there are the two packed-full etchings of *Christ Preaching*, the "Hundred Guilder Print" of 1639–1649, and the so-called "La Petite Tombe" of 1652, either of which alone would justify a long chapter of commentary and both of which are discussed later (chap. 6).

I turn, however, in concluding this consideration of Rembrandt's meaning to a painting that only *may* have any biblical connection. I do so in part as a reminder that Rembrandt's meaning is certainly not a feature only of his works on biblical subjects. There are many drawings, etchings, and paintings in his vast legacy that have little or nothing to do with the Bible or with Rembrandt's faith that are nevertheless laden with meaning, meaning that can often only be guessed at, from what little we know of his life.

I also turn to this work because it presents in so undeniable a manner the wholly intangible quality and content that I am attempting to suggest by the admittedly inadequate term "meaning." This painting, done in the last decade of Rembrandt's life, probably as late as 1666, is *The Jewish Bride*, now in Amsterdam. It has been so called for well over a hundred years, mainly because the pair pictured cannot be specifically identified. They have been variously named, in order to establish a biblical connection, Boaz and Ruth, Isaac and Rebekah, Tobias and Sarah, and even, astonishingly, Judah and Tamar. Attempts have been made to identify the pair as a couple who commissioned the portrait, and even as characters in a play popular in Rembrandt's time.

The Jewish Bride, 1666, Rijksmuseum, Amsterdam

Any firm identification of the couple is impossible, and an unnecessary distraction as well. What Rembrandt has given us here is biblical in a way that transcends any one particular moment and any one particular couple. Though he no doubt used real individuals, perhaps good friends, as his models in this work, he has presented in this masterpiece on a painted surface a truth truer than any facts we can recover and analyze.

Portrait of Saskia in a Straw Hat, Benesch 427, 1633, Kupferstichkabinett, Staatliche Museen, Berlin

Whether the couple in this painting is in any way "Jewish" *or* "bridal" is wholly beside the point. Rembrandt's meaning this time is the love between a woman and a man that cannot be understood unless it has been experienced, the love that cannot be seen unless it has been known, and that cannot then be missed.

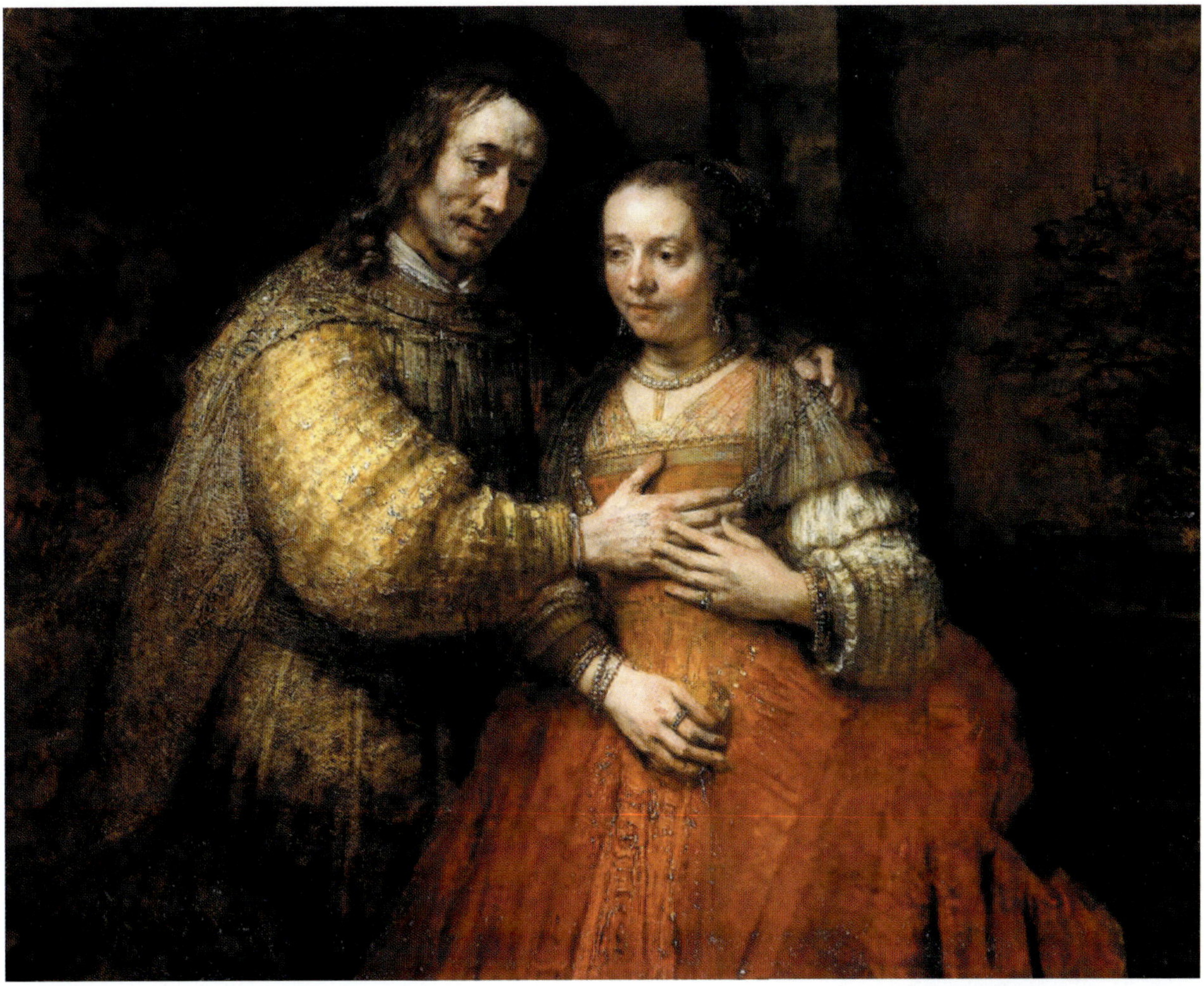

On 8 June 1633, Rembrandt drew in silverpoint on vellum what may be called an engagement portrait of his wife-to-be, Saskia van Uylenburgh. His use of such an expensive medium, coupled with an inscription (a rarity for Rembrandt) in which he refers to Saskia as "mijn huysvrou," hints that he was a goner. "Huysvrou" may be translated "betrothed," but its more common meaning is "wife." This latter translation has been questioned because Rembrandt and Saskia were not married until 22 June 1634, but may it not have been the understandable slip of an eager young man in love?

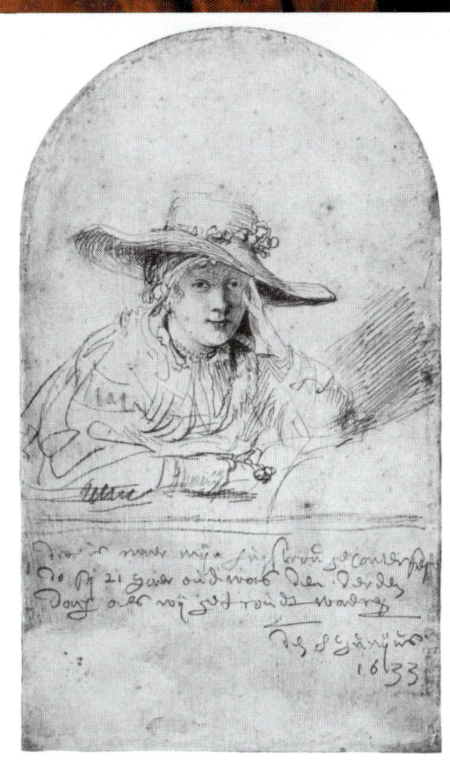

Such a possibility is surely borne out by the portrait itself. Rembrandt repeatedly drew and etched and

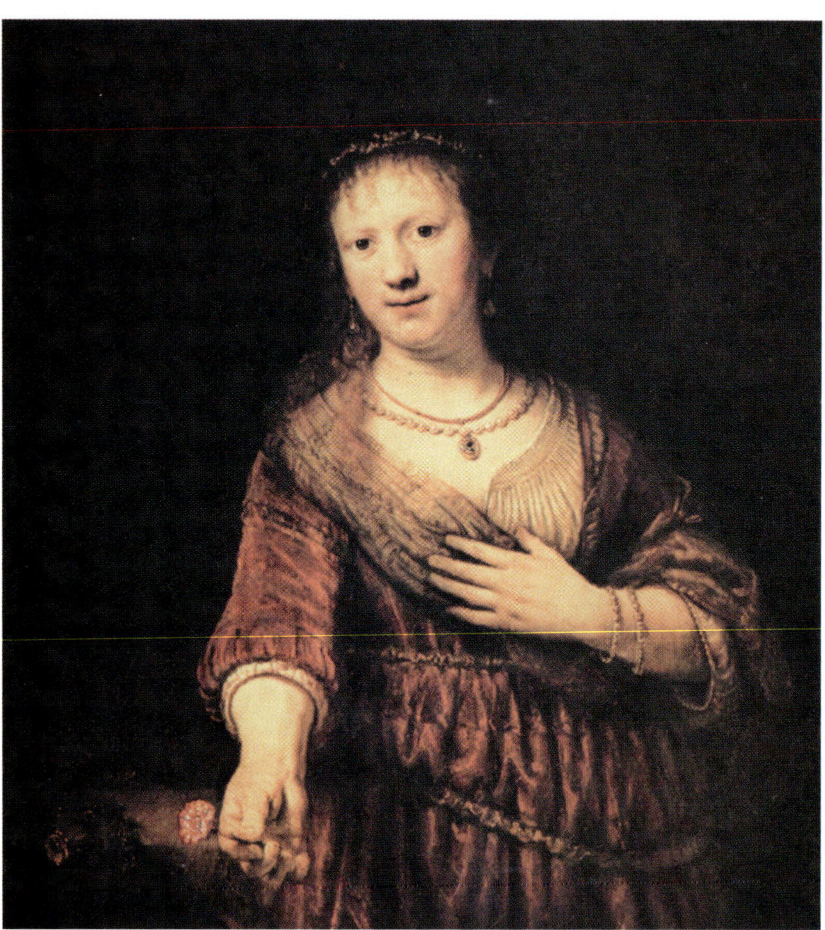

Saskia as Flora, 1641, Gemäldegalerie Alter Meister, Dresden

painted Saskia, but never is she so lovely and so delicately drawn as in this little portrait, with flowers in her hat, her left hand at her head, and her right hand holding the stem of a single blossom.

Above is a portrait of *Saskia as Flora* (one of several), now in Dresden, that Rembrandt painted in 1641, the year before her death. It may be considered Rembrandt's final painting of his wife from life, and in it, as in the engagement drawing, Saskia is holding in her right hand a single flower.

A more formal portrait of Saskia, now in Kassel, *Half-Length of Saskia van Uylenburgh in Rich Apparel*, begun perhaps in the same year as the little silverpoint drawing of 1633, was completed by Rembrandt only in 1642, the year in which his wife died. Despite repairs to the oak panel on which Rembrandt painted this portrait, and some overpainting at a later time, one has the impression that Saskia's face and even parts of her lavish costume were painted by a series of caresses. From the evidence of all the known depictions of Saskia, by Rembrandt and by his pupils, she was not a beautiful woman, yet she is certainly beautiful here.

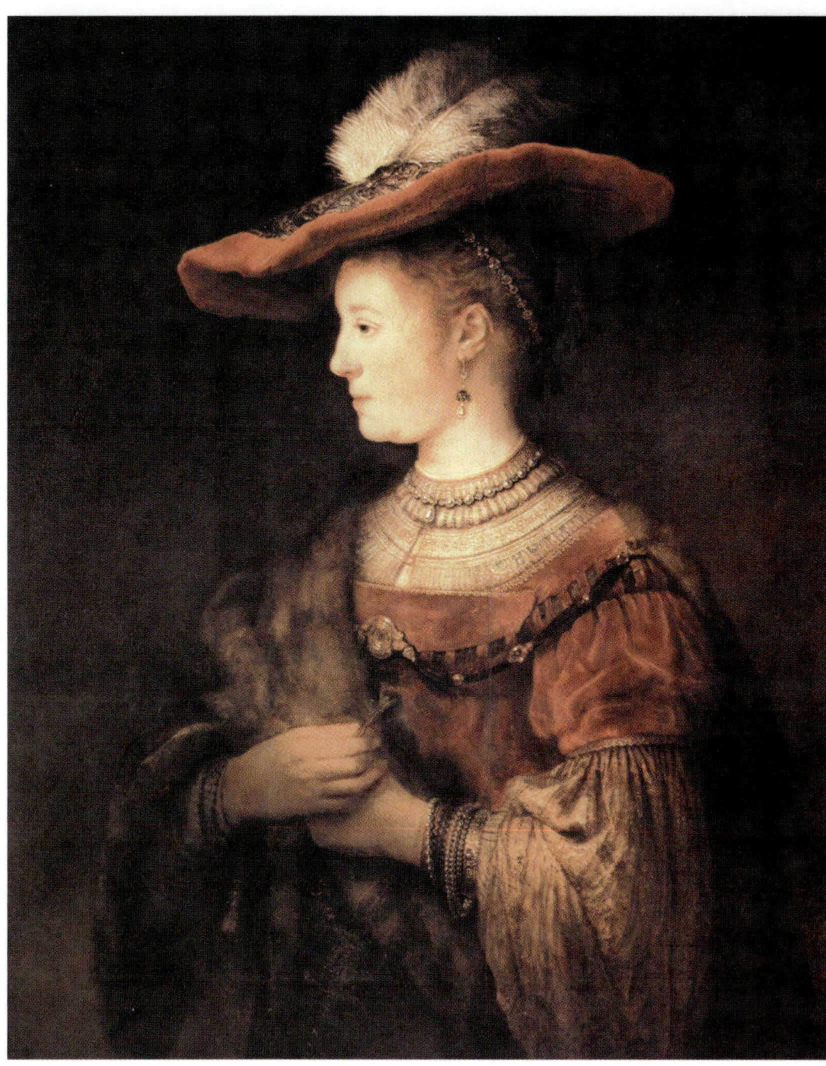

Half-Length of Saskia van Uylenburgh in Rich Apparel, 1642, Staatliche Kunstsammlungen, Schloss Wilhelmshöhe, Kassel

The hair about her temple falls in gentle wisps. Her face has a kind of glow from the inside that outshines even her lustrous pearl earring and necklace. Her hands, sometimes an important feature of Rembrandt's portraits, are delicate, though by no means small. Her expression is contentment. She is presented as a woman who is loved and who knows that she is loved. She looks beyond the moment of her sitting, beyond the discomfort of posing, beyond all the pains and griefs of her short life with the satisfaction of one who might come to say, "I cannot have had more, though I might have had it for a longer time."

I think it not too much to say that this painting, on which Rembrandt lavished love for almost a decade, is his farewell portrait of Saskia, with whom he was never out of love, from the time of their early meetings together. X-ray photographs suggest a series of subtle changes in the portrait across the years of its genesis, an evidence of

Saskia with Pearls, B 347, 1634, Prentenkabinet, Rijksmuseum, Amsterdam, detail (left)

Studies of the Head of Saskia and Others, B 365, 1636, Prentenkabinett, Rijksmuseum, Amsterdam, detail (right)

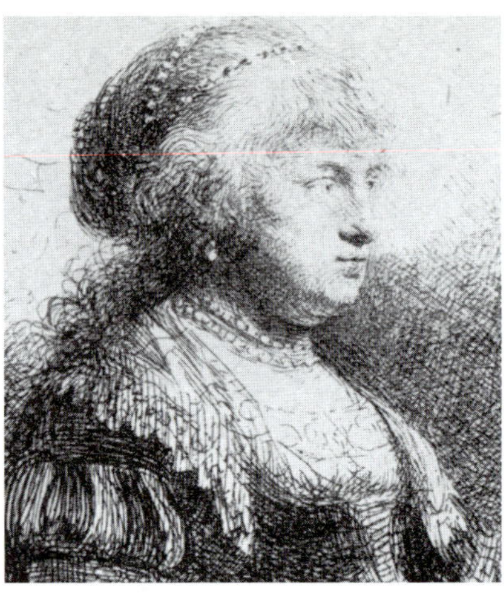

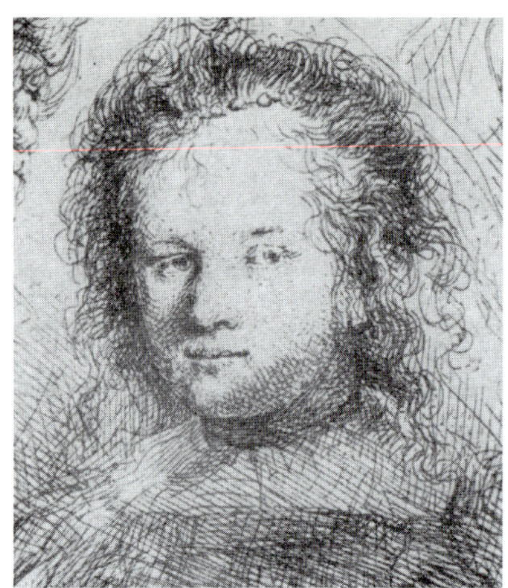

Young Woman Leaning Against a Door, 1656-1658, Gemäldegalerie, Staatliche Museen, Berlin, detail (left)

Bathsheba with King David's Letter, 1654, Musée du Louvre, Paris, detail (right)

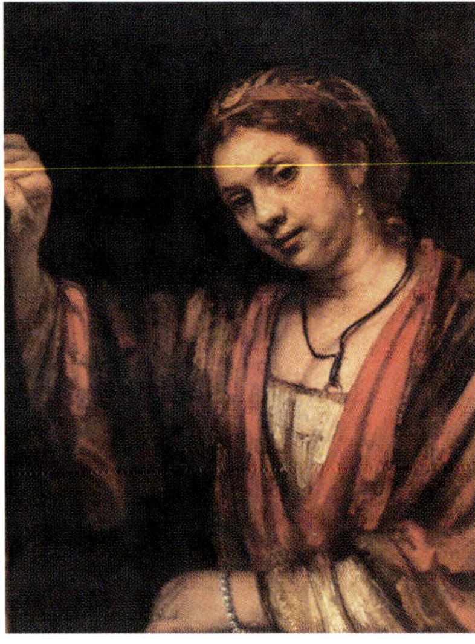

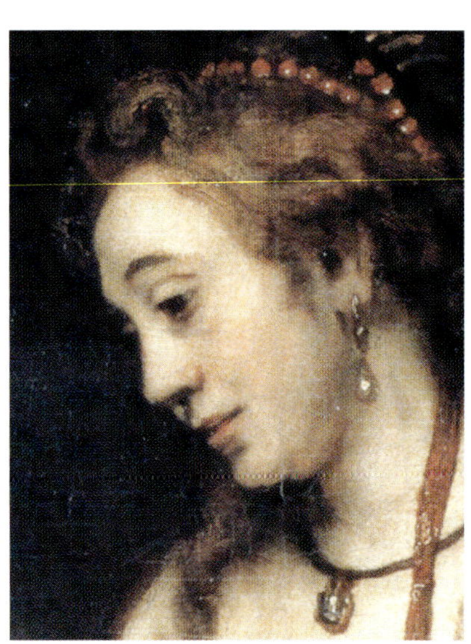

Rembrandt's desire to achieve exactly the result he wanted. These x-rays also reveal that to begin with he painted in Saskia's right hand the stem of a single blossom, perhaps an echo of the silverpoint engagement drawing on vellum and the painting of 1641. By 1642, when he completed the portrait, he had changed the flower to a sprig of rosemary, the symbol of faithfulness. One wonders whether the final touches were put to the panel after Saskia's death.

Rembrandt's meaning in *The Jewish Bride* may be experienced more fully if this more famous and well-known painting is considered with these three portraits of Saskia in mind, for the essential meaning of all four works is the same. Rembrandt and Saskia were engaged on 8 June 1633 and married on 22 June 1634. Rembrandt was twenty-seven, Saskia twenty-two. At the time of her death on 14 June 1642, a week before the eighth anniversary of their wedding, Saskia was just seven weeks shy of her thirtieth birthday.

When Rembrandt painted *The Jewish Bride* in 1666, he was sixty, and but three years from the end of his life. In the twenty-four years that had passed since Saskia's death, he had known the special love of his son, Titus; the love of his common-law wife, Hendrickje Stoeffels; and the love of his daughter with Hendrickje, Cornelia. He had also known loss and much trouble, including bankruptcy, the sale at a deficit of his house, the sale of paintings special to him, including the *Half-Length Figure of Saskia van Uylenburgh in Rich Apparel*, and even the sale and transfer of Saskia's grave plot in the Oude Kerk. And he had suffered the death, in July of 1663, of Hendrickje.

A number of likenesses of Hendrickje have survived, including the justly famous *Bathsheba with King David's Letter* of 1654, now in Paris. They reveal both respect and affection, and Hendrickje appears clearly to have been the more physically attractive of the two women, judging from these probable likenesses of each of them, Saskia in the etchings, Hendrickje the sitter for the two paintings.

Yet not one of the probable likenesses of Hendrickje seems to me to possess the glow of the silverpoint drawing or the *Saskia as Flora* of 1641 or the *Half-Length of Saskia van Uylenburgh in Rich Apparel.* The difference lies, I believe, in the love that is given in this life but once, to any man, to any woman.

And that, precisely, is what shines from *The Jewish Bride.* The man and the woman painted by Rembrandt are not "beautiful people." They are not even attractive. Their rich outfits, so gorgeously painted, are far more interesting, in terms artistic, than their faces or their pose. And all of this, I suggest, is entirely intentional, for what Rembrandt has presented is a picture of love. This pair is oblivious to us. They do not look at anything we are able to see. They do not even look toward each other.

They do not have to look at each other. They are looking into the trusting security of a love totally shared, and what they are seeing in that distant nearness, reflected in their comfortable and affectionate touching, is what draws us

The Jewish Bride, 1666, Rijksmuseum, Amsterdam

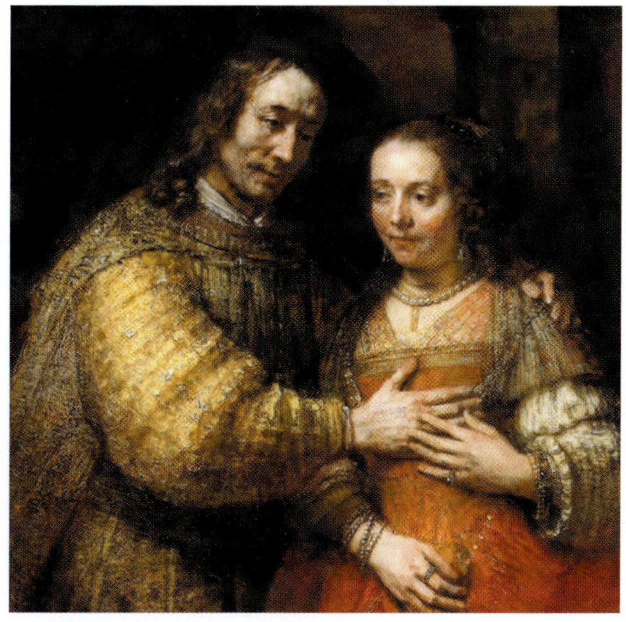

irresistibly to this wonderful picture. Those who have never known such love cannot explain the painting's attraction. Those who *have* known such love can feel its warmth and joy shining forth as if from within the work itself.

I believe that Rembrandt was remembering Saskia as he created *The Jewish Bride*. Because of Saskia, he understood what love can be. He had known and so still knew what real love means. And in this painting from the last years of his life, he worked the miracle of putting that meaning onto canvas.

As Saskia in her little silverpoint engagement drawing and in the 1641 *Saskia as Flora* is holding in her right hand a flower, and in the portrait on which Rembrandt worked for ten years a sprig of rosemary, so the woman in *The Jewish Bride* holds in her right hand the blossom of a flower. This is surely no accident, just as it was surely more, for Rembrandt, than a mere symbol of feminine devotion.

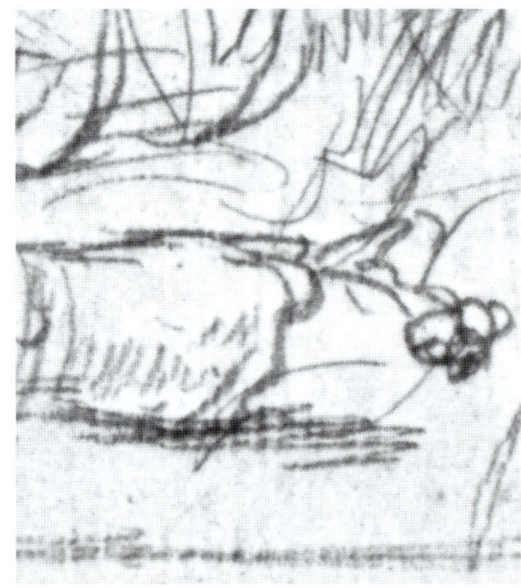
Benesch 427, detail

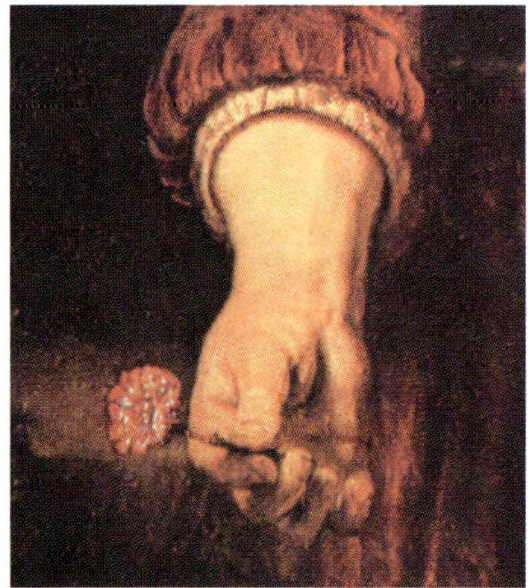
Saskia as Flora, detail

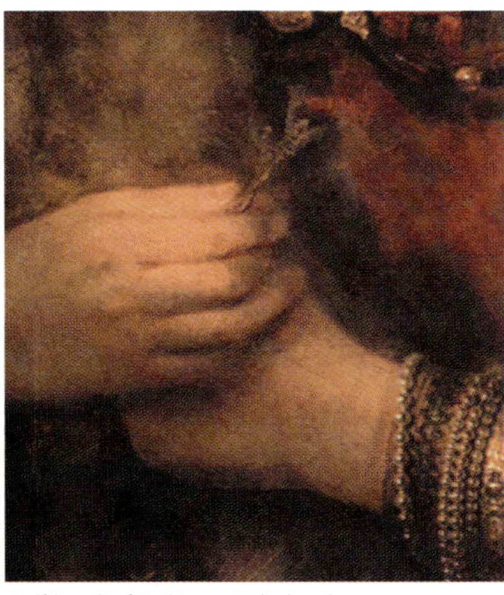
Half-length of Saskia van Uylenburgh in Rich Apparel, detail

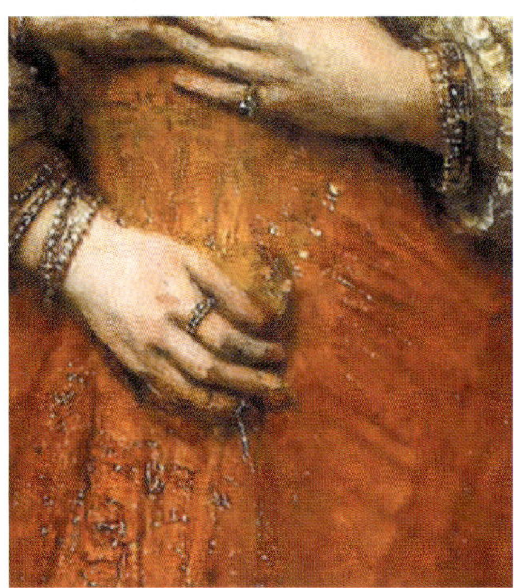
The Jewish Bride, detail

SOME SOURCES AND SUGGESTIONS

The three additional drawings that Rembrandt made of the moment when Christ was about to raise Jairus's daughter. The Benesch comment suggesting the presence by Jairus's daughter of a physician is made on page 21 of volume 1 of *The Drawings of Rembrandt.*

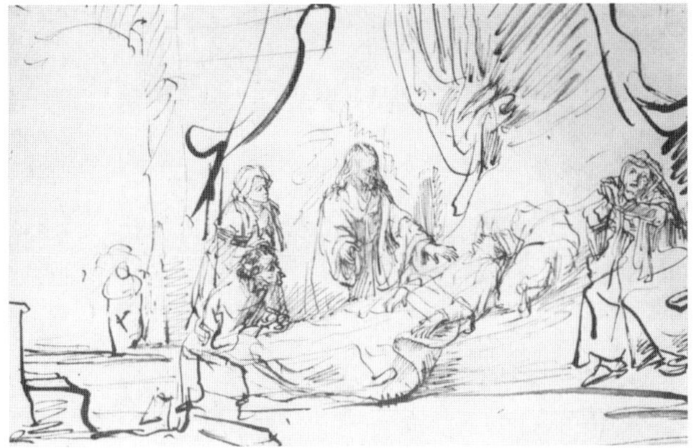

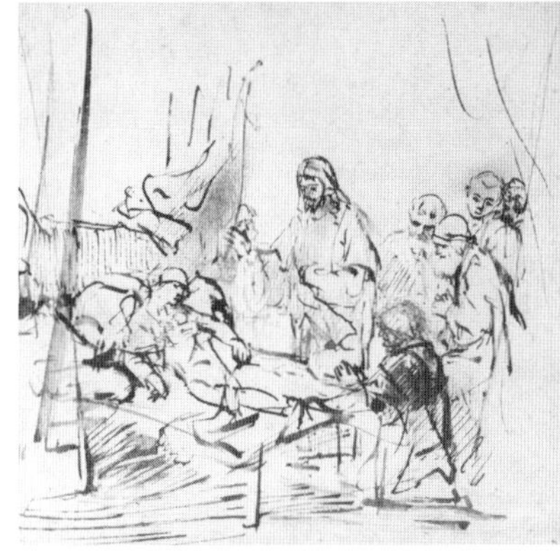

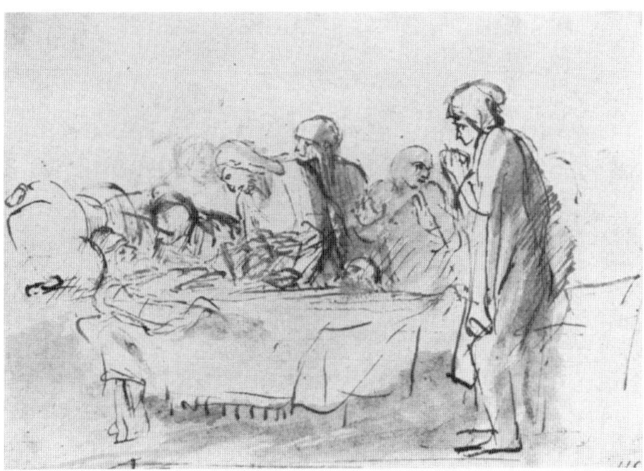

The Raising of the Daughter of Jairus, Benesch 62, 1632-1633, Berlin (private collection) (left)

The Raising of the Daughter of Jairus, Benesch 1064, 1660-1662, Kupferstichkabinett, Staatliche Museen, Berlin (right)

The Raising of the Daughter of Jairus, Benesch 1002, 1656, Kobberstiksamling, Statens Museum for Kunst, Copenhagen (below)

The seven extant letters of Rembrandt to Constantin Huygens regarding the Passion paintings done for Prince Frederick Hendrick are printed in facsimile, in transcription, and with translations in RD. They make for interesting reading, not least because they reflect the usual difficulty involved in obtaining payment from bureaucracy. The first of them was written in February 1636, the seventh in February 1639, and the order for payment, finally issued by the prince's treasurer (and also reproduced in RD), is dated 17 February 1639.

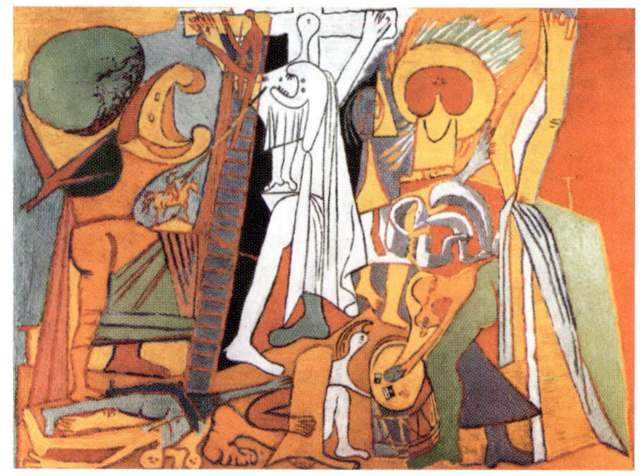

Pablo Picasso, **Crucifixion**, 1930, Musée Picasso, Paris

Picasso's 1930 *Crucifixion*, now in Paris, at the Musée Picasso (Rembrandt's spade-handle is at the far right; there are also other borrowings from Rembrandt's painting—the man with the lance among them.)

In 1990, the Rembrandt House Museum in Amsterdam mounted a fascinating exhibition titled "Picasso Rembrandt Picasso." The catalog for that exhibition provides an intriguing survey of a number of works by Rembrandt from which Picasso derived works of his own. This practice became more and more common in the last years of Picasso's life and included in particular the painting *Bathsheba with King David's Letter* and the etchings *Christ Shown to the People* and *The Three Crosses.* Also helpful is an article by Janie Cohen, "Picasso's Dialogue with Rembrandt's Art," in the catalog to an exhibition in 2000 of the Rembrandt House Museum titled "Etched on the Memory."

The discussion of the condition of *The Raising of the Cross* in volume 2 of *Corpus*, p. 316 (see also p. 280 on *The Descent from the Cross*) suggests that the "poor preservation" of the work was "probably due to some calamity about the middle of the 18th century."

On Rembrandt's self-portraits, both as self-portraits *per se* and as they occur in his "history paintings," see *Rembrandt by Himself* and the other works cited on p. 20.

Self-Portrait, 1628, Rijksmuseum, Amsterdam (left)

Self-Portrait, 1629, Alte Pinakothek, Munich (right)

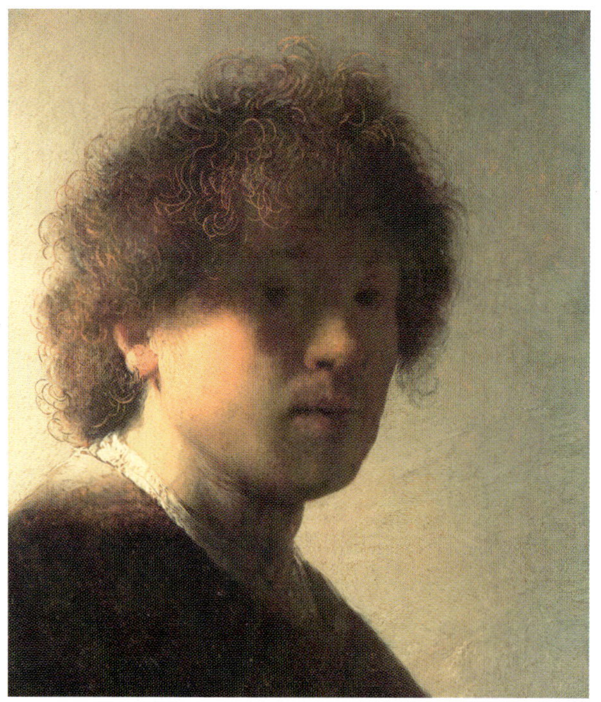

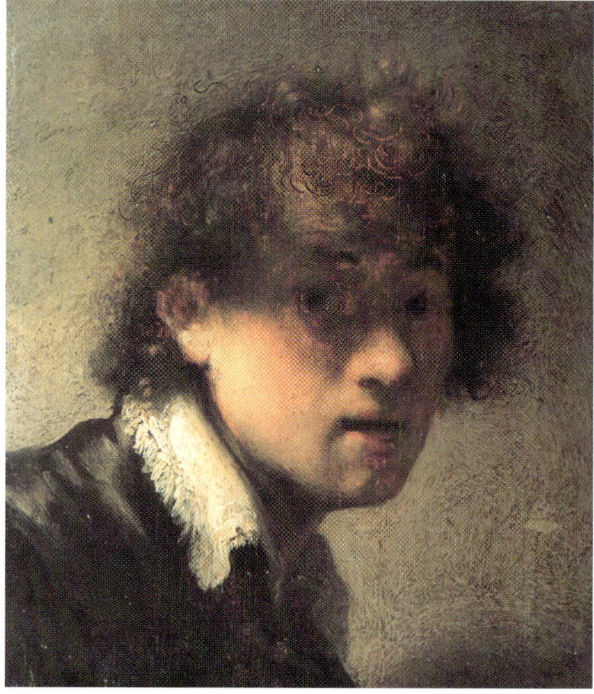

A brief summary on the mechanics of the etching of copper plates, with an extended quotation of material from the English edition of Abraham Bosse's famous treatise of 1645, is provided by Gary Schwartz in *Rembrandt: All the Etchings Reproduced in True Size* (pp. 13–18). Also very helpful is Christopher White's more detailed essay on "Technique" in *Rembrandt as an Etcher* (pp. 5–18).

A. Hyatt Major's *Rembrandt and the Bible* includes some greatly enlarged details from *The Three Crosses* (see pp. 40–41) and *Christ Presented to the People* (see pp. 32–37).

Kenneth Clark links the tall hat of the horseman in *The Three Crosses,* B 78:IV, to a medal struck by Pisanello (*Rembrandt and the Italian Renaissance,* p. 170, on which also Clark's comment about "the mechanism of the unconscious" is to be found). Christopher White's commentary on this etching (*Rembrandt as an Etcher,* pp. 77–88) is brilliantly illuminating; on page 83, he compares *The Three Crosses* to the Rondanini *Pietá* of Michelangelo.

The determination of Rembrandt to make his portrait of Saskia the special painting it became is made clear not only by the amount of time he gave to it, nearly ten years, but also by the changes he made across that period of time, particularly on his representation of his wife's face. These changes are visible in the x-ray photographs and are discussed in great detail in volume 2 of *Corpus* (pp. 423, 426–35).

On 27 October 1662, Rembrandt signed, in the presence of appropriate witnesses, a document of sale provided by Willem van Veen, notary, transferring Saskia's grave plot in the Oude Kerk to Pieter van Gerven, warden of the church. The financial squeeze prompting him to so extreme (and no doubt difficult) a step is reflected in the language of the instrument: He "let it be known that he has sold, ceded, and transferred...a certain single grave plot...[that] he has received payment and reimbursement in full...the last penny with the first" (RD, pp. 504–505).

6

REMBRANDT'S FAITH

"So faith puts a foundation under our hopes, giving reality to what we have not seen," writes the author of the Letter to the Hebrews (11:1). This assertion comes at the beginning of that long recommendation of faith celebrating those heroes at believing who "were too good for a world like this" (Heb. 11:38 as translated by C. H. Dodd).

At some point in Rembrandt's life, I believe his faith became this kind of sight, and his illustration of biblical moments moved beyond even his statements of meaning to what I call his confessions of faith.

The highly subjective, even hubristic character of such a statement, regarding what can only be speculation, is of course obvious. One's own beliefs are difficult to determine and describe, in serious and truly personal terms, and any attempt to suggest what even a contemporary and intimate friend believes is at best an iffy business. Hinting at what someone as notoriously wordless as Rembrandt might have believed, a man who lived over three and a half centuries ago and whose religious affiliations are quite unknown, may well be thought the writer's equivalent of a snipe hunt.

Yet Rembrandt is well known to have given us an unparalleled autobiography in self-portraiture, and his lifelong obsession with the Bible may surely be taken as more than mere picture-making. There are too many drawings, too many etchings, too many paintings across the entire range of his career for us to believe that the Bible was for him merely a handy source of subject matter. Rembrandt's biblical oeuvre, moreover, is quite unparalleled, both in his time and beyond it, despite his powerful influence on his pupils, of whom only a few show more than a passing interest in biblical subjects (see p. 79).

My view is that Rembrandt's biblical works, considered through the texts that attracted him, can tell us much about what he believed, just as his self-portraits can tell us much about what he thought about himself. Though he may well have turned to the Bible to begin with because his teachers did, and because the works of art he saw and studied frequently depicted biblical moments, I believe he came to do so as time passed for reasons of his own. Those reasons were no doubt related to his upbringing and his education at Leiden's Latin School, but they came more and more to be personal reasons. What began as imitative art became for him an art that took on a life, a direction, of its own. His choice of biblical moments becomes increasingly instructive, as does his progression from illustration to meaning, and ultimately, in my view, to confession.

The transitions are gradual. There is no sharp line, no moment of dramatic turning. As Rembrandt grew older, however, there is an undoubted increase of focus on biblical sequences that are less action-centered and more belief-centered, and moments that tumble with movement in their early versions become more serene in their later versions.

His depiction of the moment when Cleopas and his companion recognized the risen Christ in the Emmaus story (Luke 24) gives us, in a drawing of 1629, two very frightened disciples, rising and turning over chairs, as a blaze of light appears to explode from the face of Christ just as he is breaking the bread of the meal.

In a painting of the same year, *The Supper at Emmaus*, now in the Musée Jacquemart-André in Paris, the disciple across the table from

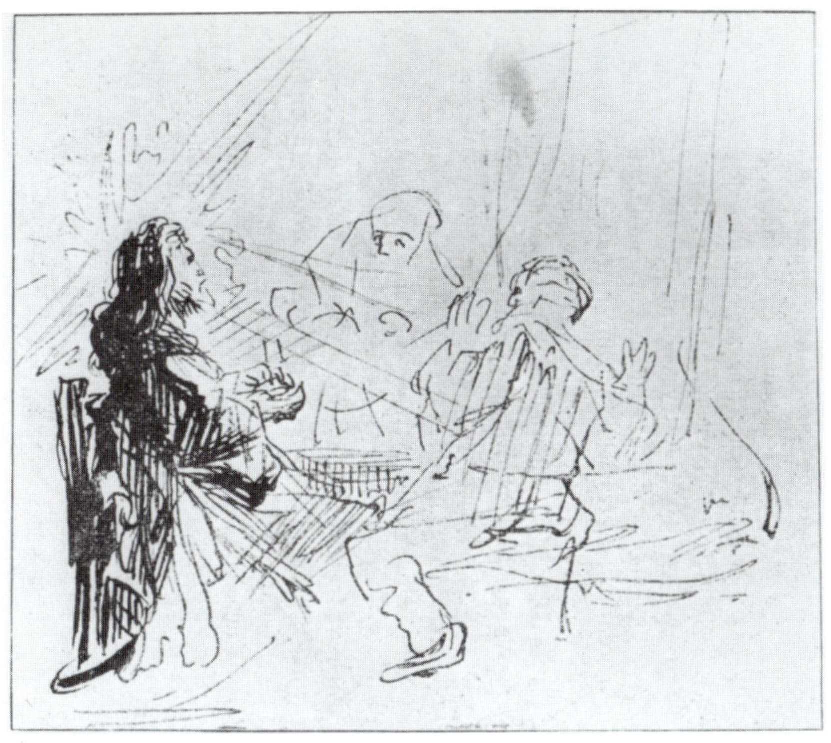

The Supper at Emmaus, Benesch 11, 1629, Fogg Museum of Art, Cambridge

Christ shrinks back in bug-eyed terror, his hands and arms thrown up as if to protect himself, while the disciple nearer to Christ has fallen to his knees, overturning his chair, and has bowed his head toward Christ's feet as if in adoration. In a room far to the back, a servant who appears to be a woman is busy, perhaps preparing the meal, and notices nothing of what is taking place. It is possible that the drawing above was a part of Rembrandt's preparation for the painting, which is a far more detailed presentation of the same composition, turned 180 degrees.

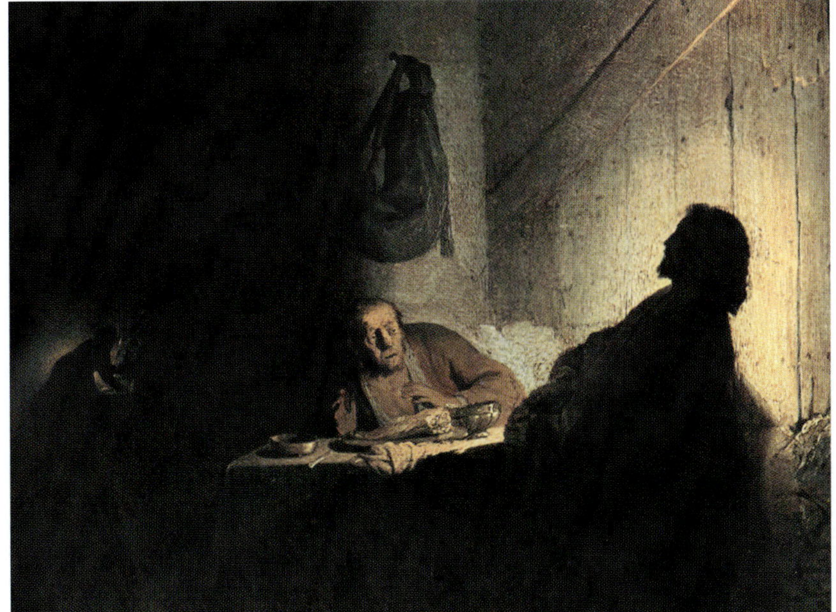

Supper at Emmaus, 1629, Musée Jacquemart-André, Paris

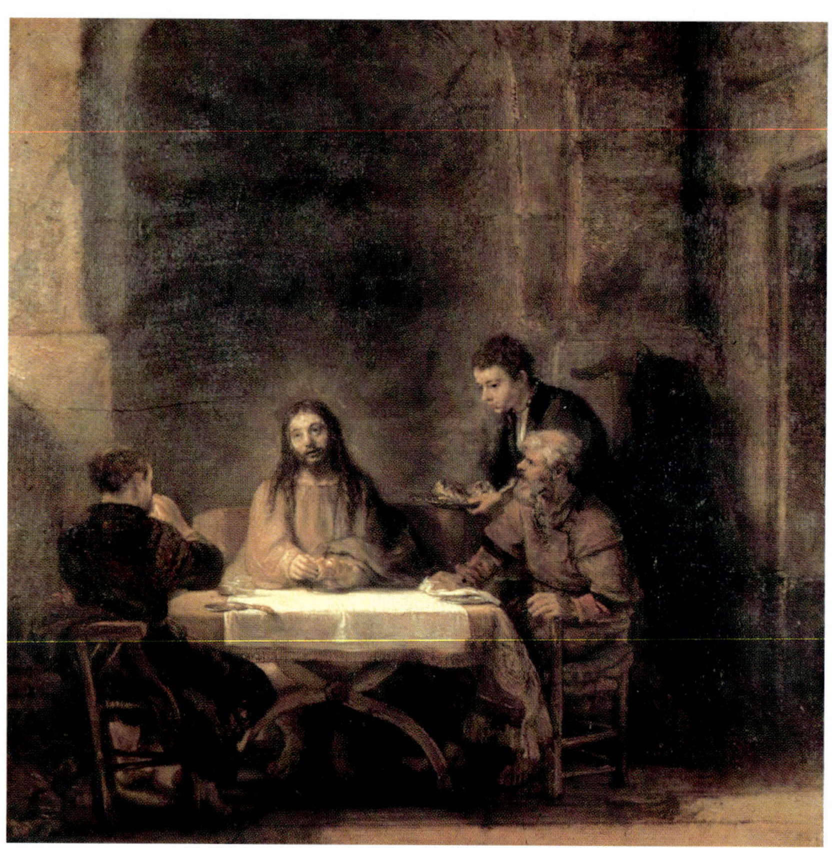

Christ at Emmaus, 1648, Musée du Louvre, Paris

In the painting of 1648 now in the Louvre, *Christ at Emmaus*, as in an etching of 1654, this same moment is calmer and more spiritual, with a softer astonishment and a heightened adoration: the disciples are still startled, but they are in awe, not fear. In the painting, the disciple on the left has a hand raised to his face in surprise, while the disciple on the right appears to be contemplating the reality, before his very eyes, of the risen Christ, one hand grasping his napkin, the other hand at rest on the chair arm. And the young servant, about to place a tray of food on the table, notices nothing unusual and is concentrating on his task.

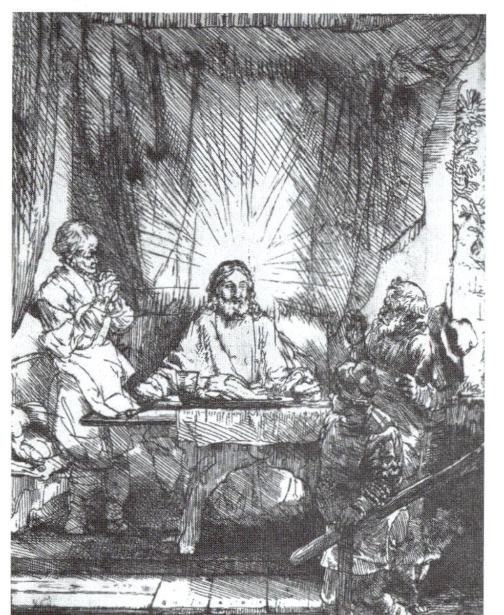

Christ at Emmaus (the Large Plate), B 87, 1654, Prentenkabinett, Rijksmuseum, Amsterdam

In the etching from six years later, the disciple on the left has risen and has clasped his hands, as if in prayer, perhaps a prayer of thanksgiving. The disciple on the right, his mouth gaped open, has raised both his hands in amazement. The servant, a much older person this time, is moving down a step, and as he does (once again apparently unaware of the theophanic moment taking place at the table), he turns to look at the disciple who has stood.

This servant is followed by another one of Rembrandt's dogs, which appears to be turning as it walks to look at something to its left. In this etching, as in the painting from 1648, Rembrandt has given us works that have much less to do with a moment of action and much more to do with a moment of recognition, exactly the note sounded by the narrative of Luke 24—as the two disciples of Emmaus reported in Jerusalem, "he had been recognized by them in the breaking of the bread" (Luke 24:35).

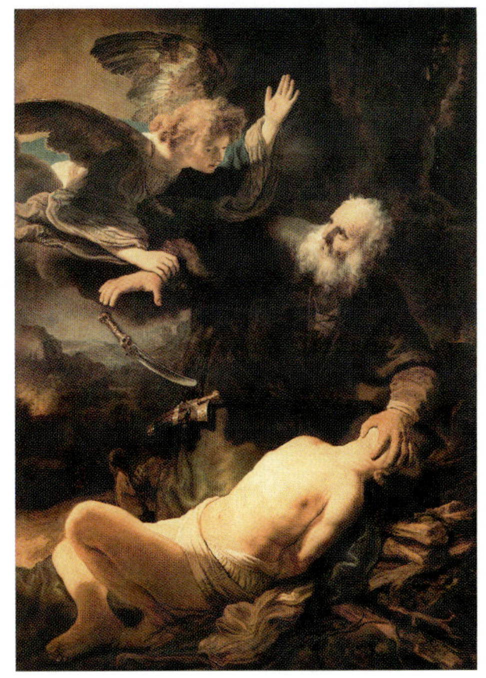

Abraham's Sacrifice, 1635, State Hermitage, The Winter Palace, St. Petersburg

A similar transition may be seen from the drama of this 1635 *Abraham's Sacrifice*, now in St. Petersburg (see chap. 4), to the much more reflective etching of 1655. Here, the emphasis is on action and emotion—the angel grabs as he speaks; Abraham turns, weeping; the knife falls from his hand through the air. Only Isaac is still, awaiting the death he knows to be coming.

The etching, by contrast, has the feel of stillness, a holy moment in "stop-action": the angel grips both of Abraham's arms, the one covering Isaac's face and the one holding the knife. Abraham turns toward this angelic interruption, his mouth open as he tries to hear and understand this new and canceling command, his body tense with resistance. And Isaac, this time not obviously bound, and kneeling instead of lying across the wood for the sacrifice, is also open-mouthed: has he too heard the words of the angel?

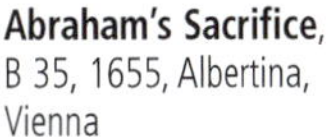

Abraham's Sacrifice, B 35, 1655, Albertina, Vienna

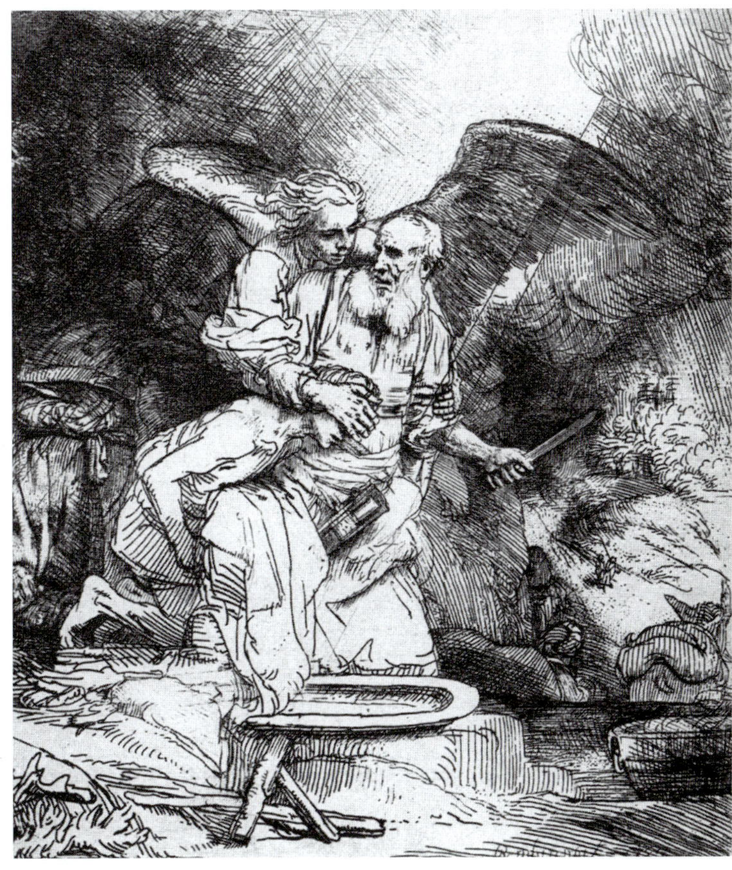

At the bottom right corner of the plate, Rembrandt has included even the two young servants and the donkey of Genesis 22:3, at a distance as ordered (Gen. 22:5), and at rest, their backs turned toward the sacrifice they never expected. And the two travelers walking in the distance beyond them also seem a part of a moment frozen in time.

Beneath Abraham, and Isaac's exposed throat, the salver that was to have caught his blood stands empty. And from above, a glow of heavenly light illumines the angelic messenger, the obedient Abraham, and the waiting Isaac. Again, Rembrandt has an inner view of a powerful story, stopping the action to suggest the meaning behind that action.

Then there is the dramatic shift from the malevolently glaring Saul in the 1629–1630 *David Playing the Harp to Saul*, now in Frankfurt, to the weeping, tragically poignant Saul wiping his tears on the drapery in the 1657–1658 painting now in the Mauritshuis Museum, currently assigned to Rembrandt's workshop rather than solely to Rembrandt. In the earlier painting, Rembrandt apparently has in mind the text of 1 Samuel 18:10–11, the second of the three accounts of David playing the harp to soothe the king's troubled spirit:

> And so it was that from the very next morning a destructive spirit of God came over Saul, so that he became distraught even at home. Then David put his hand to the harp, as he did day by day. Saul was holding a spear, and he thrust the spear, intending to nail David to the wall! David however dodged his blow, two times.

Saul sits in regal splendor above David, who is intent on the music he hopes will calm the king. David's face is turned toward the harp strings he plucks so that we see his profile only slightly. Saul holds the spear with a massive fist, and though his face is turned away from David, his eyes turn toward David, and his scowl suggests both his disturbed mind and the violent outburst about to occur.

The third account of Saul attempting to spear David as he plays the harp to relax his manic king is in 1 Samuel 19:9–10. It comes after Saul's promise to Jonathan that he will spare David's life, and following another of David's victories over the Philistines, and is described in nearly the same words as the second account, translated above. While it is possible that Rembrandt had this third text in mind, or perhaps even both of these very similar narratives, I believe the

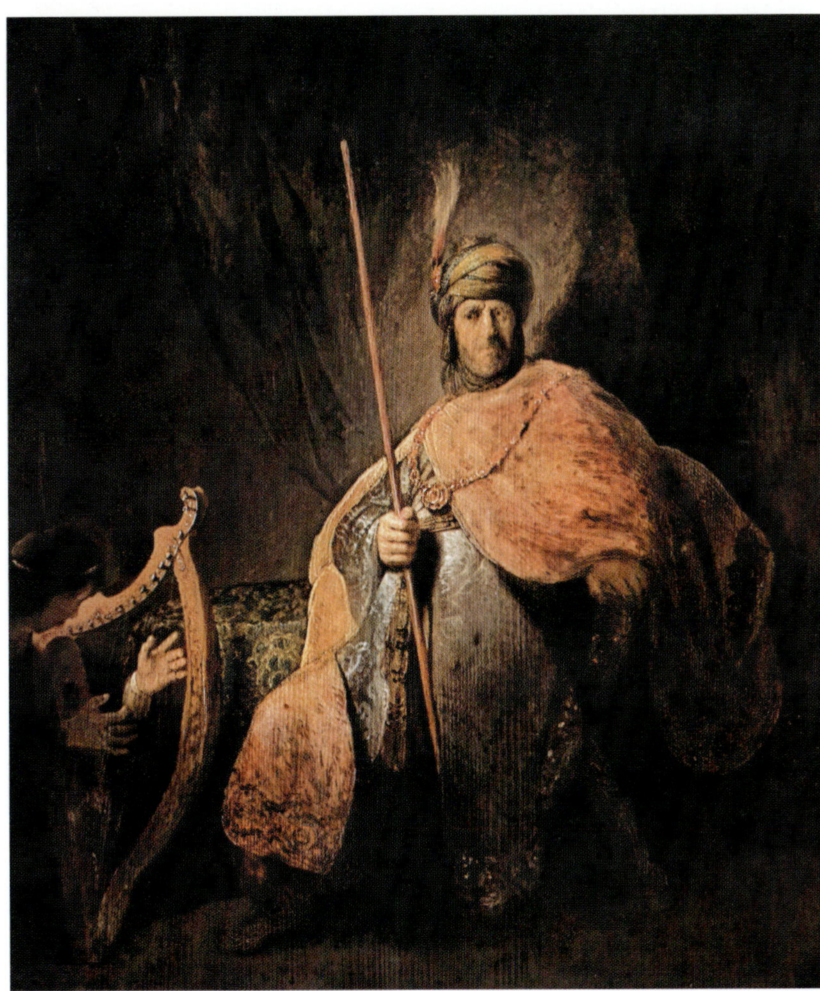

David Playing the Harp to Saul, 1629-1630, Städelisches Kunstinstitut, Frankfurt

former of the two accounts, which may carry a stronger hint of surprise, is more likely the one he had in mind.

Some twenty-eight years later, Rembrandt took up once more the David/Saul story, this time with reference to the first account of David's harp playing before the disturbed Saul, recorded in 1 Samuel 16:23: "And when a spirit from God was upon Saul, David picked up a harp and put his hand to its strings—then Saul calmed down and felt better, and the evil spirit turned away from oppressing him."

There is no reference in the passage to which this verse is the conclusion to any jealousy of David on Saul's part. The depression brought on by the evil spirit sent by God when he withdrew from Saul his own spirit has not yet found a target in David. Indeed, the young David, newly anointed by Samuel (1 Sam. 16:1–13), has just come into Saul's court at the king's request: "So David came to Saul, and stood waiting in his presence, and Saul loved him very much, and appointed him his aide." (1 Sam. 16:21)

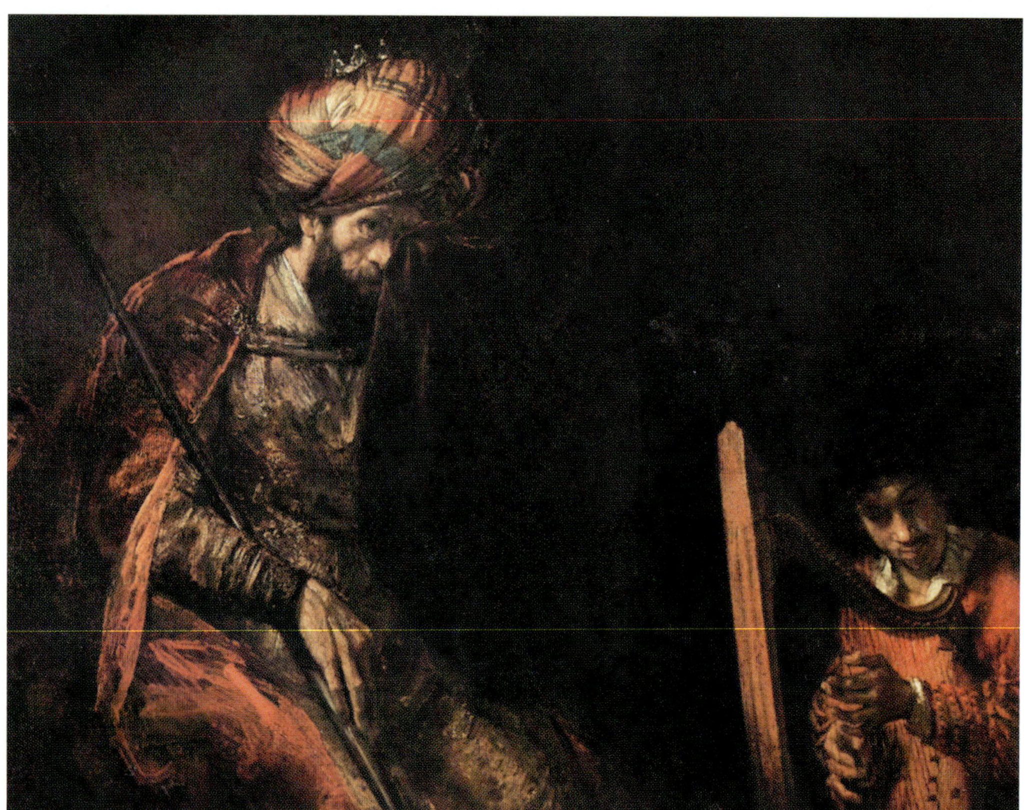

David Playing the Harp before Saul, 1657-1658, Mauritshuis, The Hague

In this later work, *David Playing the Harp before Saul*, a very Jewish-looking David (a Michelangelesque David would have made no sense whatever to Rembrandt) is intent upon his music making, but is seen this time face on rather than in profile. He is now more nearly on the same level as the king, instead of on a level beneath him. And Saul, still more regal in costume than in the earlier painting, does not look toward David; indeed, he does not appear to look at anything we can see, a recurring device of Rembrandt to suggest deep reflection. There is no grimace on Saul's face, no glare of hatred in his one visible eye, and there is about him no hint of any impending violence. This Saul is a tragic, even pathetic figure who, moved by David's music and by the grief (regret?) in his mind, reaches out and pulls a heavy curtain to wipe from his eye a tear. This is the Saul of 1 Samuel 16, who loves the young David "very much" and who is still soothed and calmed by the music of a shepherd lad's harp. The outer Saul of 1629–1630, all anger and bitter violence, has given way in 1658–1659 to the inner Saul, humped of shoulder, cradling his spear in the crook of his arm, and with his hand resting, relaxed, upon the weapon he is later to use in an attempt to kill David.

What is known of the history of this work is a history of abuse. The painting was even cut in half at one point, making two pictures, and further marred by additional revisions when it was put back together. Originally ascribed solely to Rembrandt, it is now viewed as a creation of his workshop, sometime between 1655 and 1660. I find it difficult to believe that the idea for the work was not Rembrandt's, and I think it very likely that he had a hand in the painting itself in its unknown original form. His physical involvement in the work of his pupils is well known, and he was too interested in the David/Saul narrative to have left a work produced in his workshop entirely to his apprentice painters. If we could see the work in its undamaged state, we might well agree with Abraham Bredius, who cataloged it as a work of Rembrandt, sold his coach and four to buy it, and willed it along with other works to Mauritshuis.

This list of contrasts, illustrating what may be called a transition from action-oriented moments to more contemplative moments, could readily be expanded, but Rembrandt's movement from meaning to confession may be seen more clearly still in the contrast between two etchings, one from the decade of the 1640s with one from the early 1650s.

Christ Preaching (the "Hundred Guilder Print"), B 74, 1640-1650, Prentenkabinet, Rijksmuseum, Amsterdam

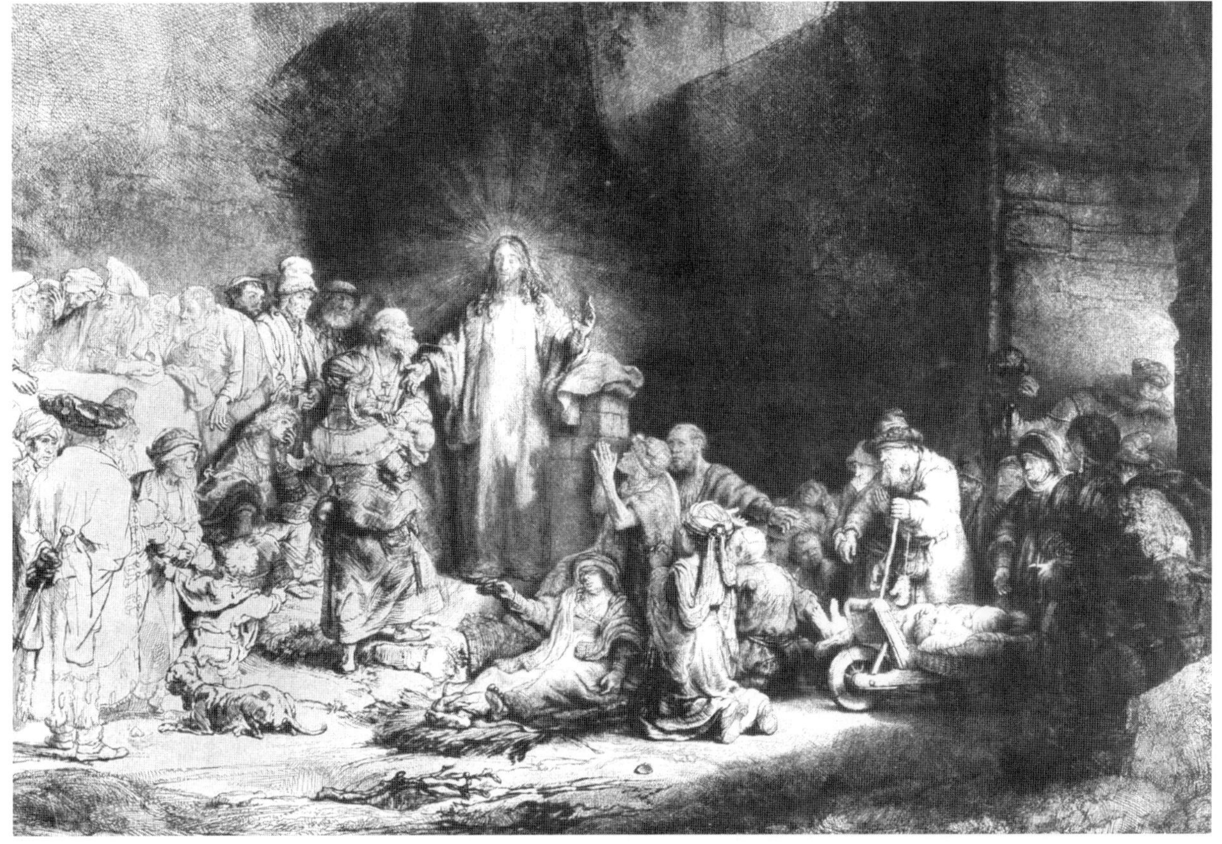

The first of these two works is the so-called "Hundred Guilder Print," a work that appears to have occupied Rembrandt, in view of drawings that reflect its gestation, for the better part of ten years. Christopher White describes it as a work that became, for Rembrandt, "a personal act of faith." In a departure from his usual choice of a biblical moment, Rembrandt presents in this work most of an entire biblical chapter, Matthew 19, and he does so in one of his larger plates.

The Pharisees, questioning Jesus about marriage and divorce (Matt. 19:3–12), are there, along the wall to the left; the children brought for Christ's blessing (Matt. 19:13–15) are there at Jesus' right hand, one in its mother's arms and one with patched trousers pulling his mother along; the rich young man asking about eternal life (Matt. 19:16–22) is there, seated at the end of the wall; the crowd pushing in to be healed (Matt. 19:2) is there, moving in from the right; and even a camel is present, in a reference to Christ's teaching about the rich entering the kingdom of God (Matt. 19:23–24).

Rembrandt omits from his plate only the dialogue between Jesus and his astonished disciples following the teaching about entry into the kingdom of heaven (Matt. 19:25–30). I have long wondered if several unexplained features of the "Hundred Guilder Print" may not in some way allude to these final six verses of Matthew 19—there is the curious hole in what is apparently the street at the bottom of the plate, with a warning branch thrown over it, for example. And there is the massive figure holding his cane behind his back in the left corner—is he one of the rich men for whom entry into the kingdom of heaven is so unlikely? Does he represent those who are indifferent to Christ or "the eternal looker-on," as Visser 'T Hooft suggested? He appears just to have entered the scene and stopped. He is barely into the moment, and he appears to be curious about this man speaking. His body is turned toward Christ, though his head is turned toward the persons to his immediate left, of whom he is perhaps asking what is going on. Did Rembrandt intend him as a representative of those in between acceptance and denial? I wonder whether he stands for those who do not yet believe, but are curious and may still come to belief. And there in front of this man, another of Rembrandt's dogs—why here?

The amount of detail Rembrandt has crammed into this plate is amazing. Yet Christ is the dominating center of every movement,

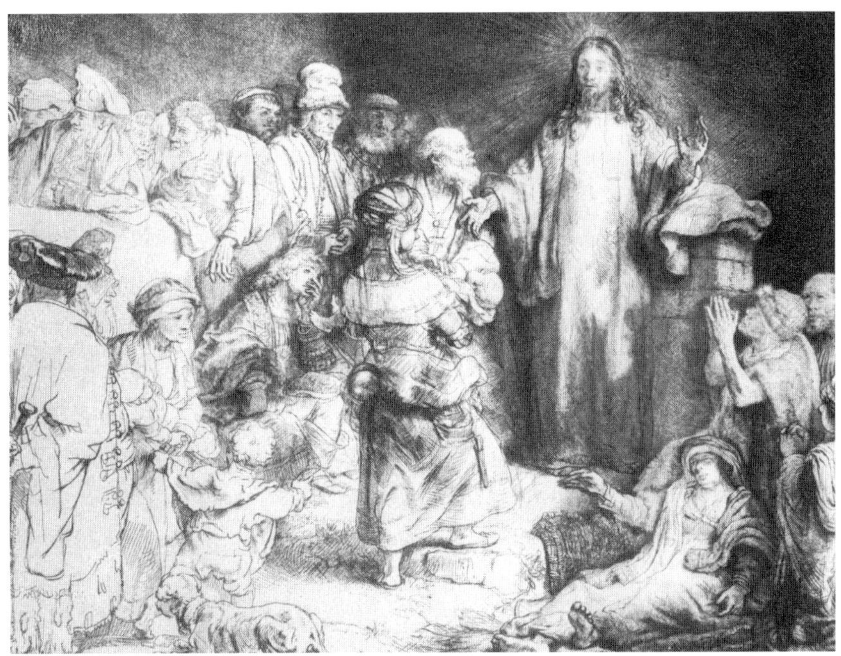

every action, every reaction, every reflection, even every apparently casual and minor detail. Every line in the etching, including even those that appear at first to head elsewhere, leads the eye to Jesus, whom Rembrandt has drawn taller than every other figure present. What appears to be a milling mass of humanity moving in a variety of different directions is pulled into a unity of composition by the figure of Christ. Light falls upon him out of darkness behind us so that we almost expect to see our own shadow across the scene, along with that of the supplicant woman whose silhouette falls onto Christ's robe. And the range of response to the teaching, preaching, healing Jesus is the range of the response of every time, our own time included. The true believers are there, in the disciples to Jesus' right attempting, with touching devotion, to protect him from both the criticism of the Pharisees and the approach of the children. Six of these followers

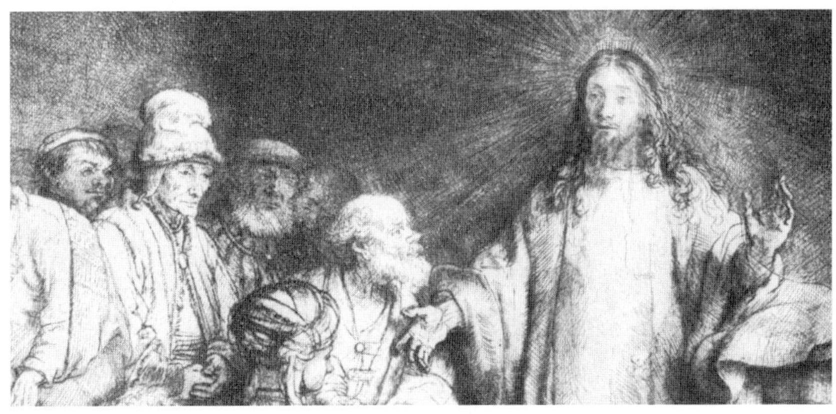

(Rembrandt himself is among them) crowd in between Jesus and his critics, with Peter reaching out a hand to restrain the well-dressed woman bringing her baby forward, and Jesus reaching out a hand to restrain Peter: "Jesus however said, 'Don't send away the children, let them approach me: for to such as they are, the Kingdom of Heaven belongs'" (Matt. 19:14).

The desperately ill are there, grasping with nervous hope at what may be to them only a long shot. They stream in through the archway at Jesus' left, a moving mass of pitiful affliction. There is the woman lying on the pallet at the feet of Christ who appears to have suffered a stroke, with her mother and her sister (consider the noses of the two younger women) pleading with Christ for help. There is the solid and well-clad man pointing with both hands toward a young man lying crosswise on a padded wheelbarrow: the young man appears to be a son, and in a touching gesture of heart-stopping expectancy, a woman who must be his mother watches Jesus for some sign of permission and reaches for the handles of the barrow surely too heavy for her to lift. There is the crippled hunchback hobbling forward with his crutch under his left arm, steadying himself with his right arm. There is the struggling old couple trying to move forward, the wife supporting her

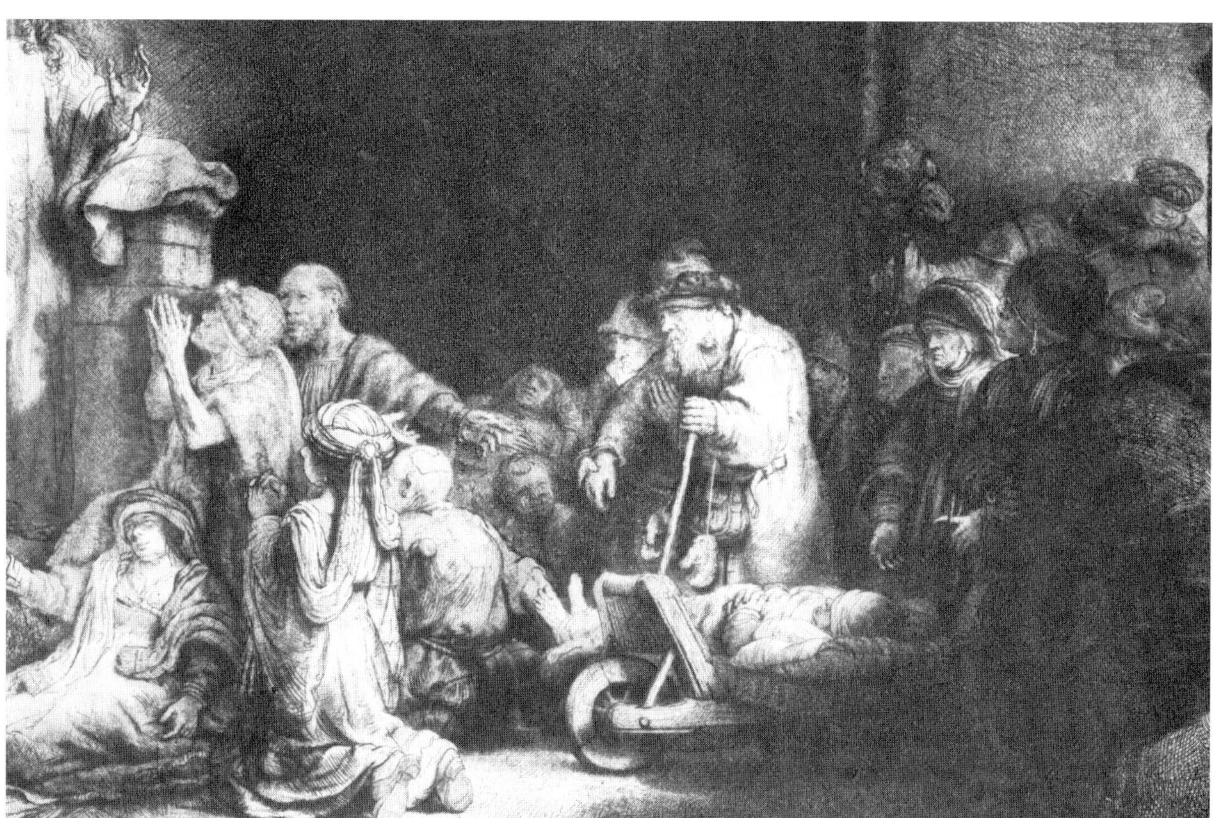

heavy husband, holding his right hand and arm as he leans with a stagger toward Christ, a testimony of the indiscriminate ravages of illness.

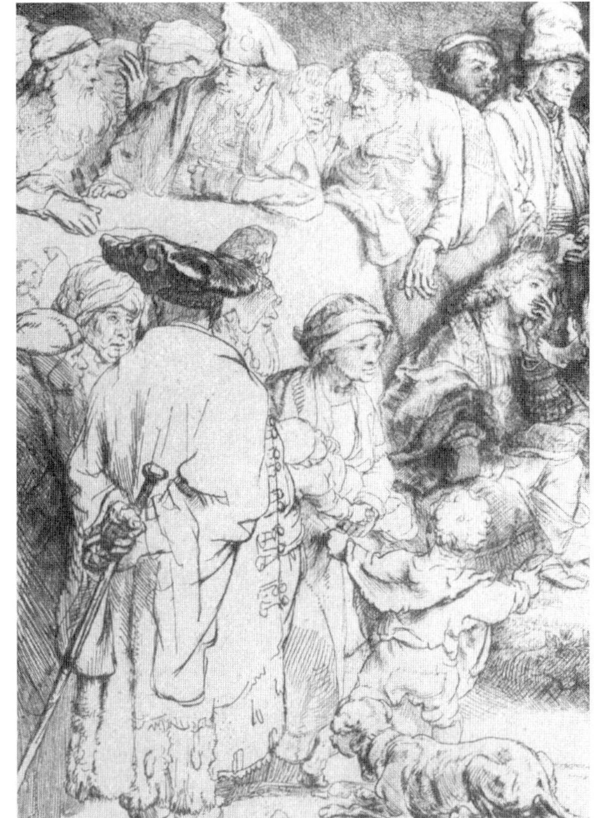

The critics and the sophists are there, huddled to the left of Christ, working on their attack and displaying expressions of both cunning in their plotting and shock at what they are hearing—one even has his hand over his face, as if the teaching of Jesus is altogether too much to bear.

The rich young man is there, elegantly dressed and coiffured, in a turmoil of indecision, placed midway between those who have decided they cannot believe and those who know that they do believe, his right hand seeming to hold his leg to the ground, his left hand covering his mouth as if he is afraid of speaking some commitment.

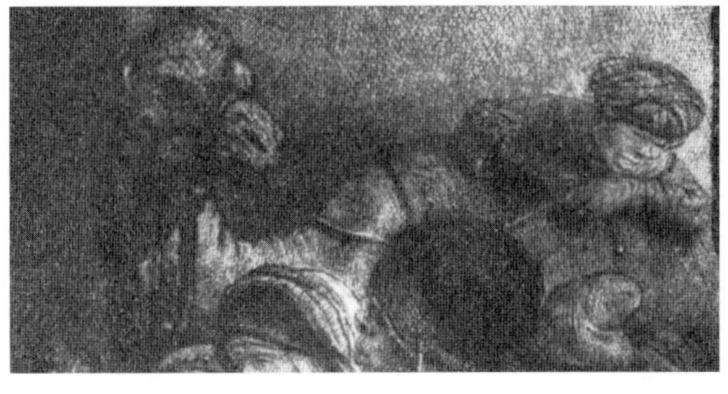

And, of course, the curious and the indifferent are there, to the right and to the left of Jesus, ranging from the massive figure with the walking staff, who is looking away from Jesus, to the grinning camel-driver who appears to be laughing at something or someone passing through the archway.

Rembrandt has presented in a single compressed scene the considerable action and movement of Matthew 19, but even so, the impression this work gives is one of serenity and contemplation, despite its undeniable action of gesture and movement. We almost seem to be looking at a tableau in which all movement and all sound have suddenly been suspended, a "freeze frame" in which every feature has become subsidiary to the significance of the person of Christ. What Christ is has become of greater importance than what he is saying and doing. We find ourselves suddenly seeing faith.

I wonder whether this incredible achievement is what kept Rembrandt at this plate for ten years. Beginning with an entire chapter of biblical narrative, he first summarized the action, with its great variety of movement. Then, as is so often the case with the Bible, the real significance of the text reached out and took hold of Rembrandt: in that moment, or perhaps in a series of moments, the Bible's confession became Rembrandt's confession. And he made everything in the plate secondary to his own statement of that confession. At the end of a long process of reflection and struggle to present what he was feeling, Rembrandt finally knew, perhaps, where he had been heading and why he could not leave this *Christ Preaching* until he "got it right."

About three years later, Rembrandt made another *Christ Preaching*, and the contrast between it and the "Hundred Guilder" *Christ Preaching* is dramatic. This time, and somewhat exceptionally so for Rembrandt, there is no particular biblical text. The movement of the earlier plate is gone; the only apparent motions Rembrandt presents are the gestures of Christ and the finger of the little boy who has abandoned his top and is drawing in the dust.

Christ Preaching, B 67, 1652, Prentenkabinet, Rijksmuseum, Amsterdam

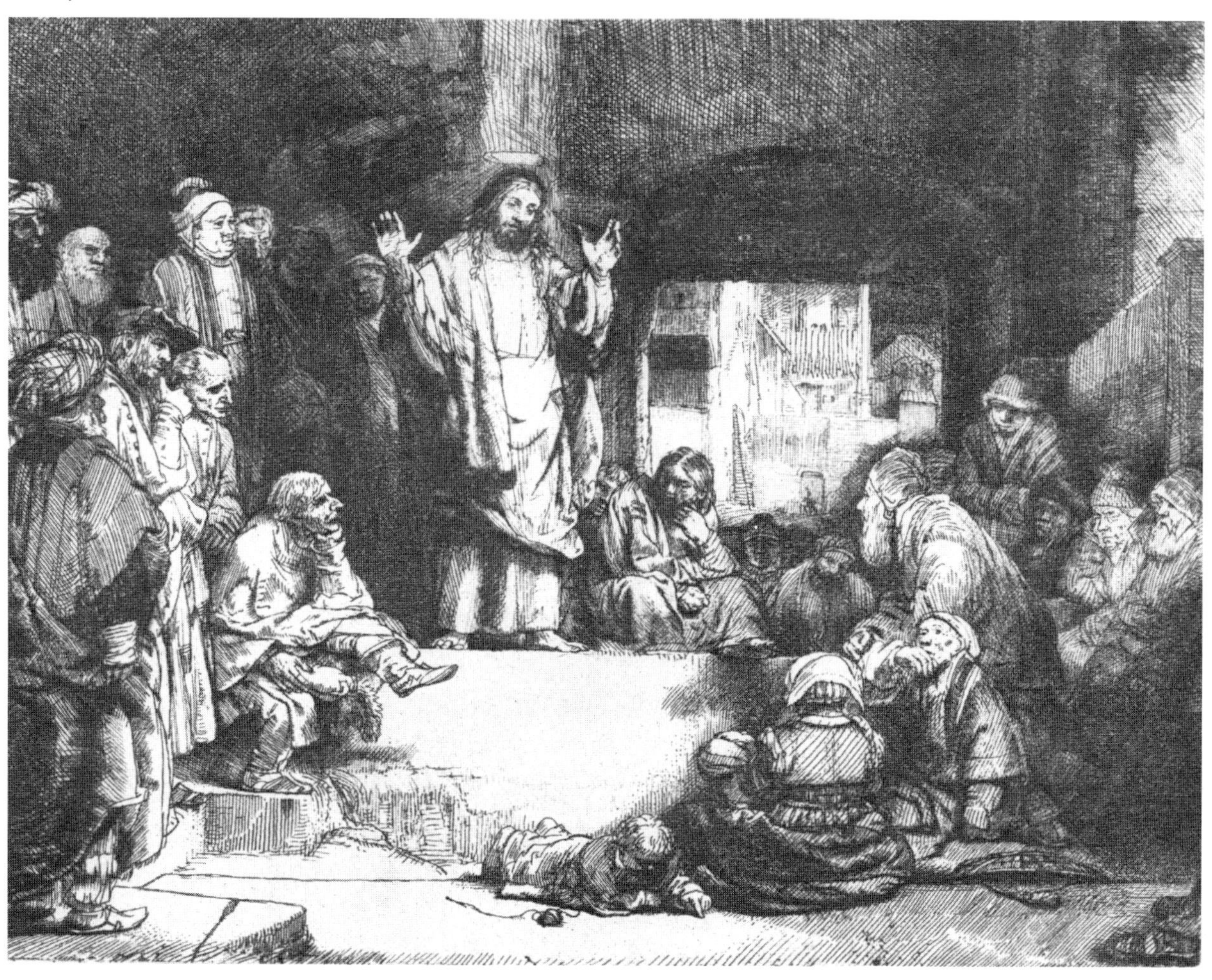

The audience is now a collection of believers, and they are drawn in postures of rapt and reflective attention to the words Christ is speaking. No one has come for miraculous healing; no one seems disbelieving or even in a struggle between disbelief and faith. There are no doubters present now, and the intensity of listening gives the impression of an embrace.

The figure of Christ is now more nearly the size of the figures of those who stand and sit around him. The effulgence of his face is much subdued. Yet Rembrandt has still placed Christ at the center of his composition, and not even the human touch of the lad with his back to Jesus is a distraction from this moment of concentration in which everyone except the little lad seems almost not to be breathing for fear of missing even one word.

Rembrandt has here come straight to the heart of the matter. In a work that is almost abstract in its concentration on faith, he presents Christ at the center of an intimate gathering. And the faith, in this version, is not the faith provoked by a miracle, or by loyalty against attack, or even by the appearance of divinity. It is the faith that sees what cannot be seen by reason, or by tradition, or by the allegiance of anyone else. It is the faith that is not the result of doctrine, or of the organizations of the church, or of the keeping of ritual observance. It is the faith of personal belief, the faith that simply knows, with no need for any explanation. In his *Christ Preaching* of 1652, I believe Rembrandt has given us the endpoint of the "Hundred Guilder" *Christ Preaching*, with a minimum of fuss and a total concentration.

Though no other biblical etching is so direct a statement of Rembrandt's faith as these two, there are others from the decade of the 1650s that must at least be mentioned in passing. *Abraham Entertaining the Angels*, from 1656, even includes a representation of God the Father, though in the guise of a patriarchal figure older still than Abraham, who was ninety-nine at the time (Gen. 17:1). As in the narrative of Genesis 18:1–15, Abraham serves the meal to God and the two angels while Sarah eavesdrops behind the door. Atypically for Rembrandt, the tent of Genesis has here become a house, and Ishmael, not mentioned in Genesis 18, leans over a wall practicing his shooting, an allusion to Genesis 21:20: "So God was with the young lad, and thus he became a man, lived in the wilderness, and became an expert archer."

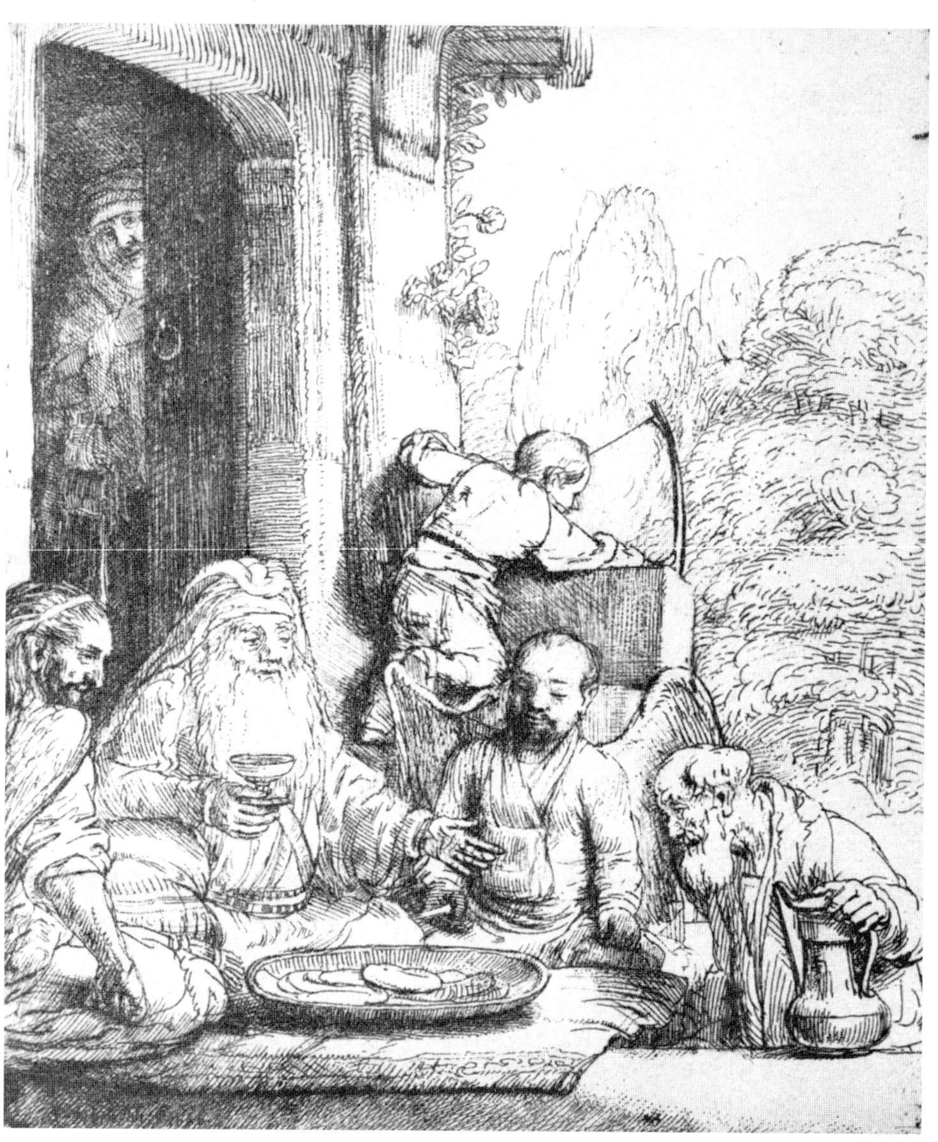

Abraham Entertaining the Angels, B 29, 1656, Prentenkabinet, Rijksmuseum, Amsterdam

There is no mistaking the figure of God in this etching—he presides over the meal Abraham is serving, speaking to Abraham, who bows in an appearance of astonished obeisance. The meal itself, with the chalice in God's hand and the tray of flat bread, resembles a Communion meal, and Rembrandt's presentation of this holy moment has a reverence that goes beyond narrative alone.

From 1654 there is *The Adoration of the Shepherds with the Lamp*, a glowing nativity plate. The awestruck shepherds ease into the stable and bask in the brightness of this divine child, while Mary lifts her cloak tenderly to show him off and Joseph, sitting on an overturned wheelbarrow, presents this son with a gesture and an expression of

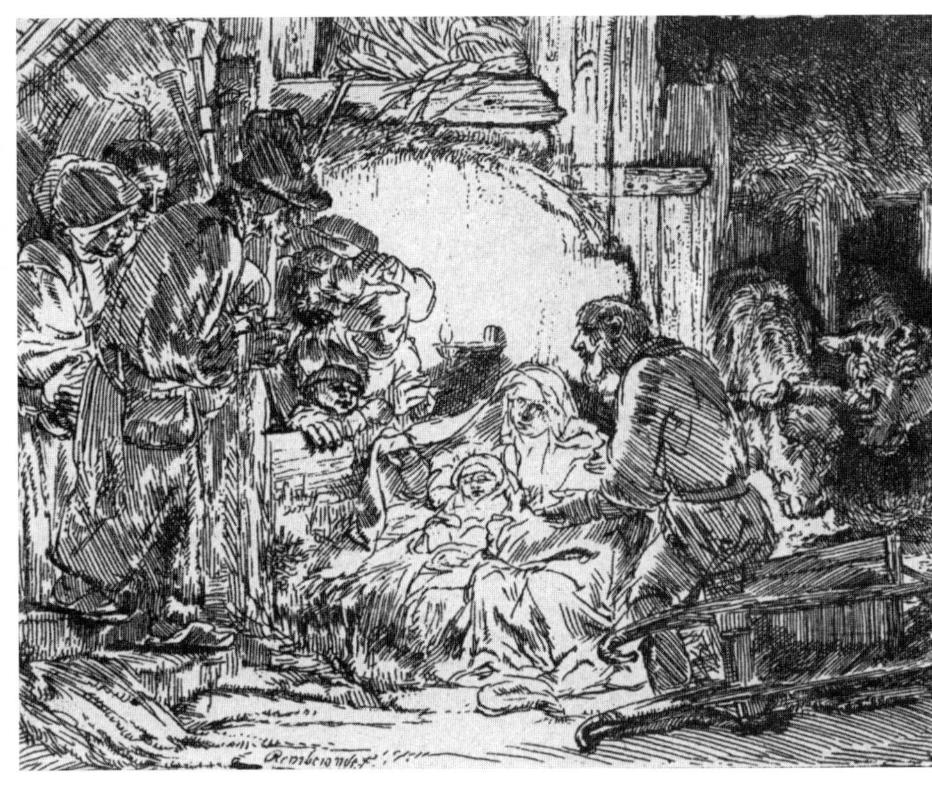

The Adoration of the Shepherds with the Lamp, B 45, 1654, Prentenkabinet, Rijksmuseum, Amsterdam

weary humility. The shepherd boy peeping over the edge of the manger and the cows quietly munching add somehow to the holiness of the moment.

The imperfectly etched *Christ Disputing with the Doctors* from 1652 and a more finished plate on the same theme from 1654 also suggest this quality of astonished awe, though without the hush of silence of *The Adoration of the Shepherds with the Lamp.*

Here, the lad Jesus is responding to the learned teachers (see next page), and there is a buzz of amazement going around those nearby who listen in on the conversation, while some skeptics above on the right show finger-wagging disapproval. Rembrandt gives us a young Jesus wholly caught up in the dialogue, without the least appearance of intimidation or distraction (or divinity: precisely the point of the learned teachers' astonishment).

The face of Jesus is the same in *Christ Returning from the Temple with His Parents* from 1654, a moment farther along in the narrative of Luke 2:41–52 when the lad answers the parental rebuke with a kind of calm, even surprised innocence, "But why were you looking for me? Didn't you know that I was sure to be in my Father's house?" (v. 49)

Christ Disputing with the Doctors: A Sketch, B 65, 1652, British Museum, London

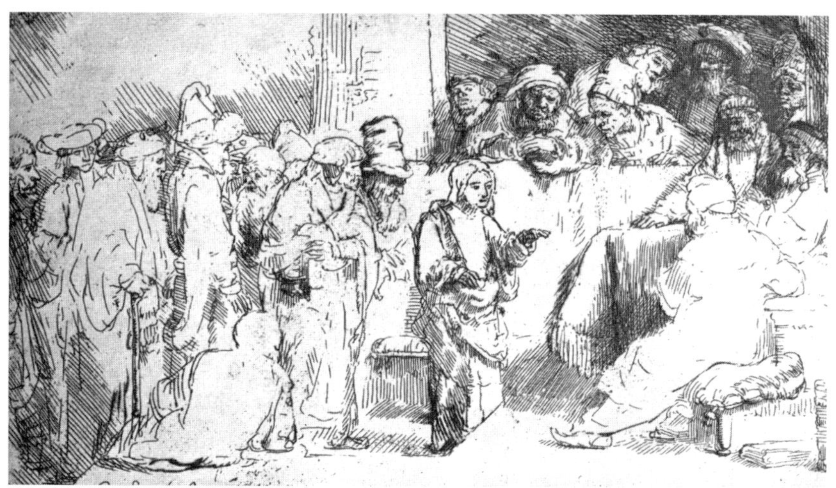

Christ Disputing with the Doctors, B 64, 1654, Teylers Museum, Haarlem

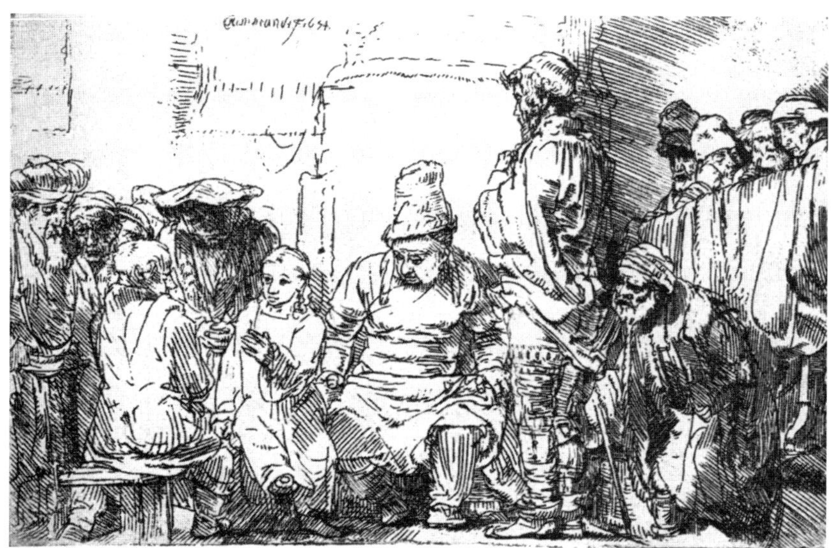

Christ Returning from the Temple with His Parents, B 60, 1654, Teylers Museum, Haarlem

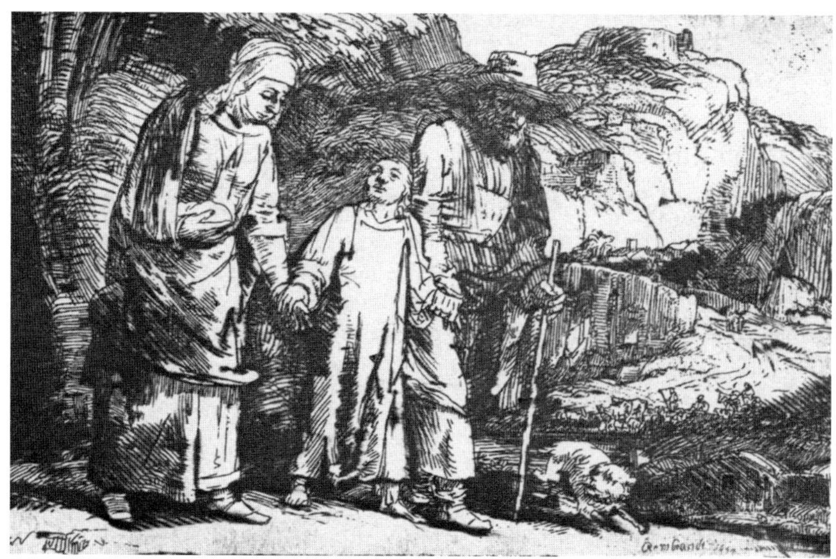

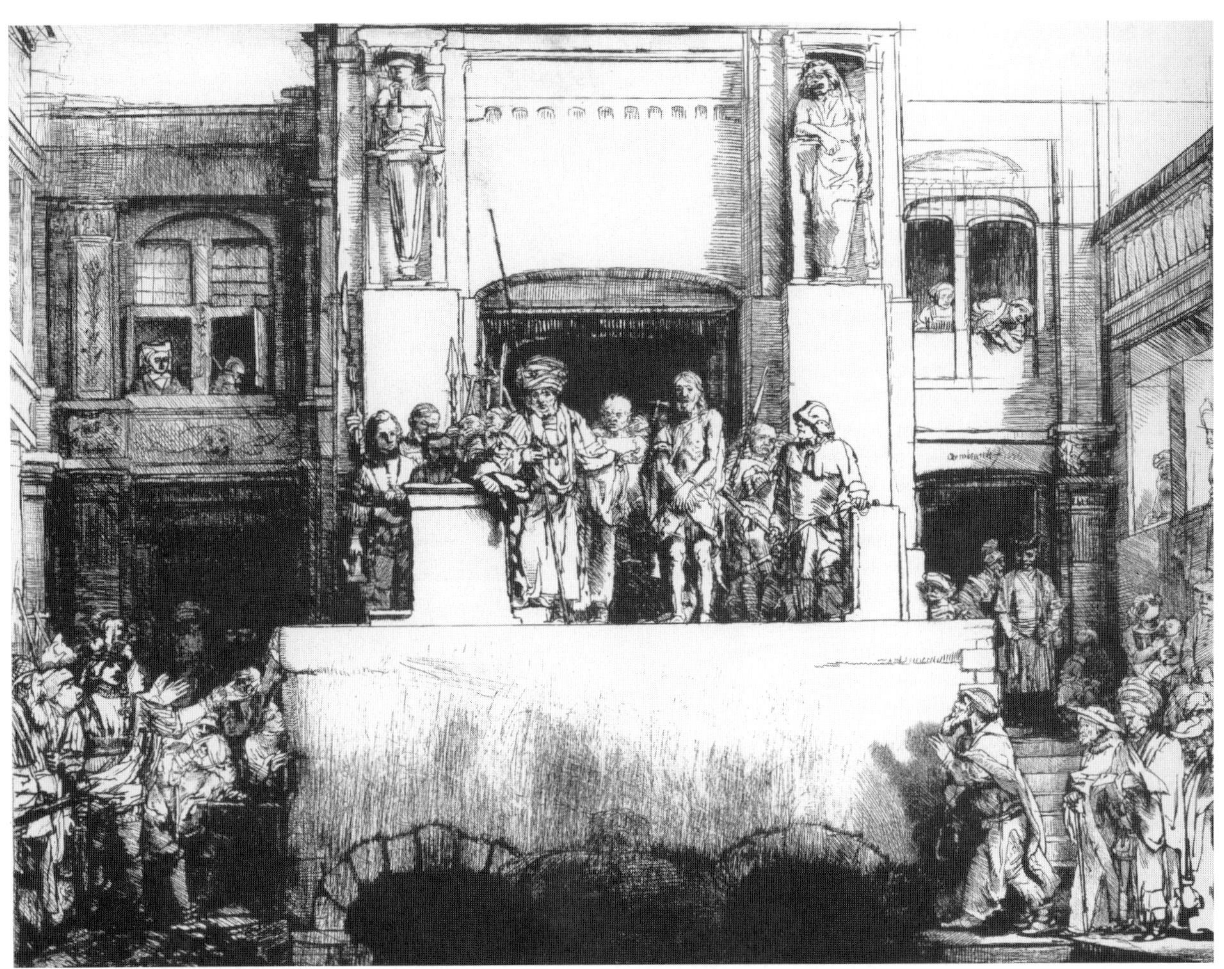

Christ Presented to the People, B 76:VIII, 1655, Prentenkabinet, Rijksmuseum, Amsterdam

Running ahead and turning with an adoring look at his young master is still another of Rembrandt's dogs, that repeated presence in so many of his biblical works.

Rembrandt gives us in these works a boy, but a boy who is already Christ. In the temple, his hands make gestures of explanation. On the road, one of his hands is grasped by Joseph, holding on to this son he has back and does not intend to lose again; his other hand holds his mother's hand, as if to comfort her, and her face bears the expression of Luke 2:51d: "And his mother kept all these matters as a treasure in her heart."

I have referred already to the astonishing clarification Rembrandt brought to his *Christ Presented to the People* of 1655 (see chap. 5). The final four of the eight states of this etching are clearly an attempt to achieve the single-minded, concentrated focus of *The Three Crosses.* That Rembrandt did not achieve this goal does not in any way reduce the overwhelming sense of sadness surrounding this Christ, bound

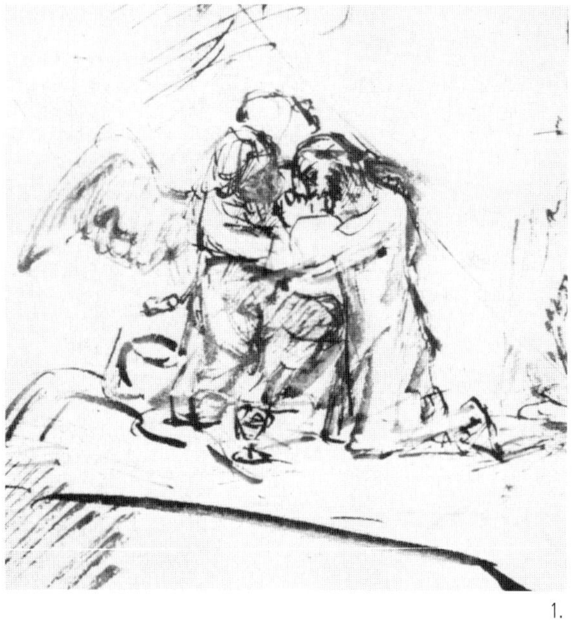

1.

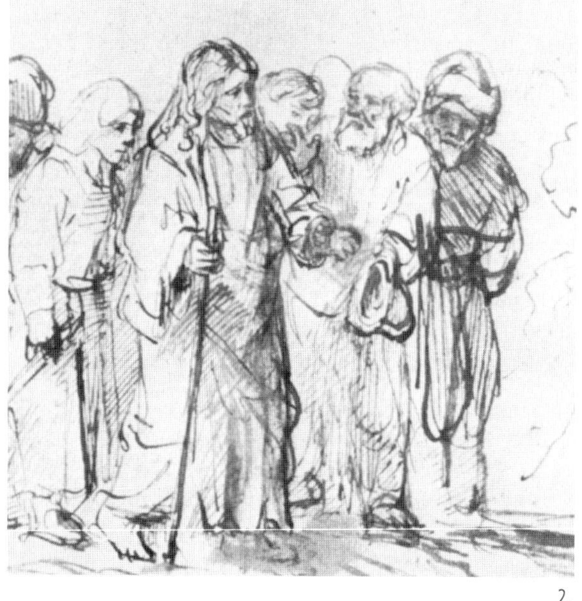

2.

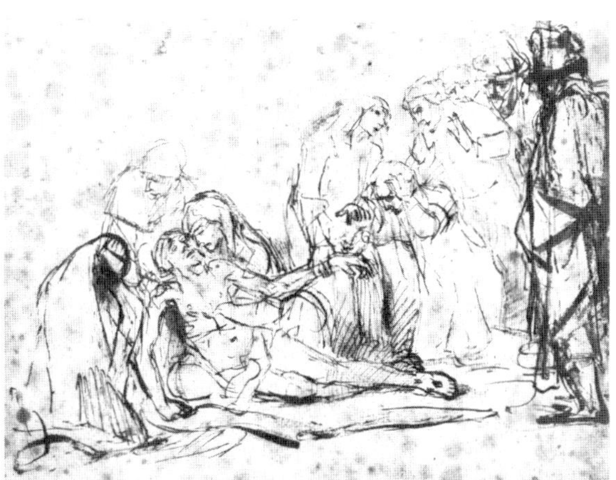

3.

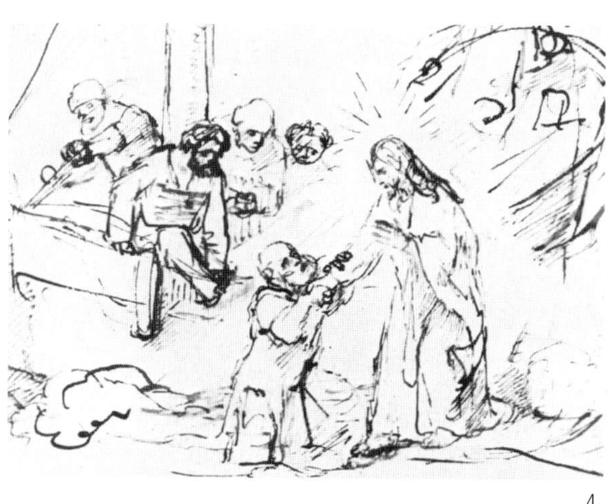

4.

1. **Christ Consoled by the Angel**, Benesch 899, around 1652 Kunsthalle, Hamburg, detail

2. **Christ and the Canaanite Woman**, Benesch 921, 1652-1653, private collection? (Sold by Sotheby's, London, 4 December 1969), detail

3. **The Lamentation for Christ**, Benesch 883, 1651-1652, Wessenberg Gallery, Constance (Germany)

4. **Christ Walking on the Waves**, Benesch 1043, 1659-1660 British Museum, London, detail

and nearly naked, standing on what feels like the edge of an abyss, and surrounded by an array of detractors.

There are many drawings that are radiant with what can only be Rembrandt's emotional belief in what he was depicting, in particular the large number of drawings dealing with the Passion and the resurrection. The gripping pain of Rembrandt's thoughts on Christ's scourging and crucifixion, the pathetic tenderness of the drawings of the deposition, and the blazing light of the resurrection sequence are not the creation of a mind and a hand simply making pictures.

I think, for example, of the tender gesture of the angel comforting a distraught Christ in the garden of Gethsemane (Luke 22:41–44). Or the poignancy of the grief of Jesus' mother and the two Marys echoed by the devastation and disbelief of the disciples over his dead body. Or the panic of Peter sinking and the saving grasp and the gentle admonition of Christ walking on the water of the Lake of Galilee. Or the absorbed concentration of the disciples walking along with Jesus as he teaches them.

Among the biblical paintings of the final decade and a half of Rembrandt's life, a number may be mentioned as reflecting his experience of faith. In a way, indeed, no work on a biblical theme from Rembrandt's later years can be said to be devoid of a sense of belief, belief that sustained him amidst trouble and grief, and belief that raised his considerable genius to transcendent levels.

Bathsheba with King David's Letter, 1654, Musée du Louvre, Paris

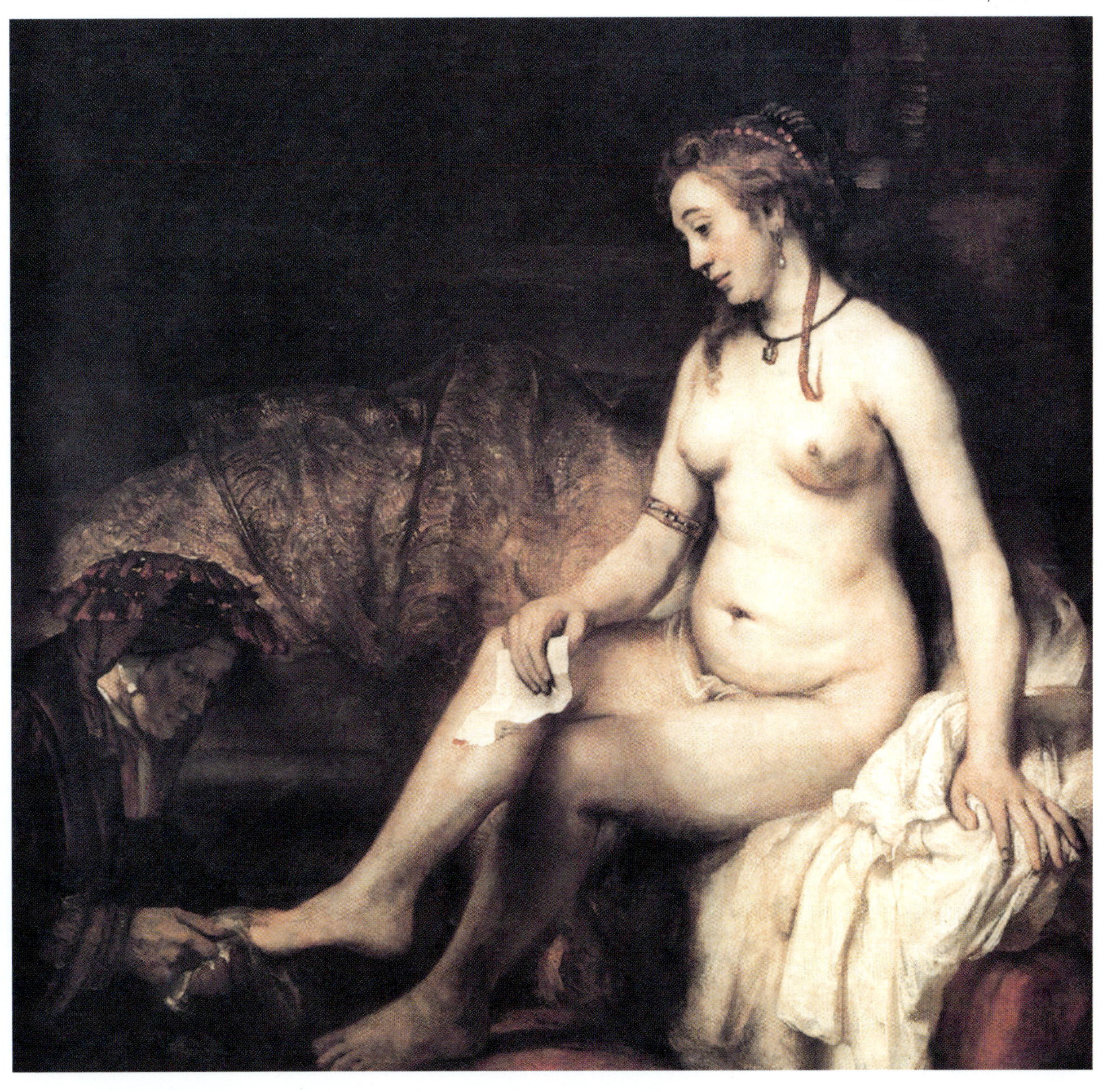

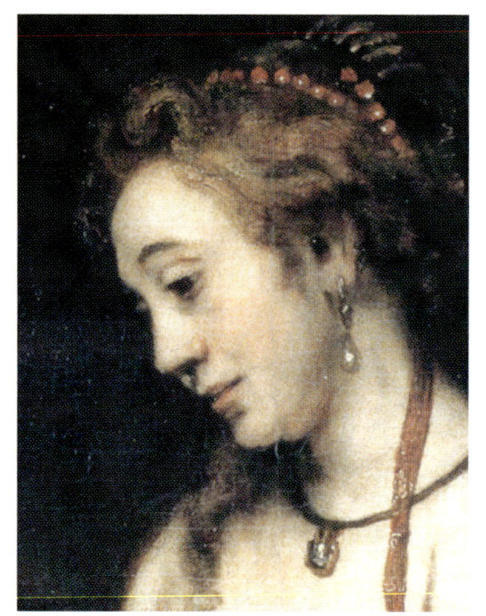

The luminous *Bathsheba with King David's Letter* of 1654, now in the Louvre, may well attest to Rembrandt's perception of biblical narrative as parallel to his own life. X-ray photographs reveal that he labored to achieve in Bathsheba's face exactly the correct expression of regret and resignation, and perhaps also the pride of being chosen.

Some part of Rembrandt's depiction of Bathsheba's reflection on what she is about to do may well have come from Rembrandt's own reflection on his personal experience with Hendrickje Stoeffels, who was probably the model for this painting. I think it likely that Rembrandt felt both guilt and inevitability about his liaison with Hendrickje. And guilt and inevitability peer into the distance from his Bathsheba's face—she is not looking at anything we can see in the painting, or at anything any eyes save hers can see.

Rembrandt's confession of guilt may be clearer still in a painting of 1660, *The Apostle Peter Denying Christ*, now in Amsterdam. Peter, who had sworn to die rather than betray Jesus (Matt. 26:35), is depicted in the moment of the first of his three denials. Confronted

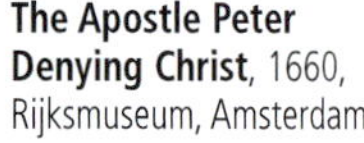

The Apostle Peter Denying Christ, 1660, Rijksmuseum, Amsterdam

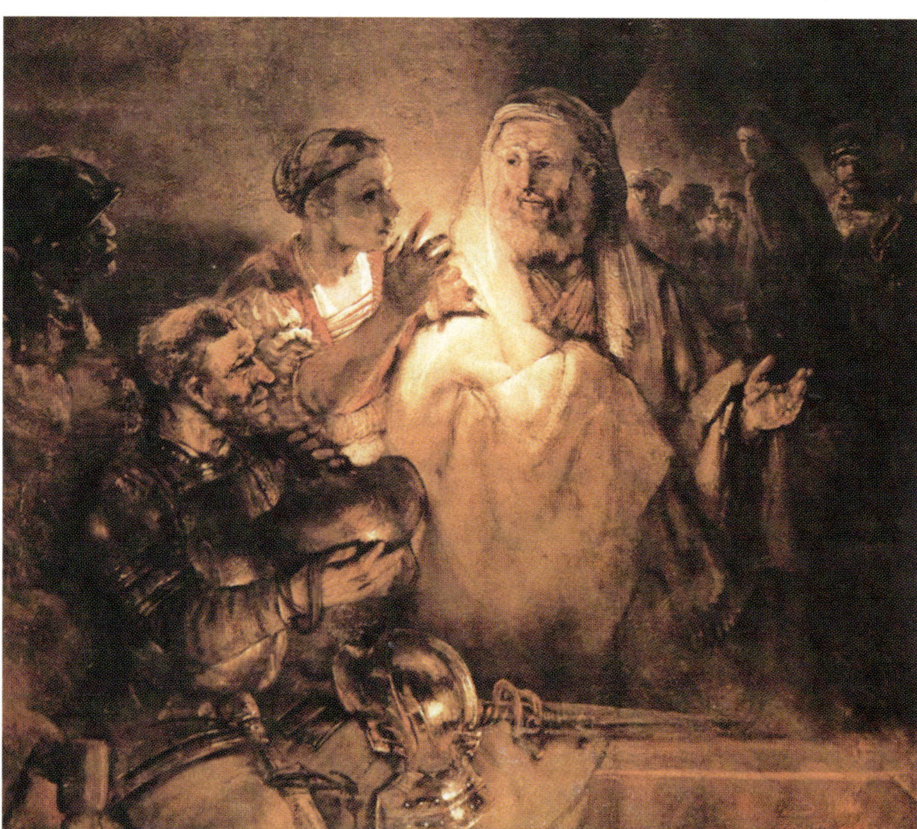

by a maid who recognizes him as one of Jesus' followers, Peter lies, pretending ignorance (Matt. 26:60–70). Rembrandt presents the maid, illuminating Peter's face with a candle, two soldiers looking with suspicion as Peter speaks, and Christ in the distance, his hands bound behind him, turning to look at Peter, whose denial he has predicted (Matt. 26:34). Peter's face is turned away from Christ, and he gestures with his left hand, but his expression suggests no defiance. It has the same pensive guilt, the same look beyond the moment into memory and prospect, as the 1654 *Bathsheba with King David's Letter*. Rembrandt has confronted the account of Peter's denial as every believer must. We have all "fallen away" at one time or another, and sometimes again and again.

From 1656, there is a moving *Jacob Blessing the Sons of Joseph*, now in Kassel. The nearly blind old Jacob—and how sympathetically Rembrandt always represents blindness—reaches out to give his blessing to Manasseh and Ephraim in the presence of their parents,

Jacob Blessing the Sons of Joseph, 1656, Staatliche Kunstsammlungen, Schloss Wilhelmshöhe, Kassel

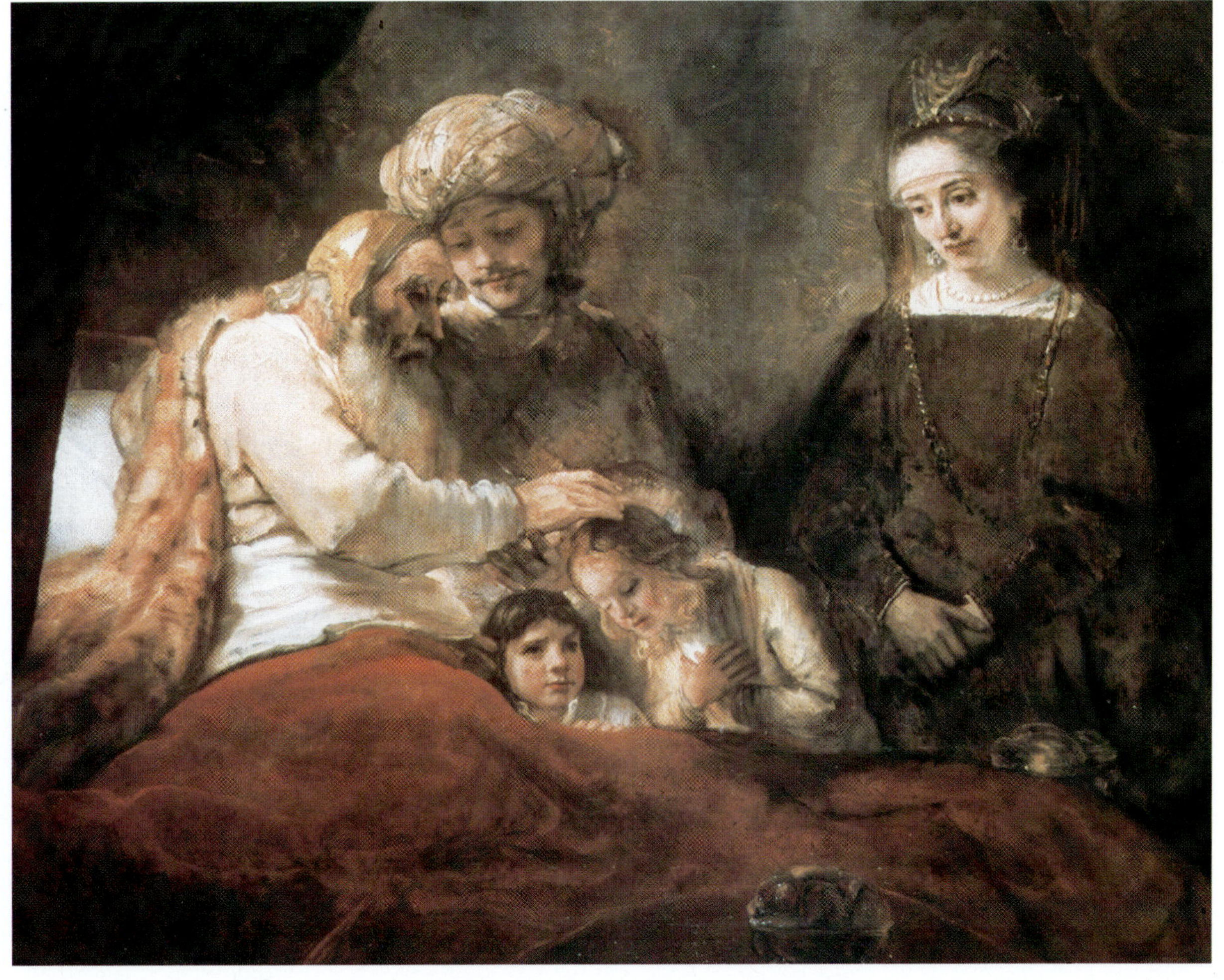

Joseph and Asenath. Jacob has reached out his right hand to Ephraim, the second-born son, and Joseph, assuming this to be a mistake of his father's failing vision, reaches out his left hand to guide the blessing hand to the correct son, the firstborn Manasseh (Gen. 48:17). Rembrandt has made Joseph's gesture of correction a gentle one, just as Jacob's hand is about to touch Ephraim's head. This is a Joseph who trusts his father's intention and who watches his sons with tender affection, as does their mother, not mentioned as present for this moment of blessing in the text of Genesis.

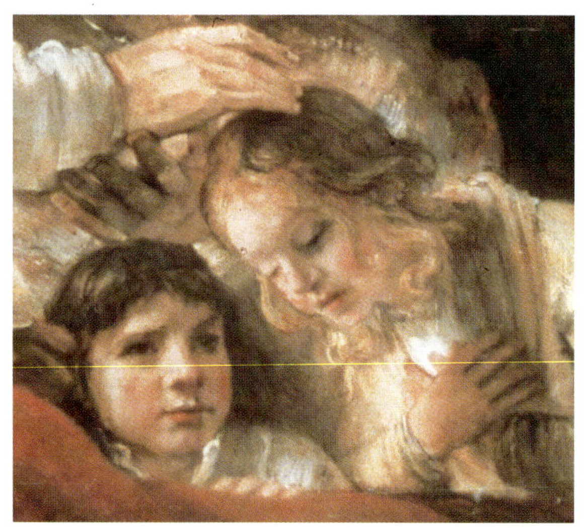

The fingers caressing Manasseh's hair just above the red covering, usually said to be Jacob's in a sort of second-best blessing, may perhaps better be seen as the fingers of Joseph's right hand, given his position so close to Jacob, and thus another gesture of correction, in parallel to that of his more visible left hand. Joseph, seeking to guide his old father's right hand with his left hand, is thus also with *his* right hand nudging Manasseh's head nearer, at the same time, to the blessing hand of his grandfather.

Rembrandt has given us an intimate family moment, a kind of ideal family leave-taking and lean into the future that in 1656 he must have felt had all but slipped from his own life irretrievably. The faith of this peaceful painting is no protest, however, but rather the assurance that there will be blessing, beyond every trouble, for no two biblical characters made more mistakes and suffered more for them than Jacob and his spoiled love-son Joseph. Both tenderness and hope shine in this lovely work. It had just been cleaned when I saw it in 1984, and I found it a hypnotic testament of Rembrandt's serenity amidst the troubles that pressed him in the 1650s.

A series of representations of the twelve apostles, identified as such by W. R. Valentiner in the 1920s, may also be said to reflect Rembrandt's belief in what may be called the faith of real life. Though some of these apostle paintings are now lost, and some can no longer be identified, those that remain present what Christian Tümpel called "exalted moods," and also what Simon Schama has so aptly termed

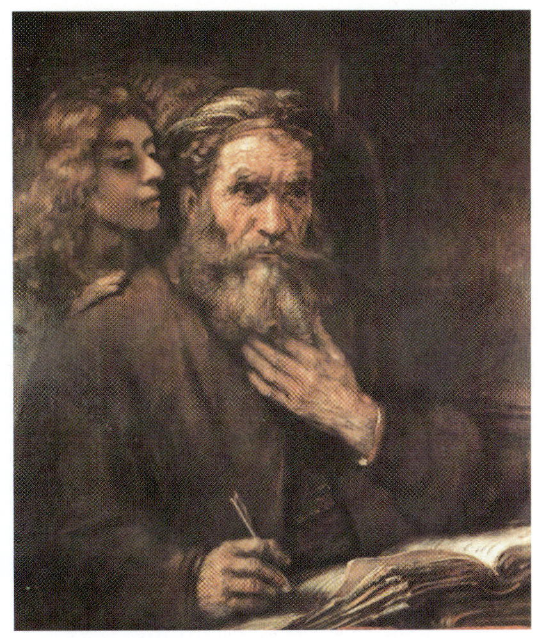
The Apostle Matthew, 1661, Musée du Louvre, Paris

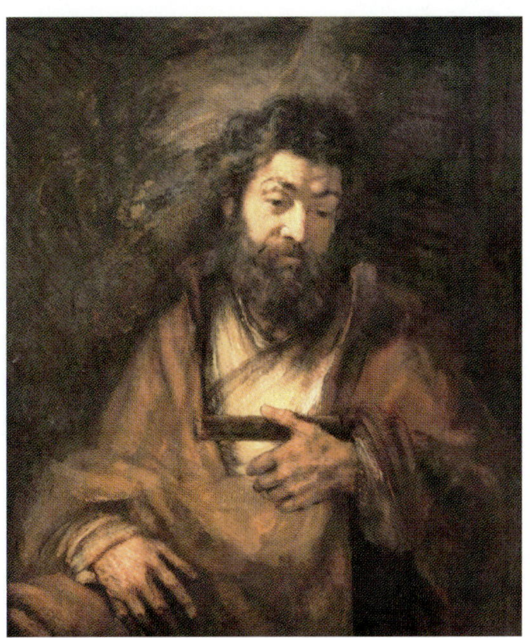
The Apostle Simon, 1661, Kunsthaus, Zurich

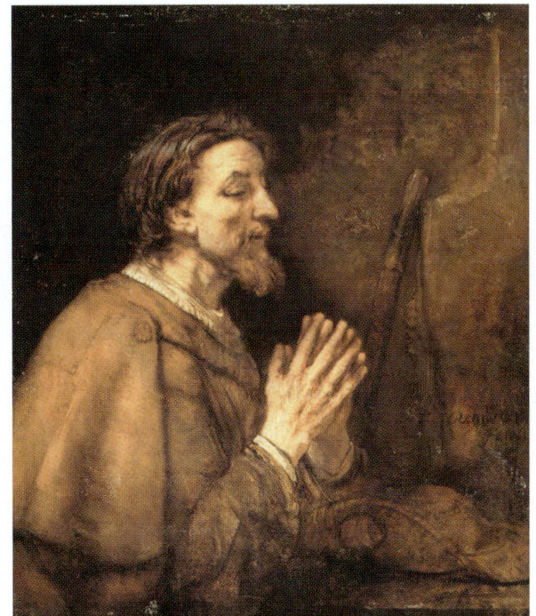
The Apostle James, 1661, The Israel Museum, Jerusalem

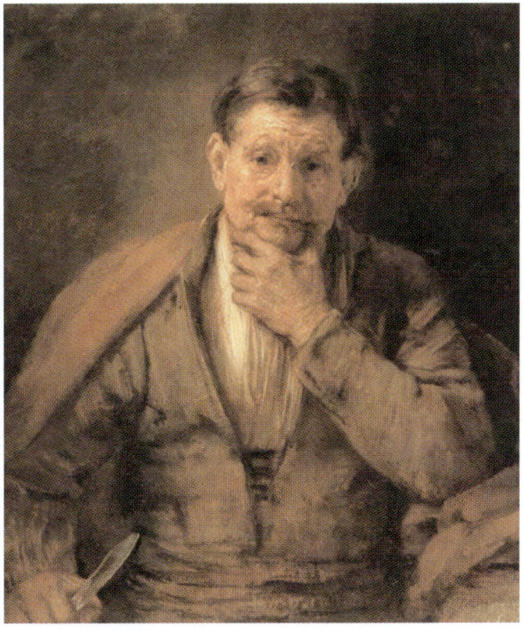
The Apostle Bartholomew, 1661, The J. Paul Getty Museum, Malibu

the "collapse of boundaries between saints and sinners." The *Matthew* in the Louvre, the *Simon* in Zurich, the *James* in Jerusalem, the *Bartholomew* in Malibu are without more than a subdued hint of the symbols of their sainthood, but their worn faces and wrinkled hands present to us the faith that is a confrontation of the world, not an escape from it.

What is most remarkable about this series of paintings is not the humanity of these apostles, nor their expressions of worn faith, but the fact that Rembrandt painted them at all. Twelve portraits of such considerable size (the ones extant average in size more than 35.43 x 29.54 in.) amount to a time-consuming labor. Further, apostle portraits were of no interest to the Dutch Reformed Church, and such defiantly non-traditional works as these Rembrandt created would hardly have elicited a second glance from the Roman Catholic Church.

Nor would any but a most unusual patron have had any interest in such an everyday-looking bunch: the four I mention, apart from Matthew receiving angelic dictation, might be next-door neighbors. I suspect that Rembrandt did these paintings for himself and that they are a part of his lifelong interest in knowing the world of the Bible as

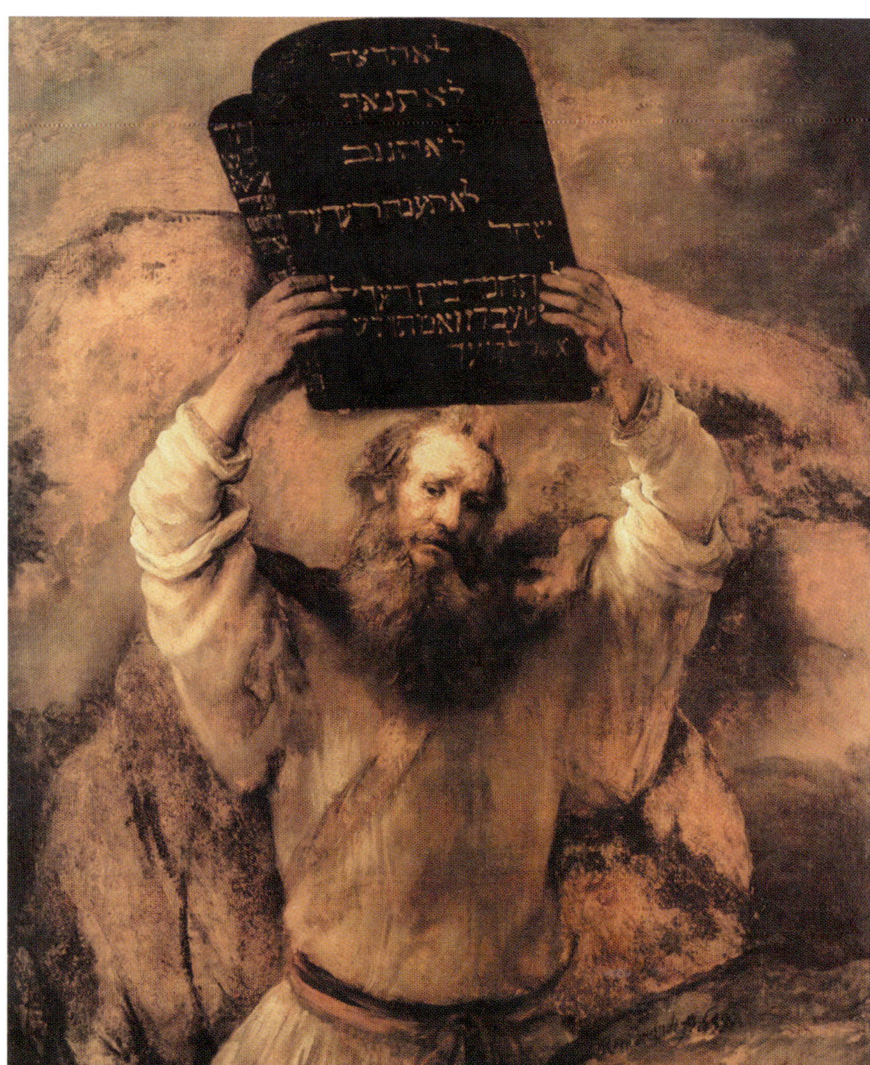

Moses with the Tablets of the Law, 1659, Gemäldegalerie, Staatliche Museen, Berlin

real because it is a world no different than, and certainly no holier than, his own world. As such, they amount to an expression of belief, a statement of a faith that can be lived, indeed *must* be lived, as opposed to one that can only be looked at from a distance, admired and even adored but never attained.

There are other biblical paintings of Rembrandt's final decade that fairly glow with faith. The 1659 *Moses with the Tables of the Law*, now in Berlin, with his last (and mostly correct) attempt at writing Hebrew, is arresting in its conception of the shining face of Moses.

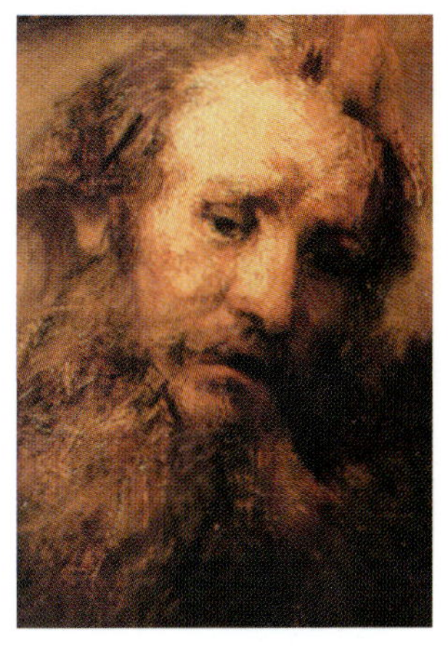

This Moses is clearly not enjoying a moment of triumph. His expression has led some to the assumption that he is here about to cast the stone tablets bearing the Ten Commandments to the ground, breaking them to bits (Exod. 32:19). Others have suggested that these are the tablets cut by Moses and written by God to replace those Moses had smashed, because here Moses has the shining face mentioned in that narrative (Exod. 34:29). I doubt both these interpretations. The shining face of Moses was the result of his being in the presence of God, and Rembrandt has given us here a somewhat abstract presentation with a general and subdued background because he intended a Moses separated from one particular narrative, a Moses whose face reveals neither anger nor beatific peace. This is the chastened and inspired Moses of Exodus 34:29–35, coming down from Sinai with the replacement pair of the "tablets of the testimony."

Thus is his face the face of reflective memory and regret and humble astonishment at the granting, by God, of such intimacy. Moses' expression resembles the face of *Bathsheba with King David's Letter* and the face of *The Apostle Peter Denying Christ.* Perhaps Rembrandt painted Moses here the way he thought of himself: flawed, and amazed at what he had been given.

There is the curious *Jacob Wrestling with the Angel* (next page), also in Berlin and also from 1659 or perhaps 1660. It has the same abstract quality as the *Moses with the Tables of the Law*, despite the frightening violence of the moment from Jacob's life that it recalls (Gen. 32:22–32). Rembrandt presents Jacob with his eyes shut, as though the whole business might be some sort of dream. The angel who holds him and looks at his face with such affection is far more a blessing presence than a harming one, despite his pulling right knee and his pushing left hand. This painting is much more about seeing

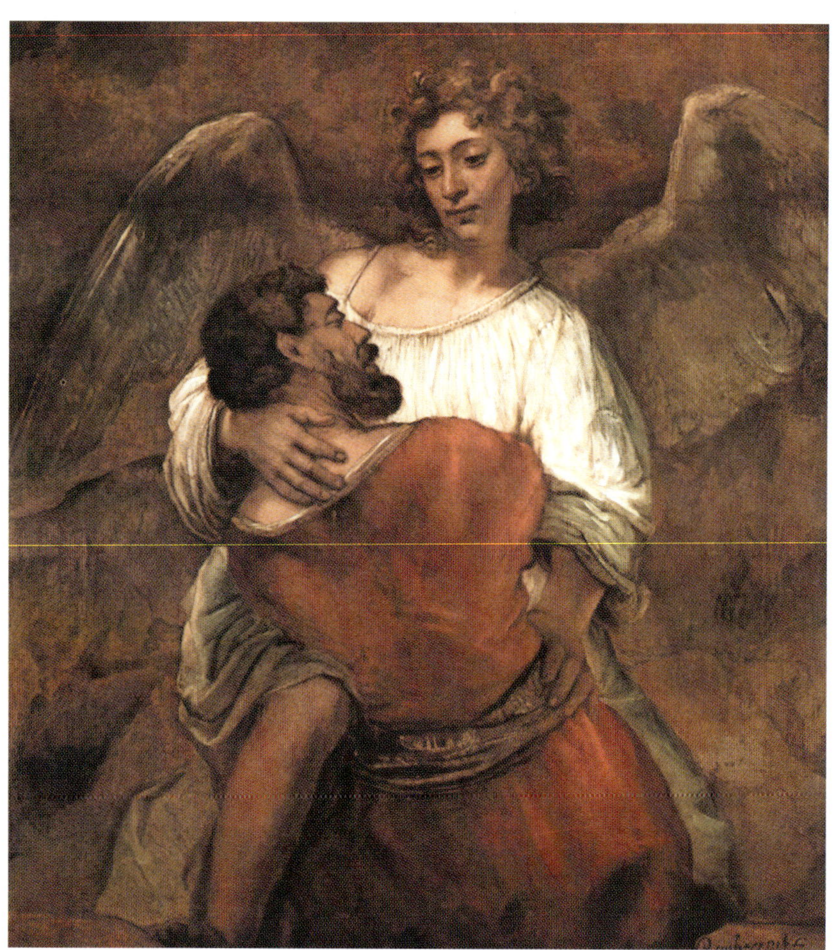

Jacob Wrestling with the Angel, 1659 or 1660, Gemäldegalerie, Staatliche Museen, Berlin

God than about dislocating a hip. And this emphasis of Rembrandt is exactly in tune with the text, for Jacob, having asked the angel ("man" in the Hebrew text) his name (the very question Moses is to tell God the Israelites in Egypt will want answered, Exod. 3:13), calls the place of his night experience "Face-of-God": "Because I have seen God, face to face, but I am still alive!" (Gen. 32:30; v. 31 in the Hebrew text).

It is amusing to consider what the thirty-year-old Rembrandt who painted *The Blinding of Samson* would have made of this moment from the narrative of Genesis. What the fifty-four-year-old Rembrandt has given us is a moment of theophany. His Jacob is one who, despite the lifetime of cheating recalled by his very name (Jacob = "Deceiver"), has been given the blessing of a vision of God. His Jacob is one whose name is about to be changed to "Israel," "God-Struggler." Rembrandt knew that blessing, from what he must have considered an equal unworthiness, and the painting he has created is a self-portrait of experience as opposed to a self-portrait of appearance.

The discipline required for the choice of these works among the many that may be said to attest Rembrandt's faith is a difficult one. One's list of favorites changes with each experience of the canon, in part because one's understanding increases. And Rembrandt's genius at engaging our involvement in the biblical stories that moved him is not unlike many of the stories themselves, which pull at our minds, at our souls, by what is left undescribed, unsaid.

One choice, however, is an easy one, easy because it is the obvious culmination of more than thirty years of Rembrandt's reflection on a single biblical story, and easy because it is in itself a kind of summary conclusion to Rembrandt's own pilgrimage of faith. The story is found only in the Gospel of Luke, at 15:11–32, and the work is *The Return of the Prodigal Son*, now in St. Petersburg.

Rembrandt's earliest known comment on the parable of the prodigal son is a drawing from 1632 or 1633, *The Departure of the Prodigal Son*, a depiction of the moment described in Luke 15:13a: "And after not many days [i.e., as soon as possible], the younger son put together everything and took off for a distant region."

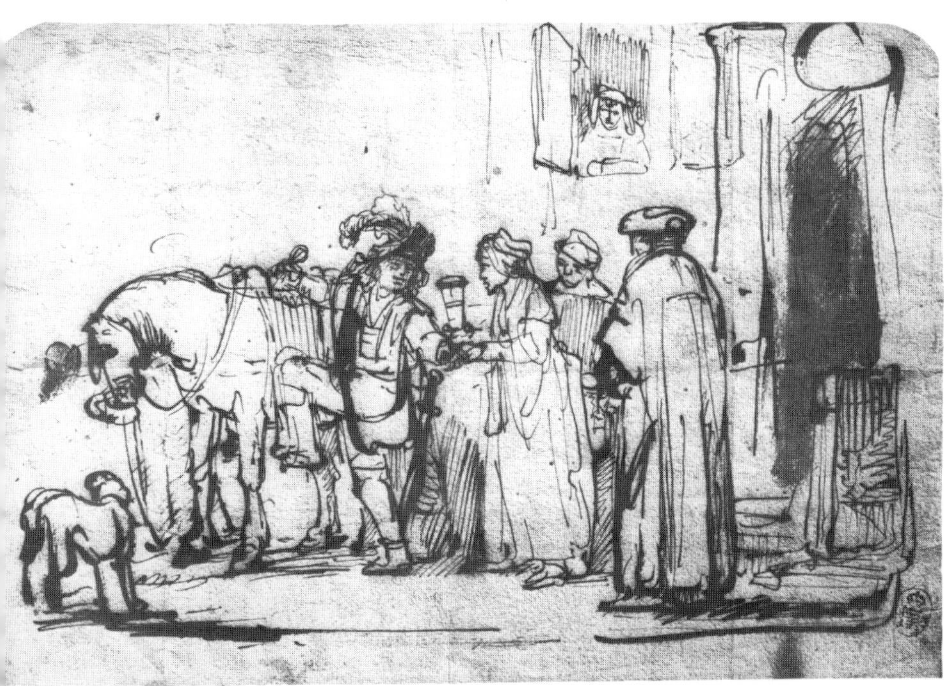

The Departure of the Prodigal Son, Benesch 81, 1632 or 1633, Kupferstichkabinett, Gemäldegalerie Alter Meister, Berlin

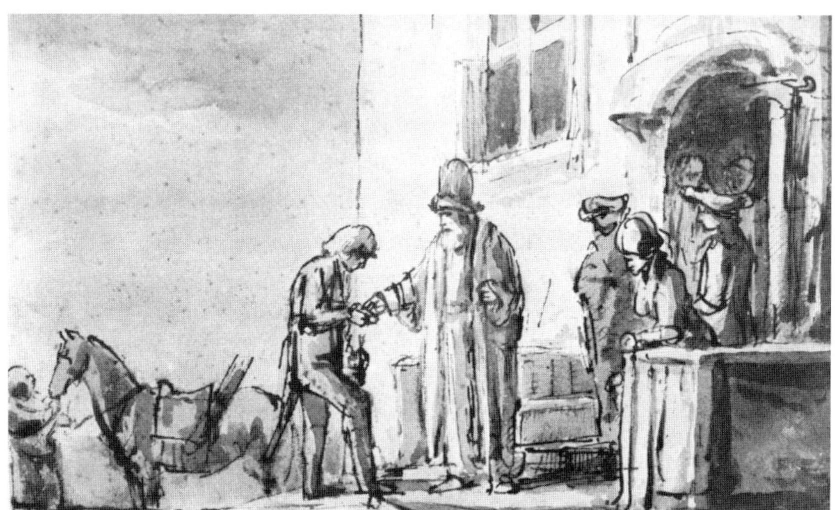

The Departure of the Prodigal Son, Benesch 651, 1649 or 1650, Groninger Museum voor Staden Lande, Groningen

Rembrandt returned once more to this moment in a drawing he made more than sixteen years later, in 1649 or 1650. In the earlier drawing, the younger son is about to mount his horse, with his mother still holding his hand. In the later drawing, his father solemnly hands the son something, probably the inheritance of gold. This father has on a tall hat and was apparently drawn again by Rembrandt as a solitary figure around 1662 or 1663, perhaps as he began thinking about the painting now in St. Petersburg.

In 1635 or 1636, Rembrandt painted *The Prodigal Son in the Tavern*, now in Dresden, in which he presents himself as the jolly partying younger son with his wife Saskia as his companion. This work has elicited a wide range of comment, stretching from the view that Rembrandt was putting down his in-laws and celebrating the first flush of his success, through the proposal that he was warning against excess while confessing his own sinful behavior, all the way to the suggestion that no allusion to the parable of the prodigal son was even intended by this work in the first place.

1. **The Prodigal Son in the Tavern**, 1635, Gemäldegalerie Alter Meister, Dresden

2. **Three Couples of Soldiers and Women**, Benesch 100, verso, 1635, Kupferstichkabinett, Staatliche Museen, Berlin

3. **The Prodigal Son with Loose Women**, Benesch 528a, 1642, Musée des Beaux-Arts, Orléans

4. **The Prodigal Son with Loose Women**, Benesch 529, 1642 or1643, Basel (private collection)

I think this painting is unquestionably a work on the parable of the prodigal son, and certainly based on the reference in Luke 15:13b to "debauched living" and on the words of the elder son in Luke 15:30, "this son of yours who has thrown away your retirement with his whores."

The symbols of high living are here, in the peacock pie, the billboard on the wall at the top of the painting on the left, the measure-marked glass half-empty of its wine, and the designer

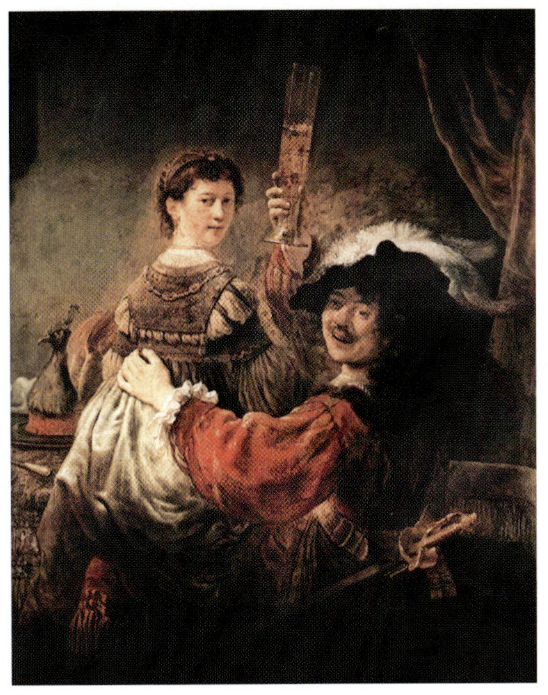
1.

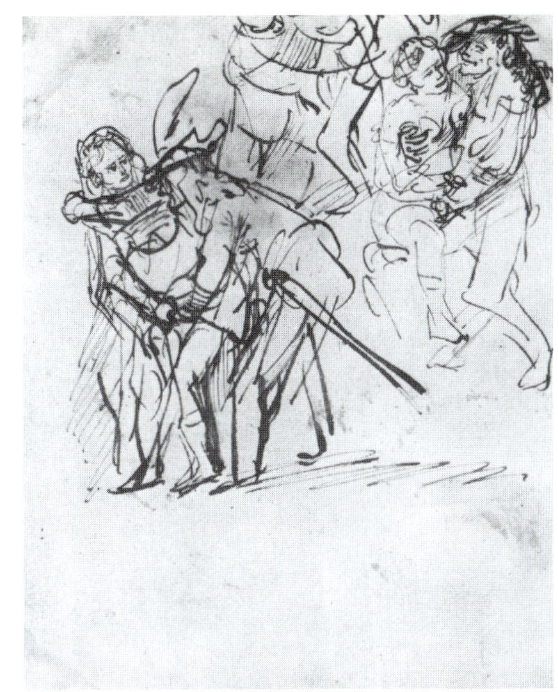
2.

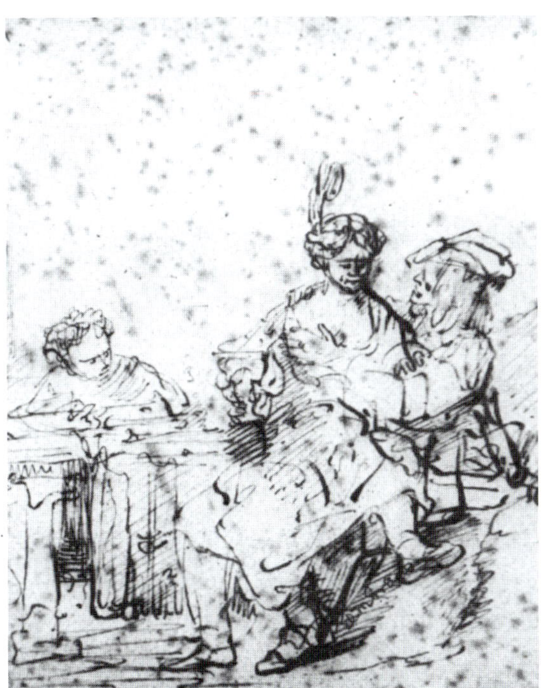
3.

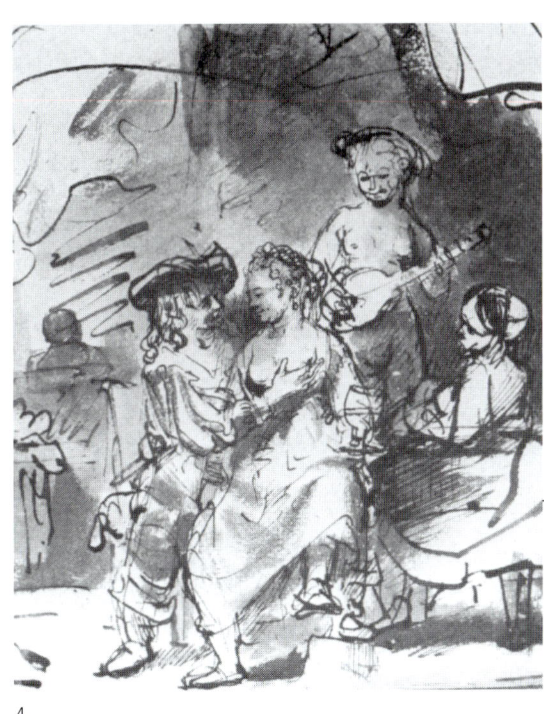
4.

clothing of the couple. Such an interpretation is supported by x-ray photography, which reveals the presence of a topless woman playing a lute just behind and between the partying pair, and by three drawings, one from around 1635, one from around 1642, and one from 1642 or 1643 that includes a nude woman playing a lute.

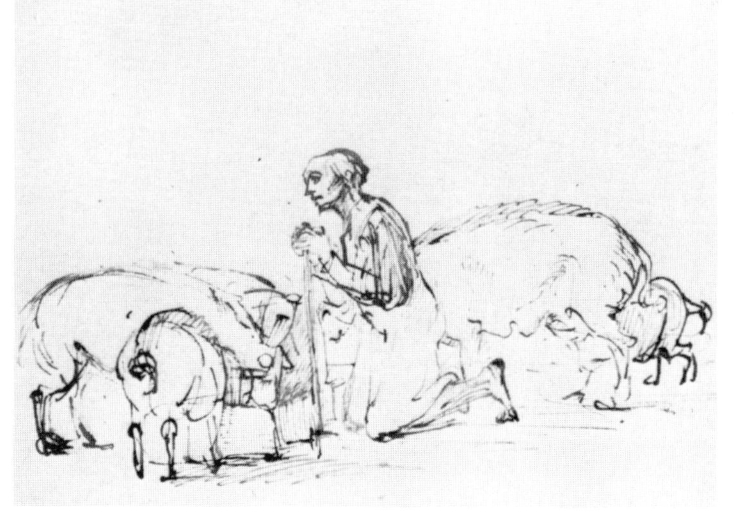

The Prodigal Son among the Swine,
Benesch 601, 1647-1648, British Museum, London

I also think it doubtful that Rembrandt intended any specific message, either of braggartry or warning, in the inclusion of his and his wife's likeness in this painting, apart perhaps from a suggestion that none of us is immune to the temptation of prodigality. (See chap. 3.)

From 1647–1648 comes Rembrandt's sole reference to the prodigal son's most complete and humiliating debasement, *The Prodigal Son Among the Swine.* Already the prodigal has lost his rich clothing and even his shoes, and already he has become emaciated in his hunger: "He longed to eat even the hogs' feed, but no one gave him anything" (Luke 15:16). Rembrandt gives us here a reflective prodigal, looking beyond the eating hogs, perhaps even in prayer for some rescue, and about to begin thinking more clearly (Luke 15:17a).

As early as 1636, however, the one moment from the parable of the prodigal son that came to Rembrandt most often began to take on a variety of shapes in his mind: the moment of the father's forgiving embrace of the son "who was dead, yet now lives, and was gone, but is now here" (Luke 15:32bc). Rembrandt's use of a sixteenth-century woodcut of Martin van Heemskerk in his earliest etched version of *The Return of the Prodigal Son* is well known and often mentioned in discussions of the etching. A comparison of the two works suggests however that Rembrandt's real inspiration was the story itself, which he presents with far greater emotional impact and a much clearer summary of the parable's real point than does van Heemskerk's somewhat crowded conception.

Rembrandt has given us a son who has lost every vestige of his upbringing in well-to-do circumstances and nearly every appearance of civilized humanity. Even his tattered rags excite far less pity than his ravaged, animal-like face. The sole sign of his status is the knife that still hangs at his side. And the father, almost losing a shoe in his rush to receive and embrace and raise his kneeling son, has a face so suffused with compassion and love and humanity that one can feel forgiveness just looking at it.

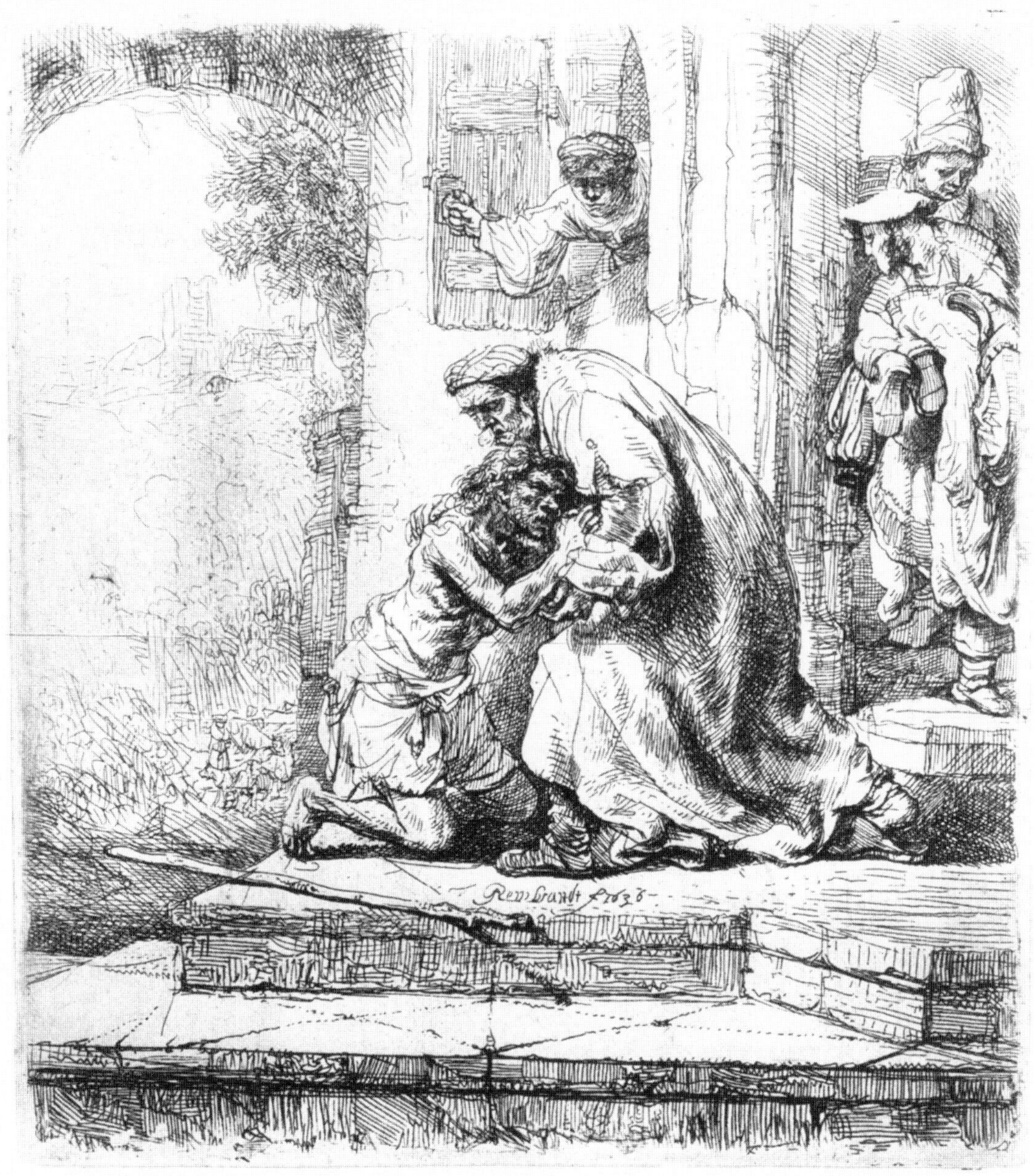

The Return of the Prodigal Son, B 91, 1636, Prentenkabinet, Rijksmuseum, Amsterdam

Other business of the story in Luke is there in this etching: servants bringing the shoes and the robe the father has ordered (Luke 15:22) and the elder brother at work in the distance (Luke 15:25a). The servants appear almost embarrassed to look on the emotional reunion—the one nearest the father and his younger son has turned his head toward the wall, and his companion looks down at the steps they are descending. Rembrandt has even put in a serving maid with no such scruples, hanging as she stares with understandable but rude curiosity from a window, a realistic and human, if non-biblical, touch.

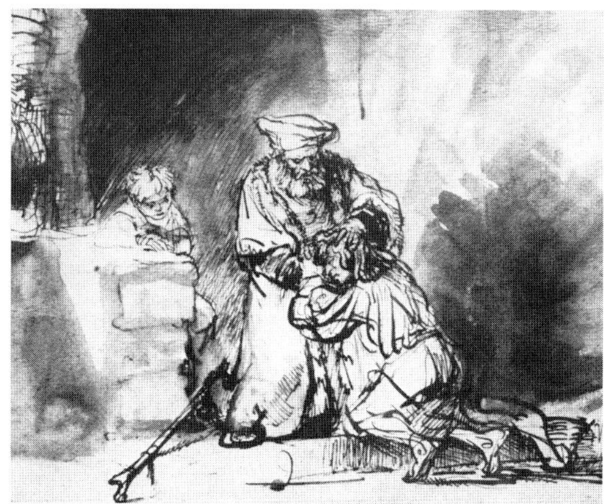

The Return of the Prodigal Son, Benesch 519, 1642, Teylers Museum, Haarlem

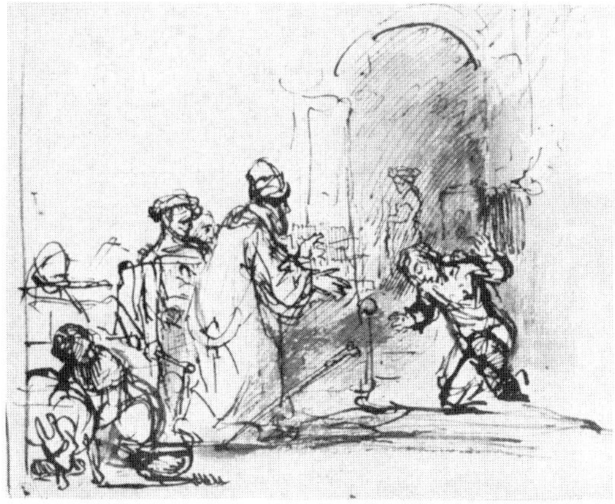

The Return of the Prodigal Son, Benesch 562, 1644 or 1645, Museum Boymans-van Beuningen, Rotterdam

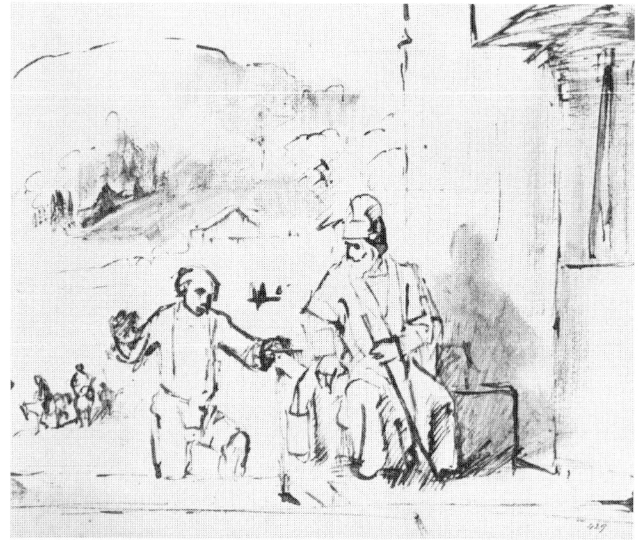

The Return of the Prodigal Son, Benesch 1011, around 1656, Victoria and Albert Museum, London

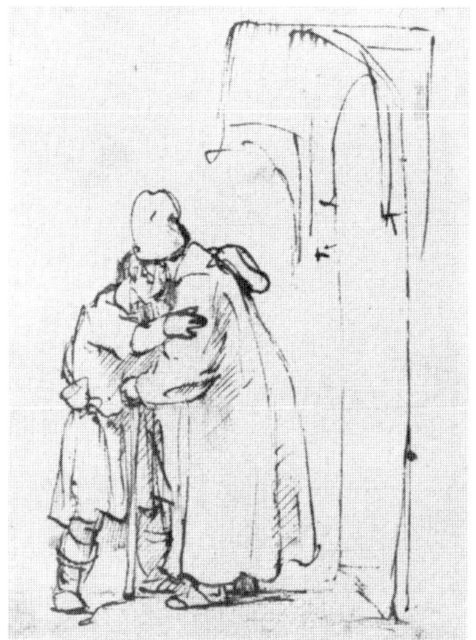

The Return of the Prodigal Son, Benesch 983, 1655-1666, F. Lugt Collection, Fondation Custodia, Paris

Despite these features, however, the clear center of the etching is the repentant son and the forgiving father. All other movement in the story is already beginning to slip into the background, and it slipped more and more as Rembrandt returned again and again to this moment in the parable of the prodigal son. A drawing from 1642 has a far less savage-looking son being received by a father whose cane has fallen in his rush out the door, and whose left hand caresses and blesses the head of his shamed son while a small boy looks solemnly on.

Two or three years later, there is a drawing in which the son, unable to look his father in the face, is falling to his knees as the father rushes toward him with his hands reaching out, his walking stick falling. There are four other persons present, and a rabbit-looking

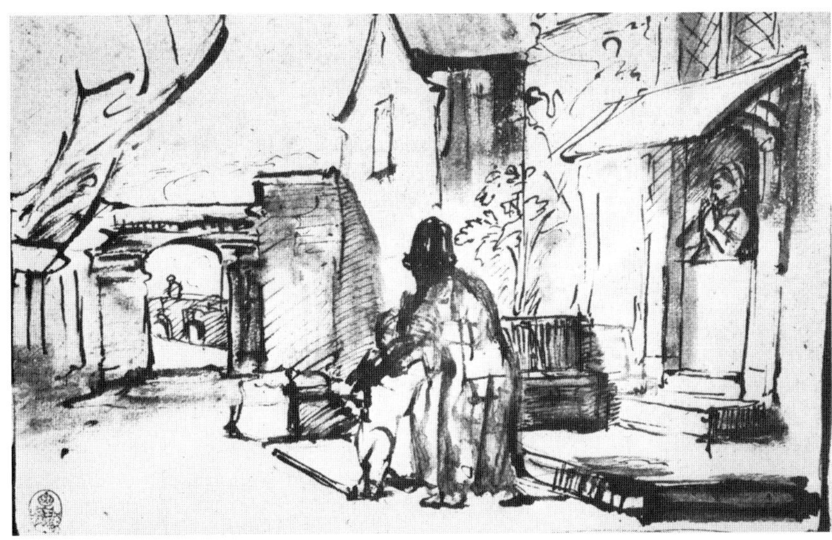

The Return of the Prodigal Son, Benesch 1017, 1656, Kupferstichkabinett, Gemäldegalerie Alten Meister, Dresden

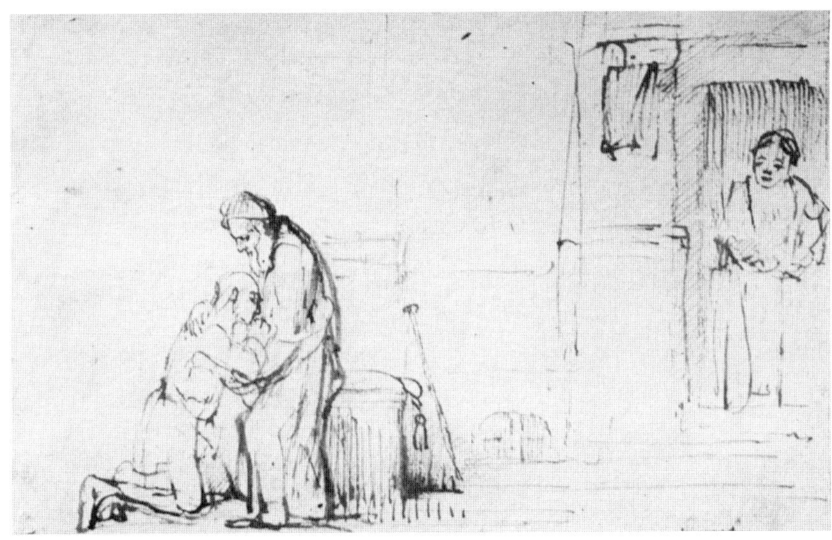

The Return of the Prodigal Son, Benesch 1037, 1658 or 1659, Albertina, Vienna

goat, but they are only scenery, now *inside* the house. From 1655 or 1656, there is a drawing of the son embracing the father, the father leaning into the hug, still holding his cane in his left hand. Both are standing this time, and the son is fully clothed. From 1656, a drawing shows the son fully clothed and coming up steps behind a seated father, who is just turning to see who is approaching. There are two horsemen in the distance, but once again they are setting only, as is the minimal architecture. Also from 1656, there is a drawing depicting a kneeling son and an embracing father that includes as well the prodigal's mother, standing in the doorway, her hands clasped together in thanksgiving. From the same year, or perhaps the next, the mother watches the father rising from his seat to embrace his kneeling son.

This inclusion of what appears to be the prodigal's mother, who is nowhere mentioned in Luke's text, is entirely atypical of Rembrandt, but once again is a feature that is in no way a distraction from the central action and meaning of what was for Rembrandt the supreme moment of the story of the prodigal son. My guess is that he was thinking more and more about this moment, and above all about its meaning, as particularly relevant for his own life and faith. This series of drawings—and there may have been other drawings as well, now lost to us—is evidence of an ongoing search to say what he felt about a moment from the Bible that he could not leave alone. Perhaps it was even more a moment that would not leave *him* alone.

This search was concluded sometime between 1661 and 1669, the year of Rembrandt's death, when the battered old artist painted *The Return of the Prodigal Son*, the glowing work now in St. Petersburg. I lean toward the final two years of that nine-year period as the time in which this painting was done. It has suffered some wear and tear and some retouching of the secondary figures to the right of the father and his prodigal son. Some Rembrandt scholars consider these figures and that of the woman at the top left of the painting the work of later hands, in part on the assumption that Rembrandt himself had not finished the work before his death and in part on the quality of the figures themselves.

The extended array of works preceding this painting may well suggest that these secondary figures, albeit fussed over by later hands after Rembrandt's death, are nevertheless a part of his own conception of the moment of the father's reception of his prodigal son. And I believe Rembrandt finished the painting, as he intended it, before his death. In a way this speculation is as unnecessary as it is subjective, for by the time Rembrandt painted this work, any feature apart from the father and his son has to be considered setting alone.

The woman just visible in the background, at the top left of the painting, may suggest the prodigal's mother, as in the drawings from 1656 and 1657. The standing man with the cane, the full beard, and the red cloak echoing the cloak of the father must be the elder brother. The seated man with crossed legs and the gold-rimmed hat, given his rich costume, may suggest the steward of the estate. And the young

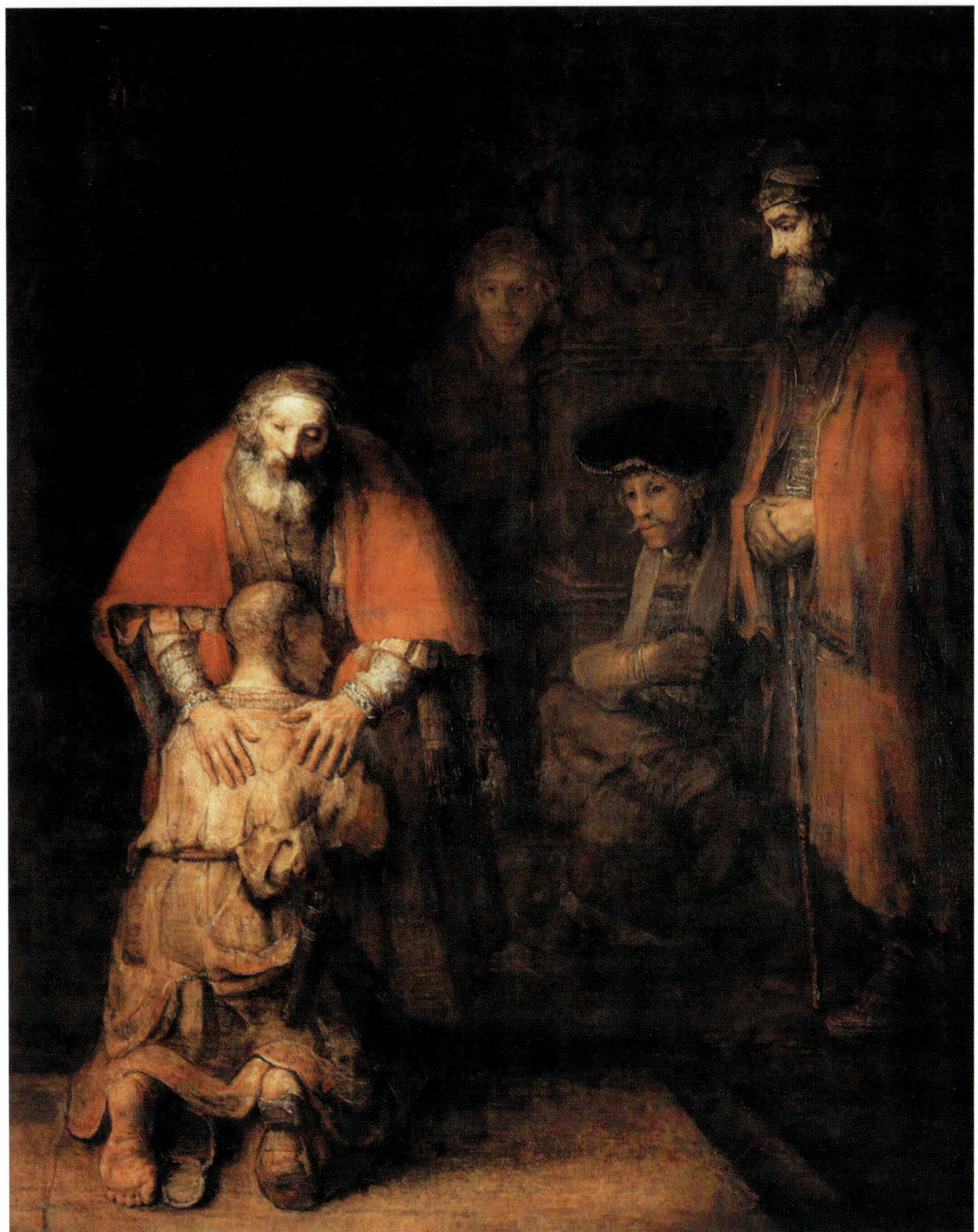

Return of the Prodigal Son, 1661-1669, State Hermitage, St. Petersburg

man (or girl) peering around the archway is perhaps to be taken as a servant.

The two men seem almost not to know where to look; the servant stares, manners pushed aside by curiosity. But all of them are there to redouble our gaze upon what is the holy moment in front of us. Rembrandt had no intention of giving these secondary figures the quality he has lavished even on the prodigal, much less still the father. They are, by intention I believe, suggestions only, even abstract representations of the rest of us, perhaps the rest of us on our own journeys toward faith and forgiveness. The figure of the elder son brings to mind the stout figure with the cane in the left foreground of the "Hundred Guilder Print" and even the man with arms akimbo in the left corner of the 1652 *Christ Preaching* (B 67) and the rotund figure with the cane in *The Descent from the Cross: The Second Plate* of 1633 (in this chapter and chapter 5).

Everything in this *Return of the Prodigal Son* is about the one single moment that Rembrandt presents as concerning every one of us, whether we know it or not. Everything in the painting, including even the figure of the prodigal son and his bending, leaning old father, is secondary to what Rembrandt here confesses.

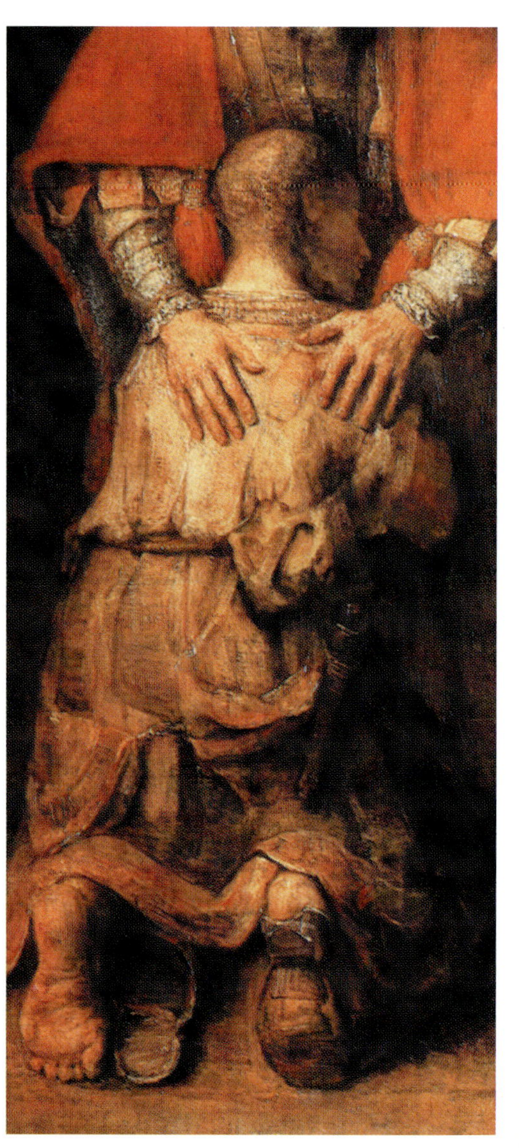

The ragged, ravaged son, his once elegant clothes worn and torn, his young man's knife in its sheath at his side as in the etching of 1636, his disintegrating shoes, his feet lacerated by his miles of travel, his head nearly bald from malnutrition and tearing despair, has fallen to his knees, as in most of Rembrandt's earlier depictions of this moment. His face is visible to us only in profile, as he leans his tired head into the peace that passes all understanding. We can see that his eyes are closed and that his lips are slightly parted, perhaps murmuring a prayer of thanks; his hands and arms are not visible to us—they may be lifted in prayer, but I think it more likely that this son is grasping his father. Rembrandt, in these last two years of his life, Saskia long dead, Hendrickje dead for five years, and Titus, the sole living memory of Saskia, dead in September of 1668, was certainly reaching for this same father himself.

This same father: the beautiful old man leaning over his ravaged son in *The Return of the Prodigal* is clearly far more than a character in a parable in the New Testament. His elegant clothing, with its tasseled cloak and its frilled, golden sleeves, is all but sculpted by Rembrandt in layer after layer of paint. The father's tender gesture, both hands blessing the son even as he pulls him closer to his bending body, is a visible summary of the blessing of Aaron and his sons:

> The Lord bless you and take care of you;
> the Lord shine his face on you and grant you grace;
> the Lord look right at you and make you whole.
> (Num. 6:24–26)

The holding hands of the father are a reminder of the touching, trusting hands in *The Jewish Bride*, which Rembrandt had painted perhaps two years before, remembering Saskia as he did (see chap. 5). They are strong but gentle hands, the hands of a father pressing his son to himself as though never to let him beyond his reach again. They are hands that love and forgive, love and bless, love and hold, love and enjoy, all at the same time. And they are hands that no longer reach to raise the prodigal from his kneeling position, as in the etching of 1636. This father has become strong enough to avoid avoiding his son's shame, strong enough to leave off attempting to change what he cannot change, and strong enough to accept and love his son as he is.

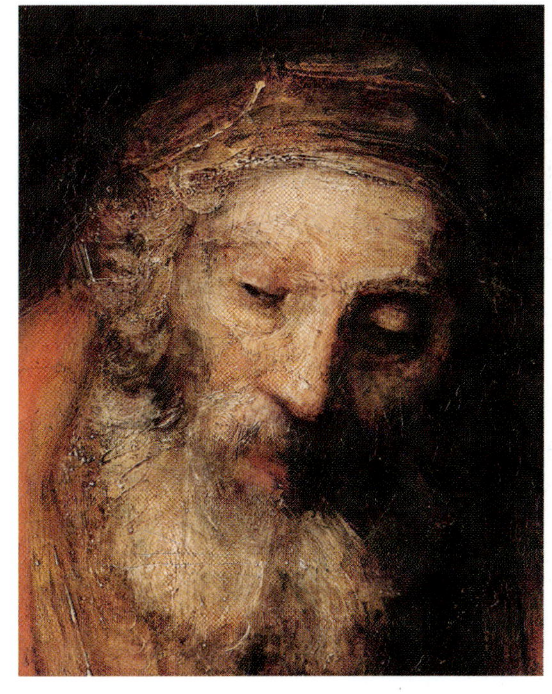

Yet it is the father's face that is the heart of this painting: a face of such compassion and tenderness, a face suffused with so much relief mingled with love, a face glowing with a transcendent light. His lips closed, his head bent over with his body, this father is looking, not down at his son whom he loves so much and whom he has back again as from the dead, but off to his right and into some distance of memory and thanksgiving and hope beyond this moment, though rooted in it. His plainly visible right eye is turned into that distance, and it recalls the look of Bathsheba's eyes in *Bathsheba with King David's Letter* and

Peter's eyes in *The Apostle Peter Denying Christ* and Moses' eyes in *Moses with the Tables of the Law.*

I believe that Rembrandt has given us here more than a universal figure, more than a sort of ideal father receiving every returning penitent child. His confession is a far more personal one. Rembrandt was here remembering his own need, the need only God can meet, the need no amount of genius or achievement or repentance or any church or any man can satisfy. He was thinking of his own life and of one special biblical story of the many that he could understand only as autobiography, peopled not by saints and figures in remote antiquity, but by himself and by those he loved and by some he knew only in passing.

I have three times stood before this profoundly moving painting, and for as long as possible each time, drawn into it, warmed by it, blessed and forgiven in the immeasurable sense of grace pouring out from its surface. I thought then, as I have while studying this painting so often, both before and since, of Rembrandt and his life, poured into and out through this re-presentation of one moment from the parable of the prodigal son. What is there about this work, undoubted masterpiece that it is, that gives us the feeling of theophany? Why has so simple a combination of gesture and expression drawn so emotional and so deep a reaction from everyone who has ever really looked at the painting, even in the vast reduction of its likeness on a printed page?

I believe now that I know the answer to these questions, though I must admit that it is an answer heard by faith. What Rembrandt gives us in *The Return of the Prodigal Son*, painted toward the end of his life, is the human face of God: the only face, finally, that any of us can ever really look upon and see. The father in *The Return of the Prodigal Son* is thus far more than one shamed son's forgiving and loving parent, far more even than some universal and impersonal notion of forgiving grace. This father is God, Rembrandt's own God, by whom he knew himself loved, received, accepted, and forgiven. And in this confession of a painting, Rembrandt has caught exactly the point and meaning of Jesus' parable of a father and his two sons, and he has summed up that point in a vision beyond any words—a vision that opens the parable to the rest of us, prodigals all, in a way no sermon, no lecture, no commentary, no scolding ever could.

So the human old painter Rembrandt van Rijn, living and moving in his landscape of faith, scolded by the church, avoided by some of his colleagues and many of his pupils, pitied by some of his friends, and deserted by most of his patrons, read his Bible, looked into the face of God, and said to us all with a direct clarity that has never been surpassed and only rarely equaled, "This is what God is really like."

SOME SOURCES AND SUGGESTIONS

The felicitous translation of Hebrews 11:38 appears in the 1961 edition of the New English Bible (NEB) New Testament. C. H. Dodd was both vice-chairman and director of the entire NEB translation project, and I believe I recognize his voice in this translation, which alas has been replaced by a more generic rendering in the Revised English Bible of 1989.

The details are very difficult to make out in the reproductions of the Musée Jacquemart-André *Emmaus*, owing to the dark foreground. This sepia-toned reproduction helps a bit, though the full impact of the work can only be felt before the painting itself (the Jacquemart-André was re-opened at the end of March in 1996 after renovation). Questions have been raised concerning the date and authenticity of the supper at Emmaus drawing (Benesch 11), though not concerning the 1629 painting; I believe they go together, as Otto Benesch suggested, following Bode and Valentiner (Benesch I:6).

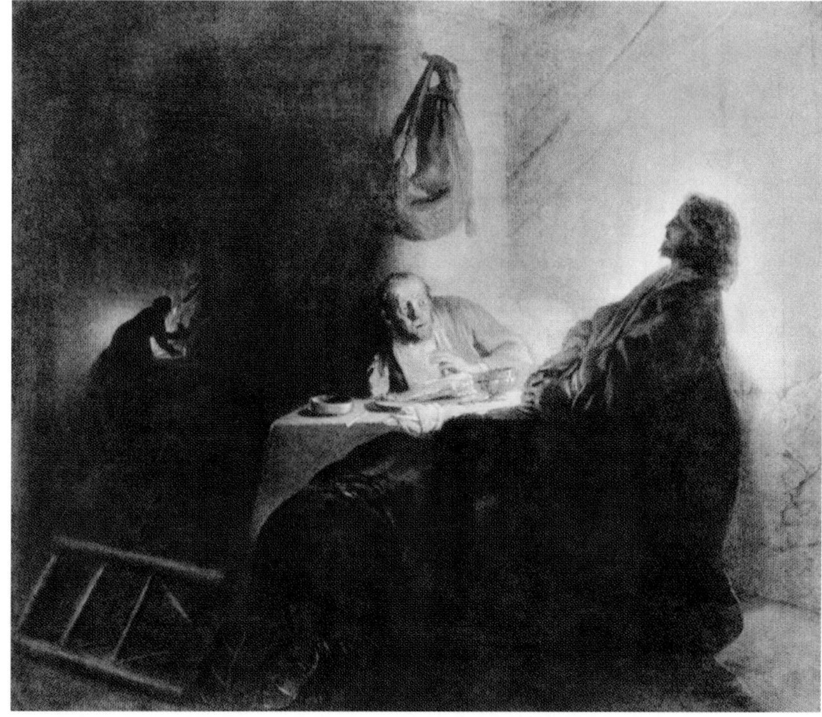

Sepia photograph of the Jacquemart-André **Supper at Emmaus**, published in A. Bredius, The Paintings of Rembrandt, 1935, Phaidon Edition: no. 539

A fascinating article on the Mauritshuis *Saul and David* by Ben Broos may be found in *Intimacies and Intrigues: History Painting in the Mauritshuis* (pp. 279–90). Broos notes that Bredius confessed that he had been forced to raise the 200,000-franc purchase price for the painting by the sale of "his coach-and-four," and after a helpful review of some of the theories of attribution, comments (pp. 289) "that Rembrandt must at the very least have contributed to the final result."

Christopher White's comment on the "Hundred Guilder Print" comes following his detailed analysis of the plate, at the beginning of his "History: Part II" section in *Rembrandt as an Etcher* (p. 65). He goes on to refer to this work as the one that "liberated" Rembrandt as the master etcher he became. A helpful monograph devoted wholly to this work was published in 1969 by Gerhard and Helmut Gollwitzer under the title *Rembrandt van Rijn: Hundertguldenblatt Die Grosse Krankenheilung.* It includes an elaborate analysis of the plate's composition and seventeen reproductions of individual figures and groups greatly enlarged. Visser 'T Hooft's discussion of the print in *Rembrandt and the Gospel* is titled "A Sermon: The Hundred Guilder Print," and his comment on "the big, fat man" in the left foreground of the print appears on page 57—"If we could find a name for him, it might be Pilate."

Bob Haak provides an x-ray photograph of Bathsheba's face, showing that Rembrandt originally painted her head lifted higher, in *Rembrandt: His Life, His Work, His Time.* Jacques Foucart, in a 1982 publication, *Les Peintures de Rembrandt au Louvre,* comments (p. 59) that Rembrandt made this adjustment to express "*la culpabilté, le regret et le remords de Bethsabée.*" Foucart also provides some excellent detailed photographs of the painting. A significant collection of essays dealing with this painting was published by Ann Jensen Adams in 1998 under the title *Rembrandt's Bathsheba Reading King David's Letter.* Particularly valuable are the essays by Ernst van de Wetering, Svetlana Alpers, and Margaret D. Carroll. The painting is reproduced in color on the back cover of this volume, and a detail, Bathsheba's face, forms two-thirds of the front cover—both reproductions have unfortunately been reversed.

W. R. Valentiner's proposal that Rembrandt painted a series of apostle portraits was made in *Kunstchronik und Kunstmarkt,* 1920–1921 (new series); Christian Tümpel has affirmed Valentiner's suggestion and given further examples of such a series (*Rembrandt,* pp. 338–43; his reference to "exalted moods" is on p. 339 of this work). Schama's comment on the series comes in *Rembrandt's Eyes* (p. 657).

Of the two tablets Moses is holding aloft in Rembrandt's painting, it is the second that is fully visible, apart from the letters covered by the grasp of Moses' hands. This tablet contains the sixth through the tenth commandments, Exodus 20:13–17; of these, commandments six through nine are completely visible, and Rembrandt's only slip appears to have been the omission of the letter (ב), "against," before "your neighbor," thus giving the reading of verse 16 as "You are not to give your neighbor a lying testimony."

The words of the tenth commandment that are visible appear to be correct. A painting from around 1650, now in Edinburgh, *Hannah and Samuel,* also includes the Ten Commandments, hanging on the wall, along with a likeness of the brazen serpent of Numbers 21, both reminders of salvation (and the need for obedience). Behind the boy Samuel and his mother, a baby is being presented to an old man: Simeon may be the suggestion here, an interesting linking of Hannah to Anna, and the boy Samuel to the infant Jesus. The Hebrew of the Ten Commandments is difficult to make out in places, and the painting in any case appears to be a work of one of Rembrandt's pupils.

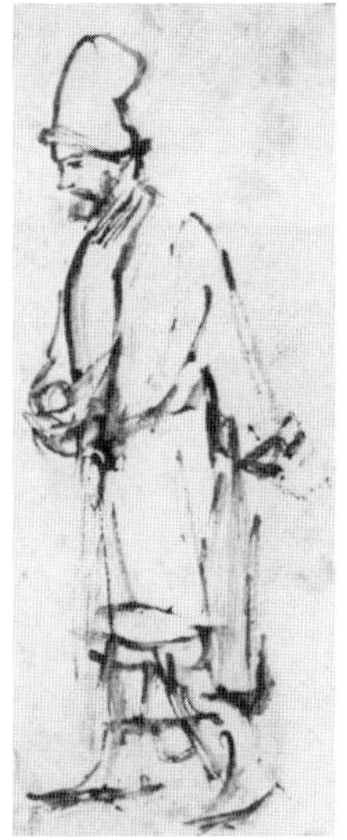

Oriental Walking,
Benesch 1068B, 1662 or 1663 Prentenkabinet, Rijksmuseum, Amsterdam

Sumowski's assignment of *The Departure of the Prodigal Son* (Benesch 81) to Philips Koninck is unconvincing. He is swimming upstream against a waterfall of critical opinion agreeing with Benesch. Noting that the drawing may "possibly" be based on an earlier drawing by Rembrandt that is now lost, he puts it into his most subjective category, as a "hypothetical attribution."

The solitary figure with the tall hat from 1662–1665, given by Benesch (1068B) to Rembrandt. Sumowski, who earlier made the same attribution, now assigns the drawing to Rembrandt's pupil Nicolaes Maes (Sumowski No. 1993x, a "substantiated drawing" – see p. 79).

There is an x-ray of *The Prodigal Son in the Tavern* and a detailed discussion of what it reveals in volume 3 of *Corpus* (A 111); the woman playing the lute can be clearly seen.

The elder son in the distance is difficult to make out in reproductions of B 91, *The Return of the Prodigal Son*, but he is present, minding the flock, as this enlarged detail shows. The parable of the prodigal son has inspired a great many sermons, meditations, and works of literature and art, from the moving "Parable for Church Performance" of Benjamin Britten to a range of paintings across the centuries from the Renaissance forward. No work of art, however, beyond this parable of Jesus itself, has so moved so many and so captured the essence of Jesus' description of God as has *The Return of the Prodigal Son* from Rembrandt's last years. Kenneth Clark aptly described it as "a picture which those who have seen the original in Leningrad may be forgiven for claiming as the greatest picture ever painted" (*An Introduction to Rembrandt*, p. 137). Henri Nouwen published in 1992 a "meditation" of nearly 150 pages (*The Return of the Prodigal Son: A Meditation on Fathers, Brothers, and Sons*), interleafing his own spiritual pilgrimage with his perception of this work of Rembrandt, which he first saw in reproduction on a poster in 1983. While Nouwen's book understandably reveals a great deal more about Nouwen than about Rembrandt and his painting, it is nonetheless an eloquent example of the living impact of a great work of art as both a declaration and a provocation of faith. No one, however, has captured in words the feeling this painting imparts so well as Clark, who said in his Rede Lecture at Cambridge University in 1972, "In Rembrandt's *Prodigal Son* in the Hermitage we feel that the whole of humanity has been enfolded in an act of forgiveness, beyond good and evil." This essay, "The Artist Grows Old," has been published in Clark's *Moments of Vision and Other Essays* (1981); the quotation is from p. 173.

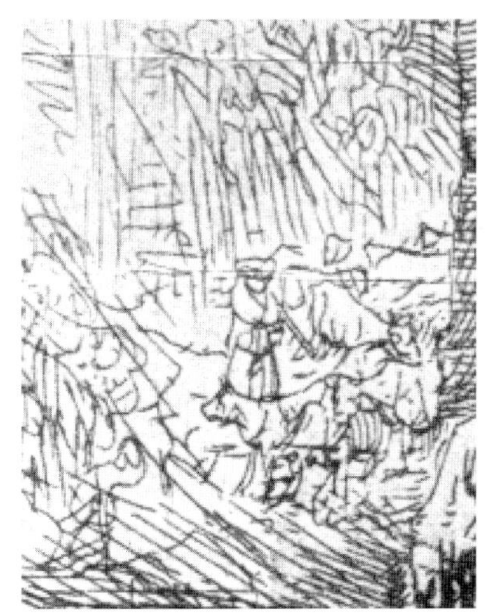

7

REMBRANDT'S DIARY

Rembrandt Harmenszoon van Rijn kept no diary, at least none that we have at hand. And about the particulars of his life we know very little. The genius of his art has inevitably stimulated much curiosity about his biography, and this curiosity has just as inevitably called forth volumes of speculation about Rembrandt's life story. Perhaps never, and certainly rarely, has so little concrete data given rise to such an endless stream of guesswork about the sixty-three years of a man who was born almost four centuries ago.

The most valuable resource for the bare facts of Rembrandt's life is a work that attempts to gather together every known scrap of public data referring to him, beginning with a record of payment to his great-grandfather, Gerit Roelofszoon, for grinding grain in 1484, and ending with the notice of his burial on 8 October 1669: *The Rembrandt Documents*, 569 pages of officialdom and commentary. Along with the notices of births and marriages and deaths, contracts and legal actions, references to paintings and etchings, statements of praise and complaint, and inventories of Rembrandt's possessions, there are the seven surviving letters written by Rembrandt, all to Constantin Huygens, concerning the series of paintings on the Passion done for Prince Frederick Hendrick of Orange. Five of the letters mention payment for these works.

Invaluable as these documents are, however, which of us would choose to have the tale of our lives told by what the bureaucrats have considered significant? There is far more to life lived (and far less as well) than legal notices and public announcements and "press releases" reveal.

Yet beyond these recorded facts, when there is no correspondence to speak of, no autobiography, no personal diary, no Boswellian adulation, and not even any consistent memoirs from contemporaries, where is a biographer to turn? One is left with the bare documents of the public record, with such scraps of contemporary reference as may be extant and, unavoidably, with a liberal admixture of speculation. Seymore Slive's *Rembrandt and His Critics 1630–1730* is an invaluable assemblage of this regrettably limited material.

Then there is whatever may remain of the subject's own nonliterary legacy. This legacy is considerable in Rembrandt's case, for few artists ever have left behind such a personal and candid and deeply-felt array of works, and his biographers have turned to these works, especially to his extensive series of self-portraits, to fill out the sparse outline of his life available to us from other sources.

Such a procedure is a threat to accuracy because of the tendency to make Rembrandt's drawings and etchings and paintings say what we want them to say, and thus to present to the world a biography of Rembrandt as we want him to have been, whatever that may be. This approach has produced a variety of Rembrandts, ranging from a sort of peasant genius possessed by a holy power to an arrogant, self-centered, contumelious cynic driven by greed. The truth of course lies, as usual, somewhere between the extremes and remains undiscoverable, given the limited information available to us.

So what can I possibly intend by "Rembrandt's Diary," as no such document is known to exist? The bare facts of Rembrandt's life, plus some of his works, in this case his works on biblical themes, seem to me to present a kind of diary. It may well be more *my* diary of

Rembrandt than *his* diary, but I reckon I am entitled to speculate along with all the other fiction writers. What follows, therefore, is a brief summary of Rembrandt's *curriculum vitae*, fleshed out a bit with suggestions I draw from some of his drawings, etchings, and paintings. No artist, no composer, no author can make a creative expression devoid of his or her own humanity and personhood, any more than any of us can do or say anything at all in a vacuum, wholly apart from who and what we are. Not even scientists can be wholly objective, and artists, who must create their legacy from the air of imagination and feeling and spirit and experience, would have little to say if they could speak only bare facts. Creativity, after all, deals with the truth that so frequently transcends fact, the truth that is truer than mere history.

Rembrandt was (probably) born on 15 July 1606, the ninth of ten children, to Harmen Gerritszoon van Rijn and Neeltje (or Cornelia) Willemsdochter van Suyttbroeck. None of his six siblings who survived infancy appears to have shown the least hint of Rembrandt's genius. Each of the other boys of the family was apprenticed in trades. Rembrandt, however, was enrolled in the Latin School in Leiden at the age of seven. There, he learned Latin, the language of scholarship and professional life, and there he was exposed to the strict Protestant theology of John Calvin. On 20 May 1620, he was registered as a student in the University of Leiden, just under two months prior to his fourteenth birthday. He apparently did not long remain a university student, though there is no record of any official withdrawal, for late in 1620 or early in 1621, he began a three-year period of study with the painter Jacob Isaacszoon van Swanenburgh, with whom he must have learned at least the mechanics of drawing and painting.

Sometime in 1624, in his eighteenth year, Rembrandt left Leiden for a six-month period of study in Amsterdam with a famous "history painter," Pieter Lastman. Despite the brevity of this time with Lastman, the young artist from Leiden was greatly influenced. His early work is obviously derivative of Lastman's, in both theme and style, and his lasting affection for Lastman is shown in the presence among his possessions in 1656 of two paintings (one a "Tobias" and one of an ox) and two books of sketches by Lastman. Indeed, the first pages of what I am calling Rembrandt's diary might be said to be filled with admiration for Lastman, while there seems to be no reflection whatsoever of Swanenburgh, apart perhaps from Rembrandt's increasingly informed use of the materials of his art.

In 1625, Rembrandt returned to Leiden and set up a studio in a room attached to his father's mill. He began an association with another alumnus of Lastman's studio, also a Leidener, Jan Lievens, and he began taking pupils himself—by 1665, he would have taught more than fifty of them. His influence on them was strong, and many of these students imitated his work so thoroughly (and even signed his name to their paintings) that the canon of Rembrandt's work was mistakenly inflated well into the twentieth century.

Rembrandt's diary in these Leiden years includes some affectionate portraits of his mother, the only known portrait of his father, and an amusingly honest series of self-portraits.

Also in the Leiden years, the stream of works on biblical subjects begins to flow. The earliest of them depend heavily on Lastman, but the emergence of Rembrandt's own mind and emotion can be detected from the start.

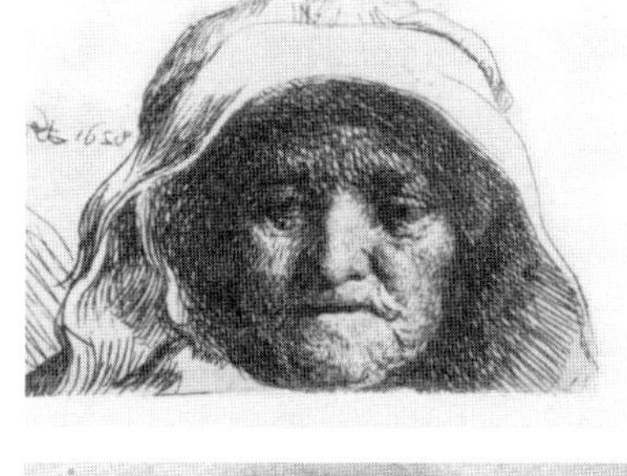

Rembrandt's Mother: Head, B 352, 1628, Prentenkabinet, Rijksmuseum, Amsterdam (right)

Rembrandt's Mother with Her Hand on Her Chest, B 349, 1631, Prentenkabinet, Rijksmuseum, Amsterdam (bottom left)

Rembrandt's Father, Benesch 56, recto, around 1630, Ashmolean Museum (bottom right)

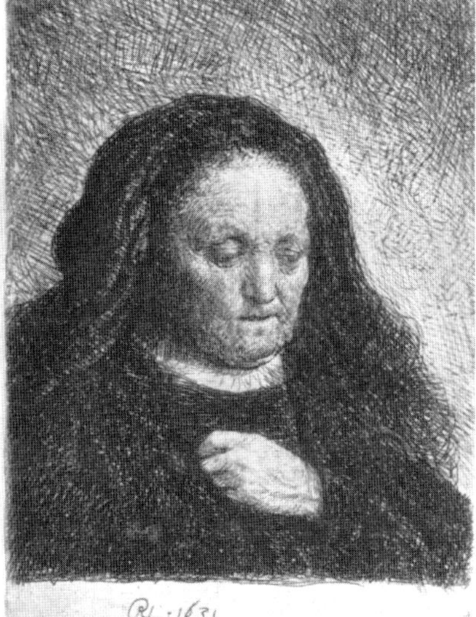

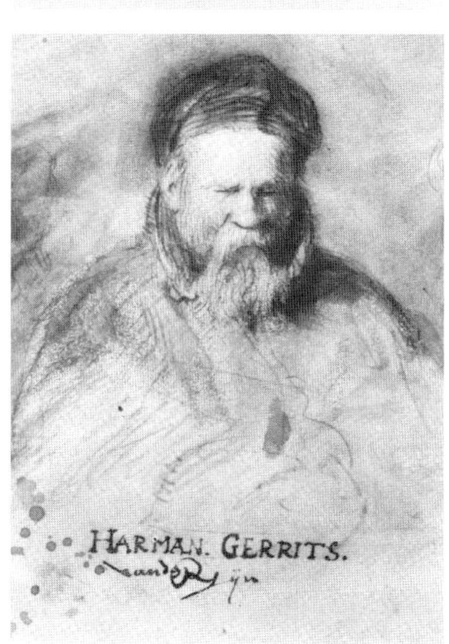

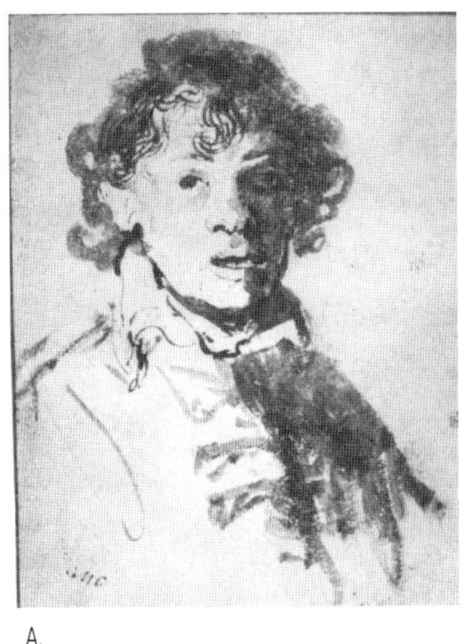

A.

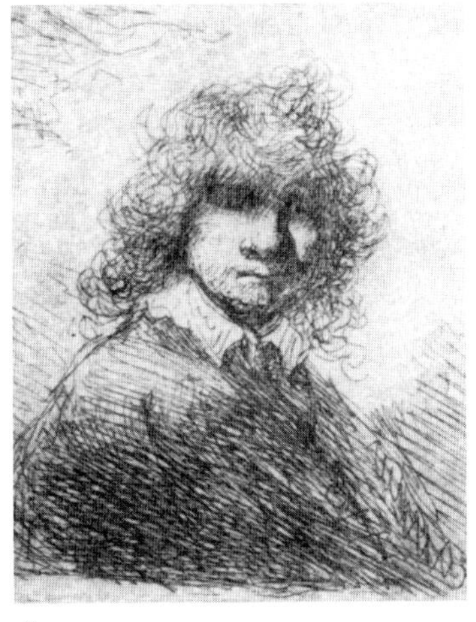

B.

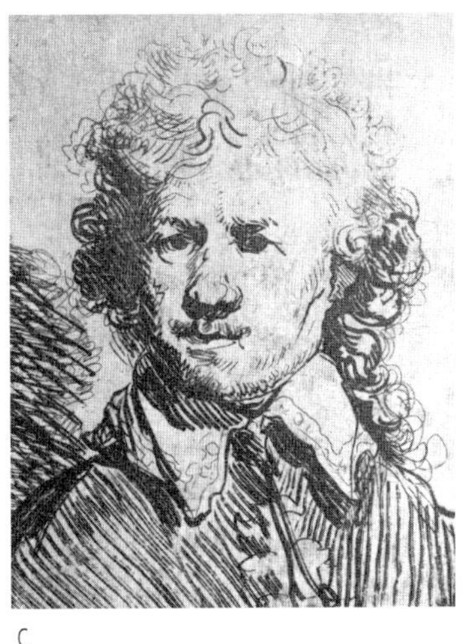

C.

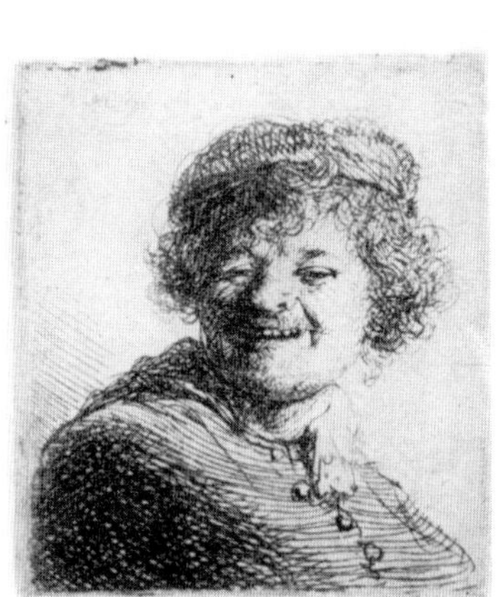

D.

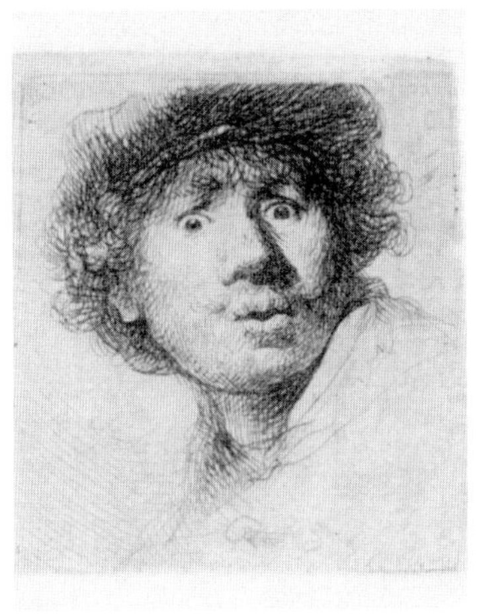

E.

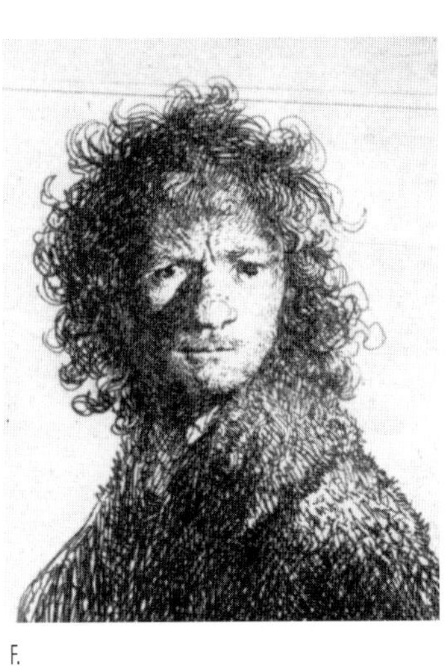

F.

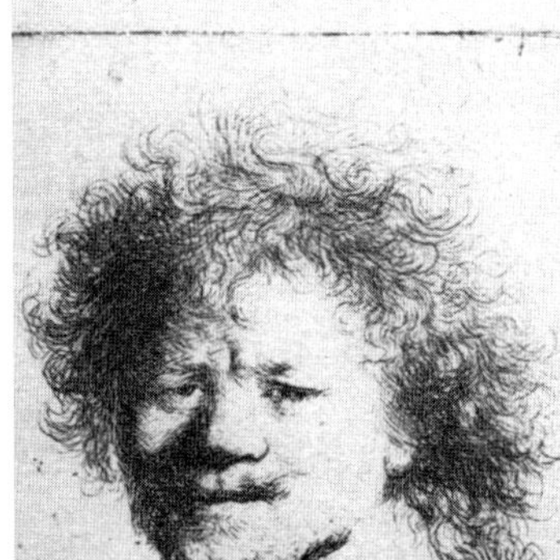

G.

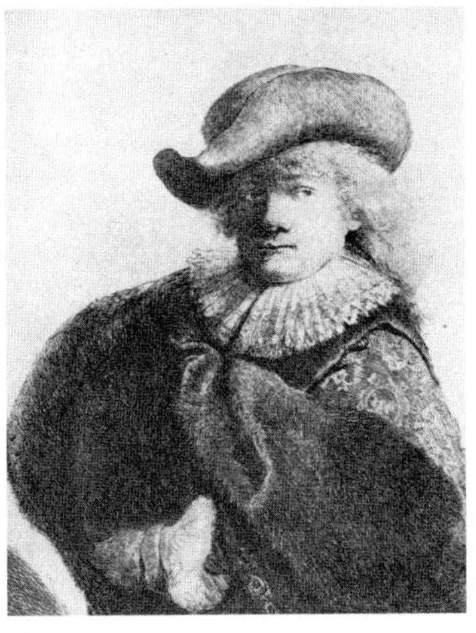

H.

A. **Self-Portrait**, Benesch 53, 1627-1628, British Museum, London

B. **Self-Portrait with High, Curly Hair**, B 27, 1628, British Museum, London

C. **Self-Portrait Bareheaded**, Roughly Sketched, B 338, 1629, Prentenkabinet, Rijksmuseum, Amsterdam

D. **Self-Portrait in a Cap, Laughing,** B 316, 1630, Prentenkabinet, Rijksmuseum, Amsterdam

E. **Self-Portrait in a Cap, Eyes Wide Open**, B 320, 1630, Prentenkabinet, Rijksmuseum, Amsterdam

F. **Self-Portrait, Scowling**, B 10, 1630, Prentenkabinet, Rijksmuseum, Amsterdam

G. **Self-Portrait with Long Bushy Hair**, B 8, 1631, Prentenkabinet, Rijksmuseum, Amsterdam

H. **Self-Portrait in a Soft Hat and an Embroidered Cloak**, B 7, 1631, Prentenkabinet, Rijksmuseum, Amsterdam

Late in 1631, or very early in 1632, Rembrandt moved from Leiden to Amsterdam, most likely to be nearer the source of his growing number of commissions and certainly to be at the center of Dutch commerce and Dutch art. He had invested money in the Amsterdam art dealership of Hendrick van Uylenburgh, and upon his arrival in the big city, Rembrandt moved in with van Uylenburgh and soon became a business partner of sorts.

Perhaps the greatest benison of this association, from Rembrandt's point of view, was meeting Hendrick's cousin Saskia, who soon became Rembrandt's lifelong love, and whom he married on 22 June 1634. Many pages of Rembrandt's diary are devoted to Saskia, from the marvelously tender engagement drawing of 8 June 1633 to his drawings, etchings, and paintings of Saskia in a variety of guises.

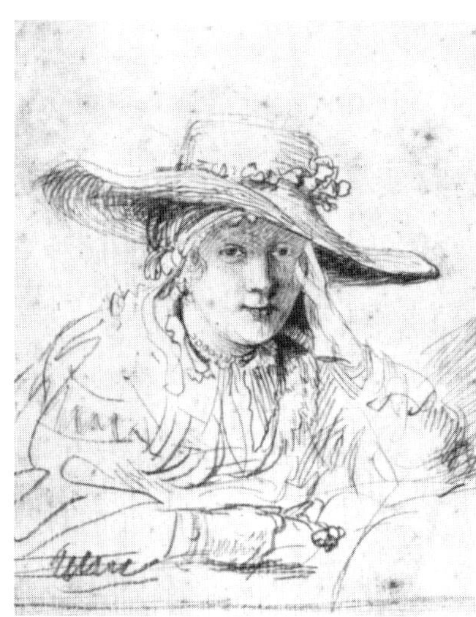
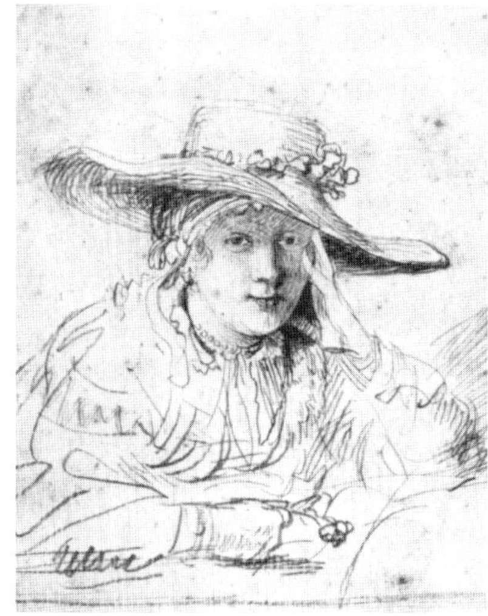

Portrait of Saskia in a Straw Hat, Benesch 427, 1633, Kupferstichkabinett, Staatliche Museen, Berlin, detail (left)

Young Woman at Her Toilet, Benesch 395, 1632-1634, Albertina, Vienna (right)

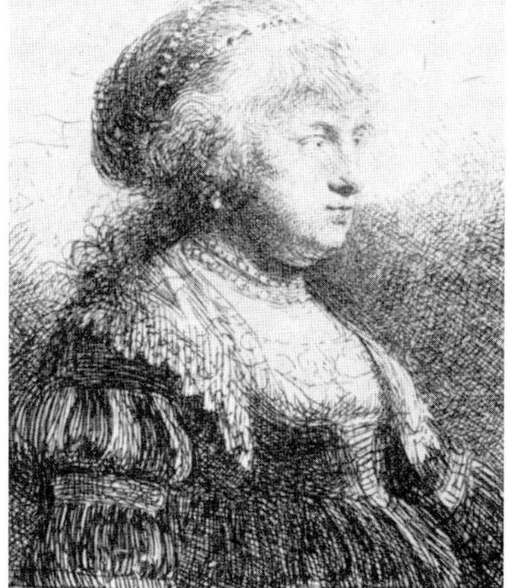

B 347, 1634, detail

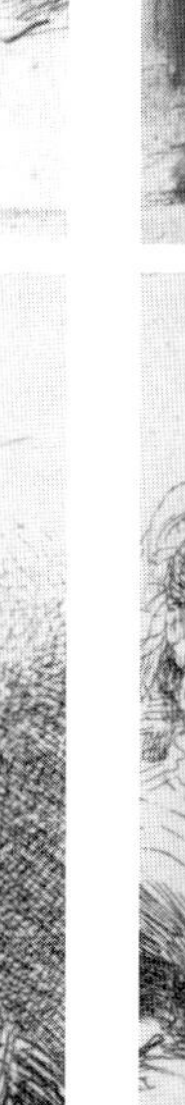
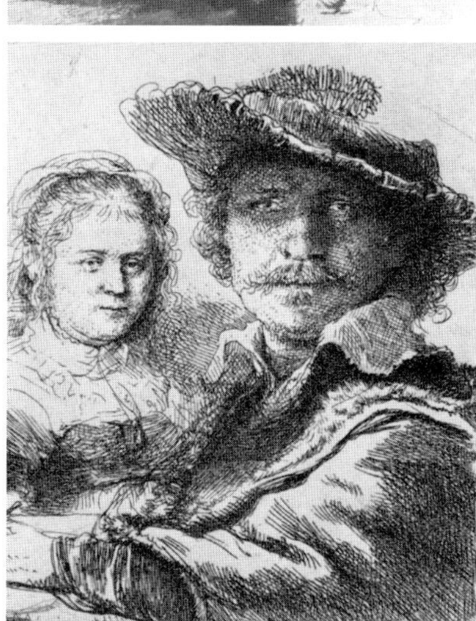

B 19, 1636, detail

Saskia with Pearls, B 347, 1634, Prentenkabinet, Rijksmuseum, Amsterdam, detail (left)

Self-Portrait with Saskia, B 19, 1636, British Museum, London (right)

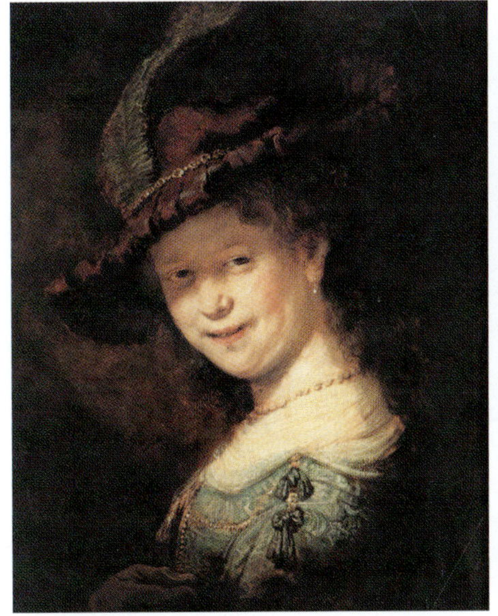

Bust of a Young Woman Smiling (possibly the Artist's Wife, Saskia), 1633, Gemäldegalerie Alter Meister, Dresden

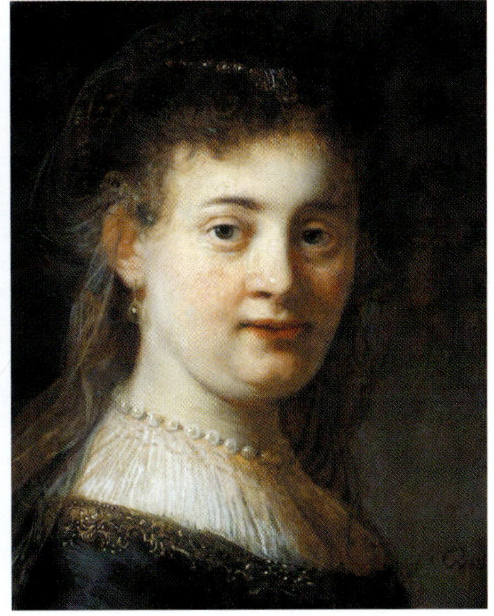

Bust of a Young Woman (commonly called the Artist's Wife, Saskia), 1633, Rijksmuseum, Amsterdam, detail

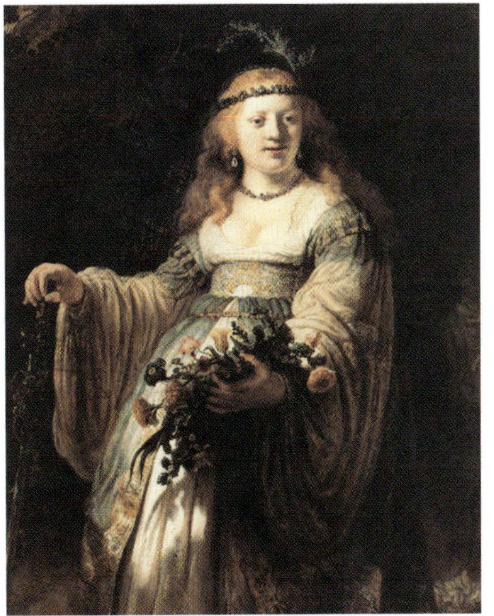

Saskia as Flora, 1635, The National Gallery, London

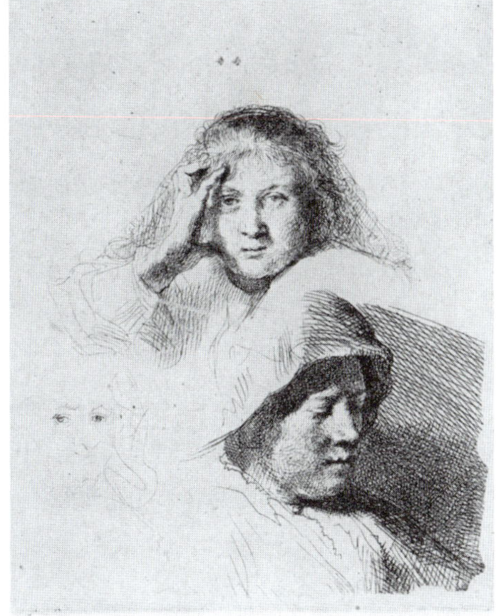

Three Heads of Women (probably three views of Saskia), B 367, 1637,Teylers Museum, Haarlem

Much too soon, however, indeed within less than two years of their life together, Rembrandt began a series of heart-wrenching drawings of Saskia ill at home in their rented house in the Niewe Doelenstraat. It was a series that he continued through their move to roomier quarters in a building known as the *Suyckerbackerij* right up to her death in their grand house in St. Anthoniesbreestraat. Their years of happiness were all too short—Saskia died on 14 June 1642, just a week shy of their eighth wedding anniversary.

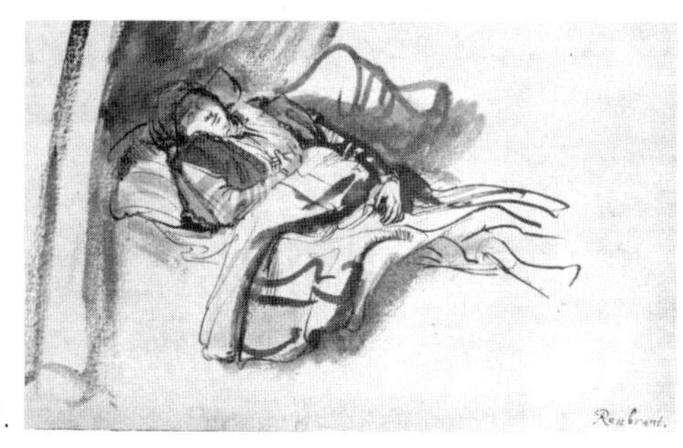

1.

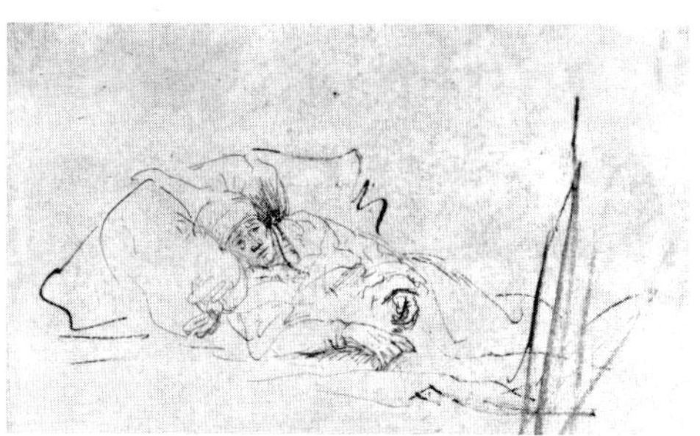

2.

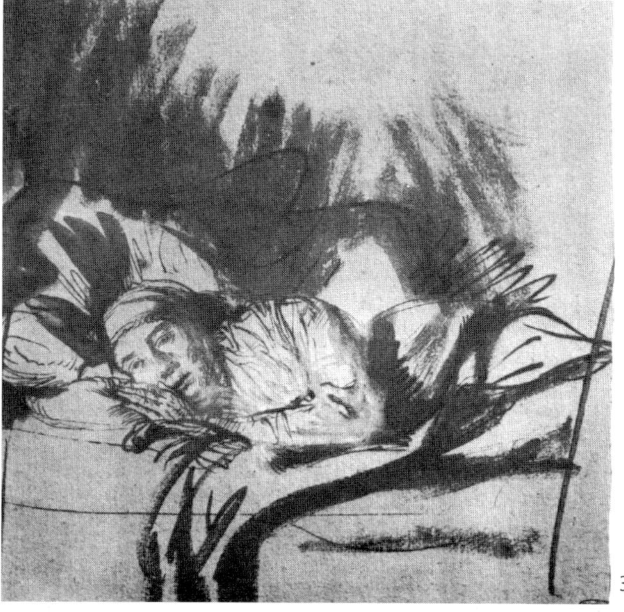

3.

1. **Saskia Asleep in Bed,** Benesch 281A, around 1635, Ashmolean Museum, Oxford

2. **Woman Ill in Bed,** Probably Saskia, Benesch 380, around 1639, British Museum, London

3. **Sick Woman Lying in Bed,** Probably Saskia, Benesch 283, around 1635, Collection Dutuit, Musée du Petit Palais, Paris

Saskia and Rembrandt had four children; their first, a son they named Rombartus after Saskia's father, they buried after two months on 15 February 1636; their second, a daughter named Cornelia, for Rembrandt's mother, they buried after two weeks on 13 August 1638; their third, also named Cornelia, they also buried after two weeks on 12 August 1640, barely a month before the death of Rembrandt's mother on 14 September 1640; their fourth, a son, was born just over a year later and was baptized on 22 September 1641. They named the boy Titus, after Saskia's sister Titia, who had died just over three months earlier.

Rembrandt's diary contains a number of affectionate drawings of children, including some of Saskia holding a baby, though any exact identification of the child depicted is impossible apart from assumption based on the probable date of each work.

Saskia Sitting Up in Bed, Benesch 280a, around 1635, private collection, London (left)

Four Studies of Saskia, Benesch 360 recto, around 1636, Museum Boymans-van Beuningen, Rotterdam, detail (right)

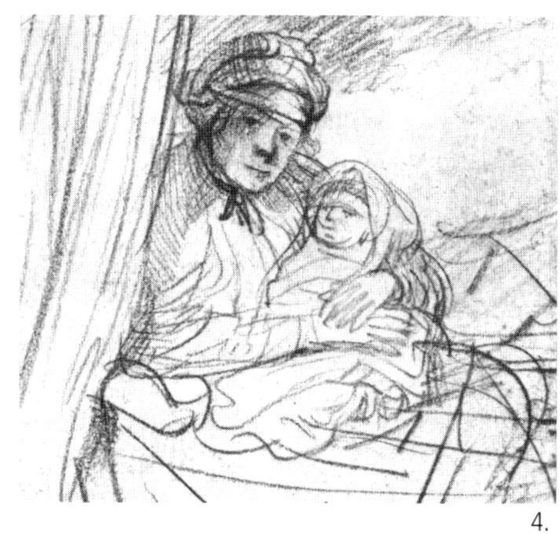

4.

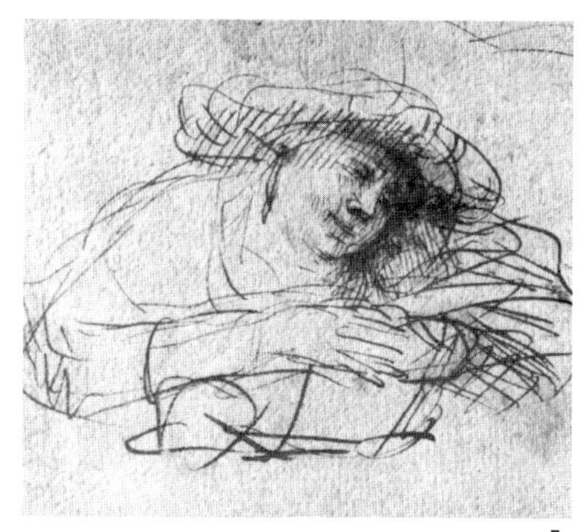

5.

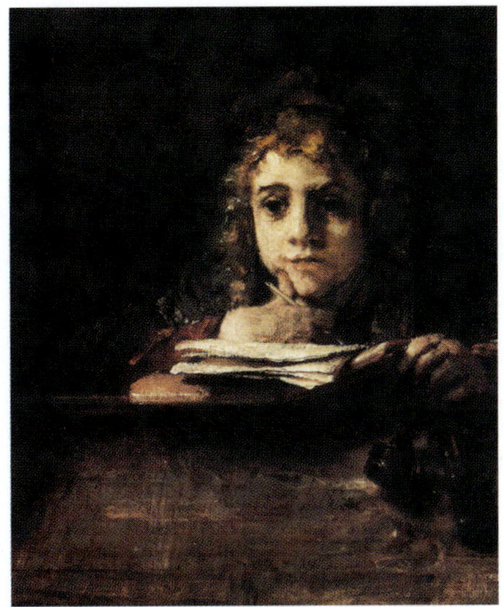

Titus at His Writing-Desk, 1655, Museum Boymans-van Beuningen, Rotterdam

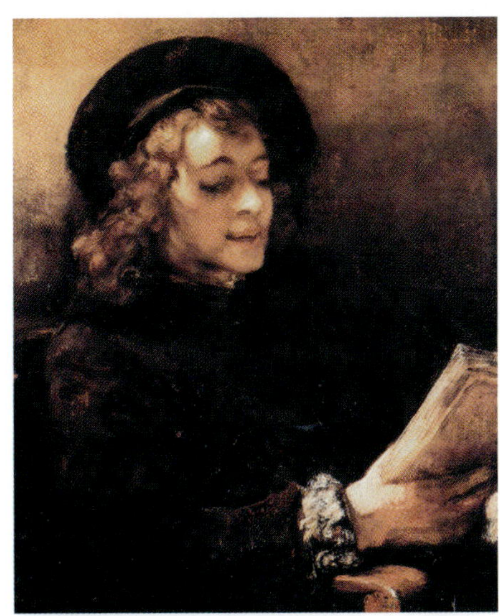

Titus Reading, 1658, Kunsthistorisches Museum, Vienna

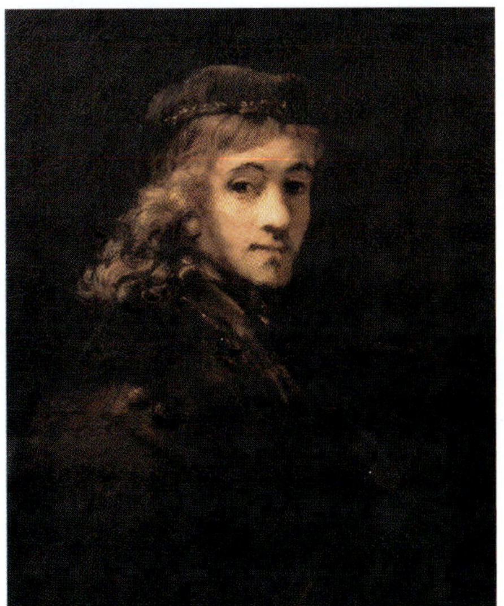

Titus van Rijn, 1660 (perhaps Rembrandt's Circle), Musée du Louvre, Paris

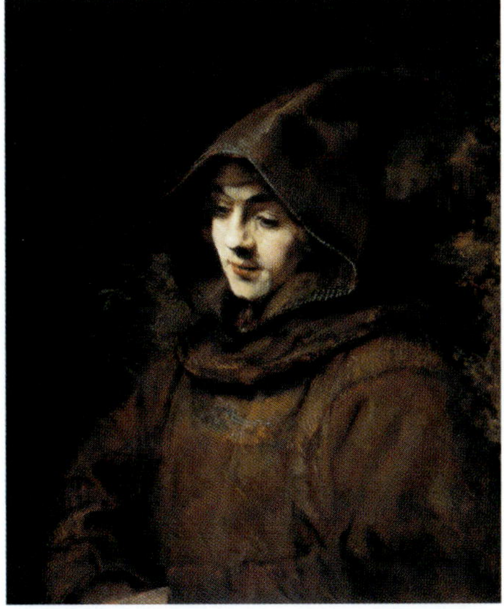

Titus as St. Francis, 1660, Rijksmuseum, Amsterdam

Titus was the only child born to Rembrandt and Saskia who survived infancy, and Rembrandt's diary, not surprisingly, contains affectionate portraits of him as boy and as man. Yet even Titus did not survive his father—he died of the plague in September of 1668, just two weeks before his twenty-seventh birthday, just over six months after his marriage to Magdalena van Loo, and just over a year before Rembrandt's death.

There are many additional drawings from the years 1636 to 1642 that may reflect the sadness of so many losses; those reflecting the grief of Saskia's declining health and early death especially may be

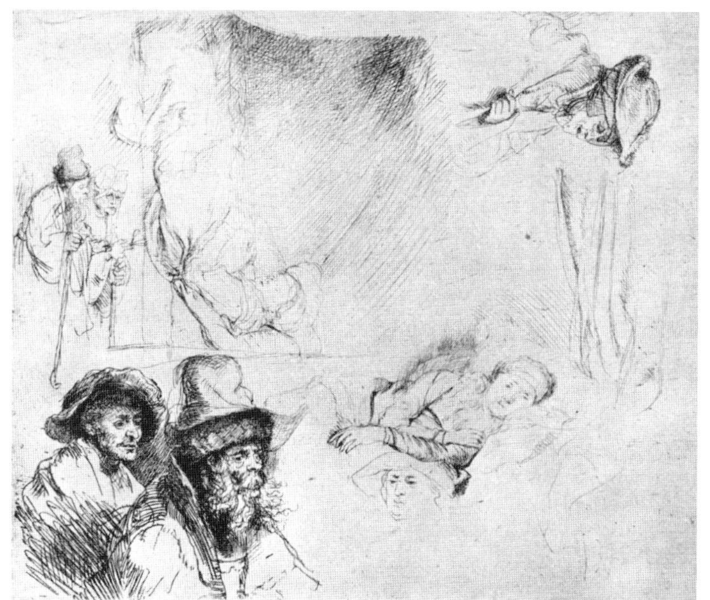

Studies, with Saskia Lying Ill in Bed, B 369, 1641-1642, Prentenkabinet, Rijksmuseum, Amsterdam

considered leaves from what I am calling Rembrandt's diary. His drawings of children are unfailingly lively and real; considered all together, they give an unmistakable impression of attraction, perhaps attraction tinged with longing. And the extensive series of drawings of Saskia in a wide range of attitudes—alone, with babies, with nurses, and then alone and obviously ill in bed—is a vivid chronicle of increasing sadness. An etching from the final months of those years, apparently intended as a scene depicting a group of men, is turned instead into two representations of Saskia on her sickbed. Given his deep love for his wife, it is unreasonable to think that Rembrandt could pull his mind away from her for long in those last weeks, and this etching may attest as much.

Despite the growing sadness of the years of their time together, however, there must also have been a great deal of happiness, a happiness Rembrandt's loving portraits of Saskia make clear. The tenderness Rembrandt felt for Saskia in motherhood informs his deeply moving series of works depicting Mary and the baby Jesus, both those made when Saskia was still alive and those made across the years after her death. The two drawings from 1635 and 1636 of Saskia in bed with a baby (see above) may well anticipate the 1652 etching of Mary and the Christ child in *The Adoration of the Shepherds, a Night Piece.*

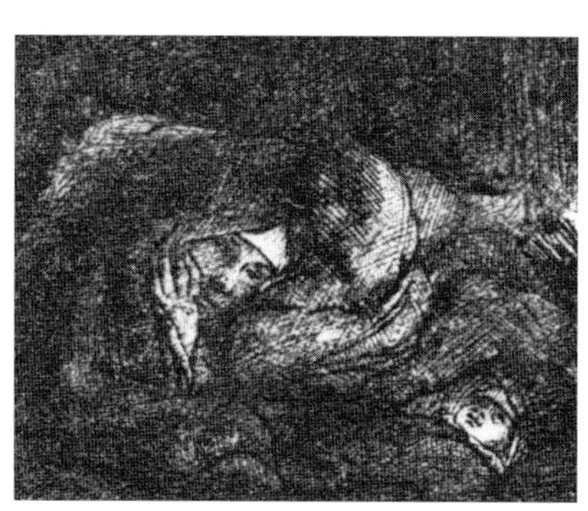

B 46, detail

The years of Rembrandt's greatest domestic happiness, despite their increasing sadness of loss and Saskia's illness, were also years of dramatic personal success. From the time of his move to Amsterdam until 1642, he produced no less than thirty-four drawings, ten etchings, and fourteen paintings on biblical themes alone. As Rembrandt's world increasingly turns up in his depictions of the biblical world, many of these works may be said to be pages from what I am calling Rembrandt's diary; I mention three in particular.

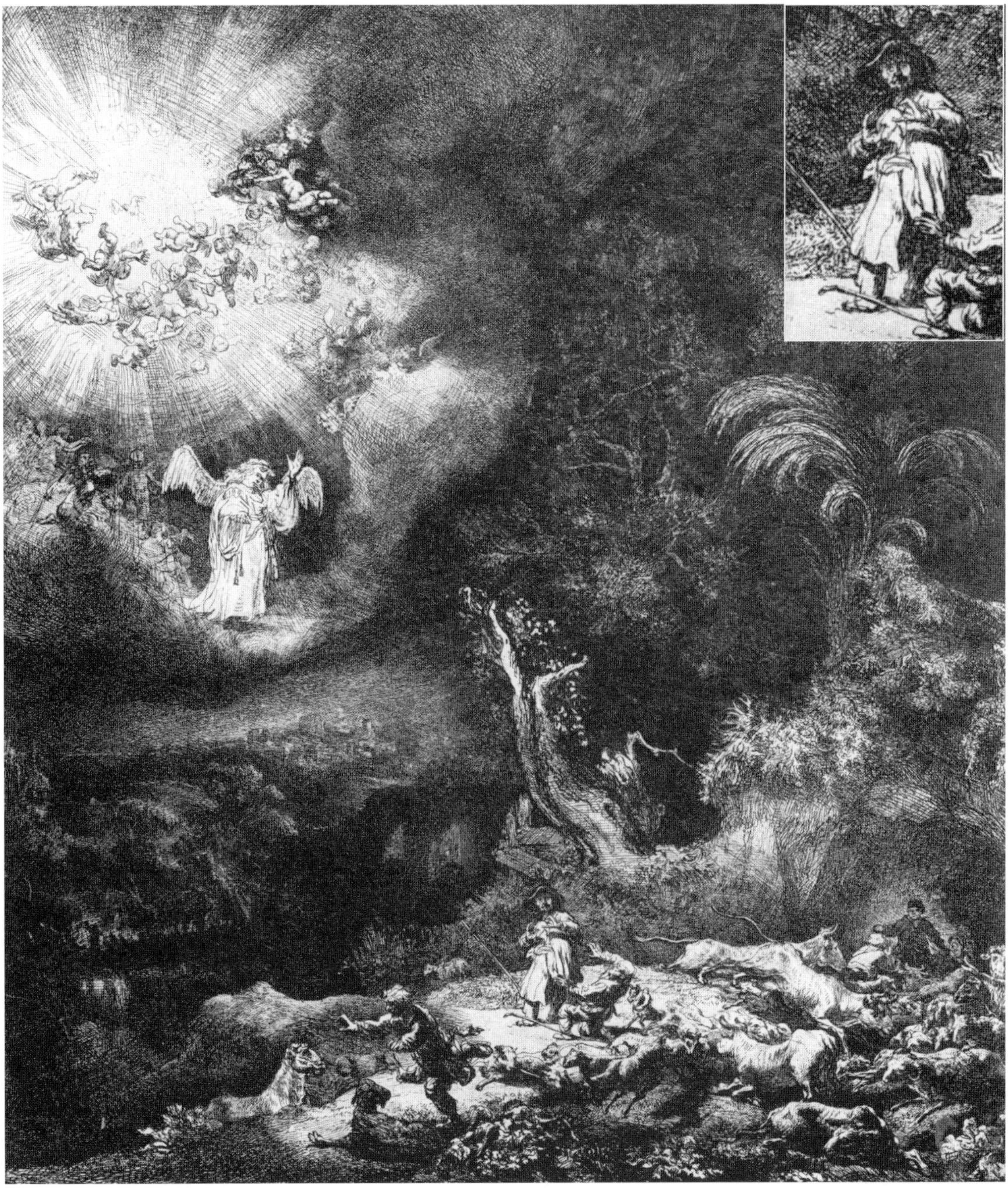

The Angel Appearing to the Shepherds, B 44, 1634, Prentenkabinet, Rijksmuseum, Amsterdam

There is an etching from 1634, *The Angel Appearing to the Shepherds*, into which Rembrandt has placed himself in the midst of the turmoil of frightened shepherds and stampeding livestock, his hands raised in astonishment, his staff falling, and his face turned out toward the viewer, as if to check on our reaction and to remind us that this event is about us as well.

There is *The Prodigal Son in the Tavern* of 1636, with its clear *double entendre*: Rembrandt and Saskia are enjoying prosperity, but there is the warning that the story of the prodigal son provides against

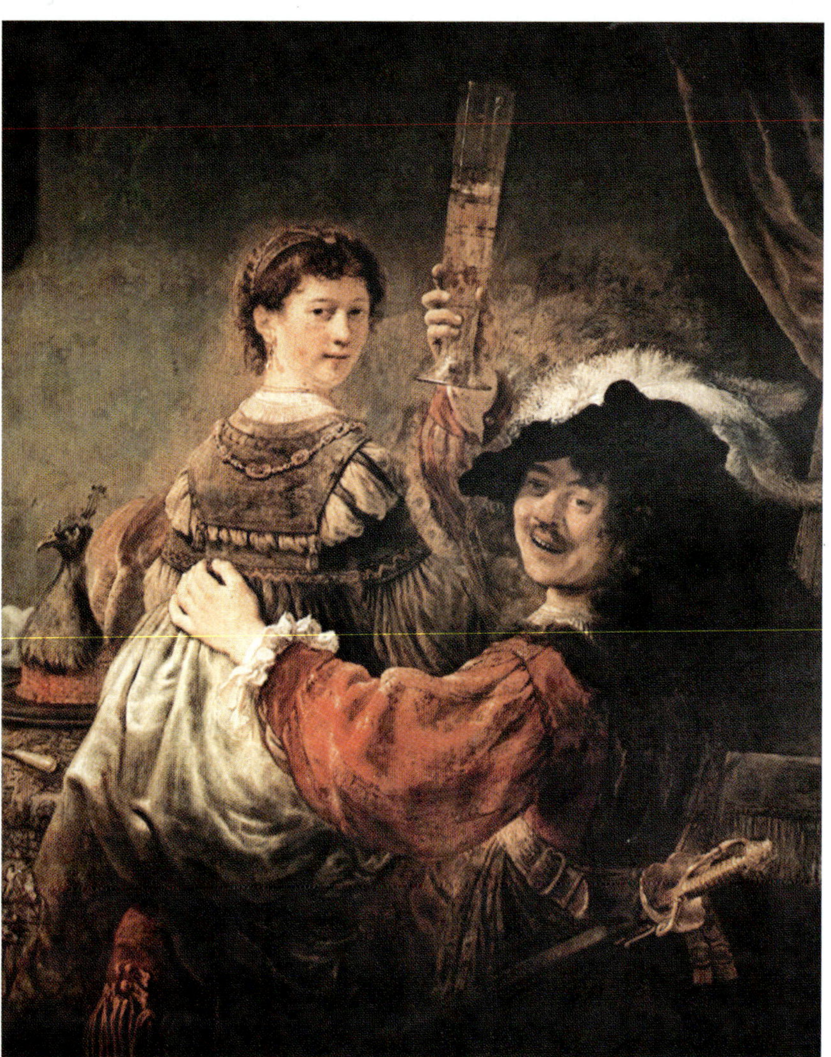

The Prodigal Son in the Tavern, 1635, Gemäldegalerie Alter Meister, Dresden

the unwise use of one's wealth (see chap. 6). In 1636, Rembrandt was just beginning to come into serious money.

And then there is *The Death of the Virgin* of 1639, a work that presents death, even the death of a holy person, as a reality to be met without panic and without hysteria, but with an honest finality despite unavoidable pain. This etching is crammed with nearly every possible reaction to death, from the tender care of the apostle supporting Mary's head, to the medical attention of the physician taking her pulse, to the weeping grief of the woman behind him, to the swooning plea of the woman standing by the bedpost, to the fervent petition of the young apostle standing behind her, to the accepting prayer before inevitable death of the woman kneeling in front of him, to the plain curiosity of the fellow parting the curtain to look in, to the gossiping distraction of the two serving maids seated on the step, to the indifference of the man at the lower right corner, to

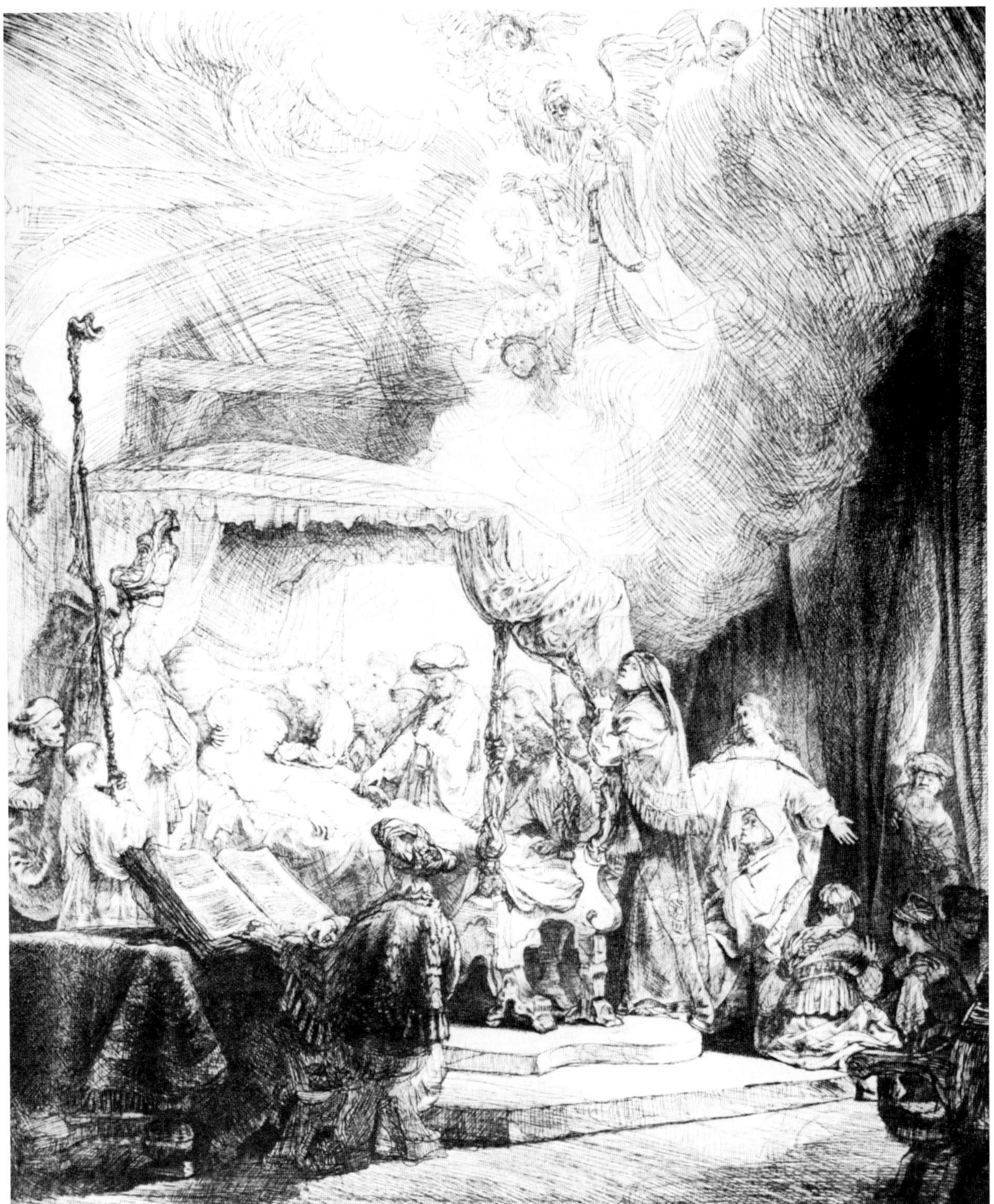

The Death of the Virgin, B 99, 1639, Prentenkabinet, Rijksmuseum, Amsterdam

the official solemnity of the reader and the pompous priest at the left corner of the bed, to the heavenly swarm of reaching, receptive angels. The range of expressions on the faces of those who gather on the far side of Mary's bed is a catalog of human reaction to death.

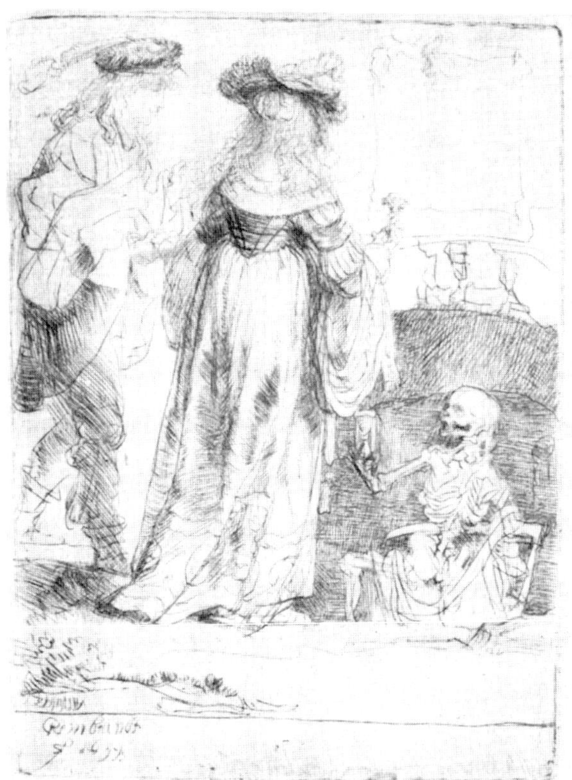

The Married Couple and Death, B 109, 1639, Prentenkabinet, Rijksmuseum, Amsterdam

Another etching from the same year, though it has no specific biblical connection, is a companion leaf from the diary of Rembrandt. It is *Death Appearing to a Wedded Couple from an Open Grave*, a macabre representation of Death coming from a tomb, his scythe behind him, and an hourglass in his skeletal right hand. Meeting Death is a well-dressed young couple holding hands. The woman advances toward Death, holding out a flower; the young man steps with her, but he has on his face a skeptical expression, as if he is at a costume ball. Rembrandt several times presented Saskia holding a flower, at least once well after her death.

By 1639, Rembrandt and Saskia had buried two children, and his drawings of his wife from these months show her to have been seriously ill. I wonder whether *The Death of the Virgin* and *Death Appearing to a Wedded Couple from an Open Grave* may represent Rembrandt's struggle between acceptance and denial, two pages from his diary that tell us something of what must have been going through his mind in 1639.

Sometime shortly before Saskia's death, or certainly very soon thereafter, Rembrandt hired a widow, Geertghe Dircx, to help out with the care of Titus, who was not quite nine months old when his mother died. Rembrandt himself was much involved in his little son's care, and that fact, coupled with his deep sadness at his loss of Saskia, may account for the fact that his prodigious output during the years of his happiness, reduced during Saskia's years of increasing illness, was now reduced still further. What I have called his diary grows notably thinner during the next decade, and his self-portraits grow fewer and more serious, even somber, in the years after Saskia's death.

Saskia had brought to her marriage with Rembrandt a considerable dowry; her will assigns all her possessions to Titus and Rembrandt, and under Rembrandt's supervision, unless he should

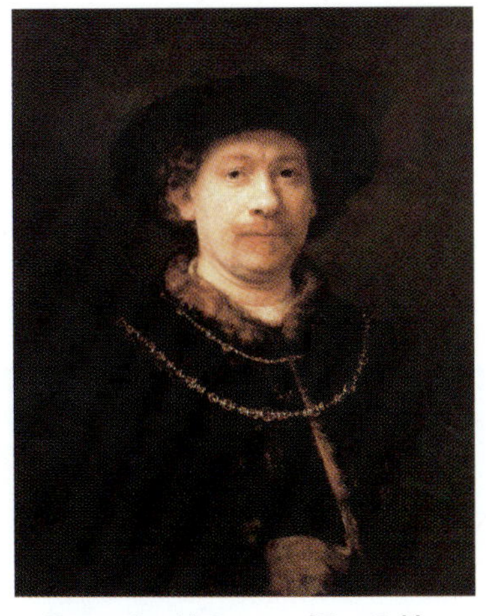

Self-Portrait with Beret and Two Gold Chains, 1642-1645, Museo Thyssen-Bornemisza, Madrid

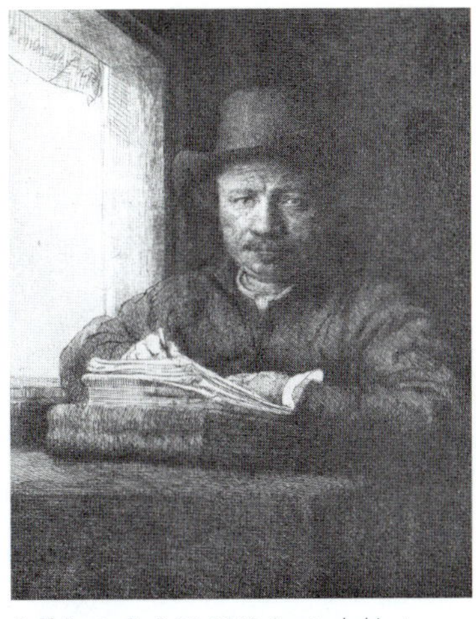

Self-Portrait, B 22, 1648, Prentenkabinet, Rijksmuseum, Amsterdam

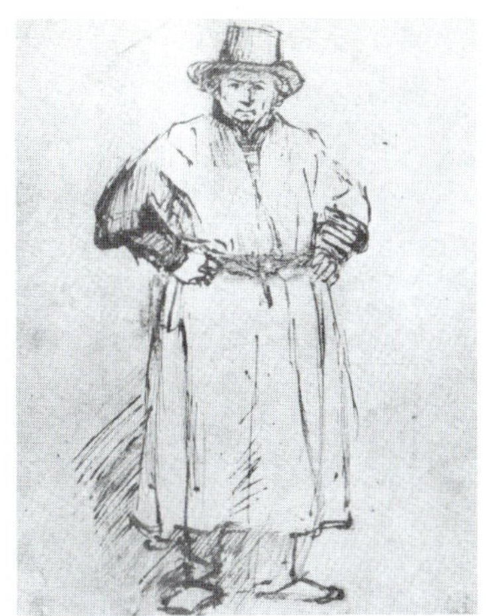

Self-Portrait in Studio Attire, Benesch 1171, around 1655-1656, Rembrandthuis Museum, Amsterdam

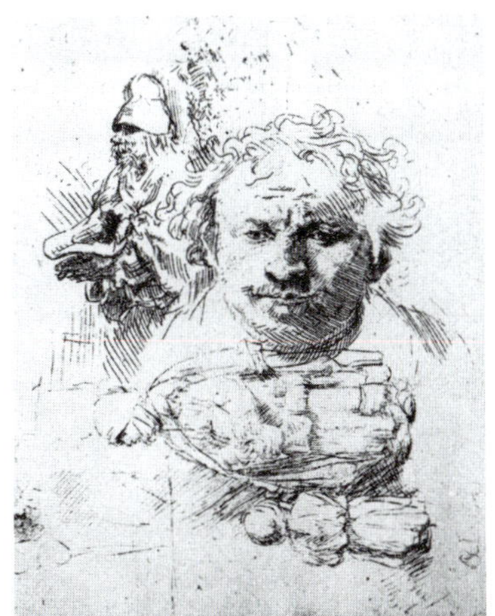

Studies, with a Self-Portrait, B 370, 1651, Prentenkabinet, Rijksmuseum, Amsterdam

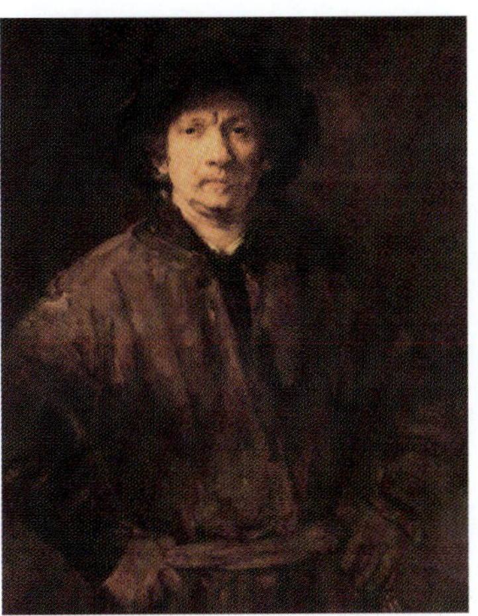

Self-Portrait, 1652, Kunsthistoriches Museum, Vienna

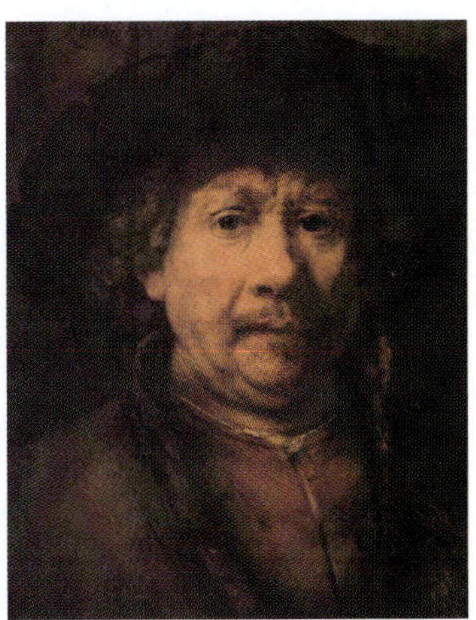

Self-Portrait, 1655, Kunsthistoriches Museum, Vienna

remarry, "because she is confident that he will acquit himself very well in good conscience" (RD 1642/2, p. 224).

In the event, though Saskia's confidence as recorded is her will "in the morning at about 9 o'clock" on 5 June 1642 was well intended, and though Rembrandt himself would have believed it then to be so, it was a confidence that proved misplaced. Rembrandt began a troubled relationship with Geertghe Dircx that ended very badly. He spent money carelessly and amassed debts he was increasingly unable to meet. He came under mounting criticism from his friends, from the Dutch Reformed Church, from his patrons and his clients, and of course from those who were jealous of his talent and of his achievements.

An important page from his biblical diary in these years is a painting from 1644, now in London, *Christ and the Woman Taken in*

Adultery, based on the narrative of John 8:2–11. This passage is not present in the oldest manuscripts and versions of the Gospel of John and is judged on stylistic grounds to have been inserted there from an

Christ and the Woman Taken in Adultery, 1644, The National Gallery, London

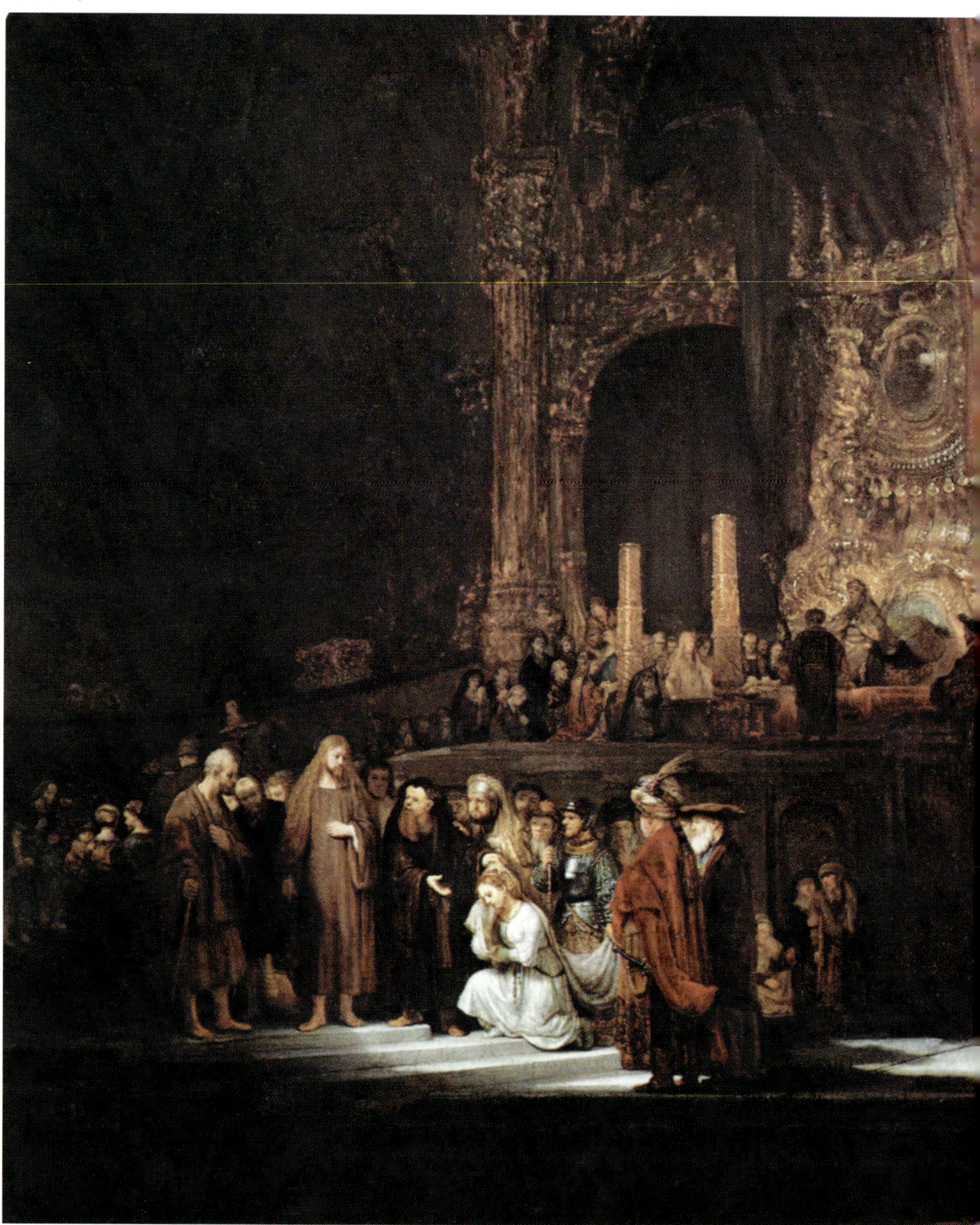

original location in one of the Synoptic Gospels, possibly the Gospel of Luke, just before the Passion narrative, at 21:38. None of this would have posed any problem for Rembrandt, even if he had been aware of it.

Rembrandt gives us his customary temple interior of vast and impersonal proportions, with two scenes of activity: the high priest holding hieratic court in the background at the right, with a line of supplicants awaiting his ruling, and Christ and his disciples confronted by "the scribes and the Pharisees" in the center foreground.

The high priest sits on a golden throne of vast dimensions and is separated from the pollution of the sinners who approach him by a deep raised platform and also by a long space between himself and those who approach. He is physically above any criticism, guarded from any unpleasant proximity by attendants left and right.

Christ, in obvious contrast, stands in a far more public area that suggests the entryway through which the woman's accusers have just brought her for condemnation. He is dressed no differently from those who follow him, and his coarse brown robe and bare feet are made all the more dramatic by the sumptuous dress and fancy leather boots of the scribes and the Pharisees.

The spokesman of the accusers lifts the woman's veil with a delicate touch of thumb and forefinger, while gesturing toward her with his right hand. Just behind him, a bearded official encourages and nudges him forward with a hand on his shoulder. The heavily armored soldier holding the woman's train as though it was a piece of lumber adds to the ludicrous pomposity of the scribes and the Pharisees, as does the Pharisee with the high hat who is shushing with a finger to his lips the massive red-cloaked figure standing in the right foreground (the aggrieved husband?).

A shaft of light falls onto the accused woman, who is gorgeously clad in a white dress with a blue and gold sash and blue satin slippers. And at the edge of this circle of light, Christ stands, the upper two-thirds of his body in the light. Christ has no halo, no unearthly glow, no idealized handsome face. This is Christ beginning to have the appearance of inner divinity that Rembrandt was to bring to a peak in the marvelous series of portraits of Christ that he ended with *The Risen Christ* of 1661. Here, Christ listens quietly, as the charges against the weeping woman are made, but there is no question who is in command of the scene or who is to utter the authoritative word in this place of so much speaking.

Rembrandt leaves no doubt about where his sympathies lie nor about which utterance, that of the organized and official religion or that of God's own son, is the one to be followed. The point of the story in John's Gospel is compassion and forgiveness, not condemnation, and Rembrandt knew he needed compassion and forgiveness as much as he resented all the criticism and condemnation he was getting from people he must have felt had no right to be casting stones. I doubt that Rembrandt was attempting to defend his behavior with Geertghe Dircx with this painting, not least because of his choice of this particular story from the Gospel of John. But he was certainly protesting religious officialdom and self-righteous criticism, and his contrast between the accusation of the scribes and Pharisees and the gentle forgiveness of Christ, along with the tenderly painted young woman, may well be an indication of his thoughts and emotions in a difficult time.

At some point during the late 1640s, Hendrickje Stoeffels became a part of the Rembrandt household, probably as a serving maid. Rembrandt's earlier affection for Geertghe Dircx had already begun to cool, in part perhaps because of what appears to have been an instability of mind that led eventually to her confinement, and in part because she began to make assumptions about her status in his household that he considered groundless. As Geertghe became more and more unreasonable, Rembrandt turned his attention at home more and more toward Hendrickje, who probably had also suffered abuse from Geertghe's behavior.

We have no way of recovering the details of the story, as what we have left of it has to do mostly with the legal actions taken by Geertghe against Rembrandt and his responses to her various suits. We do not know Geertghe's exact age when she entered Rembrandt's service; we may estimate, from her parents' wedding date in 1599 and the date of her own wedding in November 1634, that she was around thirty. Geertghe left her position in the grand house on St. Anthoniesbreestraat in 1649, having agreed to accept from Rembrandt an annual payment toward her living expense. At that time Hendrickje, who succeeded her as Rembrandt's housekeeper, would have been in her early twenties.

The year 1649 was a difficult one for the three of them, with Geertghe changing her mind not long after her departure and taking legal action against Rembrandt, demanding either marriage or more money than he had agreed to supply. Hendrickje gave a deposition affirming the terms of Geertghe's parting agreement, and Rembrandt resisted and then fought Geertghe's new demands in every way possible. Though a few drawings can be tentatively dated 1649, there is no etching and no painting from Rembrandt in that year, the only such year in his career as an artist.

The trouble with Geertghe dragged on at least until the autumn of 1656. Hendrickje remained with Rembrandt until her death by plague in July 1663. She bore Rembrandt a daughter, whom they named Cornelia, in October of 1654, and suffered the condemnation of the Dutch Reformed Church for living with him without benefit of clergy.

Hendrickje appears to have been devoted to Rembrandt and willing to bear the criticism made inevitable by that devotion. She took his side in the difficulties with Geertghe, and she was apparently a mainstay for both Rembrandt and Titus in the period of financial reverse and professional disappointment that began a few years after Saskia's death. Rembrandt, for his part, seems to have had real affection for Hendrickje and to have depended upon her. His likenesses of her, either in drawings or as his model in a variety of paintings, suggest that she was both kind and attractive.

Yet Rembrandt never married Hendrickje, a step that would have made life much easier for her. The reasons usually suggested have to do with Saskia's will, the terms of which would have brought even greater financial trouble to Rembrandt if he had remarried, and with the great disparity in social position between the master painter and the housemaid. Given what we can surmise of Rembrandt's character, this second reason has not a scrap of support. The financial problems remarriage would have brought are much more likely to have been a consideration for Rembrandt, but I suggest that the real reason he did not marry Hendrickje was that he never stopped loving Saskia, that he could never bring himself to think of marrying any other woman, even one so caring and devoted as Hendrickje Stoeffels. He could live

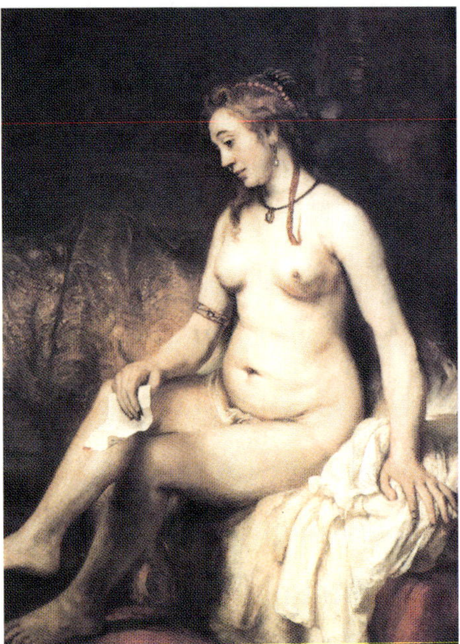

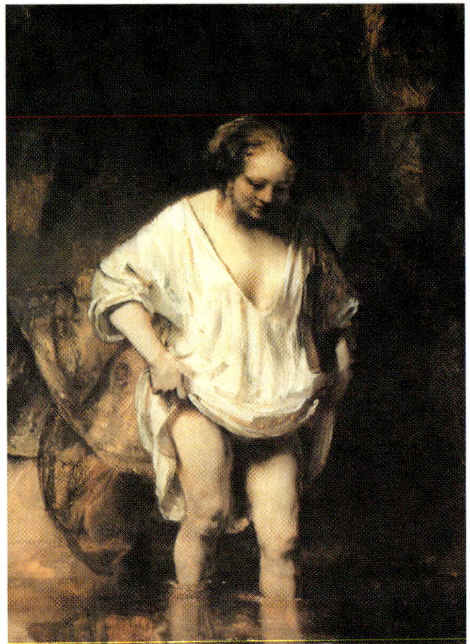

Bathsheba with King David's Letter, 1654, Musée du Louvre, Paris, detail (left)

Woman Bathing in a Stream, 1654 or 1655, The National Gallery, London (right)

with her, and even have with her a child whom he loved enough to name after his mother, but he could not bring himself to marry again. The fact that he painted no protest to the church's condemnation of Hendrickje similar to the *Christ and the Woman Taken in Adultery* of 1644 suggests that he had moved to a different level in his response to the world about him. And his likenesses of Hendrickje suggest that he thought of her more as a partner and model, even a colleague, than as a wife. One cannot imagine Rembrandt painting Saskia as the nude *Bathsheba* of 1654 now in the Louvre, or even as the *Woman Bathing in a Stream* of 1654 or 1655 now in London's National Gallery, both works for which Hendrickje was the model.

Even as the female companion of *The Prodigal Son in the Tavern* of 1636, Saskia is clothed right up to her chin (see chap. 6). And when Rembrandt painted what I have called a picture of love, *The Jewish Bride* of 1666, twenty-four years after Saskia's death, I believe he was thinking still of Saskia, only Saskia. That painting is the second most moving of the final pages of his diary, first place belonging of course to *The Return of the Prodigal Son*, which he finished toward the end of his life.

Among Rembrandt's extensive array of drawings, works that he created in the main for his own eyes, there are but three that are generally regarded as likenesses of Hendrickje; of Saskia, there are more than forty. There are no etchings of Hendrickje; of Saskia, there are nearly twenty different representations. Rembrandt never

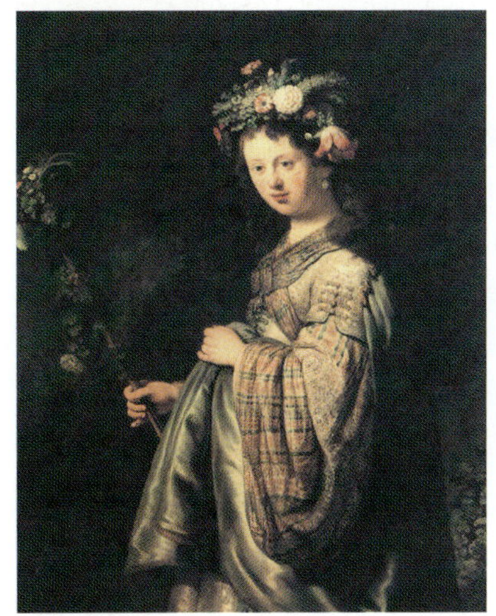

Saskia as Flora, 1634, State Hermitage, Winter Palace, St. Petersburg

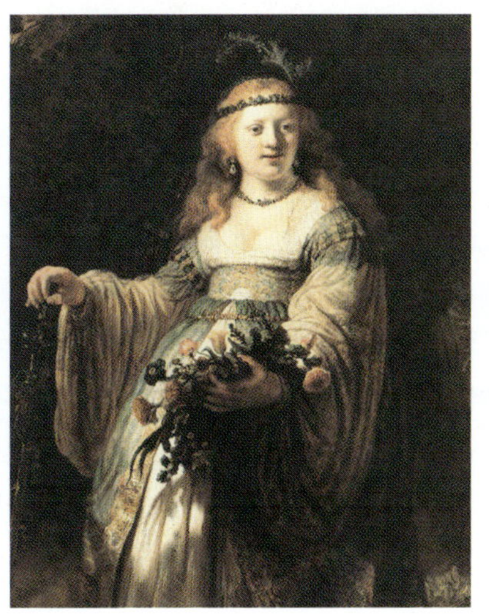

Saskia as Flora, 1636, The National Gallery, London

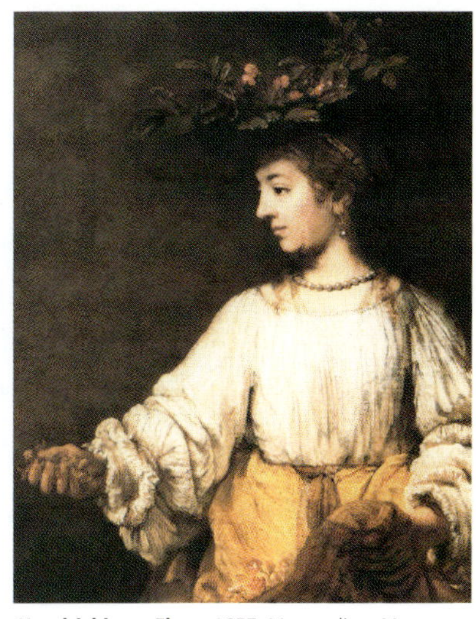

Hendrickje as Flora, 1657, Metropolitan Museum of Art, New York

depicted himself with Hendrickje, as he did with Saskia, and the paintings that present Saskia, either as herself or in various guises, have a quality of affection, of intensity, of caring, that seem to me to be lacking in the paintings that present Hendrickje. Compare, for instance, his two paintings of Saskia (above left) as the goddess Flora, with that of Hendrickje as the goddess Flora (above right). The difference in the elegance of presentation is obvious; but in emotional impact and in intensity, the difference is nearly palpable.

Saskia and Rembrandt had but nine years together, from 1633 to 1642. Hendrickje and Rembrandt, by contrast, were together for nineteen years, from about 1644 to 1663. Yet there are altogether about seventy likenesses of Saskia and only eight of Hendrickje. Of Geertghe, there is no known representation in any form.

The *Jacob Blessing the Children of Joseph* of 1656 may be a page from Rembrandt's diary. He had two children by the year 1656: Titus, who was fifteen, and Cornelia, who was two. Rembrandt may have been thinking of the blessing that could be given to these two, not least in that heaviest year of his financial difficulties, with his application for *cessio bonorum* "due to losses suffered in business, as well as damages and losses at sea…so much difficulty that it is impossible for him to pay his creditors" (RD 1656/10, pp. 345–47). Thee

Jacob Blessing the Sons of Joseph, 1656, Staatliche Kunstsammlungen, Schloss Wilhelmshöhe, Kassel

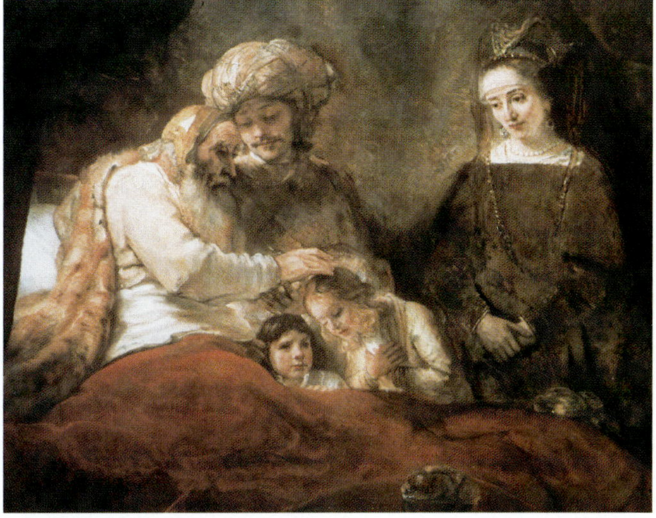

biblical narrative of Genesis 48 may have reminded Rembrandt that the source of real blessing lies beyond anything we can give, and the tenderness with which old Jacob and Joseph and his two sons are painted has the glow of personal experience.

I cannot resist including in Rembrandt's diary the grand self-portrait of 1658, now in New York in the Frick Collection. In 1658 the house in St. Anthoniesbreestraat and its furnishings were sold to repay some of Rembrandt's debt. His graphic works, including both his collection of the drawings of other artists and his own drawings, his artistic sourcebook, were sold that year as well, and for a pitifully low sum. Yet Rembrandt's only likeness of himself in that year of separation from the physical remembrances of his happy years with Saskia is that of a grandee in a rich man's outfit, complete with gold-headed cane. The fact that he and Hendrickje and the two children may have been permitted to live in the house in St. Anthoniesbreestraat for

Self-Portrait, 1658, The Frick Collection, New York

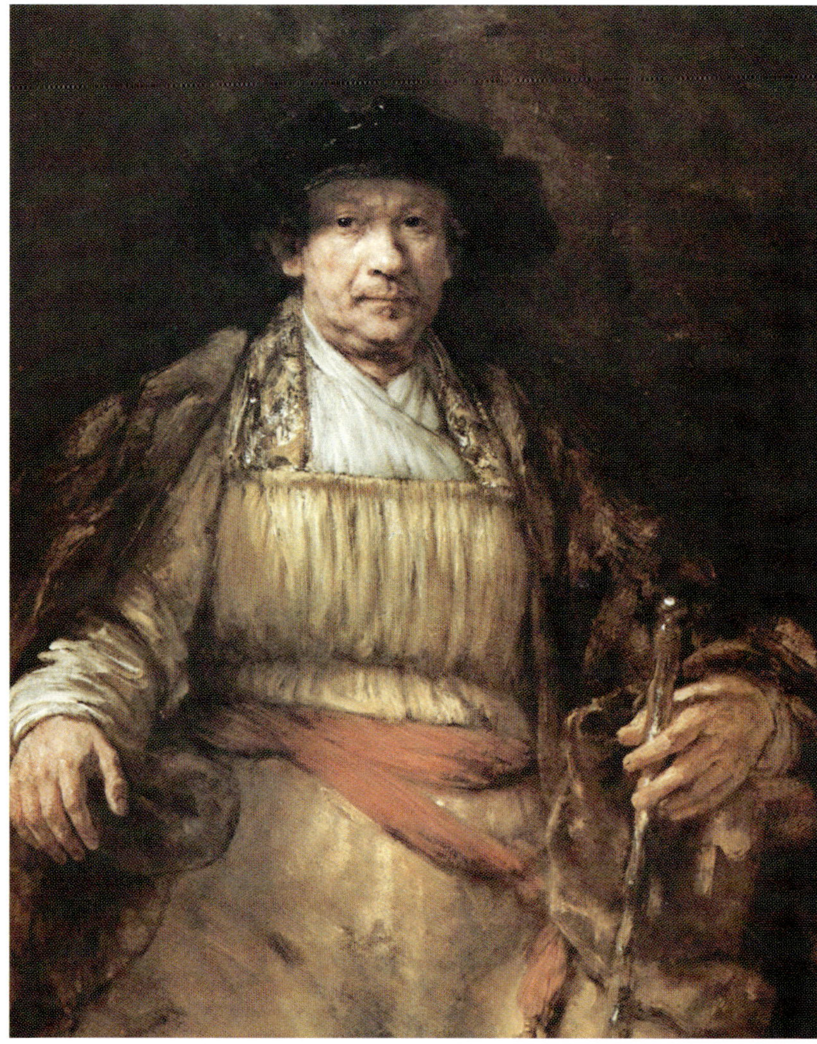

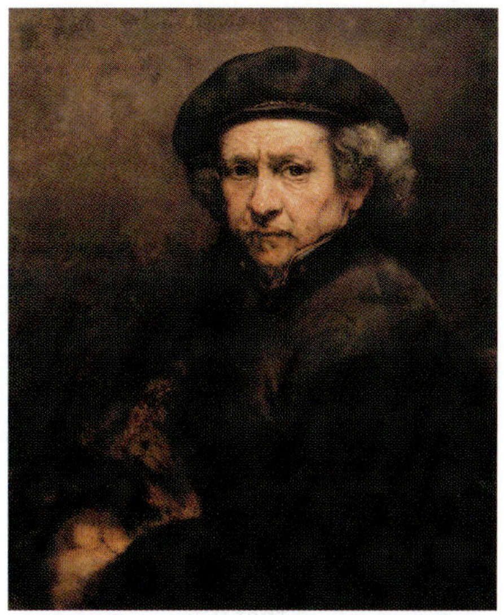

Self-Portrait, 1659, National Gallery of Art, Washington

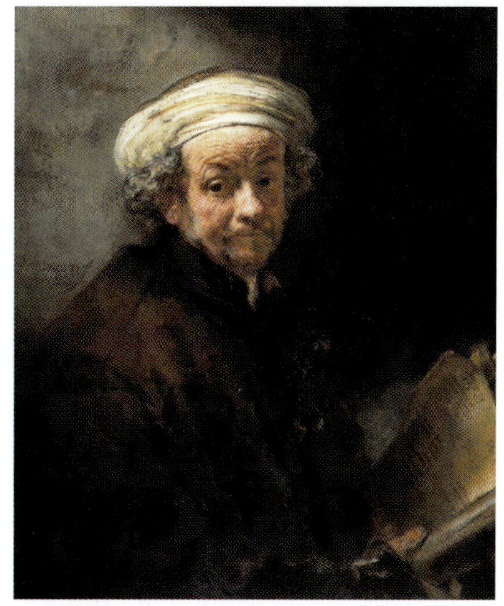

Self-Portrait as the Apostle Paul, 1661, Rijksmuseum, Amsterdam

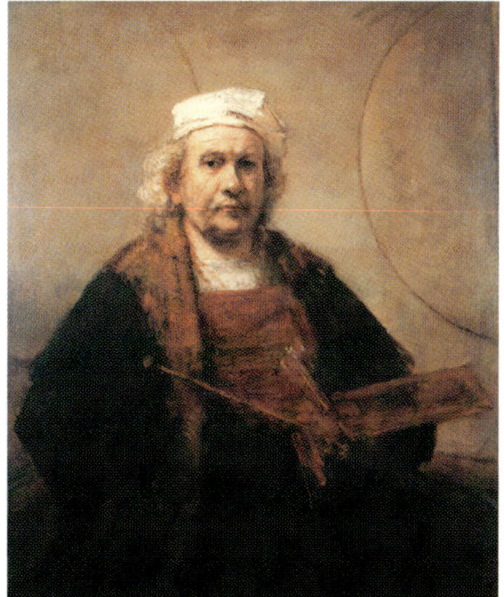

Self-Portrait, 1665-1669, The Iveagh Bequest, Kenwood House, London

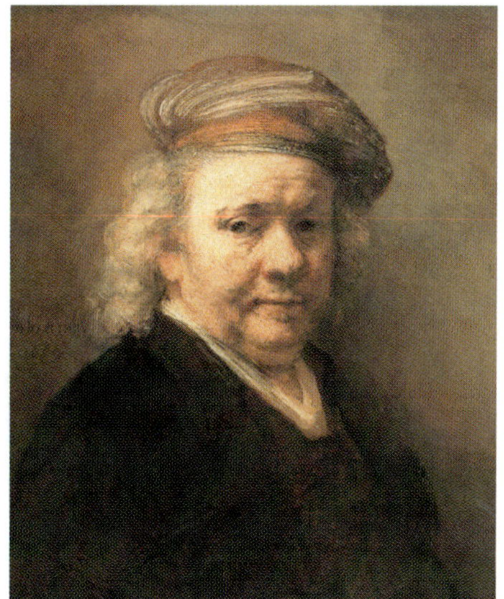

Self-Portrait, 1669, Maurithuis, The Hague

nearly two years after its sale would only have added to the pain of its loss, but Rembrandt, perhaps atypically given his penchant for honest realism, presents himself as on top of the world. The additional self-portraits of the final ten years of Rembrandt's life are more characteristically realistic, and they depict with unflinching honesty the face life had given to him.

There are at least five additional paintings on biblical themes that may give hints of Rembrandt's diary. Four of them, *Jacob Wrestling with the Angel*, *The Apostle Peter Denying Christ*, *The Jewish Bride*, and *The Return of the Prodigal Son*, have been discussed earlier (in chaps. 5 and 6). They suggest in this sequence the acceptance, the regret, the love, and the forgiveness Rembrandt came to know. A fifth painting, thought to have been on his easel at the time of his death, is *Simeon with the Christ Child in the Temple*, now in Stockholm. In this work, Rembrandt returned to a moment he had dealt with twice while he was still in Leiden, the moment described only by Luke, at 2:22–38. Verses 26–27 note that the Holy Spirit had informed Simeon that before his death he would see the Lord's Messiah (χριστός)—"And so he came to the temple under the urging of the Spirit."

In the painting below, also *Simeon in the Temple* (1627/28), now in Hamburg (and in another work on the same subject from 1631, now in Mauritshuis), Rembrandt gives us Joseph and Mary, as well as the Christ child, Simeon, and Anna. In these two paintings, the infant Christ glows, as with a heavenly light, and in the earliest of them Anna the prophetess is given the face of Rembrandt's mother Neeltje.

In the painting of 1631, now in Mauritshuis, Anna's face is hidden from view, though her hands appear once again to be raised in her astonished thanksgiving; Joseph's face, as well as Mary's, is seen in this

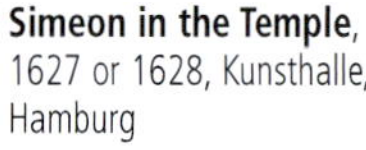

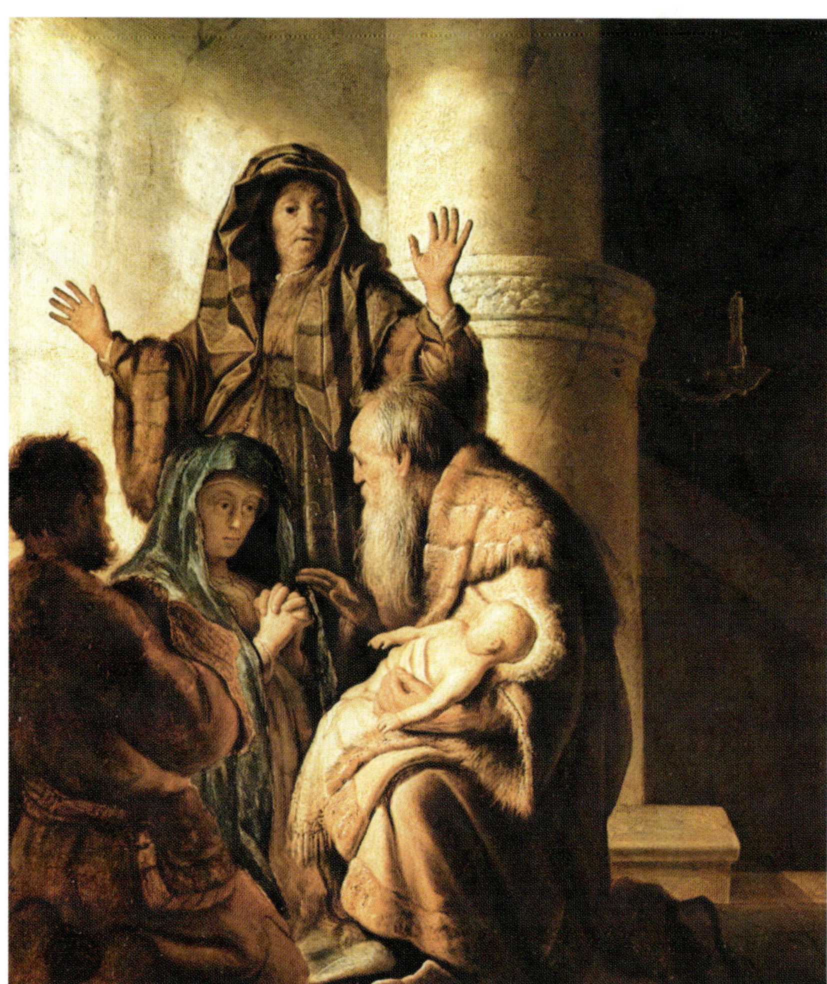

Simeon in the Temple, 1627 or 1628, Kunsthalle, Hamburg

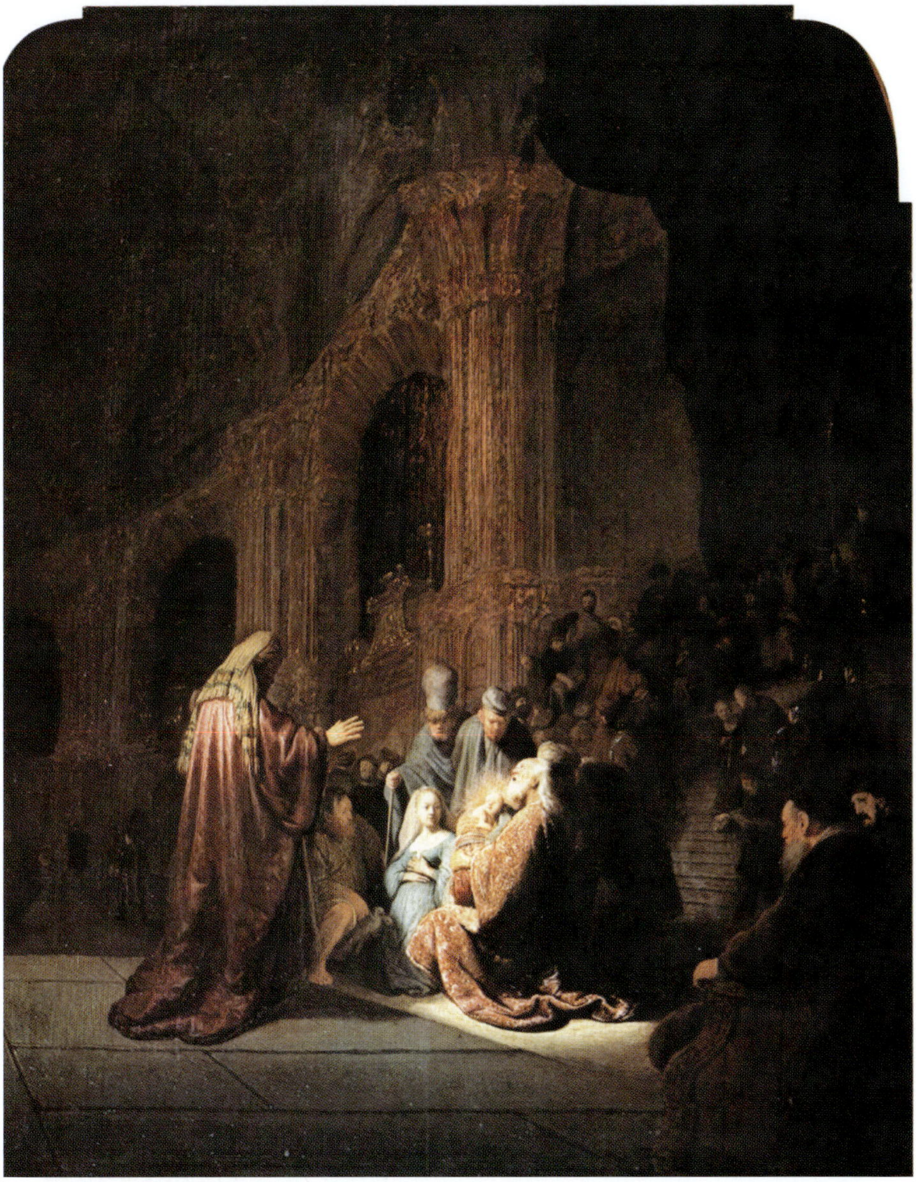

Simeon in the Temple, 1631, Mauritshuis, The Hague

work, and he holds the two turtledoves required for the sacrifice of purification (Luke 2:24; cf. Lev. 12:8).

There are two etchings of the same scene, one from 1639 and one from 1654. In the earlier plate, the heavenly light surrounds the dove of the Holy Spirit hovering over Anna, and Rembrandt has included a dog scratching its ear in the left foreground, one of his characteristic connections of the biblical world with the everyday world. In the later plate, the scene is very dark, Anna is much less prominent, and the heavenly light appears to come from both old Simeon and the infant Christ.

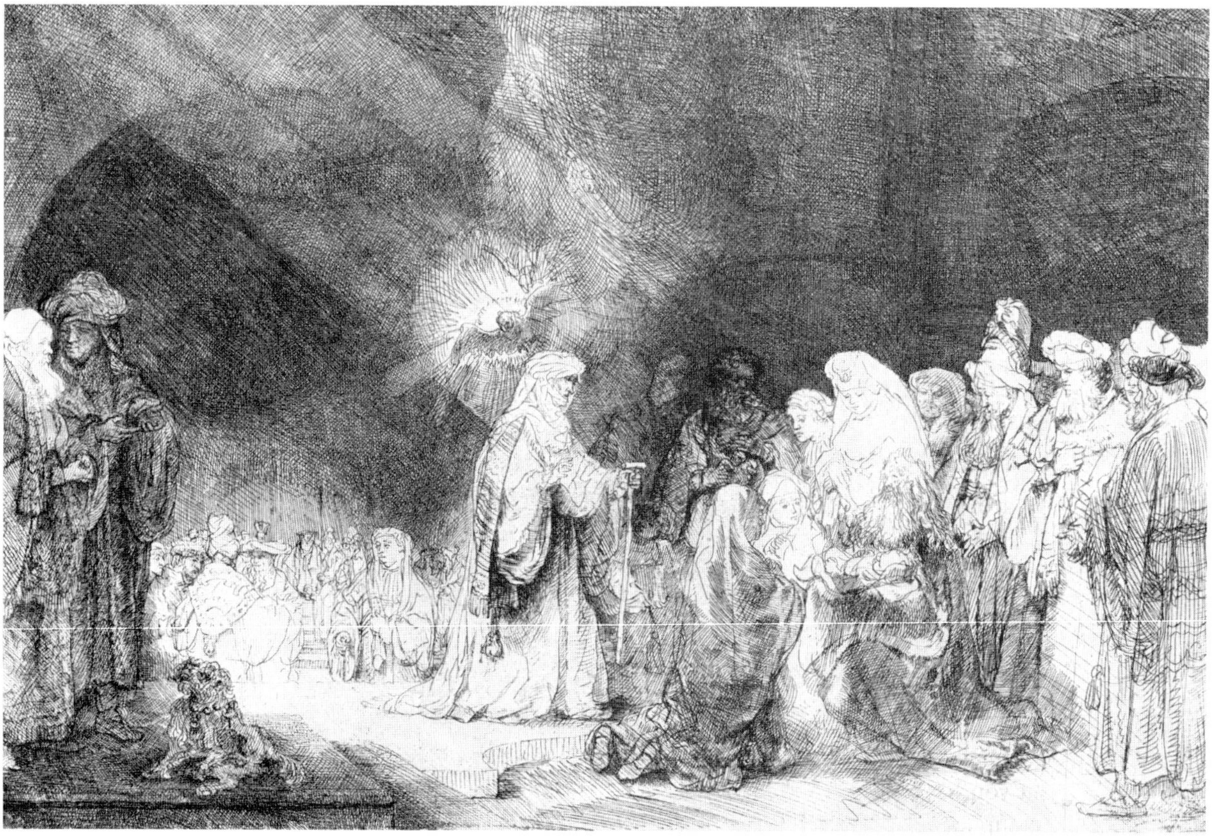

The Presentation in the Temple, B 49, 1639, Prentenkabinet, Rijksmuseum, Amsterdam

The Presentation in the Temple: in the Dark Manner, B 50, 1654, Prentenkabinet, Rijksmuseum, Amsterdam

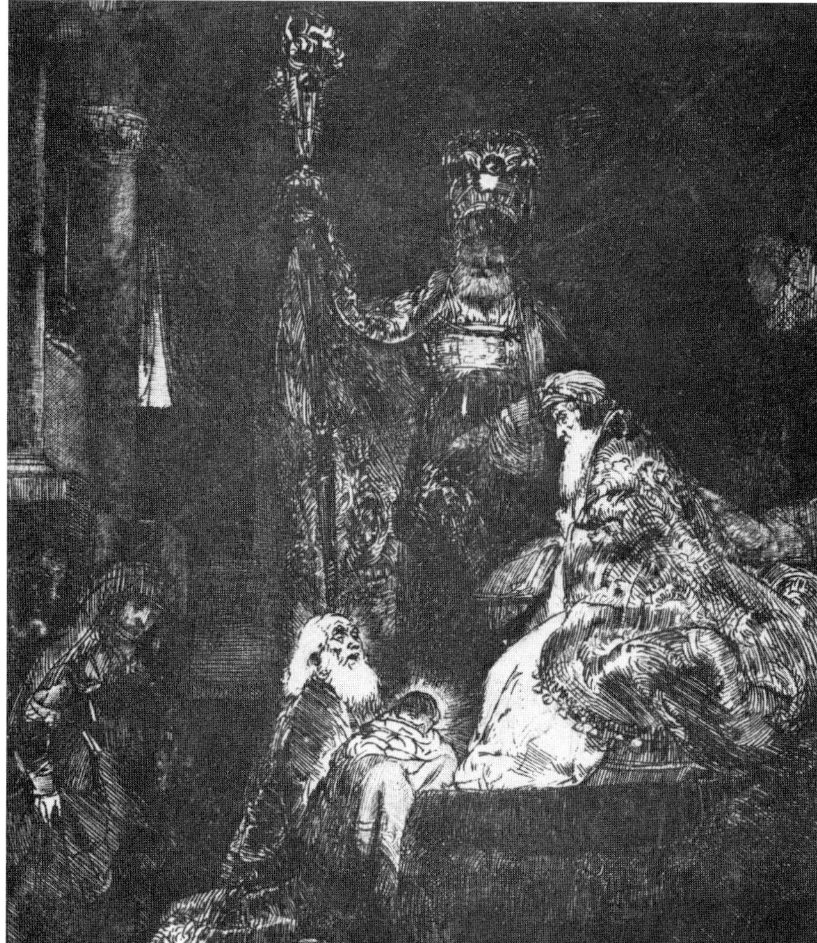

In the Stockholm painting of 1669, Mary, who has perhaps been added by a later hand, has replaced Anna altogether. The power of the work is in the likeness of Simeon and the Christ child whom he holds stiffly on outstretched arms (so Luke 2:28). The heavenly light appears now to emanate not at all from the baby, but wholly from the face of Simeon, whose eyes are nearly shut and whose lips are parted in his prayer of praise:

> Now have you set your servant free to leave, Lord, just as you promised, wholly content [literally, "in peace"] because I have seen with my own eyes your salvation that you have made ready in plain view of all peoples: a light that will make things clear to the unbelievers and bring glory to your people Israel.(Luke 2:29–32)

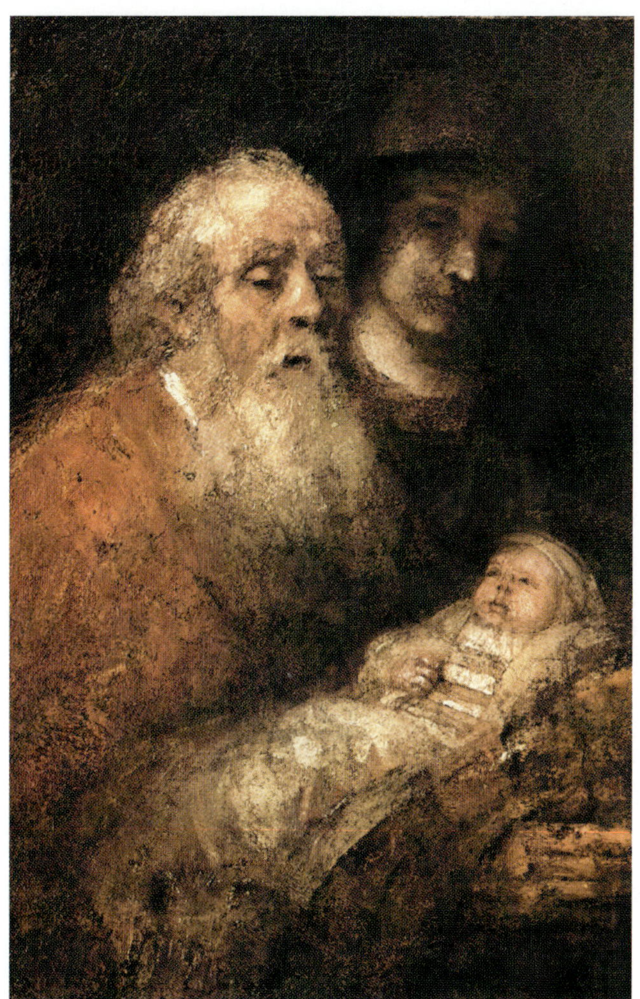

Simeon with the Christ Child in the Temple, 1669, Nationalmuseum, Stockholm

Simeon's barely open eyes may suggest more than prayer or the dim sight of old age. For all of his life, Rembrandt was obsessed with seeing. Early on, he began his extensive series of works on the story of Tobit and Tobias, a biblical narrative that has as a central feature any artist's ultimate nightmare, the loss of vision, and ends happily ever after with the restoration of Tobit's eyesight, among other blessings. Rembrandt made over forty drawings of moments from this story, more of them dealing with Tobit's blindness and its cure than with any other event in the narrative.

There are two etchings based on texts from the Book of Tobit (see next two pages), one of them a touching depiction from 1651 of the blind Tobit, who has overturned a spinning wheel and is about to walk into the wall in his fumble for the door, but whose little dog is attempting to guide his old master.

The second etching, done ten years earlier, is a scene of thanksgiving, with Tobit and Tobias and their family in grateful awe of the ascending angel Raphael, who has guided Tobias from the beginning

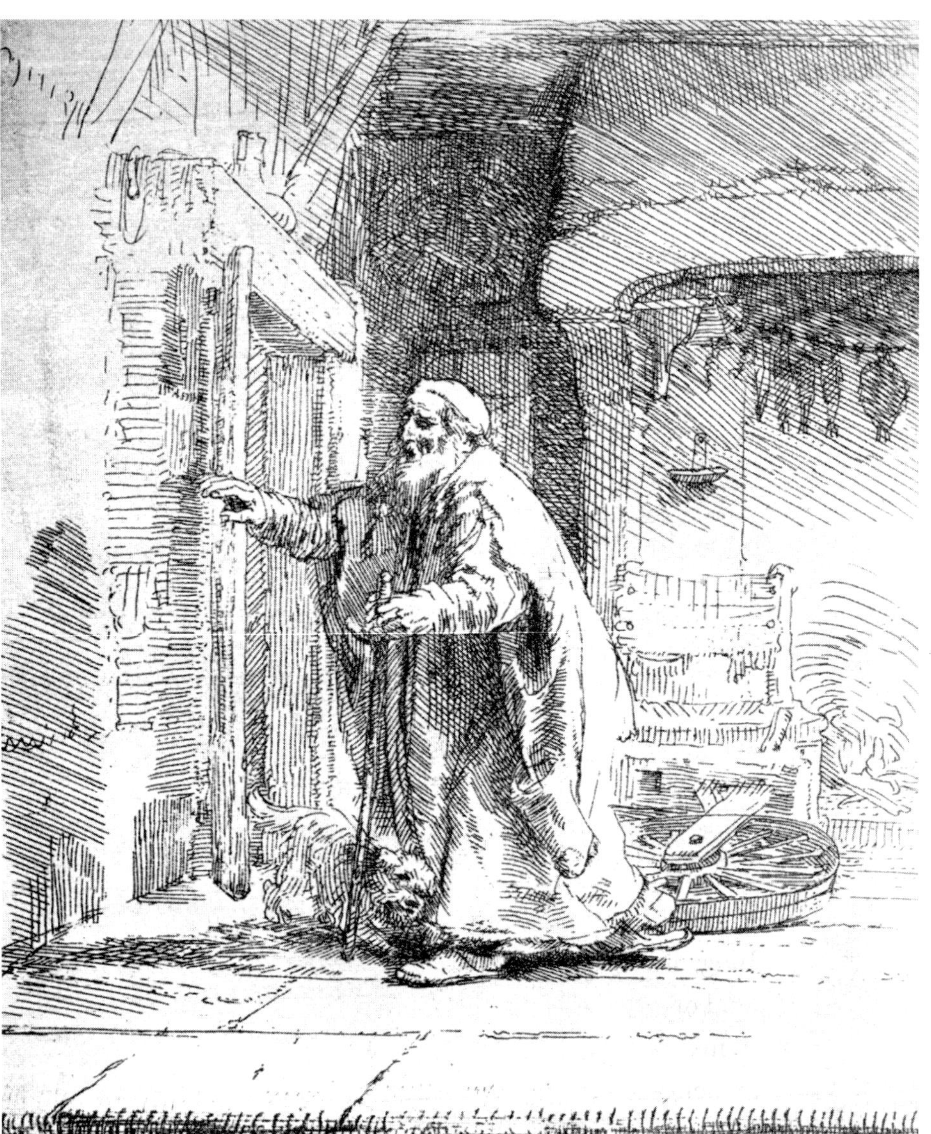

The Blindness of Tobit: the Large Plate, B 42, 1651, Teylers Museum, Haarlem

of his journey to Media (Tob. 5:4–8 and 12:6–22; see chap. 3). It is significant that Rembrandt's etchings on the Book of Tobit dealt with the happy ending of the story first, and with Tobit in his blindness a decade later.

Two paintings deal with these same moments, though in a reversed chronological sequence. The earliest of the two (1626), now in Amsterdam, is *Tobit and Anna with the Kid*; it deals with Tobit's blindness and the moment when he accuses his wife of having stolen the goat she had been given by her employer (Tob. 2:11–14).

The second painting, from 1637, is *The Angel Raphael Leaving Tobit and His Family*, now in Paris. It deals with the moment of thanksgiving as Raphael ascends to heaven, the moment Rembrandt was to depict four years later in the etching of 1641. In each of these

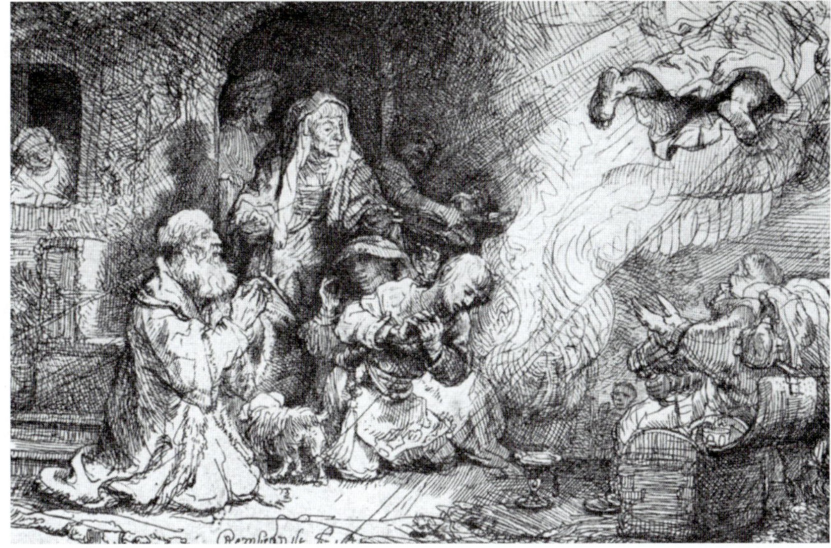

The Angel Departing from the Family of Tobias, B 43, 1641, Fitzwilliam Museum, Cambridge

works, the little dog has a prominent place, though in this painting (see next page) the animal cowers in fright, while in the etching of 1641 above, its back is turned in apparent indifference.

Altogether, in paintings and etchings as well as drawings, Rembrandt dealt with the story of Tobit nearly fifty times, from 1626 to about 1655, an interest that suggests what I would call an important theme in his diary, the theme of seeing and not seeing.

By the time he came to work on what appears to have been his final painting, however, Rembrandt may have had in his mind a different kind of seeing. The old Simeon of 1669 seems to me to be a painting finished by being unfinished. Simeon's nearly closed eyes are just a suggestion of the prayer of thanks he is uttering. The vision Rembrandt was attempting to portray is visible in the luminous glow of Simeon's face (see page 215). Here in the last days of his life, Simeon has seen the Deliverer, the Messiah, often promised and long awaited. His face shines with the knowledge of the sight, and in a remarkably bold insight, Rembrandt has given the face of the Christ child a *reflected* glow. Simeon's face shines on the face of the infant Jesus and on Mary's neck and a part of her

Tobit and Anna with the Kid, 1626, Rijksmuseum, Amsterdam

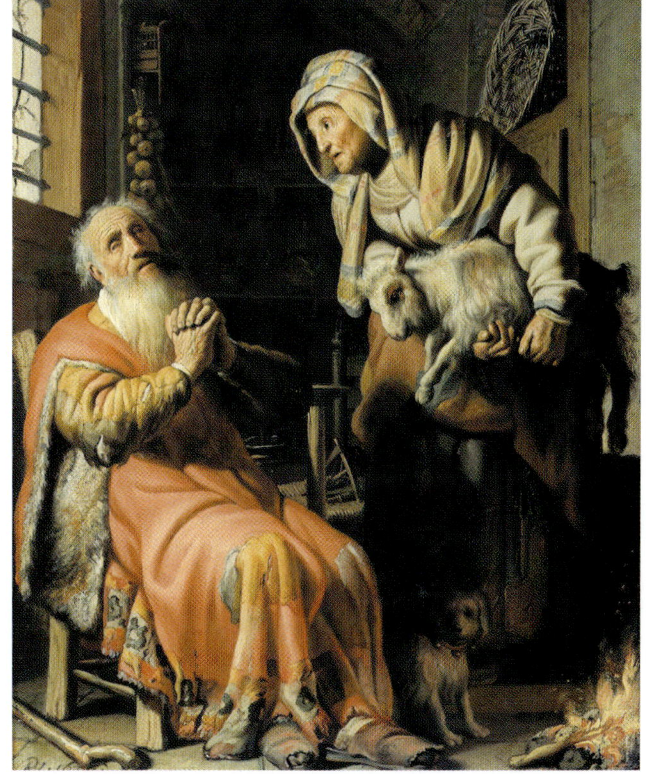

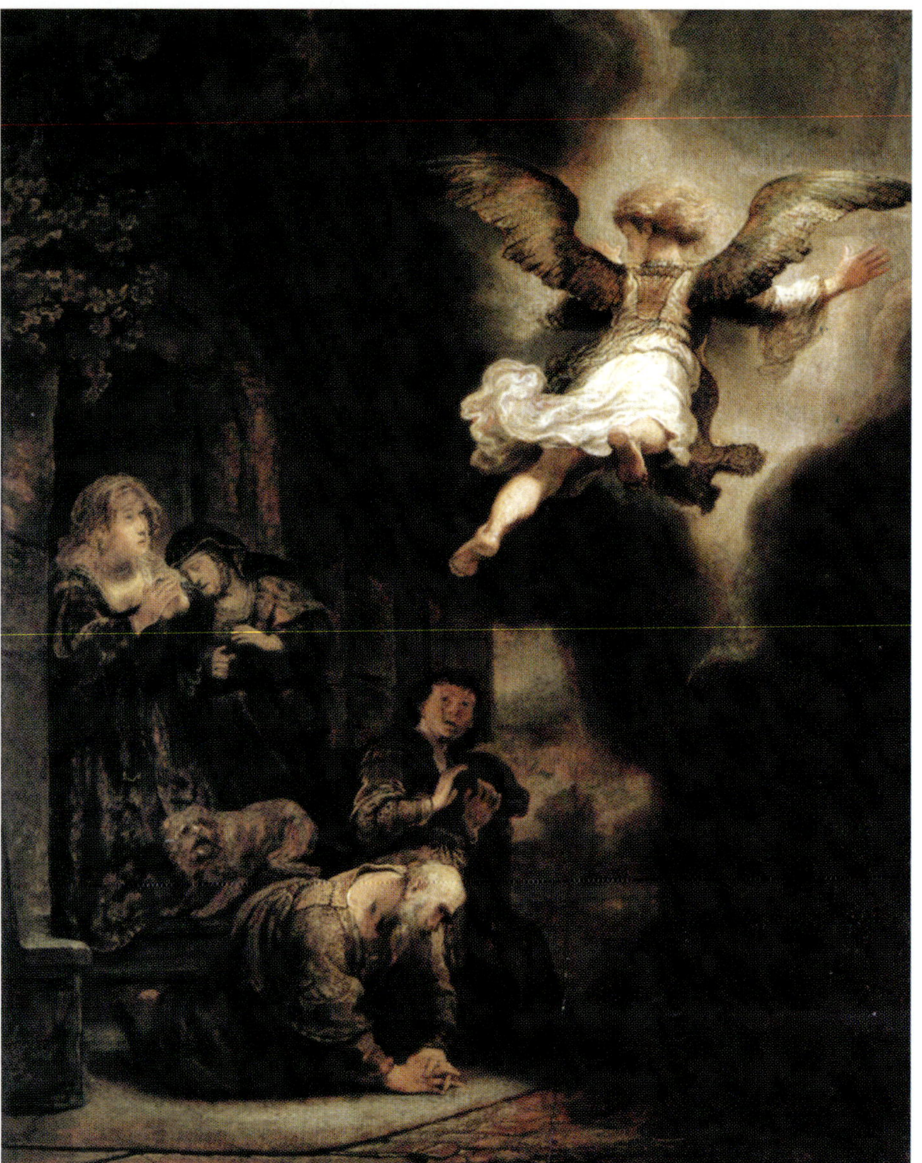

The Angel Raphael Leaving Tobit and His Family, 1637, Musée du Louvre, Paris

face as well. Here, on the final page of his diary, Rembrandt has dispensed with any hint of the glow he had so often given Christ, in drawings, in etchings, and in paintings, and has given that glow instead to Simeon, as a glow from the inside.

I suggest that Rembrandt had come to believe that the real light of knowing God comes always from the one who knows. To all others, Christ, whether a babe in arms or a man on a cross, is just a baby, just a man. If I am right, Rembrandt, like old Simeon, could depart a life full of trouble "wholly content."

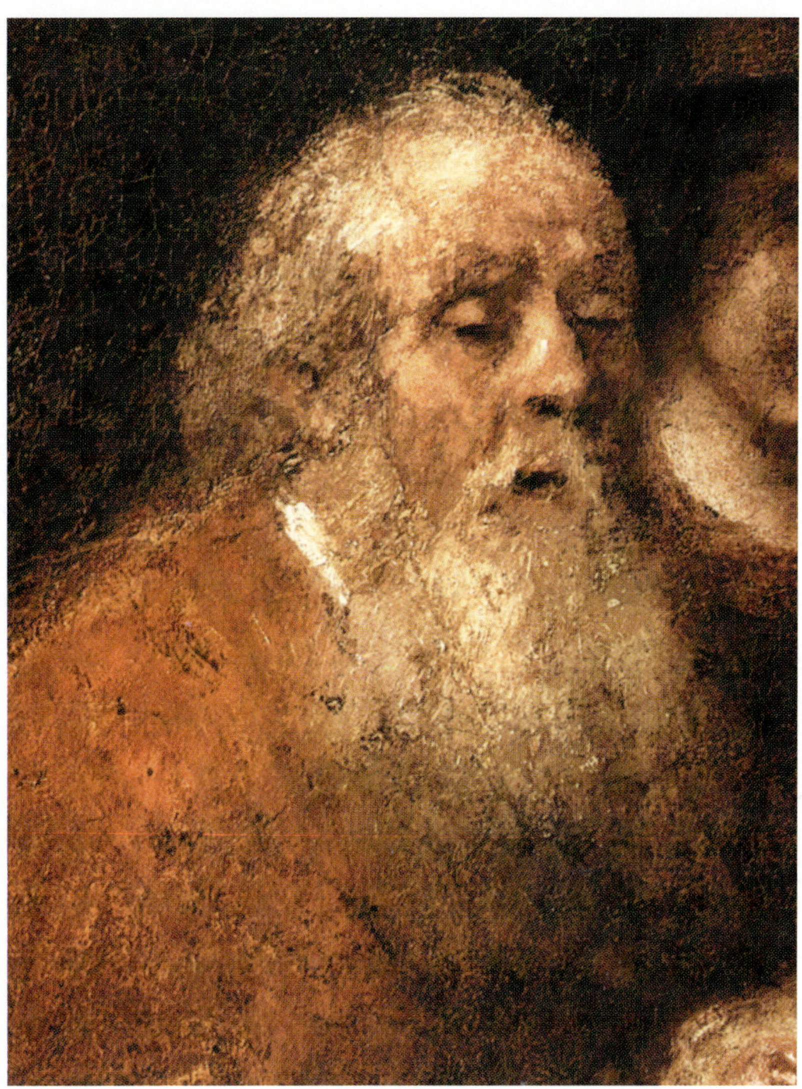

SOME SOURCES AND SUGGESTIONS

The nineteenth century approach to Rembrandt biography tended to be reverent, sometimes to the point of a sort of astonished adoration. In the first three-fourths of the twentieth century this reverence became more restrained, and the canon of Rembrandt's paintings, in particular, began increasingly to be examined much more closely, as a comparison of the catalogues of the past hundred years reveals. Abraham Bredius' list of *The Paintings of Rembrandt* published in 1935 included 620 works; the fourth edition of this work, revised by Horst Gerson and published in 1971, reduced this number to 593. Gerson's own listing, *Rembrandt Paintings*, published in 1968, pared the number to 420. And the catalogue of Christian Tümpel, *Rembrandt: All Paintings in Colour*, published in 1986, affirmed just 267 paintings that are undoubted Rembrandts. All of this numbering, and the confusion engendered both by its continued revisions and by those skeptical of its additions and, especially, its subtractions (not least the directors and curators of museums claiming works by Rembrandt) is now in process of further and systematic and authoritative revision at the hands of the Rembrandt Research Project, whose published work thus far includes 146 paintings (through *The Militia Company of Frans Banning Cocq* of 1642), and whose announced disattributions of some very famous works have stimulated fierce debate (*The Polish Rider* now in the Frick Collection and *The Man with the Golden Helmet* now in Berlin, to name two). See also pp. 17-18 above.

In the last fourth of the twentieth century, a trend toward irreverence began (albeit under the guise of deconstructionist objectivity), an irreverence typified in the work of Gary Schwartz (*Rembrandt: His Life, His Paintings*, 1985) and Svetlana Alpers (*Rembrandt's Enterprise: the Studio and the Market*, 1988). Julius Held argues, in a helpful summary-article, for a more balanced approach: "Rembrandt-*Dämmerung*?" in the 1989 revision of his *Rembrandt Studies*, pp. 3-16; and Simon Schama's *Rembrandt's Eyes* (1999) is also, on the whole, a corrective to the vilification of Rembrandt – *New York Times* art critic Michael Kimmelman called it "the longest, most effusive, most personal apologia for an artist that has been published in some time." (Feature review, *NYT Book Review* for December 12, 1999). A trenchant survey of Rembrandt criticism from 1669 to about 1990 may be found in *Rembrandt: the Master and His Workshop: Paintings*, pp. 106-123: "A Delicate Balance: a brief Survey of Rembrandt Criticism," by Jeroen Boomgaard and Robert W. Scheller.

Basic information on Jacob Swanenburgh and Pieter Lastman is included in the standard Rembrandt volumes of Bob Haak, Horst Gerson, and Christian Tümpel; the latter's "Rembrandt Studies Under Pieter Lastman" in *Rembrandt* (pp. 17-23) is especially helpful. Christian Tümpel's "Pieter Lastman and Rembrandt" in *Pieter Lastman: the Man Who Taught Rembrandt* provides a good summary review. Also of interest are two articles in the catalogue to a 2000-2001 exhibition at the Isabella Stewart Gardner Museum in Boston, *Rembrandt Creates Rembrandt: Art and Ambition in Leiden, 1629-1631*—"Making a Mark in Rembrandt's Leiden" by Mariët Westermann and "Rembrandt's Technique during the Leiden Years" by Christopher White (pp. 24-49 and 50-63, respectively).

A fascinating exhibition entitled "Rembrandt's Women" mounted in the autumn of 2001 in Edinburgh's National Gallery of Scotland and London's Royal Academy of Arts provided an excellent review of the women in Rembrandt's life and his depiction of women in his work. The catalog (*Rembrandt's Women*) to this exhibition, edited by Julia Lloyd Williams, is an example of what an exhibition catalog should be, with entries written to inform rather than to mystify. Particularly valuable are the introductory article by the editor, and the essay by S. A. C. Dudok van Heel ("Rembrandt: his life, his wife, the nursemaid and the servant").

Rembrandts Kinderzeichnungen by Doris Vogel-Köhn (1981) presents a helpful collection of ninety-nine of Rembrandt's drawings of children, arranged chronologically.

RD includes the complete 1656 inventory of Rembrandt's possessions, in facsimile and in printed form with translation (pp. 348-388); so also K. Clark, in translation only, in *Rembrandt and the Italian Renaissance* (pp. 193-209). This inventory is a document both fascinating and revealing; the works of Lastman still in Rembrandt's possession at the time of the inventory are number 43, "a Tobias" in "the antechamber," number 119, "a small ox" in "the room behind the parlor," and on the shelf among the art books in "the Art Chamber," numbers 263 and 264, a small book "full of sketches in pen" and one "in red chalk" by Lastman.

In 1956, W. R. Valentiner, then Director of the North Carolina Museum of Art, mounted an exhibition titled "Rembrandt and His Pupils" that displayed works of Rembrandt's teacher Pieter Lastman and his early partner Jan Lievens, but more importantly, some seventy-six works by twenty-one of his pupils. Valentiner's catalogue to this exhibition includes a section entitled "Rembrandt's Teachers," and a fascinating account of the rediscovery of seventy-five of Rembrandt's copper etching plates, currently on loan to the Museum in Raleigh, North Carolina. A joint exhibition of the Staatliche Museen Preussischer Kulturbesitz in Berlin, the Rijksmuseum, and London's National Gallery in 1991-1992 yielded a magnificent two-volume catalog, *Rembrandt, the Master and His Workshop* that provides a beautifully presented survey of works by Rembrandt and some of his pupils in the context of recent Rembrandt research. Bob Haak provides a most helpful chart of thirty-three of Rembrandt's pupils, arranged chronologically with the note that additional students existed, but that "little or no information exists about them" (*Rembrandt, His Life, His Work, His Time*, p. 220). The Rembrandt House Museum in Amsterdam mounted in 1984-1985 an important exhibition of more than seventy drawings and etchings by Rembrandt and his pupils entitled *Rembrandt as Teacher* – the catalogue to this exhibition provides a fascinating comparative review.

The sale of Rembrandt's graphic works on December 20, 1658, apparently the final sale in which his drawings were made available, brought a "remarkably low" amount (RD, 1658/29&30; note also the entry 1658/21). Ben Broos notes: "The proceeds for the [sale of December 20] amounted to only 470 guilders and 9 stivers." (Entry on Rembrandt in *The Grove Dictionary of Art*, I:5)

Luke 2:28 notes that Simeon "received him [the infant Jesus] in his arms and praised God." Rembrandt has taken this text quite literally, and depicted the old man holding the child on his outstretched arms, with his hands extending beyond the little body, and giving the appearance of stiff, arthritic joints and fingers.

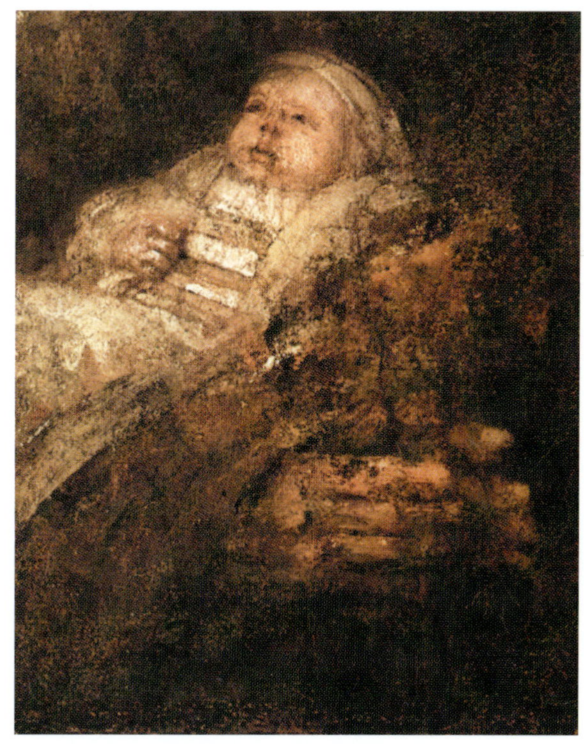

8

TO END WITH

To end with? Perhaps "to stop with" is a better expression—there are so many more works of Rembrandt on biblical moments, drawings and etchings and paintings that range from the whimsical to the profound, creations of connection between the biblical narrative and Rembrandt's own experience, that any comprehensive review and discussion would require a volume of ponderous proportions.

Of the 1,368 drawings attributed to Rembrandt in the six-volume catalog of Otto and Eva Benesch, 591 may be considered works on biblical subjects; of these, I have mentioned 49. Of the 285 or 286 etchings now attributed to Rembrandt, 72 may be seen to be works on biblical subjects; of these, I have mentioned 50. And of the 265 paintings attributed to Rembrandt in the catalog of Christian Tümpel, a number being reduced by the extensive but uncompleted work of the RRP, 89 are clearly works on biblical subjects; of these, I have mentioned 64.

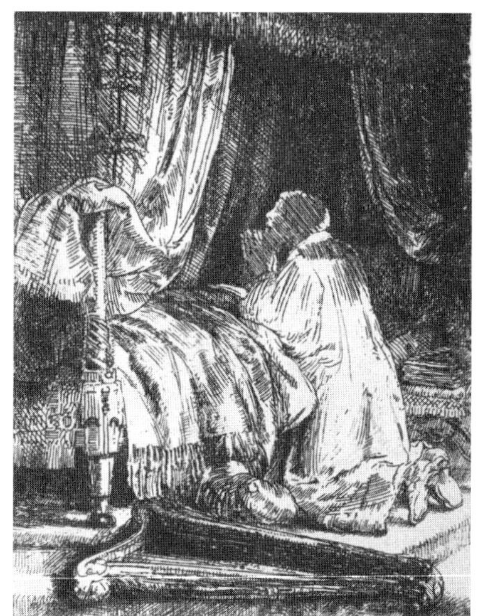

Other favorites keep calling out to me for consideration—the list changes from day to day, nearly from hour to hour. At this moment, the whimsical *David in Prayer* of 1652 floats before my eyes: an old David kneeling on a cushion by his heavily curtained, very Dutch bed, his harp at the ready and a folio volume of manuscripts (completed psalms, no doubt) on a stool to his right.

There is the grief-heavy procession of disciples and followers bearing the body of Christ to the tomb provided by Joseph of Arimathea of 1645, another scene Rembrandt imagined, as there is no mention of such a procession in the Gospels, but one of such quiet sadness and painful leave-taking that every hope seems cancelled.

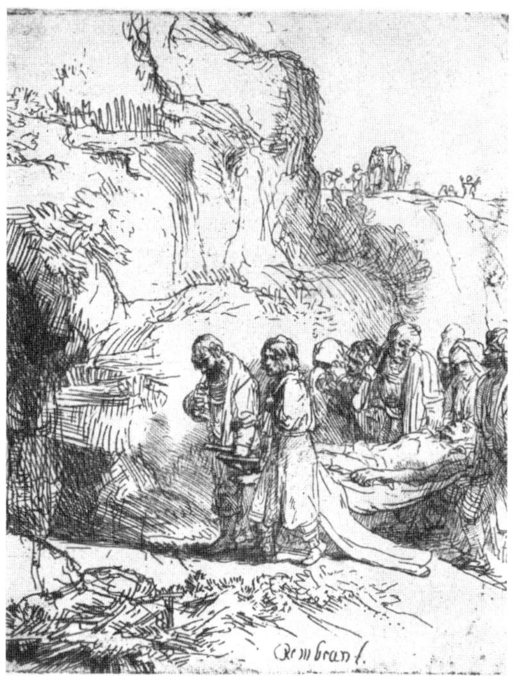

And there is the imagery-laden *Virgin and Child with the Cat and Snake* of 1654, with the touching embrace of Mary and her infant son and the poignant and wistful gaze through the window of a balding Joseph who seems sadly excluded from the holiness of *his* wife and *her* son.

A painting of 1638, *The Wedding of Samson*, now in Dresden, has always brought to my mind a chuckle since I first saw it in 1978. It is a depiction of a moment in the feast Samson gave to celebrate his marriage to a woman described in the narrative of the Book of Judges only as "a Philistine woman at Timnah," a feast to which thirty guests were invited. During the dinner, Samson put to these friends a riddle spun from his recent encounter with a lion and his subsequent harvest of honey from the lion's carcass, offering a lavish prize of clothing for each of them if they could solve it by the end of the week-long wedding celebration (Judg. 14:5–14). An important undertone of the text is that Samson had eaten of the honey (and fed some to his parents, who were unaware of its source), violating his Nazirite vow of purity and beginning the disobedience that led to his downfall—the honey was unclean because of its contact with carrion. The riddle Samson posed begins as a play on words:

David in Prayer, B 41, 1652, British Museum, London (above)

Christ Carried to the Tomb, B 84, 1645, Prentenkabinet, Rijksmuseum, Amsterdam (below)

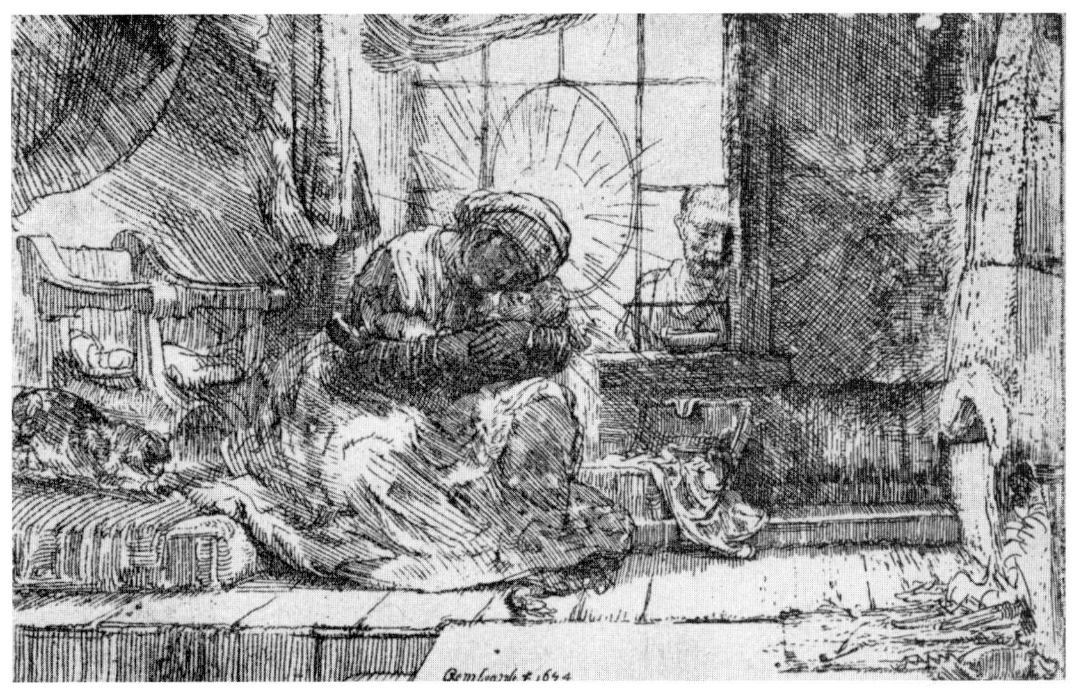

The Virgin and Child with the Cat and the Snake, B 63, 1654, Prentenkabinet, Rijksmuseum, Amsterdam

From the eater, edible came forth!
From the strong, sweet came forth! (Judges 14:14bc)

The moment from this narrative Rembrandt chose to present is the moment of Samson's statement of his puzzler. The party is well under way, and the guests in the left half of the painting (see next page) are involved in their food, their cups, and their flirtations. At the right, Samson is posing his riddle to a group of six male guests, two of whom have musical instruments and one of whom has made it into the painting literally by a nose. They are leaning in toward Samson, intent on hearing what he is saying, perhaps because of the racket at the other end of the table, and Samson is ticking off on his fingers the four points of his conundrum: eater, edible, strong, sweet—as he grasps his middle finger, he has perhaps reached "edible."

Samson's bride sits between the two groups with her hands folded across her stomach and such a dumb vacant expression on her ordinary face that one is prompted to wonder whether Rembrandt thought Samson got the better part of the deal when his new father-in-law gave this girl to Samson's best man after she betrayed the secret of the riddle to her Philistine friends (Judg. 14:15–20). Samson

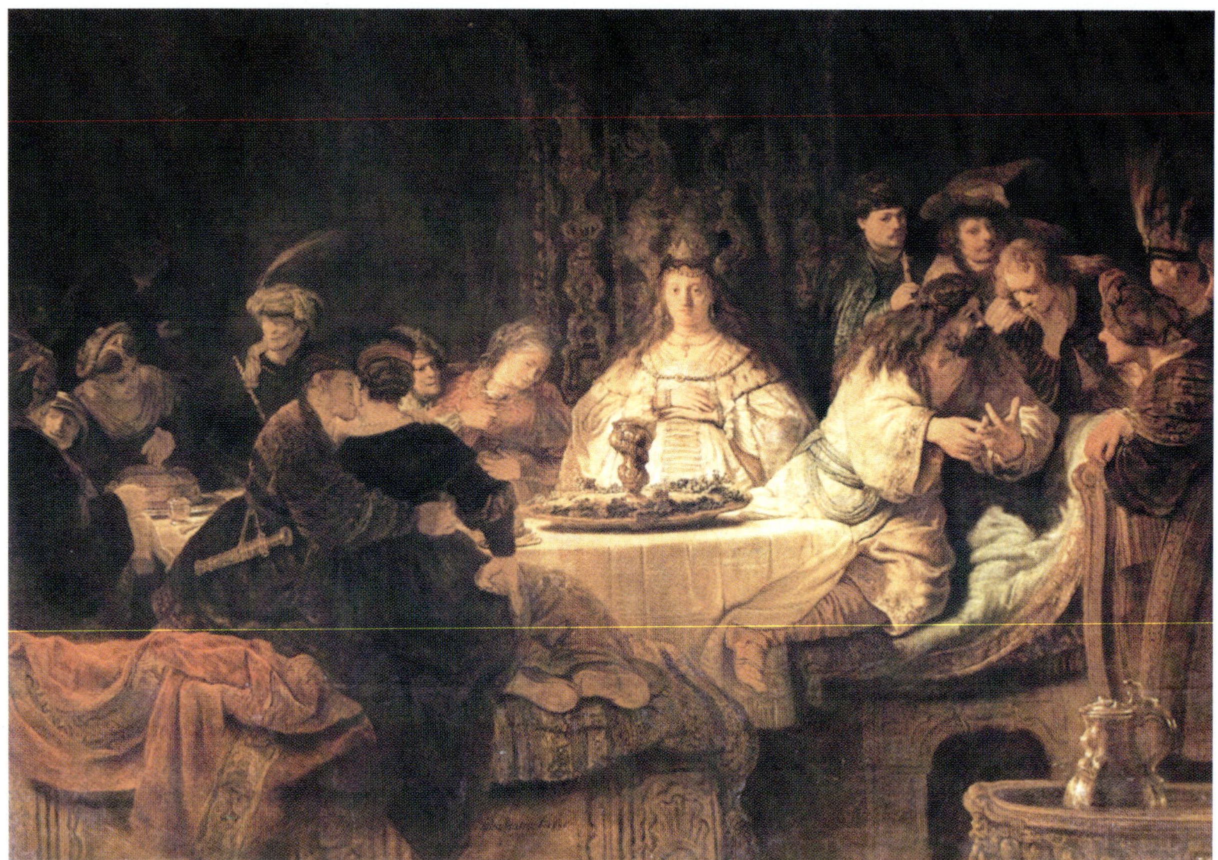

The Wedding of Samson, 1638, Gemäldegalerie Alter Meister, Dresden

appears already to be bored with her, turning his back to her to chat with his male friends.

This story clearly amused Rembrandt, as this painting and an earlier one depicting the next episode, Samson's anger at his father-in-law's presumption, suggest; the amusement shines through both works.

Then there is the lovely and somehow humorous *Christ Appearing to Mary Magdalene* of 1638, now at Buckingham Palace. Rembrandt has sought to capture the moment described in John 20:14–15, when Mary, looking around, saw Jesus and mistook him for a gardener. He has given Jesus a floppy great hat, a shovel, and a knife in his belt in reference to Mary's mistake, and Mary here appears both startled and irritated to be distracted from her grieving—it is the moment *before* she recognizes Jesus.

When Rembrandt's possessions were inventoried in 1656, the "fifth bin" of objects and art from the "small studio" contained "a Head of Christ, a study from life" ("Een Christus tronie nae 't leven" —RD, pp.382-383). Also listed in this inventory, in "the room behind the parlor," were two additional paintings titled "Head of Christ by

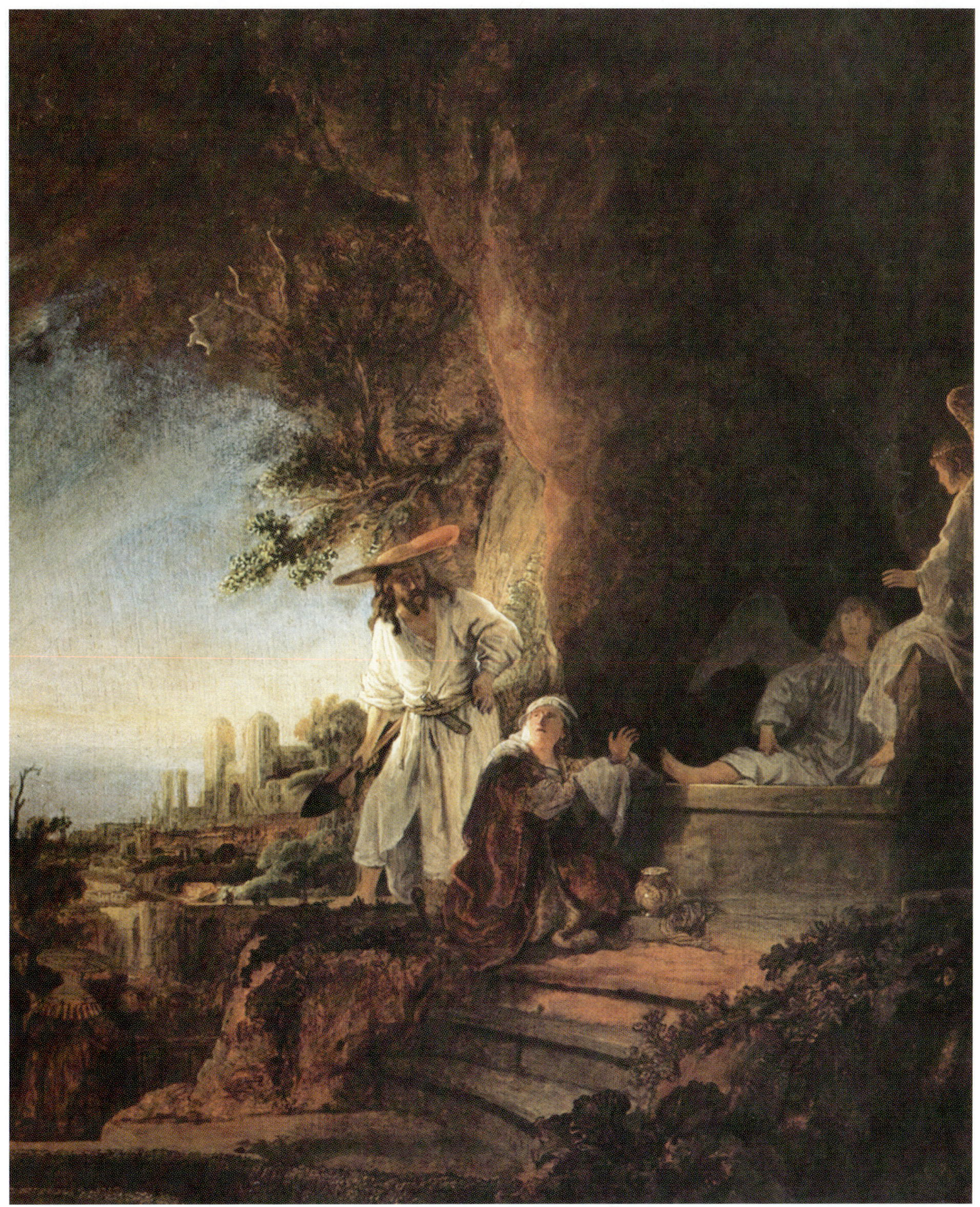

The Risen Christ Appearing to Mary Magdalene,
1638, The Queen's Gallery, Buckingham Palace, London

Rembrant" (RD pp. 360–361). To these must be added the later painting (1661) now in Munich, sometimes thought to have been intended by Rembrandt to represent the risen Christ because of the manner in which he has painted Christ's clothing. These paintings are

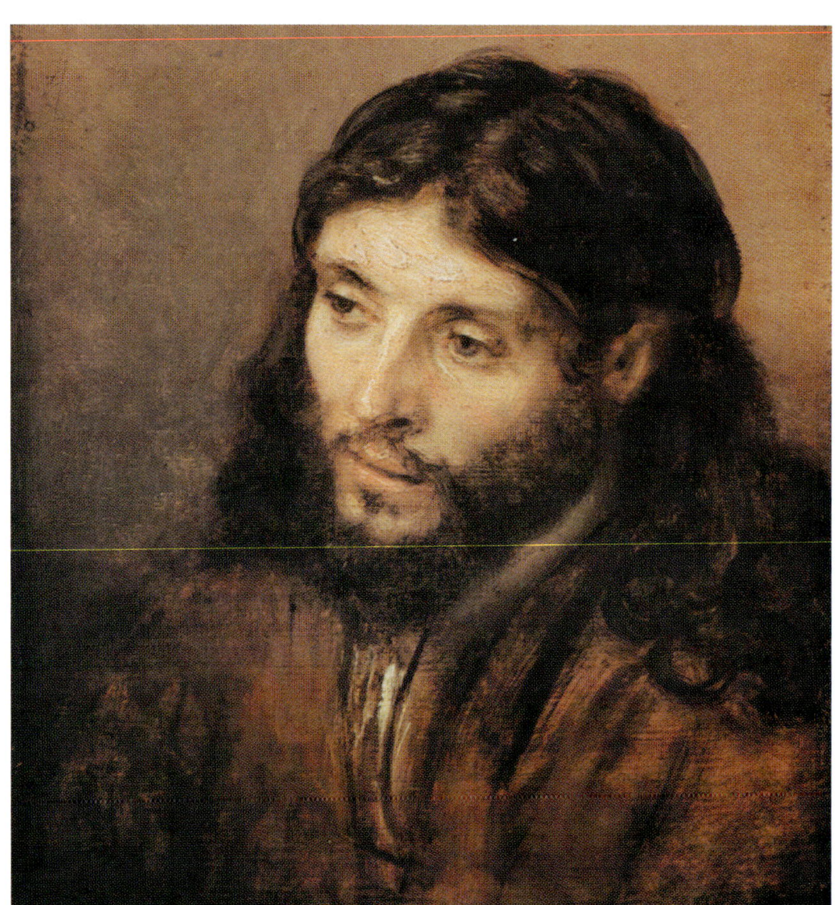

A Bust of Christ from Life, mid-1650s, Gemäldegalerie, Staatliche Museen, Berlin

not taken from any biblical description of the appearance of Christ, as no such description exists. They do, however, present arrestingly memorable images: they have done so right through their history, as the number of copies of them by Rembrandt's pupils and imitators suggests. What is striking about these paintings is not only Rembrandt's customary departure from iconic tradition in depicting Christ but also their total lack of sentimentality. Jesus is depicted simply as a Jew, for a Jew is what he was—a fact Rembrandt saw no need to obscure.

The painting usually given the inventory description "a study from life," is the work above from the mid-1650s now in Berlin, though any precise identification of this portrait or the other two portraits of Christ mentioned in the inventory is not possible at present. In my view, what these paintings tell us has to do, first of all, with Rembrandt and his own faith and, second of all, with ourselves. And by any measure, they each have visual staying power. The work

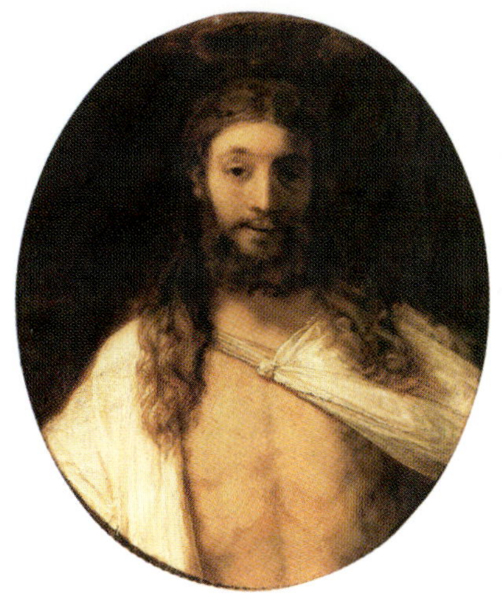

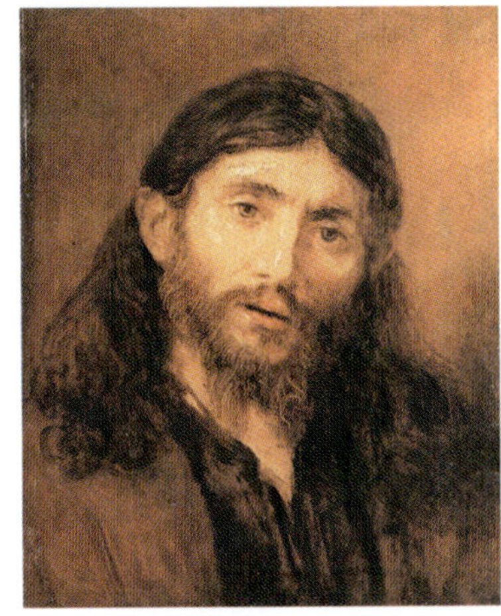

Christ, 1661, Alte Pinakothek, Munich (left)

Christ, mid-1650s, Fogg Art Museum, Cambridge (right)

now in the Fogg Art Museum in Cambridge, also from the mid-1650s, is probably one of the two "Head of Christ" paintings found in "the room behind the parlor." The work from 1661 now in Munich, depicting Christ in what may be a resurrection appearance, is the last of the series of such works, a series that may well have included a larger number of paintings than can now be attributed to Rembrandt with certainty.

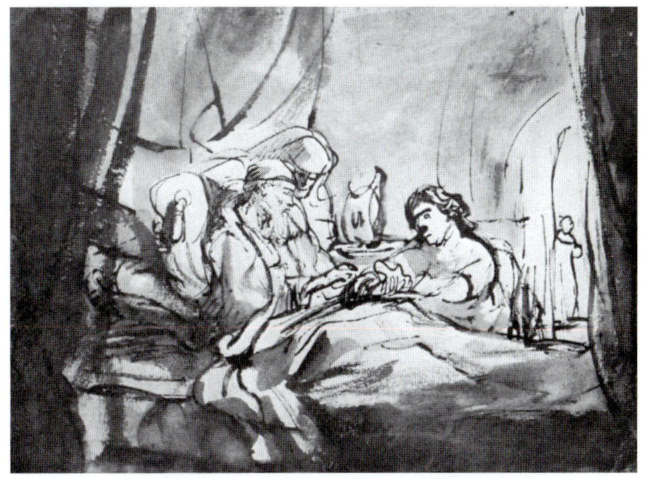

Isaac Blessing Jacob, Benesch 509, early 1640s, Vienna (private collection)

As for the drawings that haunt my mind, they are legion. The list of them changes frequently, informing and inspiriting my experience of life and the Bible. Just now, I think of blind old Isaac in a drawing from the early 1640s, blessing his scheming son Jacob, while Rebekah, scheming along with her favorite, whispers encouragement into Isaac's ear (Gen. 27:5–29).

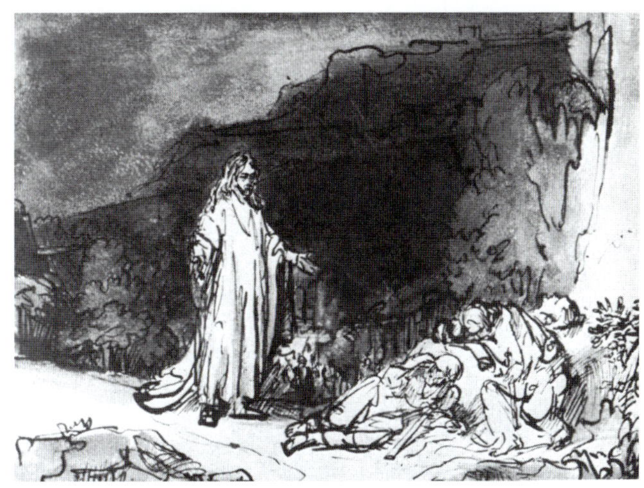

Christ Awakening the Apostles on the Mount of Olives, Benesch 513, early 1640s, Berne (private collection)

I think of another drawing from the same period, in which Christ wakes the sleeping trio in the garden of Gethsemane, his hands outstretched in both frustration and a get-up gesture, as Peter lifts himself on one elbow and attempts to claw the sleep from his eyes, while Judas and the arresting mob approach in the distance (Matt. 26:45–46).

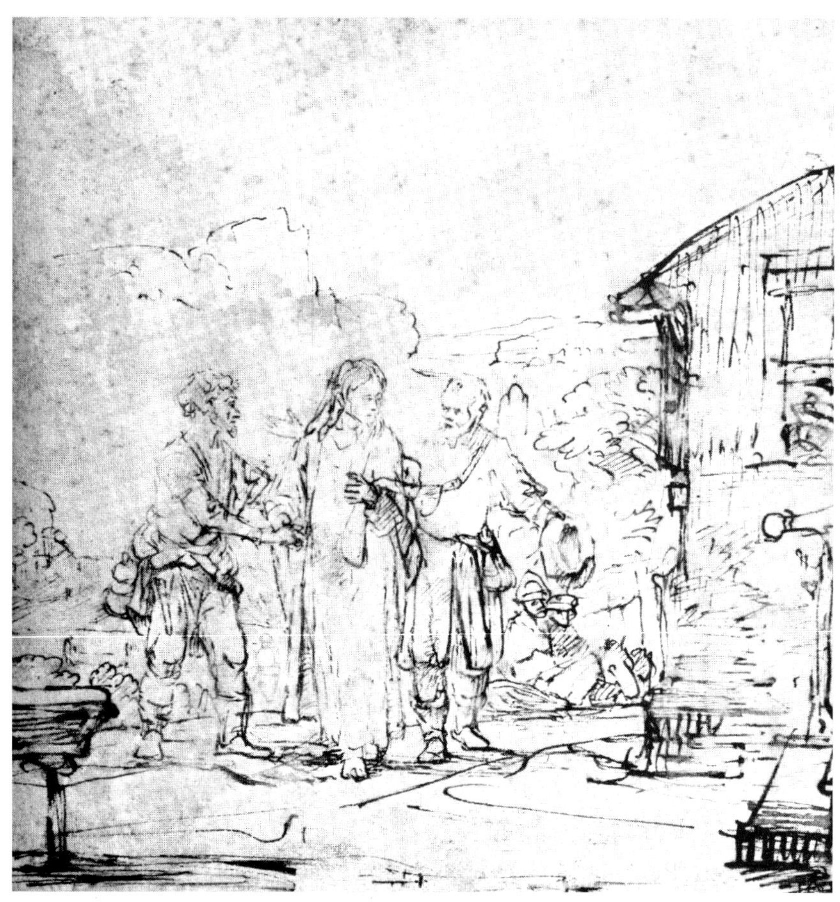

Christ and the Two Disciples on Their Way to Emmaus, Benesch 585, 1647, London (private collection)

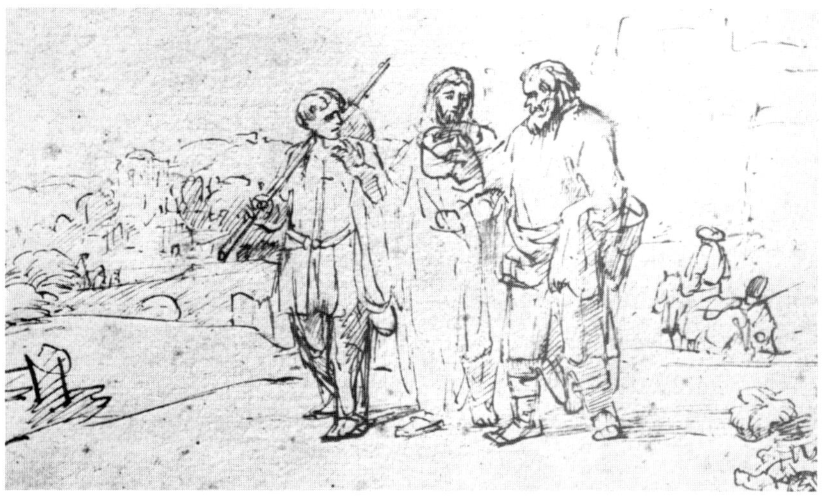

Christ and the Two Disciples on Their Way to Emmaus, Benesch 987, 1655 or 1656, Musée du Louvre, Paris

I think of a drawing from 1647 in which Cleopas and his companion all but compel their traveling companion and exegete of the road to come in to supper with them in Emmaus, and of a drawing of eight or nine years later depicting the journey itself—the number of works Rembrandt devoted to the Emmaus story (Luke 24:13–29) makes clear that it fascinated him; he returned to it across nearly three decades.

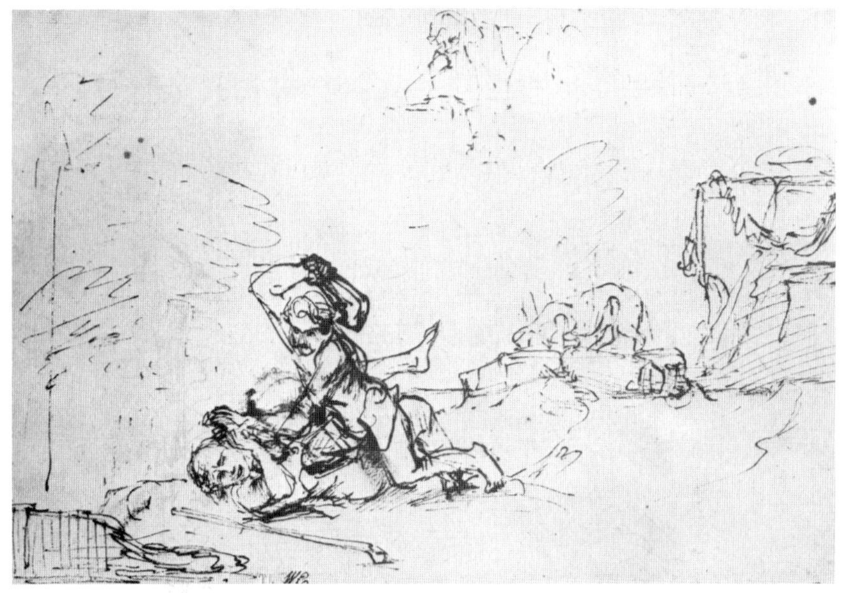

Abel Slain by Cain, Benesch 860, around 1650, Kobberstiksamling, Statens Museum for Kunst, Copenhagen

Then there is the violent image of Cain murdering his brother Abel, whom he pins to the ground with his left arm and his right knee as he raises his club for the fatal blow. In the background Cain's dog is wolfing down Abel's sacrifice, and in the distance above, God looks on in disgust, his fist clenched. Cain's ferocity and Abel's writhing alarm, along with Rembrandt's own interpretative additions, capture to perfection the feel of the Genesis text (4:3–8), and this drawing from around 1650 belies the generalization that Rembrandt gave up depicting violent scenes as he matured (so also the powerful drawing of Jael driving the tent-peg into Sisera's temple, from around 1660, Judg. 4:21). For Rembrandt, the realism of this event was in the text, and he presented it vividly.

There is the moving drawing from 1653 of Christ falling under his cross, with Veronica wiping his face, the soldiers forcing the help of Simon of Cyrene (the only feature of the drawing that has a biblical root, Luke 23:26), and a woman being restrained in her grief by a burly figure behind Christ and Veronica.

Christ Carrying the Cross, Benesch 923, 1653, Teylers Museum, Haarlem

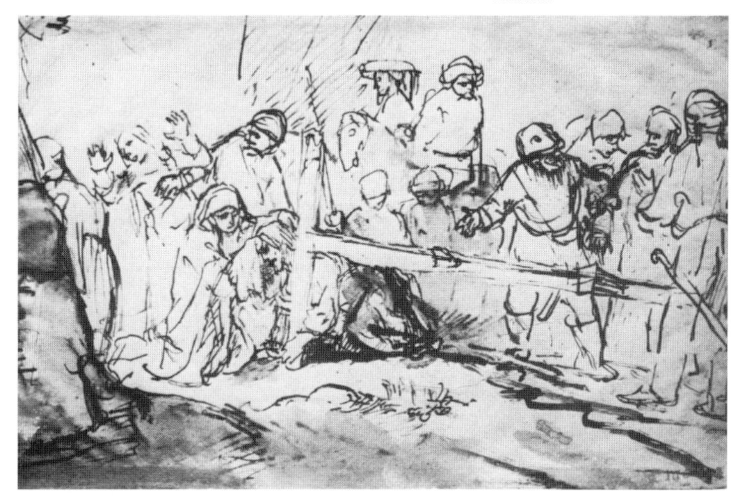

There is the dramatic representation from the mid-1650s of the call of Moses at the burning bush—Moses appears caught between his fascination and his fear, turning toward the voice and the fiery but unburned bush as his father-in-law's flock moves

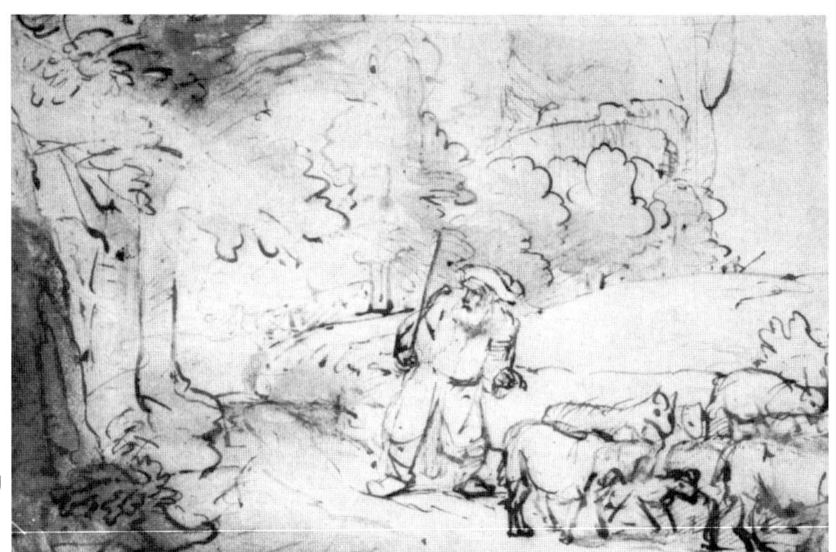

Moses and the Burning Bush, Benesch 951, mid-1650s, London (private collection)

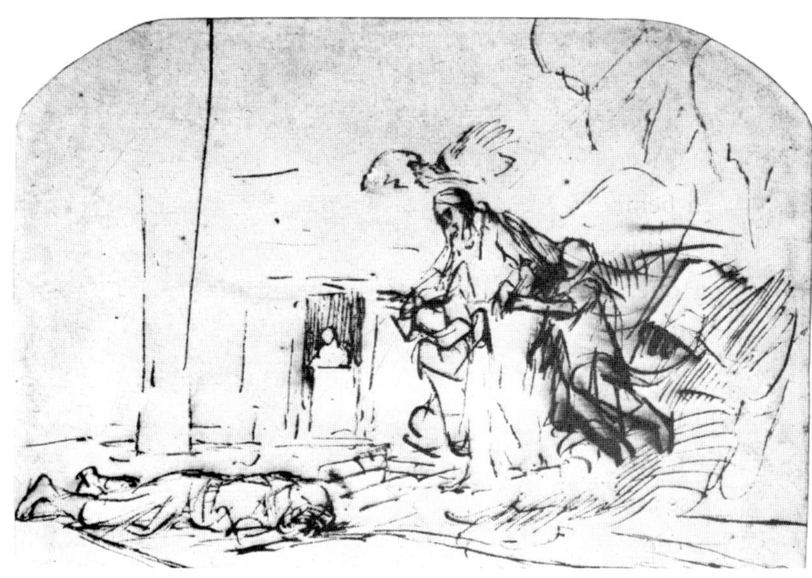

God Announcing His Covenant to Abraham, Benesch 1003, 1656, Kupferstichkabinett, Gemäldegalerie Alter Meister, Dresden

on unconcerned. The echo of the divine call, "Moses! Moses!" and Moses' reply, "I am here," can all but be heard (Exod. 3:1–4).

There is a much more palpable representation of God in a drawing of 1656 depicting the call of Abraham (Gen. 12:1–3), in which God seems to be rushing down toward the patriarch (bottom), who has fallen prostrate and is hiding his face.

And there is a drawing of the arrest of Christ in Gethsemane from that year or the next that also presents the presence of God, this time as a sudden rush of divine stillness as movement, a movement from which the weapon-carrying soldiers facing Jesus draw back, while a

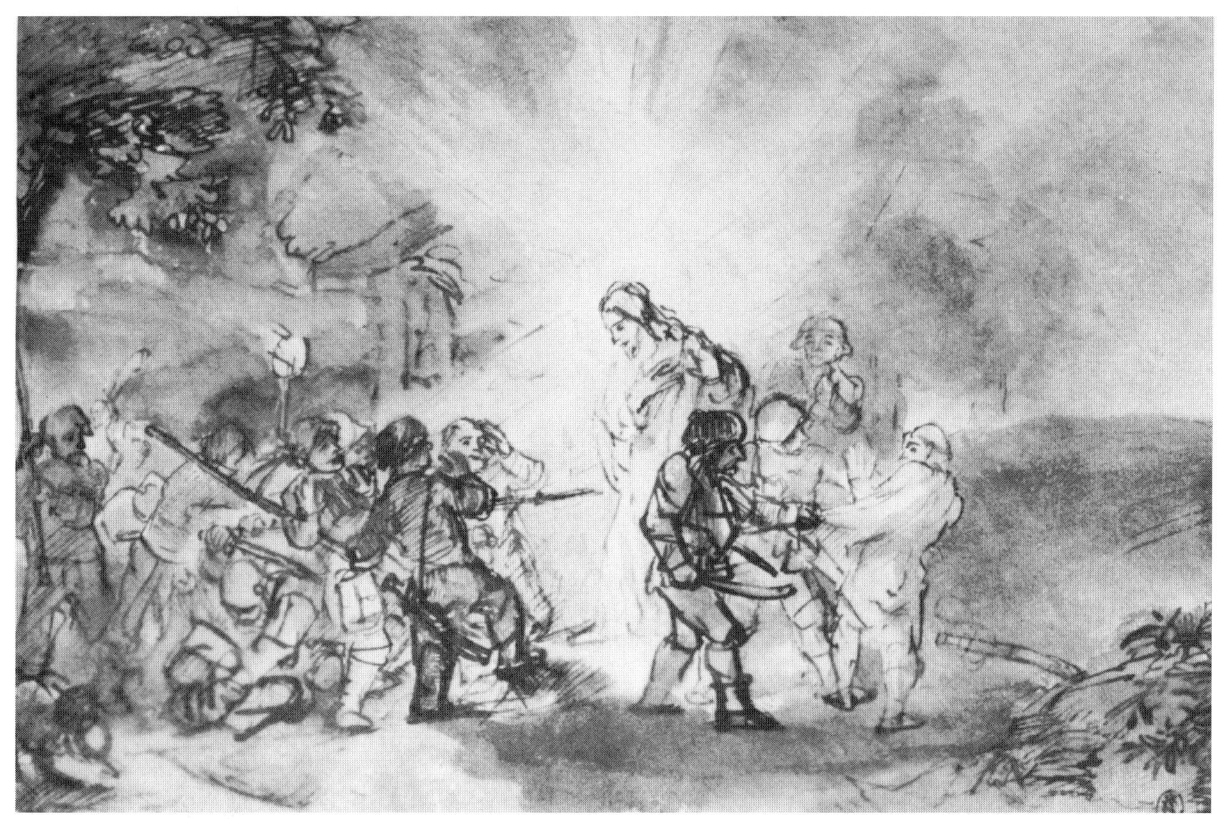

The Arrest of Christ, Benesch 1022, 1656 or 1657, London (private collection)

swordsman behind Christ grabs the robe of the disciple who fled, leaving his garment behind (Mark 14:51–52). In this drawing and the preceeding one, Rembrandt was struggling with the depiction of God's presence in a form human yet divine, the visual presentation of mystery, a visible representation of the invisible. In the one, God appears on a wisp of cloud, held up (or restrained?) by angelic forms; in the other, God appears in the Son, who is suddenly taller than everyone else and who shines with the unearthly light of Moses' face as he came down from Mount Sinai (Exod. 34:29), and with the brilliance of the figure of Jesus on the mount of transfiguration (Matt. 17:2).

As I think of these further favorites, aware at the same time that I still have so many more, I find that I am thinking also about what may be called Rembrandt's little devices, small details that he used again and again, perhaps because they gave him pleasure, perhaps because he thought he had good ideas worth repeating. I have mentioned his dogs, a device of realism, and his Jerusalem temple exteriors and interiors: the great round dome, with the two free-standing pillars outside, the cavernous spaces inside, multi-leveled and lavishly decorated—settings of awe for events that dwarf any architecture. But I

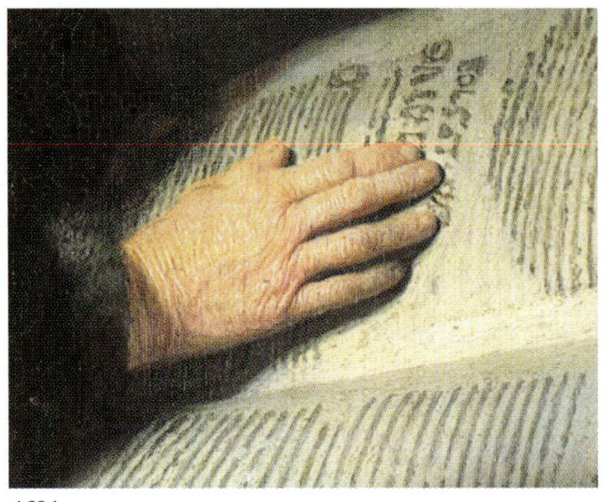

1631

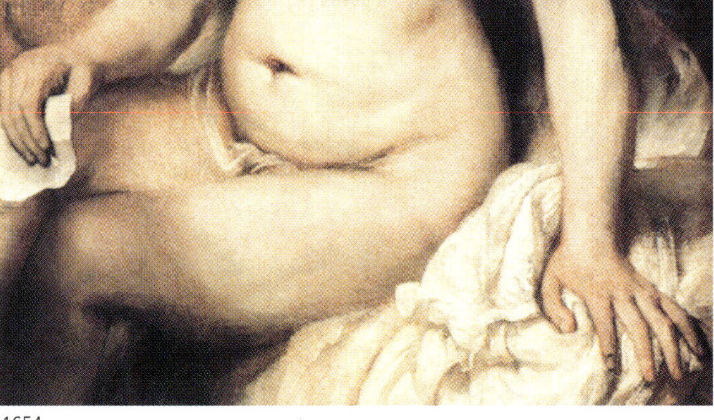

1654

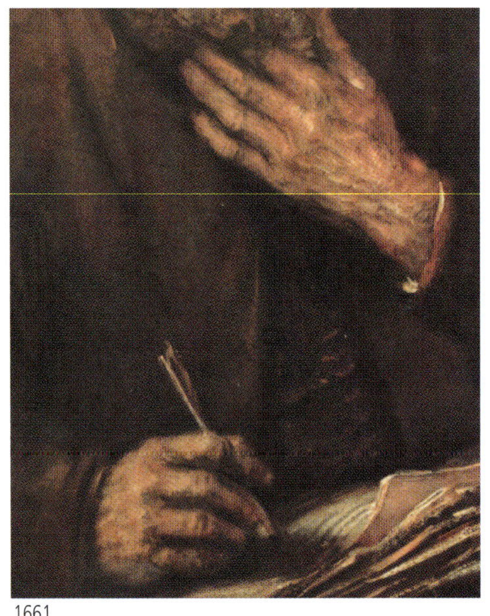

1661

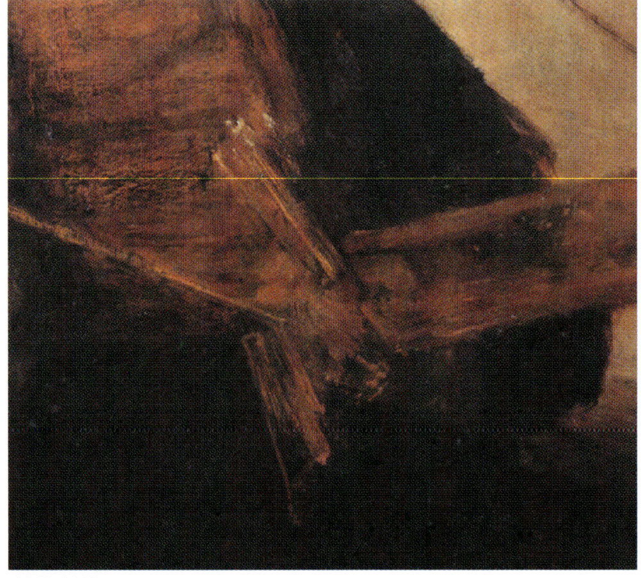

1665–1669

think also of his affection for pearls: who has ever painted such pearls, pearls with depth you can look right into? And his books and pages, inviting the touch, warm with promise. And his handling of metal, especially gold: Rembrandt's gold never looks garish or cold—it glows subtly, as with some inner warmth.

Then there are his hands: sometimes they are painted so literally that they seem to have a visible pulse, and sometimes they are almost abstract though still *there.* "Too big," say the critics of some of them, and "awkwardly placed," they say of others. But the hands Rembrandt gives us somehow always add to what he has created—they have a rightness that is beyond correctness, and they introduce us to the persons he is depicting. I include four of the many possible examples: the hand of his mother reading her Bible (see chap. 3), Bathsheba's hands (see chap. 6), the hand of the Apostle Matthew receiving the angelic dictation of the Gospel (see chap. 6), and the left hand of

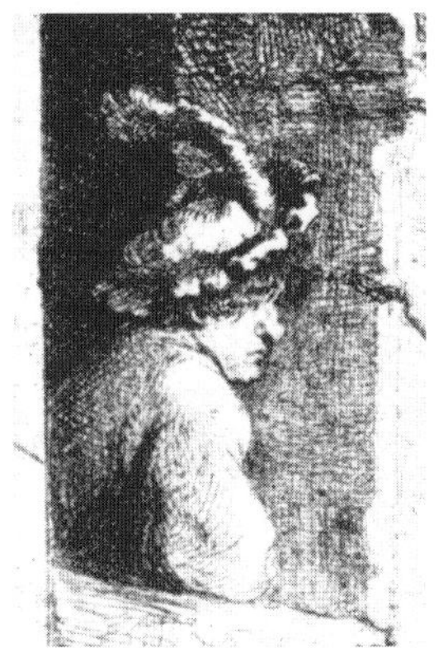
B 90, 1633, detail

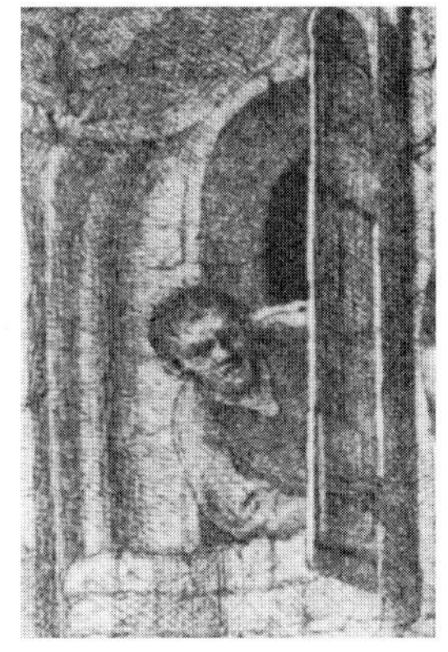
B 77, 1636, detail

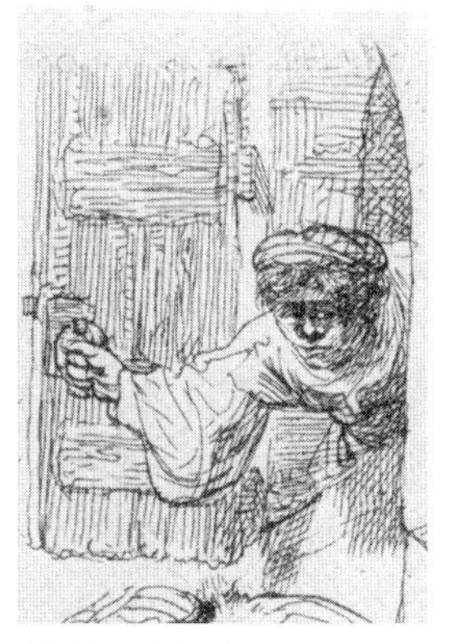
B 91, 1636, detail

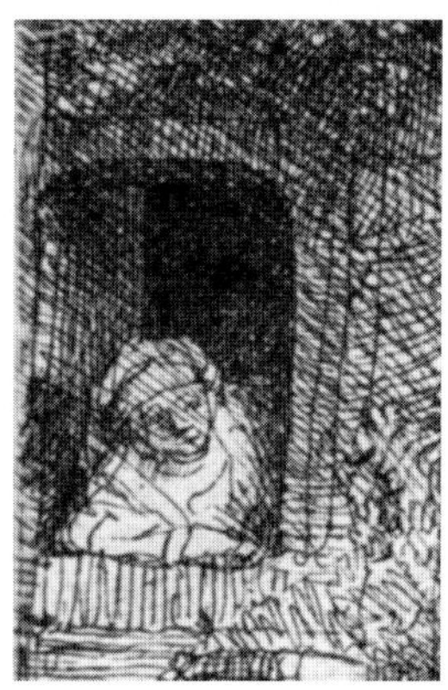
B 43, 1641, detail

Rembrandt himself holding the tools of his trade in the famous self-portrait now in London's Kenwood House.

And I cannot bring myself to leave out Rembrandt's fascination with people incidental to the narrative he was depicting looking from a window at the events taking place—a sort of human footnote. Five etchings, from 1633 to 1655, are representative: *The Good Samaritan*, B 90 (see chap. 4); *Christ Before Pilate*, B 77 (see chap. 4); *The Return of the Prodigal Son*, B 91 (see chap. 6); *The Angel Departing from the Family of Tobias*, B 43 (see chap. 7); and *Christ Presented to the People*, B 76 (see chap. 5).

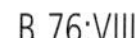
B 76:VIII

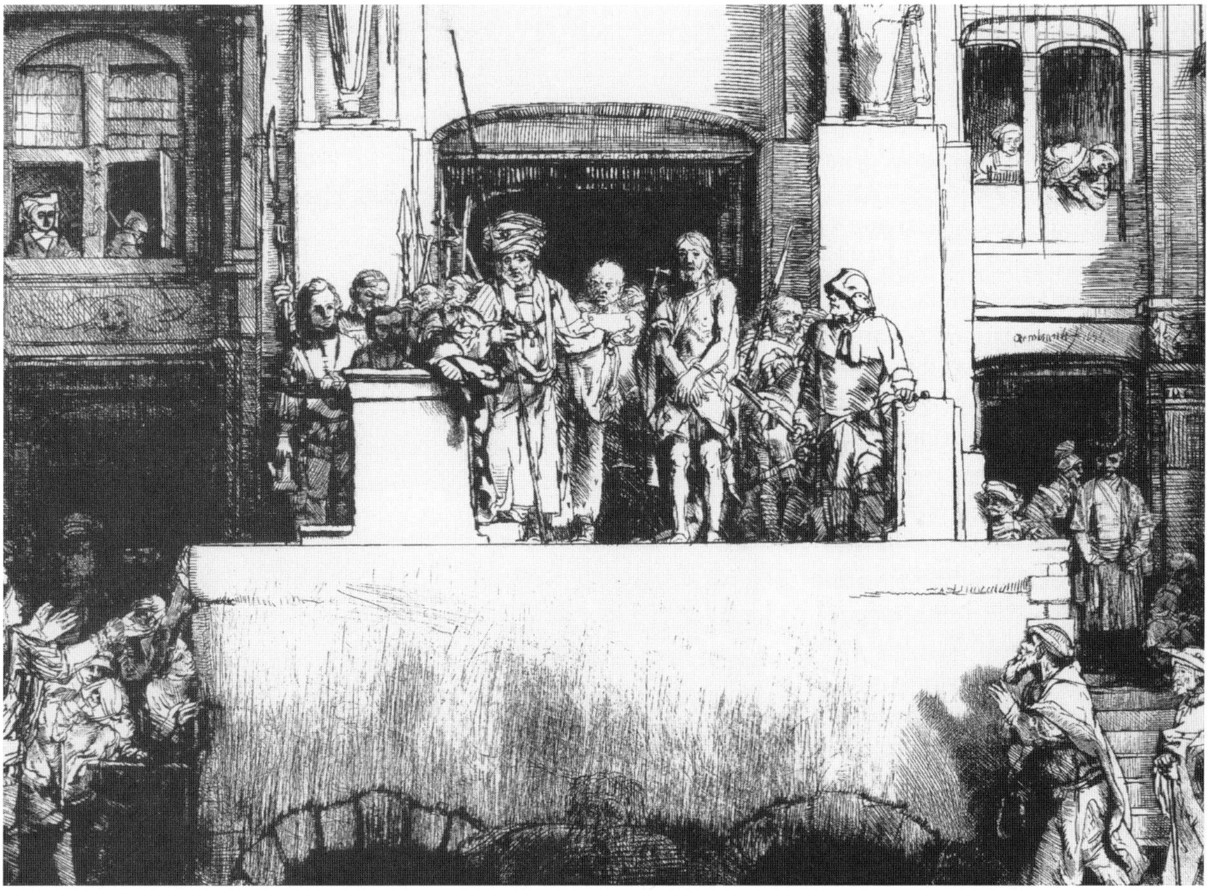

Then there is...but I promised to stop with this chapter, and stop I must. End, however, I cannot. Rembrandt's oeuvre keeps on informing, teaching, calling, reminding me. His best works have begun with me a dialogue that is ongoing—they engage my spirit and plunge me into a creative process that Rembrandt started, then let loose. His creative contribution pulls me into his idea of a given text, a given biblical moment, and I find myself in a discussion with this Dutchman who was born 327 years before I was. Biblical narratives that I have studied intensely for years have taken on added dimensions and even new meanings from Rembrandt's fascination with them, from his almost uncanny ability to go to the marrow of the text and present it as a story in and of *my* life. In a way, Rembrandt makes the Bible holier for me by making it more real, or perhaps more human. The biblical text has so entered his re-presentation of it that his images come to have a life of their own. Once you have seen them, really seen them, they become a part of your visual vocabulary and form a commentary on the texts they consider that can never be disregarded.

In a way, of course, this is what art at its best, art that transcends the artist, is about. It pulls us into its orbit, if only for a little while, and then engages us in an ongoing creativity that simply does not end. We cannot escape Rembrandt any more than we can escape Beethoven, or Shakespeare, or a biblical story that begins, "One time there was a man who had two sons." They draw us into a creative process that is ongoing—we become collaborators with genius as spirits beyond our own take us by the hand and help us along our journey through the excitement that is life.

Rembrandt learned early on that the Bible is not a book of answers and that it always stops short of telling us everything about anything so that we are drawn into its story, its inspiration, its counsel, its life. The Bible's repetitions are never superfluous, whatever the condensation vandals may hold, and its narratives and its teachings are completed by being incomplete. The Bible is a living book, as is often claimed, but by virtue of the life it takes on by the conversation to which it invites us. We become ourselves the important Scripture beyond Scripture that may well be the Bible's foremost purpose.

Rembrandt, I believe, understood this about the Bible. I find no other explanation for the clarity and the humanity of his biblical exegesis. He made the Bible an important part of his art because it was important to him, and in so doing, he has made it more important to a great many, some of whom may well have missed the Bible altogether but for Rembrandt. I doubt, somehow, that Rembrandt had any choice about his dialogue with the Bible. I know that I myself have had no choice about my own dialogue with the Bible. And I am also certain that Rembrandt has made my dialogue much richer than it otherwise would have been.

Thus have I come to feel that the Bible was real to Rembrandt: a real book about real people. He appears never to have made the Bible into what it is not and can never be, as so many have done across so many centuries. Too many who have done so, alas, are clergy and religious educators, Biblical "scholars" and harvesters of commentary and irrelevant minutiae. Not Rembrandt. His Jesus is a Jew, and not a particularly handsome one. His apostles are men who fear when they should be brave and sleep when they should stay awake, rough and rustic men, unsophisticated, often slow to catch on, men who show not the slightest hint of sainthood. His patriarchs are as flawed, as conniving, as prone to mistake and subject to weakness as the Bible reports them to have been. His prophets are as burdened by their calling as real prophets must of necessity be: Nathan addressing a guilty King David with his story of the poor man's "one little ewe lamb" (2 Sam. 12:3) in a drawing from 1654/55 appears embarrassed.

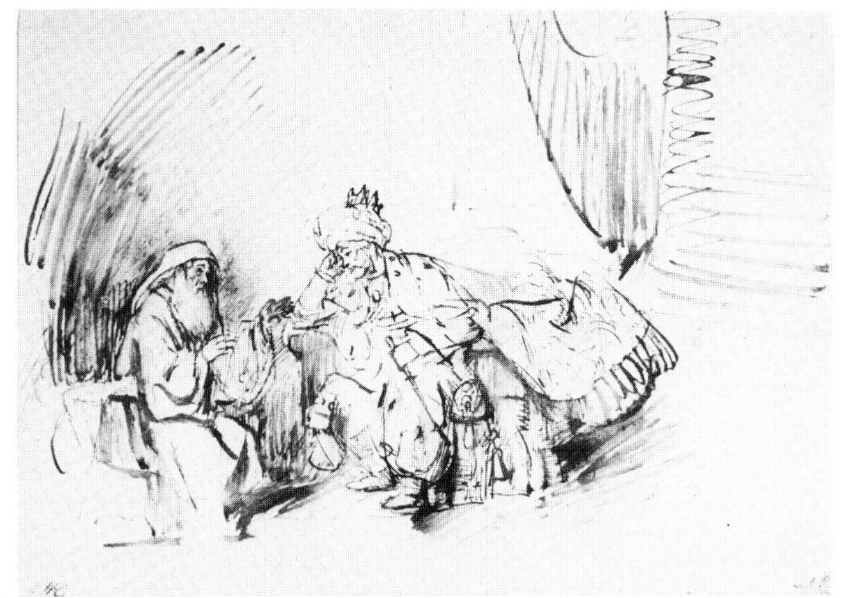

Nathan Admonishing David, Benesch 948, 1654 or 1655, Metropolitan Museum, New York

And Jeremiah grieving the Babylonian devastation of Jerusalem is more than anything else soul-weary (see chap. 4). Without exception, Rembrandt's biblical people are human; we can believe that they might understand us, not judge us—they are of our world, somehow, because they are of Rembrandt's world.

I think Rembrandt came to the Bible without pretense, read it without the pious blinkers religious people so often wear, and accepted it as a word from God, in no need of any human attempt to turn it into a talisman, an answer-book, or a rabbit's left hind foot. Thus did the Bible speak to Rembrandt, and thus does the Bible speak through Rembrandt.

If I have mis-seen and so misunderstood what Rembrandt was about, I make no apology, not to anyone, not even to Rembrandt, for art in any form has its own life, and seeing and understanding their own freedom. Rembrandt might perhaps laugh if he could read what I have written about his drawings and his paintings and his etchings, but I like to think he would even so be pleased, enough at least to say, "Well, maybe so!"

And so with these words I stop, difficult though stopping is for me. Rembrandt's paintings are so vividly human that they often seem like a mirror, a mirror of what was, what is, and what is liable to be. His etchings are so complete, so eloquently engaging, that they often seem a visible extension of one's own thoughts. And his drawings! How with such a few lines, lines that seem almost to emerge from the paper itself, Rembrandt so often summarizes emotion, brings up feelings, and summons that same "of course!" that the music of Mozart and Beethoven often suggests. All this is true of the whole of his oeuvre, but it seems somehow especially true of his biblical works, as I have attempted to suggest.

To end with? Ending a consideration of the gift Rembrandt is would be impossible for me. And for that matter, I really cannot stop either—finishing this very personal survey frees me to return without distraction to the dialogue Rembrandt and I have been carrying on about the Bible for more than forty years. Now how about that painting from 16…?

Mary's foot resting on the snake just above Rembrandt's signature is an allusion to God's curse upon the serpent in Genesis 3:15c and to the first Adam/second Adam theology of 1 Corinthians 15:45. The simple domestic setting, with the cozy fireplace and the cat pulling at Mary's skirt as Mary sits not in her chair but on the floor with her workbasket at hand reflects Rembrandt's humanity.

Three years before he painted *The Wedding of Samson*, Rembrandt had painted *Samson Threatening His Father-in-Law*, a work now in Berlin, which depicts a moment after the wedding feast when Samson returned (after a cooling-off period, Judg. 14:19e and 15:1) to Timnah. When he was refused entry to his bride's bedroom by his father-in-law, who had given his daughter to Samson's best man after the trouble of the riddle, Samson, enraged, set out to torch the Philistine grain fields, vineyards, and olive groves, ripe for harvest (Judg. 15:3–5). Rembrandt presents a menacing Samson, berating his frightened father-in-law, who understandably has a grip on the heavy handle of the window shutter in case a quick retreat is necessary. Samson's threat was actually a threat of damage to the Philistines, not his father-in-law, but as a result of his devastation of the Philistines' autumn crops, they burned to death both the father-in-law and his daughter (Judg. 15:6). Rembrandt has summed up both threat and potential result in a single moment.

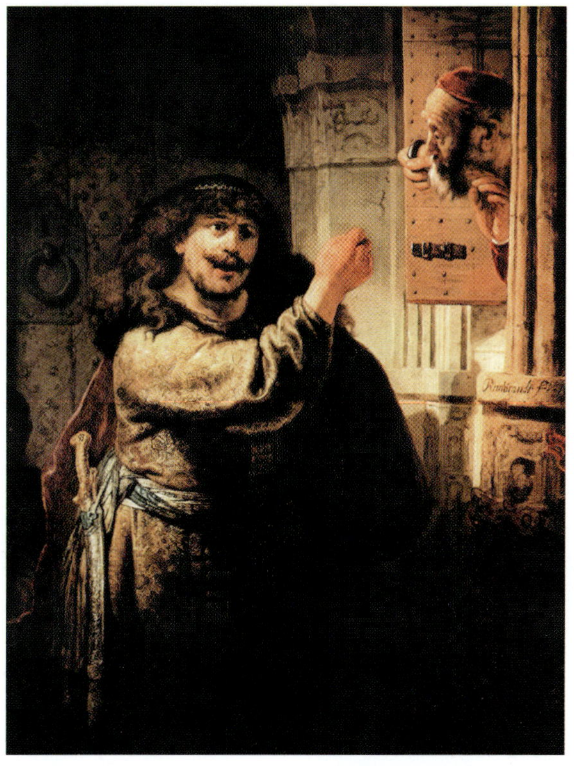

Samson Threatening His Father-in-Law, 1635, Gemäldegalerie, Staatliche Museen, Berlin

Rembrandt's inclusion of two angels sitting in the entrance of the empty tomb and Mary's pot of ointment at her knee indicates that he had considered the narrative of Luke 24:1–4, and perhaps that of Mark 16:1–6 and even Matthew 28:1–6, despite the presence in those accounts of two (Matt. 28:1) or three (Mark 16:1) or an unspecified number (Luke 24:1) of women, instead of Mary Magdalene alone, as in his primary source in John's Gospel. John does not mention either the angels or the spices for the anointment of Christ's body, hastily interred before the beginning of the Sabbath at sundown on Friday.

Franz Landsberger (*Rembrandt, the Jews and the Bible*, pp. 116–19) notes that "Rembrandt was the first artist courageous enough to show Jesus with Jewish features" and speculates that Rembrandt may have been influenced by Martin Luther's teaching and the writing of his contemporary, Hugo Grotius. I suspect that Rembrandt's friendship with the Jewish community of Amsterdam and his respect for the obvious biblical fact of Jesus' lineage were his more compelling reasons for depicting Jesus as he did.

Visser 'T Hooft has a chapter titled "Christ in Rembrandt's Work" in *Rembrandt and the Gospel* (pp. 31–41), and Hans-Martin Rotermund devotes pages 178–188 of his *Rembrandt's Drawings and Etchings for the Bible* to Rembrandt's work on the ministry of Christ.

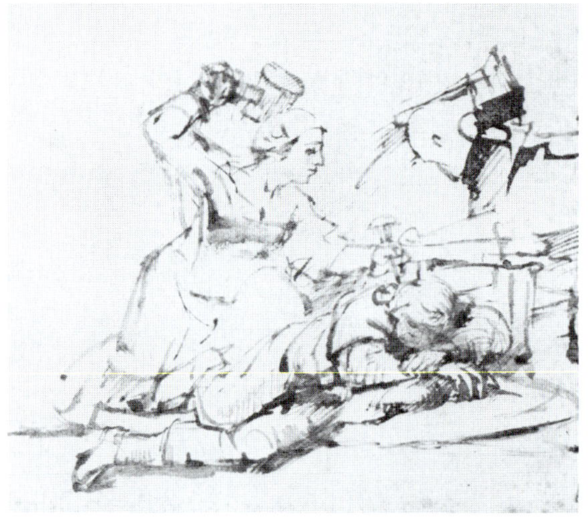

Jael and Sisera, Benesch 1042, 1659-1660, Prentenkabinet, Rijksmuseum, Amsterdam

Rembrandt's drawing of Jael's murder of Sisera, from 1659/60.

The *Self-Portrait with Two Circles* (below), now in London's Kenwood House, painted in the final years of Rembrandt's life. The enigmatic circles behind Rembrandt have been widely (and sometimes wildly) interpreted; they may perhaps best be explained as a reference to the story of the perfect circle of Giotto (see Ben Broos, *Simiolus* 4, 1971, pp. 150-184; Vasari, *Lives of the Artists,* Penguin, pp. 64-65).

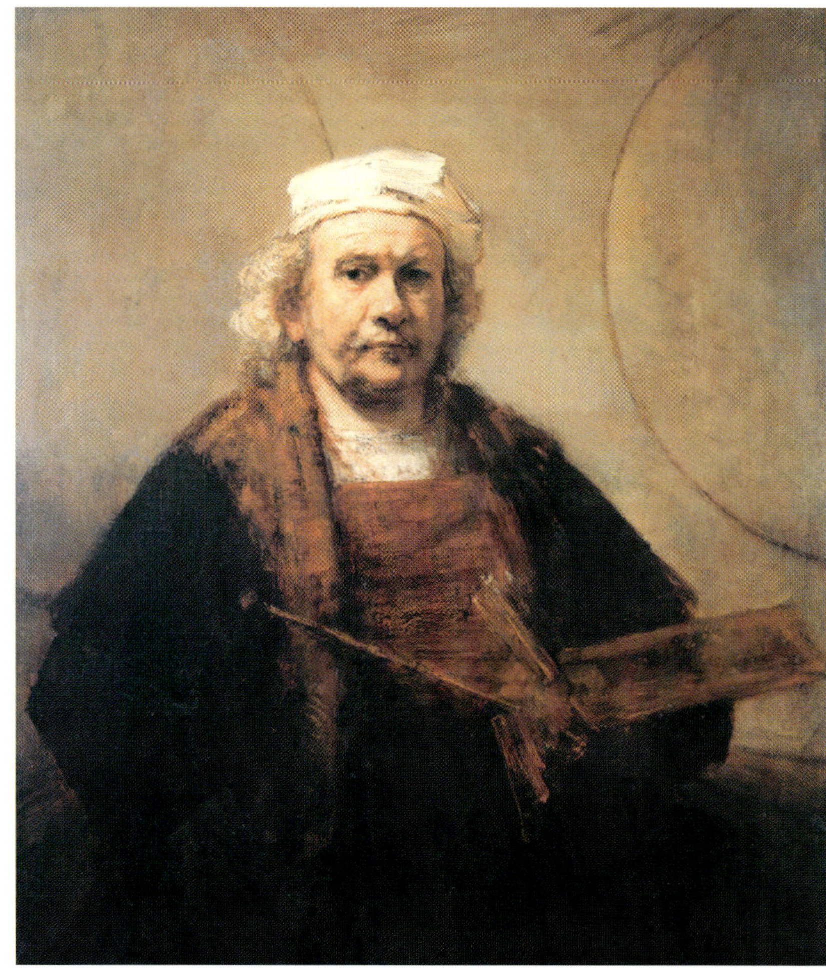

Self-Portrait, 1665-1669, The Iveagh Bequest, Kenwood House, London

A LIST OF MUSEUMS

For more than four decades, I have been devouring the works of Rembrandt in museum collections and in special exhibitions at every opportunity. To start with, I suspect I merely looked at his paintings in awe—they stood out, even among my short list of favorite pictures. In time, however, I began to *see* Rembrandt's paintings, and then his etchings, and then his drawings, a quite different experience from mere looking. And eventually, I found myself engaged in an ongoing dialogue with Rembrandt himself, as I attempted to understand how he understood and so experienced biblical narratives I had myself struggled to understand and so experience.

Thus did a casual museum-goer's acquaintance with Rembrandt stimulate an ongoing quest to see as much of his work as possible, and to possess as extensive a library dealing with that work as I could find and afford. Along the way, I have been the fortunate recipient of enthusiastic assistance from the keepers and curators of his works in an array of museums, special collections, and special exhibitions. They permitted me to hold in my own hands for study drawings Rembrandt created, etchings both pulled and touched up by his own hand, and even some of his etching plates that have survived, albeit in much abused condition. They have answered my questions, usually with an amazing gladness, and they have answered my letters and e-mails, generally, in detail and promptly. I cannot list their names, some of which I do not even know, but I thank them here by listing the museums to which they have devoted their careers. I list only the museums in which I have worked with Rembrandt materials, some of them repeatedly, and I list them by city, in alphabetical order.

AMSTERDAM

Museum "Het Rembrandthuis"
Rijksmuseum
Rijksmuseum Prentenkabinet
Rijksmuseum Vincent van Gogh

BASEL

Öffentliche Kunstsammlung

BOSTON

Isabella Stewart Gardner Museum
Museum of Fine Art

DUBLIN

National Gallery of Ireland

EDINBURGH

National Gallery of Scotland

FLORENCE

Galleria degli Uffizi

FORT WORTH

Kimbell Art Museum

FRANKFURT

Städelsches Kunstinstitut

GLASGOW

Glasgow Art Gallery and Museum

THE HAGUE

Mauritshuis
Museum Bredius

JERUSALEM

The Israel Museum

KASSEL

Staatliche Kunstsammlungen

LEIDEN

Stedelijk Museum De Lakenhal

LONDON

The British Museum

Dulwich College Picture Gallery

The Iveagh Bequest, Kenwood House

The National Gallery

The Queen's Gallery, Buckingham Palace

Victoria and Albert Museum

The Wallace Collection

Windsor Castle

LOUISVILLE

J. B. Speed Art Museum

MOSCOW

Pushkin Fine Art Museum

MUNICH

Alte Pinakothek

NEW YORK

The Frick Collection

Metropolitan Museum of Art

OXFORD

Ashmolean Museum

PARIS

Musée Cognaq-Jay

Musée Jacquemart-André

Musée du Louvre

Musée du Petit Palais

PHILADELPHIA

Philadelphia Museum of Art

RALEIGH

North Carolina Museum of Art

STOCKHOLM

Nationalmuseum

ST. PETERSBURG

State Hermitage

STUTTGART

Staatsgalerie

VIENNA

Albertina

Kunsthistoriches Museum

WASHINGTON

National Gallery of Art

ZURICH

Kunsthaus

Paintings from museums I have yet to visit have in some instances been seen and studied in loan exhibitions: I mention, in particular, works from Detroit's Institute of Fine Arts, from Dresden's Gemäldegalerie Alter Meister, from Berlin's Museum Dahlem Gemäldegalerie, and from Hamburg's Kunsthalle.

GENERAL INDEX

INDEX OF REMBRANDT ETCHINGS

Listed Alphabetically, by Title, with Bartsch Catalog Numbers

INDEX OF REMBRANDT DRAWINGS

(Listed alphabetically, by Title and Benesch Catalog Numbers)

INDEX OF REMBRANDT PAINTINGS

Listed Alphabetically, by Title, with *Corpus* and Bredius Catalog Numbers (Paintings for which no Br. Number is listed were not known to Bredius; those for which no *Corpus* Number is listed have not yet been published or have been deattributed by RRP)

INDEX OF BIBLICAL REFERENCES

Rembrandt.